Unfair Competition Law
European Union and Member States

International Competition Law Series

Volume 18.

The titles published in this series are listed at the end of this volume

Unfair Competition Law
European Union and Member States

By

Frauke Henning-Bodewig

KLUWER LAW
INTERNATIONAL

Published by:
Kluwer Law International
P.O. Box 85889
2508 CN The Hague
The Netherlands

Sold and distributed in North, Central and South America by:
Aspen Publishers, Inc.
7201 McKinney Circle
Frederick, MD 21704
USA

Sold and distributed in all other countries by:
Turpin Distribution Services Ltd
Stratton Business Park
Pegasus Drive
Biggleswade
Bedfordshire SG18 8TQ
United Kingdom

A C.I.P. catalogue record for this book is available from the Library of Congress

Printed on acid-free paper

ISBN 90-411-2329-6

Printed in the Netherlands.

Table of Contents

Preliminary Comment: Is There a European Unfair Competition Law?

The title 'Unfair competition law—European Union and Member States' raises two questions, namely: is there indeed an 'Unfair Competition Law'? And if so, how 'European' is this?

The first question can be answered in the affirmative. Despite all their differences, all European countries have developed mechanisms based on the principle of fairness to control commercial activities. The fact that details are disputed—see the first chapter—does not affect the basic common conviction that market conduct should be fair in the interests of all market participants and that there must be some rules to secure this fairness.

One may disagree whether this should be referred to as *unfair competition*, unfair trade practices or unfair commercial practices. Each of these terms has its advantages and disadvantages. The use of the term unfair competition here is based above all on the fact that it has long been the expression used at international[1] and (although not consistently) European level.[2] In addition, most Member States speak of *unlauterer Wettbewerb, concurrence déloyale, ongeoorloofde mededinging, competenzia desleal, concorrenza sleale* etc.[3] While this does not ignore the fact that the concept of unfair competition law as such has not entered the Anglo-American legal systems,[4] it nevertheless seems to be the most familiar concept in Europe. In any event, the question of terminology should not be overrated, there being no significant differences in terms of content between 'unfair competition' and other terms, such as the term frequently used by the ECJ, 'the fairness of commercial transactions'[5] or the term 'unfair commercial practices' used in Directive 2005/29/EC.

What lies behind the term 'unfair competition'? On this, there are different views (for detail see Chapter 1, I). and at this point we merely point out that it would be unhelpful to define the field of regulations at issue too narrowly solely for terminological reasons. What is regulated in one country under the law of torts is part of consumer protection law in another Member State; what one Member State leaves to the self-regulatory mechanisms is in another country a matter for the state prosecutor. This cannot be the decisive factor. What matters is that the fairness of market conduct

1. Article 10bis Paris Convention, also referred to in TRIPS (see Chapter 2, I, II)
2. For instance, Art. 14 (2) of the Council Regulation 40/94/EC on the Community Trade Mark expressly reserves the application of national laws against unfair competition; the ECJ occasionally speaks of "legislation on unfair competition" (e.g. in the "Lifting" decision, p. 32), etc.
3. See the country reports (Chapter 4).
4. See country report Great Britain (Chapter 4). It is somewhat ironic that the only international regulation on unfair competition—Art. 10bis of the Paris Convention—obviously owes its existence to initiatives of the United Kingdom; see in detail Chapter 2, I.1.
5. Established justification of the ECJ since the landmark judgment "Cassis de Dijon" (see Chapter 3, III.1.a.).

is at issue—and it is initially irrelevant where and with what instruments this is to be achieved.

This brings us to the second question: Is there a *European* unfair competition law? Definitely not, in the sense of one uniform coherent set of regulations, which for a wide variety of reasons has not yet been achieved at Community level.[6] What does exist, however, are selective regulations, regulations dealing with individual problem areas in the field of unfair competition. They have made considerable progress recently, especially through the Directive on Unfair Commercial Practices that was passed in 2005. Thus, although the '*piecemeal* approach' has predominated so far, there are a number of arguments that may justify the term 'European' unfair competition law.

Within the framework set by Community law, unfair competition law, however, is above all a matter for *national law*. National law is of importance even in situations where Community law has led to provisions that are identical in terms of language, for instance where Member States have adopted the text of a directive more or less unchanged (such as that on comparative advertising). The Community legislature necessarily uses unspecific legal terms that must be given specific meaning by the Member States. The question of what, for instance, is disparaging, misleading or harassing depends very much on the legal tradition, on cultural, linguistic and historic particularities, indeed on differences in mentality. It would be naïve to assume that the harmonisation of the legal framework necessarily leads to a completely uniform interpretation and application in all 25 Member States. As long as there are different national states and above all different cultural communities, there will be differences that European unfair competition law and even the harmonising judicial practice of the ECJ will be unable to eliminate. On the contrary, one might ask whether these differences should be eliminated at all, as long as, in the final analysis, the desired protection of competitors and consumers is achieved and the free movement of goods and services is not restricted.

Hence, anyone dealing with fairness of market conduct in Europe would be well advised to consider both the provisions at Community level—including the judicial practice of the ECJ on the fundamental freedoms—and the very lively national competition laws that, while respecting Community law, have nevertheless retained their own special features. Misunderstandings will arise above all if the focus is on the one at the expense of the other. Thus anyone who only considers, for instance, the situation at European level will be surprised to discover that an 'unfair competition case' is in practice handled quite differently in, for instance, Sweden, Poland, Great Britain or France. And anyone who only considers Swedish, Polish, British or French unfair competition law will fail to realise that these laws today are at least partly based on European directives and principles and consequently can and must be interpreted in accordance with Community law. Thus it is only the two combined, the European requirements and national laws, that create "European unfair competition law".

Accordingly, the following intends to bring the two levels together. This means that, following a number of basic considerations (Chapter 1), a brief description will be presented of the international requirements, which take priority over European and national law (Chapter 2). The next chapter then deals in more detail with Community law (Chapter 3), followed by an extensive discussion of the national unfair competition laws of all 25 Member States (Chapter 4).

6. Nor by Council Directive 2005/29/EC on unfair commercial practices, which is limited in personal ("B2C") and substantive aspects (regulation of important areas in other directives); for details see Chapter 3, III. 10). As to the reasons for this lack of coherence see Chapter 1, I.

Chapter 1. Basic Considerations

I. "UNFAIR COMPETITION" AS A SEPARATE FIELD OF LAW? SOME (HISTORICAL) OBSERVATIONS

The term "unfair competition" initially only describes a specific constellation of facts, which involves commercial or business conduct that does not satisfy the generally accepted requirements of fairness. Where, as here, the term "competition" is used, it should not be regarded too narrowly, and also include the sales activities of a monopolist, which does not have competitors.

Thus the first prerequisite is that the conduct must not be private, social or political, but must be commercial. This, however, is again still too broad. Not everything that is regarded as "unfair" in the commercial sector falls under unfair competition law. Instead, there is a wide variety of forms of unfair (commercial) conduct. To name but a few, it is certainly unfair to enter into price fixing agreements, to put unsafe products on the market, to disregard contractual obligations, to spread rumours about competitors, to infringe another's patent, to harass consumers with unsolicited emails, or to conduct misleading advertising. However, which of these are covered by unfair competition law, and which belong to other fields of law such as general tort law, intellectual property law, contract law or antitrust law?

This is a difficult question. Obviously, unfair competition law regulates only a part of what is regarded as unfair commercial practices in a broader sense. If, as in Member States, it is acknowledged as a field of law in its own right, a differentiation must be made on the basis of additional criteria. In the past, the main criterion was seen in the competitive relationship between the parties. However, this approach is regarded as too narrow today, since it excludes the impact of unfair competition on other market participants, especially consumers, and neglects the interest of the general public in the fairness of competition. Consequently, the legislation in a number of Member States is no longer directed against unfair competition only, but concerns quite broadly trade practices or market conduct generally.[1] Other Member States still, in theory, hold fast to the connection with competition, but the requirements made are becoming increasingly relaxed.[2]

The reason for this is mainly historical. The law against unfair competition is deeply rooted in the national system of law, which has developed rather differently in the countries of Europe (or at least in groups of countries). The influence of this is reflected in unfair competition law even today.[3]

1. See e.g. Belgium, Denmark, Sweden (Chapter 4).
2. For instance, in the new 2004 German Act against Unfair Competition, the scope of application depends on a competitive practice and not on a competitive relationship; see country report Germany (Chapter 4).
3. A good overview can be found in Schricker, *Twenty-Five Years of Protection Against Unfair Competition*, 26 IIC 782 [1995]; Schricker, *Unfair Competition and Consumer Protection in Western Europe*, 1 IIC 415 (1970); Bakardjieva Engelbrekt, *Fair trading law in flux? national legacies, institutional choice and the Process of Europeanisation*, 2003.

The origins of the law against unfair competition may be traced as far back as the second half of the 19th century in Europe, triggered by the introduction of free trade (in France as early as 1791). Until then the guilds had ensured fair play in commerce with an iron hand. The hope that a "reasonable" trader would conduct himself fairly towards his competitors even without such a constraint unfortunately proved to be an illusion. In most European countries, unanimity was swiftly reached over the fact that the introduction of some form of rules of play was indispensable.

Yet it was only in France that a satisfactory solution was successfully found from the outset. Here, on the basis of the general tort-law clause in Article 1382 of the Civil Code, case law quickly and flexibly developed what became known as the "action en concurrence déloyale", which guaranteed business persons legal protection against the risk of confusion, imitation, disparagement, betrayal of secrets, parasitic competition, etc.[4] Other countries had a harder time including such acts of unfair competition within the law of torts. Germany, for instance, declined to follow the path taken by France for systematic reasons, with the result that at the turn of the century German legislators were forced to enact a special law on competition.[5] Finally, the third major European industrial nation at that time, England, pursued a completely different direction.[6] Here neither a tort of unfair competition was recognized, nor was a special law enacted. Rather, England concentrated upon the familiar possibilities of claims under equity and common law, particularly the claim against passing off. Protection against unfair competition going beyond this was regarded as incompatible with the common-law system.[7]

The leading industrial nations at the turn of the 20th century thus reacted very differently to the demands of competition brought about by the introduction of free trade. The form of their reaction is in principle at the root of the current difficulties faced by the harmonisation of the law against unfair competition at European (or international) level.

This is all the more true since, on account of the different points of departure, the difficulties already existing at the outset have increased with the passing of time. This can best be illustrated by the example of the consideration of consumer interests.

In the second half of the last century all industrial nations were confronted with the problem of whether and how public interests—and in particular the interests of the consumer—could adequately be taken into consideration. One of the possibilities which presented itself was their inclusion in competition law. However, from the

4. See country report France (Chapter 4).
5. For an in-depth discussion see Beier, *The Development and Present Status of Unfair competition Law in Germany—An Outline*, 4 IIC 77 (1973); as to the New Act of 3.7.2004, see Henning-Bodewig; 4 IIC 421 (2005).
6. See country report Great Britain (Chapter 4) and Thompson, *English Law and the Concept of Unfair Competition*, in: *Unfair Competition. Some Comparative Aspects of the Law of the US, Germany, France and the UK* (London 1966); Cornish and Llewelyn, *Intellectual Property* (8th ed., London 2003, p. 583); Kamperman Sanders, *Unfair Competition Law. The protection of intellectual and industrial creativity*, 1997, p. 52 et seq. It is interesting to note that in spite of this the United Kingdom was one of the driving forces for the establishing of international protection against unfair competition within the Paris Convention; see Chapter 2.I.1.
7. A modified form of this approach may be found in US law, where additional limited possibilities of civil-law claims exist on the basis of Sec. 43 of the Lanham Act, and the different laws on fair trading in the States, and where a government agency (FTC) watches over the fairness (and simultaneously the freedom) of competition. On the American system, cf. Callmann, *Unfair Competition, Trademarks and Monopolies* (4th ed., 1984, revision 2003); Kamperman Sanders (fn. 6), p. 12 et seq.; comparing laws (with German law), e.g., Grimes, 84 *Harv. L. Rev.* 1769 (1971).

French starting point, namely the subsumption of unfair competition under the general law of torts, this was not possible, since the "action en concurrence déloyale" requires a strict perspective of individual rights, with legal protection only being granted to the competitor and only with regard to his very specific interests, while legal protection for consumers requires its own laws. Yet also in the Anglo-American system—which, as far as the civil-law protection of competitors is concerned, for the most part failed to progress beyond the claim against passing-off, likewise influenced by the emphasis on individual rights—consumer protection must appear an alien subject matter. On the other hand, the German system, with the creation of a statute specifically directed at combating unfair competition and headed by a broad general clause, was from the start also more open to the integration of interests other than those of the competitor. This had the effect that in the countries in which a special law along the lines of the German model was chosen, general interests and consumer interests could be integrated relatively straightforwardly into these laws, which in turn meant that in these countries competition law often protects competitors and consumers equally or has also generally become "market law".

This is, of course, only a very rough classification, and to make things even more complicated, in the meantime "hybrids" have developed in most countries. To mention but three: Spain has two separate laws to prevent unfair competition, both, however, involving civil-law remedies and protecting both competitors and consumers alike.[8] In Sweden and Denmark, although a particularly important role is played by an administrative authority (the ombudsman), civil law measures predominate.[9] In the Netherlands, protection is granted almost exclusively on the basis of the general tort clause, although other interests are also taken into consideration.[10]

There is thus a wide variety of approaches.[11] Most countries today have their own laws against unfair competition, the protection of competitors and consumers in some systems being brought together in one statute, in others spread over two or more statutes. Only four of the 25 Member States have no statutory provisions of any greater extent whatsoever.[12]

II. DEMARCATION FROM OTHER FIELDS OF LAW

Against this background, the question of what constitutes the "essence" of unfair competition law—a question closely related to the subject-matter covered—is not an easy one. It is first of all a question of differentiating other fields of law.

1. Tort law

As stated above, the law against unfair competition in most European countries has developed from general tort law.[13] However, this original approach was relatively

8. See country report Spain (Chapter 4).
9. See country reports Sweden and Denmark (Chapter 4).
10. See country report Netherlands (Chapter 4).
11. Kamperman Sanders (fn. 6), p. 24 et seq. distinguishes between the "civil code principles, common law and case law-approach" (e.g., by France, the Netherlands, Italy, the United Kingdom) on the one hand and the "lex specialis-approach" (e.g., by Belgium, Germany, Austria, Luxemburg, Spain, Greece, Portugal, Denmark, Sweden) on the other hand.
12. Great Britain, Ireland, Malta and Cyprus.
13. See for instance the development in Germany, discussed by Beier (fn. 5).

narrow, since it focuses on the individual rights of the "honest tradesman" and neglects the interests of the general public in the functioning of competition. Nor can it be easily reconciled with the modern aim of protecting consumers against unfair commercial practices. Although it is not impossible to base consumer rights on tort law principles, this seems to encounter systematic problems in most countries.[14] The tort law approach thus at best can explain part of the protection granted against unfair competition, namely as far as "concurrence déloyale" in the narrow sense is involved. It can hardly explain the protection actually granted in most Member States that goes far beyond this, especially if consumer protection is included or the original law against unfair competition has been extended to "market practices" in general. In any event, the original approach was transformed in most Member States in such a way that tort law principles alone, though being at the root of most national unfair competition laws, are no longer capable of explaining in dogmatic terms modern unfair competition law.

2. Intellectual property laws

In the past, considerable emphasis was given to the connection with intellectual property rights. This is expressed most strongly in the first (and only) regulation of unfair competition law at international level, the Paris Union Convention, which includes protection against unfair competition under industrial property rights.[15] This is understandable to the extent that there are close points of contact especially to trademark law. This is most obviously with respect to the issue of the likelihood of confusion, which all Member States deal with both under unfair competition law ("confusion", "passing off") and under trademark law. In addition, Directives 84/450/EC and 2005/29/EC[16] also cover confusion as to commercial origin under the aspect of misleading. This thus raises the question of the demarcation between unfair competition law and especially trademark law.

This demarcation appears all the more significant today, since in trademark law—prompted by European (Trademark Directive) and international developments (TRIPS)—a marked tendency to more extensive protection of the mark can be observed. This protection is, however, as a rule linked to certain (specific trademark law) requirements—to the formal act of registration, to secondary meaning, etc—and follows its own rules with respect to ensuring and enforcing protection. Against this background it can appear to be problematic if unfair competition law should confer protection which could undermine the standards of national (or European) trademark law. There are possibly good reasons for not providing such protection, or in any event not providing it in this manner. There are even better reasons for not disturbing the delicate balance between the freedom of competition (and imitation) and the granting of exclusive rights.[17]

14. The only Member State that succeeded in broadening the interpretation of the general tort clause to an extent that might also take into account general interests is the Netherlands. See country report Netherlands (Chapter 4).
15. See Chapter 2, I.
16. See Chapter 3, III.
17. The aspect of "pre-emption" is emphasized by Kamperman Sanders (fn. 12), p. 11 et seq., who also stresses that unfair competition law "aims to protect fairness in competition and to secure the freedom of competition structures; thus maintaining healthy competition as the foundation of the free enterprise system. Unfair competition, therefore, encompasses all aspects of "industrial property law" (p. 22, 23). This is in line with the theory developed by Ulmer (Sinnzu-sammenhänge im modernen Wettbewerbsrecht) as early as 1932.

What could be the criteria for such a demarcation? Cases in which protection is granted under both trademark and competition law should be relatively straightforward; here the trademark holder will, in his own interest, take care that the protection under trademark law, which is as a rule "safer" and stronger, takes precedence. Mainly, therefore, the problems arise with those cases in which unfair competition law would confer protection going beyond trademark law, for instance where a formal registration or secondary meaning is lacking or where marks not susceptible to trademark protection are involved.[18]

Although the principle applies in most legal systems that trademark law protection does not fundamentally preclude the supplementary application of unfair competition law,[19] it should not, however, be overlooked that despite having much in common, trademark law and unfair competition law pursue different goals of protection in sometimes quite different sometimes quite simular ways. For this reason alone, the concept of likelihood of confusion within the meaning of unfair competition law need not necessarily be identical with the same concept under trademark law, although the benchmark of the "European Consumer Model" of the ECJ is applied in both areas.[20]

Likelihood of confusion in the unfair competition sense is to be determined specifically with regard to the purpose of unfair competition law. This lies in combating unfair acts of competition, and not in conferring protection on a "property right" (as constituted by the trademark). To the extent that it concerns the confusability of goods with identical or similar designations, there must indeed be a risk of mistaken identity amongst the public in terms of the attribution of the product to a specific source. The likelihood of confusion is thus very similar to the risk of misleading the public about the source of the goods, which falls, for instance, under Article 3 of the 1984 EC Directive on misleading advertising.

The features as to confusion that are common to both trademark law and the law against unfair competition are the most obvious. However, a demarcation is also necessary in other cases, such as slavish imitation ("misappropriation"),[21] which requires a distinction being made to patent or design law, for instance. This leads to another special feature of competition law, namely its function as a supplement, filling gaps. Unfair competition law has repeatedly "jumped in" where specific protection was not (yet) available via intellectual property law but where there was felt to be a gap in protection.[22] Although this stresses the relationship between both fields of law, here too the approach was and is normally different: IP rights concern the protection of a specific position ("property right") while unfair competition law concerns protection against specific behaviour that may (or may not) lead to an infringement of property rights. Practice, however, shows that this theory is not completely unflawed; there are overlaps for which a convincing theory has yet to be found.

18. This seems to be a crucial aspect in many countries; see the reports presented at the LIDC-conference in Ghent (2005), see, e.g. country reports Chapter 4.
19. In some Member States—Belgium—such a protection is expressly prohibited; see country report Belgium (Chapter 4).
20. See, for instance, Case C-342/97 *Lloyd Schuhfabrik* v. *Klijsen Handel BV* [1997] ECR- (trademark) and Case C-210/96 *Gut Springenheide* [1998] ECR I-04657 (unfair competition).
21. On the differentiation from this point of view see, in particular, Kamperman Sanders (fn. 6).
22. As an example of many, see Dutch law, discussed for instance in van Engelen, *The Misappropriation Doctrine in the Netherlands*, 22 IIC 11 (1991).

3. Consumer (contract) law

Recent years have seen intensified attempts to ascribe unfair competition law to the field of consumer protection law and to regard the essential criterion as being the effect on consumer interests.[23] Indeed, consumer protection is one of the most important objectives of modern unfair competition law, but, in the same way as the original approach under tort law is too narrow, the aspect of "consumer affectedness" is too broad. Not everything that serves the protection of the consumer is also part of unfair competition law. Contract law and product liability law, for instance, have their own rules, even though they concern the consumer and were adopted to protect the consumer.

In particular, contract law can supplement the rules on unfair competition—and vice versa—but not replace them. This is evident as regards the trader who has no contractual relationship with his competitor. It is, however, also true for the consumer. Even in the case of misleading advertising which has the closest relationship to contract law, the focus is different. Contract law deals with the specific relationship of two (or more) parties. Within this relationship (misleading), advertising is only relevant in so far as the misleading statement influences the conclusion of a specific contract. All other misleading statement are outside the scope of contract law and can neither be prevented nor corrected by contract law.

Another major difference between contract law and unfair competition law is the fact that the law against unfair competition primarily aims at the collective, abstract protection of the consumer, while contract law, on the other hand, is more concerned with a specific and individual balancing of interests between two (or more) individuals. Of course the two concepts can overlap, with misleading advertising, for instance, possibly leading to the conclusion of a contract by misrepresentation. However, the prevention of deception as part of unfair competition law is based on a general and abstract point of view; the basis, for instance, is not the consideration of the affected individual, but rather a—standardised, normative—model of a reasonably informed and circumspect average consumer.[24]

This shows that the protection against unfair competition is a priori only granted after a balancing of interest which may also involve a correction based on the interest of the general public in the well-functioning of competition; enforcement can also be the responsibility of associations, etc.[25] In contrast, in contract law, the assessment of deception is made exclusively from the point of view of whether there has very specifically been a misunderstanding on the part of the purchaser (that has influenced the conclusion of the contract). Although this understanding is generally also standardised (only normal perceptions count) the standardisation exclusively serves the interest of the contracting party. Other value judgments (for instance the interest of the public) are of no relevance, nor are associations and the like involved in the enforcement of individual rights.

The protection of the consumer provided by unfair competition law can therefore not be replaced by the law of contract, nor be explained simply by the necessity to

23. Cf., for instance the Directive on Unfair Commercial Practices, which is restricted to consumer protection (Chapter 4.10) and in legal literature, e.g., Collins (ed.). *The forthcoming EC Directive on Unfair Commercial Practices*, 2004.
24. See the judicial practice of the ECJ, published in Chapter 3, III.
25. For this reason, the regulation of standard terms of business, in which collective interests similarly (also) play a role, and the enforcement is (also) left to organisations, is included in the legislation on fair market conduct in a number of European countries (e.g. Belgium, Switzerland).

overcome an informational deficit.[26] It is indicative that not only the unfair competition laws of the Member States but also the Directive on Unfair Commercial Practices, intended exclusively as protection for consumers, excludes consumer contract law from its scope of application (see Chapter 3.10).

4. Antitrust law

The relationship to antitrust law is more obvious (as already shown in the fact that some countries have created a separate department within their antitrust authorities to deal with unfair competition).[27] Both antitrust law and unfair competition law are concerned with the protection of competition, and both are therefore also referred to as "basic competition legislation". Even if different aspects are emphasised—for antitrust law, the freedom of competition, for unfair competition law the prevention of distortions of this competition—the common feature in both is competition. The latter can only function properly if it is both free and undistorted, with distortion resulting not only from restrictions but also from unfair market practices. Antitrust law cannot achieve this by its own; additional regulations to prevent distortions of competition particularly through unfairness are indispensable. The assumption that free competition will necessarily be also fair competition proved erroneous as early as the introduction of the freedom of trade.[28] The economic analysis of law, especially advocated in the USA, has on this point also come to differentiated results in the meantime.[29]

Moreover, the functioning of competition is one of the essential interests of the general public and must therefore also be taken into account in the interpretation of unfair competition law.[30] Finally, antitrust law and competition law offences frequently lie close together. This becomes particularly obvious in the fact that a number of legal systems regulate certain constellations—e.g. sale below costs, general market disturbance—through the laws against unfair competition, while others do the same through antitrust law.

In summary, it can be concluded that unfair competition law has close connections to tort law, from which it originated in many European countries, but also to antitrust law, consumer protection law (in particular contract law) and intellectual property law.

26. Such a premise would, for instance, not explain the protection of consumers against aggressive sales methods, which according to the Directive on Unfair Commercial Practices (Chapter 3.10) forms a central aspect of the protection of consumers against unfair commercial practices. Of course, the field of unfair competition can be defined terminologically such that the decisive aspect is an information deficit. However, this does not correspond with the actual protection provided on the basis of unfair competition, clearly demonstrated by comparative law (see the Country reports in this book in Chapter'4). Collins in: Collins (ed.) (fn. 23), therefore, rightly examines under the heading "Contract Law" the relationship to the unfair practices provisions (at Community level) exclusively from the point of view of a "potential for mutual interference" (p. 37). Such overlaps indeed exist, e.g., with a possible duty to "disclose material information". However, overlaps also exist with a number of other legal areas (e.g., IP rights). This merely shows that the genuine character of unfair competition law is "different" from those neighbouring areas of law.
27. Italy, Hungary, Estonia; the FTC in the USA etc.
28. See above (Chapter 1, I).
29. Cf., as early as 1982, van Veljanovski, *The New Law and Economics. A Research Review*, Oxford, 1982.
30. See, for instance, the clause laying down the purpose of the Swiss Act against Unfair Competition, which expressly emphasises the interests of the general public in the functioning of competition; an identical clause can be found in the new Act against Unfair Competition in Germany; for details see country report Germany (Chapter 4). The link between competition law and consumer protection against unfair commercial practices is slightly stressed by Stuyck, *EC Competition Law after Modernisation: More than ever in the Interest of Consumer*, Journal of Consumers Policy (2005) 28: 1–30.

However, it does not (or no longer) fit entirely into only one of these fields of law. Instead, in most Member States it has developed into a legal field of its own in which the focus is on the collective protection of businesses and consumers against unfair market behaviour.[31] This focus typically is on the way in which a trader behaves in promoting his goods or services; thus ensuring a level playing ground for all market participants. If competition is often compared to, for instance, a football match or a track and field race (where all participants pursue the same goal, namely to score or to come in first), then unfair competition law deals with the rules of the relevant game, preventing fouls and ensuring that the goal is reached through the participants' own efforts.

III. SUBJECT MATTERS OF UNFAIR COMPETITION LAW

As far as concerns the subject matter of unfair competition law, almost all Member States start from a core area that roughly corresponds with the traditional view of "concurrence déloyale": the creation of a likelihood of confusion, disparagement and deception. However, almost all legal systems have now gone beyond this limit. They regulate, mostly in the interests of all market participants, for instance the entire field of advertising, sales promotions, special sales, price indications, direct marketing through modern forms of communication, business secrets, slavish imitation, breach of the law and more.[32] The difference is that some Member States regulate the entire field—possibly with the addition of collective consumer protection regulations such as those concerning standard business terms—in a single law, while others distribute it across a number of laws; sometimes adopting the sanctions to the concrete purpose of protection.

These differences, in part due to history and in part to national peculiarities, should not be overrated. The fact that all regulated areas belong together is reflected in the fact that the "consumer protection laws" frequently also protect competitors—and vice versa—or that there are at least numerous "links" between the two areas.[33] Even if the regulations are distributed over a number of laws, the aim remains the regulation of market activities under the aspect of fairness. These market practices can be divided up in legal terms but not in commercial terms. Most commercial practices affect the interest of competitors and consumers equally, being two sides of one coin. This is evident in the case of misleading practices, where the deception of the consumers also harms competitors' sales. But even the harassment of consumers, without doubt a business practice primarily concerning consumers, has an effect on the sales opportunities of the offender's competitors. Conversely, slavish imitation, disparagement etc. affect indirectly the interest of consumers, at least their interest in the well-functioning of competition.[34] If the basic feature is competition,

31. As to the objective criteria of defining unfair competition law (although restricted to the aspect of misappropriation) see also Kamperman Sanders (fn. 12), p. 78 et seq.
32. Kamperman Sanders (fn. 6), p. 7 et seq., referring to the WIPO Study (see Chapter 3, III), indicates as possible subject matters: Confusion, misleading, discrediting, trade secrets, freeriding (e.g. exploitation of another's goodwill, slavish imitation, parasitic acts), comparative advertising and other acts of unfair competition, namely nuisance advertising, exploitation of fear, psychological pressure, sales promotion, impeding market activities. See also Henning-Bodewig and Schricker, 24 EIPR 271 (2002).
33. See for instance country report France (Chapter 4).
34. For this reason, most EC Directives protect consumers and competitors equally, see Chapter 3, III. The restriction on consumer protection in Directive 2005/29/EC on Unfair Commercial Practices (Chapter 3, IV.10) seems to be more due to questions of responsibilities within the

then consumers and competitors have one common goal: to prevent a distortion of competition through unfair acts or practices.

IV. THE GENERAL CLAUSE AND THE DEFINITION OF "UNFAIR"

With the exception of Great Britain, Ireland, Malta and Cyprus, all Member States consider general clauses mandatory in order to control ever-changing marketing practices and to supplement the system of express legal provisions.[35] Although these general clauses are drafted differently, the core issue is the fairness of commercial practice.

This leads to the difficult question of how commercial fairness is to be determined. Most Member States try to describe it (in the general clauses or in interpretation by the courts) through terms like "honest practices", "bones mores", "good marketing" or "good faith". This choice of words, largely historical on the whole, is only of limited relevance. The decisive factor is how judicial practice and literature interpret the respective terms. So far, this has been a matter for national law, although the requirements laid down in the new Directive 2005/29/EC on Unfair Commercial Practices, will have to be taken into account.

In most Member States, the interpretation of "fairness"—irrespective of the term actually used—is based above all on the regulatory context, hence in particular on any statutory explanation of the general clause given by means of examples. Otherwise, reference is often made to the definition in the Paris Union Convention which, since 1925, defines unfair competition as "any act of competition contrary to honest trade practices in industrial or commercial matters".[36] This clarifies two things: The starting point is what is actually usual in business life ("trade practices"), corrected by the ethical aspect of "honest". Thus the Paris Union Convention (also) refers to extra-legal standards. However, these must in turn be derived from market activity; what counts are not the "ten commandments" or other morally based requirements, but rather the business ethics of the trade in question. To this extent, one may speak of a functional interpretation.

The attempt to arrive at a more precise definition is made in Directive 2005/29/EC of 11 May 2005.[37] Article 5(2) describes unfair commercial practices as practices that are "contrary to the requirements of professional diligence" and are capable of materially distorting the economic behaviour of the average consumer. The concept of professional diligence (better known in the field of tort law) was originally defined as "the measure of special skill and care exercised by a trader commensurate with the requirements of normal market practices towards consumers…".[38] Following criticism, this wording was extended through the addition of "honest market practices and/or the general principle of good faith in the trader's field of activity", which ultimately brings us back to the wording of the Paris Union Convention. The definition used in the Directive contains the additional clarification that what matters is the effect on the economic behaviour of the addressee.[39]

Commission. Recital 8 itself acknowledges the fact that the interests of consumers and competitors are intertwined.

35. See the country reports in Chapter 4; see also Henning-Bodewig and Schricker, 24 EIPR 271 (2002).
36. For details see Chapter 2, I.
37. See Chapter 3, IV.10.
38. Cf. Micklitz, "A general framework directive on fair trading", in Collins (ed.) (fn. 23), p. 43 et seq.
39. This corresponds with the general opinion at Community level and with national law, cf. Directive 84/450/EC (presented in Chapter 3, IV.3) and in particular the interpretation by the ECJ in the "Nissan" decision (Case C-373/90 [1992] ECR-I-00131).

Despite these difficulties of terminology, the concept of unfairness is not entirely "vague". On the contrary, there are a number of approaches to its determination that are generally accepted in most Member States:

- Reference points are actual commercial practices;
- In the individual case, these practices may be corrected by an extra-legal value judgment;
- The "ethical criteria" are to be taken from business life (self-regulatory agreements can provide valuable indications, provided that they take account of all interests);[40]
- The interpretation is "functional", i.e. takes into account both the importance of any express regulation of unfair competition and the specific context of the general clause, in particular its connection with the purpose of the protection;
- Unfair practices must be able to influence the commercial conduct of the addressee;
- there is a balancing of interests which also includes the balancing of constitutional positions.[41]

In addition, it must be remembered that every further decision by the national courts, and in cases of conflict by the ECJ, gives more contours to the concept of fairness. The disadvantage of the general clause being open to a certain extent—as is necessary if the aim of flexibility is not to be endangered—is thus considerably mitigated. Such a concept is familiar in almost all Member States; even in the Anglo-American legal systems there are no reservations against, for instance, a "fair-use" doctrine. At Community level, general clauses are familiar in particular in cartel law; for instance in Article 82 of the EC Treaty. It is the task of such general clauses in cartel law as well as in the law of unfair competition to mark the borderline between legitimate use of the freedom of competition and the misuse of this freedom.[42]

V. ENFORCEMENT

The question of the most suitable remedies for preventing unfair competition is answered differently in the different Member States; there being a mixture of remedies in almost all countries, with a focus on one particular type of remedy. According to current Community law, this is permissible.[43]

In most countries, criminal law is regarded as too cumbersome to do justice to the requirements of modern competitive life. For this reason, all Member States (also) provide for civil-law remedies.[44] Of the civil-law remedies, the action for an injunction, irrespective of fault and damages, has prevailed especially in interlocutory proceedings, it coming closest to the pragmatic need to prevent unfair competitive activity without delay. It is indicative that in the countries where the action for damages

40. For instance, the IIC Codex is often used in the Scandinavian countries to assist interpretation of "good marketing behaviour"; see the country reports in Chapter 4.
41. This aspect will increase upon the adoption of the Charta of Fundamental Rights; see Chapter 3, I.
42. Henning-Bodewig and Schricker, EIPR [2002] 271, 274.
43. See, in particular, the enforcement provisions of Directive 84/450/EC and Directive 2005/29/EC (Chapter 3, IV.3 and 10).
44. See the country reports, Chapter 4.

still predominates, the specific requirements are construed in such a way that the result tends to depend on objective criteria.[45]

Put very simply, all Member States rely on civil-law remedies, in particular injunctive relief, if the primary interest is that of business. However, in contrast there are differences as to the question whether the protection of the (collective) interests of the consumers requires (additional) public-law remedies.

- In a number of Member States, consumer protection through unfair competition law is likewise a purely civil-law matter;[46]
- Usually, the predominant civil-law remedies are, however, supplemented by administrative law remedies;[47]
- In some Member States, the focus is on administrative and criminal-law protection, although there are always some connections to civil-law protection.[48]

Where consumer protection is supplemented by administrative and criminal-law remedies, the latter can take very different forms. It remains to be seen whether the Regulation concerning Cooperation on Consumer Protection[49] will indirectly lead to any degree of harmonisation.

It is the overwhelming view that self-regulation does not, from the point of view of unfair competition law, constitute a substitute for legal remedies. In a (rather small) number of countries,[50] it has nevertheless de facto almost assumed the function of the law, while in most other countries it has only supplementary effect. This difference in significance leads to misunderstandings, for instance about the importance of judicial decisions in unfair competition law. In countries with an efficient self-regulatory system, this is often used to satisfy the need for a rapid and simple termination of unfair trade behaviour (although the reason may naturally also be the difficulty of pursuing actions before the courts). In countries without any significant self-regulation, the desired "arbitration ruling" can only be issued by the courts, and here the action for a preliminary injunction (the results of which are usually accepted by the parties) frequently fulfils the same function as self-regulation.[51]

VI. APPLICABLE LAW, MULTI-STATE CONFLICTS, COUNTRY-OF-ORIGIN PRINCIPLE

1. The "market-place" principle

Since competition law is primarily national law, constellations of fact that take place entirely within the borders of one Member State are to be determined also entirely

45. See, for instance, the interpretation of the general tort clause in cases of "concurrence déloyale" in France, country report France (Chapter 4).
46. E.g. Germany, Austria, the Netherlands, Spain, Luxemburg.
47. E.g. Belgium, Denmark, Sweden.
48. E.g. France, Italy.
49. Chapter 3, IV.11. The Regulation only relates to inner-Community cases. This can indirectly also have an impact on the national system of enforcement.
50. In particular Great Britain, Ireland and in part also the Netherlands, see the corresponding country reports (Chapter 4).
51. A comparison of the number of judicial decisions in unfair competition matters is thus not always conclusive. One of the thousands of interlocutory injunctions in Germany is of different importance than one of the few court decisions in Great Britain, for instance.

according to the laws of that Member State. This does not mean that the national judges do not keep an eye on the secondary Community legislation implemented in national law, submitting cases of doubt to the ECJ.

As trade intensifies, however, more and more cross-border market activities are taking place. Thus, advertising and marketing (for instance on the internet) increasingly ignores national borders. If a market activity affects a number of Member States, the question arises of which country enjoys jurisdiction and what law is to be applied.

International jurisdiction is determined by Council Regulation 44/2001/EC of 22 December 2000 on Jurisdiction and Recognition and Enforcement of Judgments in Civil and Commercial Matters,[52] which entered into effect on 1 March 2002. Article 5(3) lays down the jurisdiction of the courts of the country "where the harmful event occurred or may occur". Hence, the primary point of departure is the market place.

The international jurisdiction has, at least in theory, nothing to do with the question of the law that the (competent) court must apply. This is determined according to international private law, hitherto the national law of the Member States.[53] International private law in probably all Member States likewise applies the market-place-principle, i.e. the law of the place where the interests protected by competition law conflict is applicable.

In multi-state competition affecting a number of countries and legal systems, it is possible that a decision could be adopted in a number of countries applying different laws, which can lead to different results. As stated at the beginning, even a harmonisation of substantive law does not always exclude differing interpretations. The approach proposed by the EC Treaty in such cases is to submit the case to the ECJ. This gradually leads to the clarification of individual issues, thereby increasing harmonisation of the interpretation of the law. One (successful) example of this is trademark law, where "vague" terms such as the likelihood of confusion have been filled out by an increasingly dense net of ECJ decisions.

2. Country-of-origin principle

Harmonising the law by means of the approximation of substantive law and by interpretation from the ECJ does, however, have one disadvantage: it requires time. To compensate for this disadvantage, the EU Commission has recently attempted to introduce the so-called country-of-origin principle.[54] However, it should be noted that the term "country-of-origin principle" is being used for a number of different factual and legal constellations depending on context.

a. Article 28 EC and the country-of-origin-principle

Thus, the principle of the free movement of goods established in Article 28 EC is in part already being referred to as the "country-of-origin principle". This is correct to the extent that the aim of the free movement of goods implies that products legally marketed in one Member State should be able to circulate as a matter of principle in

52. OJ L 012, 16.1.2001, p. 1; see also Case C-68/93 *Fiona Shevill* [1995] ECR I-00415.
53. Harmonisation is intended, but the so-called Rome II Agreement has as yet not been adopted; see Leistner, "The Rome II-Regulation Proposal and its relation to the country-of-origin-principle", in Drexl/Kur (eds.), *Intellectual Property and Private International Law*, 2005, p. 177 et seq.
54. On the country-of-origin principle, cf., e.g., Leistner (fn. 53).

other Member States. Hence, the product must be capable of being marketed lawfully (or the service being provided lawfully) in at least one Member State. If it is prohibited everywhere, the principle of the free movement of goods or services cannot be infringed.

Nevertheless, the point of departure is not the lawful putting into circulation in the country of export. Article 28 of the EC Treaty takes as its starting point the receiving country, and lays down the principle that a Member State cannot prevent or impede the import of goods from another Member State. In contrast, the starting point is not whether these are goods that have been lawfully produced and marketed especially in this Member State. For example, the ECJ does not examine whether the term "Clinique" is permissible especially according to the law of France (as the country of export), but merely determines that "Clinique" is lawfully marketed in other Member States. The focus is on the laws of the country of import (here Germany).[55]

Moreover, Article 28 EC is a priori subject to restrictions. A Member State may prohibit imports despite this being an obstacle to the free movement of goods if either the exceptions of Article 30 of the Treaty apply or if there are "mandatory requirements" (see Chapter 3.III.1). The restriction of a "lawful putting into circulation" in another Member State is neither a restriction in Article 30 of the Treaty nor an inherent restriction. If, for instance, an insecticide is marketed in Italy in breach of Italian regulations and is then exported to Hungary, the import to Hungary cannot be prevented using the argument that the product was unlawfully put into circulation in Italy. It could only be prohibited if the product breaches Hungarian law and if the regulations of Hungarian law are covered by Article 30 or "mandatory requirements."

b. Secondary Community law

Of course, taking into account the above considerations, Article 28 of the EC Treaty can be qualified as the country-of-origin principle in a broader sense. However, it has to be made clear that the Commission also uses the term "country-of-origin principle" in a different sense. Thus the country-of-origin principle of secondary Community law, to the extent implemented so far, takes a different approach, with the primary issue being not the recipient country's right to prevent imports but rather the fact that an enterprise resident in one Member State should be able to rely on compliance with its own national law being sufficient in all other Member State.

The use of the term country-of-origin principle becomes even more confusing by the fact that there are also different types of country-of-origin principle in secondary law.

- Thus, in secondary Community law, the country-of-origin principle was first introduced in the Television Directive 89/552/EEC dated 17 October 1989.[56] According to Article 3, the country-of-origin principle applies to all "sectors coordinated" by the Directive, which means the factual constellations harmonised by the Directive itself. As the ECJ[57] has expressly held,

55. See Case C-315/92 *Verband Sozialer Wettbewerb* v. *Clinique and Estée Lauder* [1994] ECR I-317 (also Chapter 3.III.2).
56. OJ 1989 L 298, p. 23; discussed in Chapter 3, IV.4.
57. Joined cases C=34/95, C=35/95 and C=36/95 *Konsumentenombudsmannen* v. *De Agostini* [1997] ECR I-03843.

the Directive does not contain a general harmonisation as far as concerns, for instance, the field of advertising. For this reason, misleading television advertising is not covered by the country-of-origin principle, while in contrast advertising to and with children is covered, since the latter is harmonised by the TV Directive itself. The TV Directive obliges the country of origin to monitor at source (in accordance with the harmonised regulations) and in return prohibits the recipient country banning the broadcast by applying national law.

- Another kind of country-of-origin principle is to be found in the E-Commerce Directive adopted on 8 June 2000.[58] This Directive deals inter alia with "commercial communications" (advertising, marketing, sponsoring, etc.), but itself regulates only few aspects. It also lays down the country-of-origin principle for the "coordinated area" and links this to an obligation to monitor at source (Article 3). However, the scope of the country-of-origin principle is significantly broader than that of the Television Directive. These differences are due to the fact that the "coordinated area" is defined differently, and covers not only the (relatively few) aspects harmonised by the Directive itself, but also all other requirements that national law applies to commercial communication. Hence the country-of-origin principle of the E-Commerce Directive also and specifically applies where the laws of the Member States have not been harmonised. It consequently represents a genuine new approach by the Commission.[59]

This new approach is not regarded as a regulation of the applicable law, which would have been the obvious solution. On the contrary, Article 1(4) emphasises that the provisions of international private law remain unaffected. The practical result is the following scenario: the applicable law is determined according to the international private law of the receiving country (hence mostly the law of the "market-place"). However, the decisive question whether the commercial communication at issue is permitted is to be determined by the law of the country of origin (if it is more liberal). This requires a comparison of the laws, hardly possible in summary proceedings that are of special importance in competition law.[60]

- Directive 2005/29/EC on Unfair Commercial Practices[61] originally contained (Article 4) an obligation on the country of origin to monitor at source and in addition an obligation on the receiving country "neither (to) restrict the freedom to provide services nor (to) restrict the free movement of goods falling within the field approximated by this Directive". The first paragraph was subsequently dropped, leaving the meaning of the remaining obligation not to impede the free movement of goods unclear.[62] A situation as in the E-Commence Directive

58. OJ L 178, 17.7.2000, p. 1; discussed in Chapter 3, IV.8.
59. Cf. Bodewig, GRUR Int. 2000, 475; Mankowski, IIC 390 (2001).
60. The complications were demonstrated in proceedings before the Hamburg Court of Appeal, Germany, of 9.2.2004 (GRUR 2004, 880 with note by Henning-Bodewig). It concerned an advertisement on the Internet from the Netherlands to Germany for a medical device; disputed was the question whether the product required a CE certification. Although this is regulated in a relatively detailed Directive, the interpretation of the Directive differed in Germany and the Netherlands. The application of the country-of-origin principle made it necessary not only to make a partial legal comparison of the exact implementation of the Directive in Germany and the Netherlands, but also of the interpretations given to it by the courts and legal literature. This required legal expertises to be obtained, etc., which normally is not done in interlocutory proceedings.
61. See in detail Chapter 3, IV.10.
62. Directive 2003/33/EC on Tobacco Advertising contains a similar clause (see Chapter 3, IV.6).

can hardly be intended because of the clear statement that the country-of-origin principle has been abandoned. That leaves two interpretations of the "internal market clause": either that the national courts apply their own law and check whether it infringes Arts. 28 and 59 of the EC Treaty, which, this being their duty anyway, gives Article 4 purely declaratory significance. Or the internal market clause is interpreted such that the principle of mutual recognition is absolute, i.e. there can be no reliance on exceptions. This, however, would be incompatible with the previous judicial practice of the ECJ, according to which Article 28 of the EC Treaty is a priori subject to inherent restrictions and that in cases of doubt EC directives must be interpreted in the light of the fundamental freedoms.[63] It is also unclear what is meant by "within the field approximated by this Directive".

Thus the country-of-origin principle of secondary Community law also proves, upon closer examination, to vary. Nevertheless, its common feature is that the focus is on the legal situation in the country of origin—the entrepreneur resident in one Member State need only take account of the law of his home country. Hence the issue is not, as with Arts. 28 and 49 of the EC Treaty, the lawfulness of the legislation of the receiving country that prevents imports from another Member State, but rather the (specific) transfer of the law of the country of origin to the receiving country.[64]

63. Case C-315/92 *Verband Sozialer Wettbewerb* v. *Clinique Lab. & Estée Lauder* [1994] ECR I-317.
64. See also the discussion on the country-of-origin principle in the proposed Services Directive.

Chapter 2. International Protection Against Unfair Competition

International protection against unfair competition is provided for by two international treaties: the Paris Convention—promulgated as early as 1883—and (in part) by the TRIPS Agreement of 1995.

I. THE PARIS CONVENTION

1. Development of unfair competition law in the Paris Convention

The Paris Convention initially (1833) served the international regulation of the "hard core" of industrial property right protection. Above all, patent law, where the principle of territoriality dominated in the individual states, was felt to be unsatisfactory because of increasing international connections and the disparity between the national laws. Since the creation of a uniform international patent law was not realizable, the route via an international treaty, the Paris Convention, was chosen as the next best solution. This international treaty was (and is) characterized by two principles: the principle of national treatment, i.e., citizens of the contracting states of the Paris Convention are to be treated like nationals in all other contracting states. Beyond this, however, in many areas the Paris Convention also stipulates a certain minimum protection, which shall be guaranteed to these foreign members of the Convention. In contrast, the Paris Convention does not mandate the introduction of corresponding provisions in national laws, and thus permits what is known as "national discrimination".

From this starting point it is understandable that in the beginning protection against unfair competition was not considered as one of the topics of the Paris Convention,[1] especially since it was at best only weakly developed in most of the contracting states.[2]

However, France, which was the first country to provide effective legal protection against "concurrence déloyale", pressed for the introduction of corresponding protection at international level as well, in order to ensure comparable protection to its own nationals abroad. It is generally assumed that the United Kingdom was strictly against any such protection and that the proposal foundered on the resistance from

1. The "classic" commentaries on the Paris Convention, namely the works by Bodenhausen, Guide to the Application of the Paris Convention of Industrial Property (1968) and Ladas, The International Protection of Industrial Property (Cambridge, Mass.) hardly discuss the topic of unfair competition. A more recent (short) introduction can be found in Kamperman Sanders, Unfair Competition Law. The protection of intellectual and industrial creativity, 1997. p. 6 et seq.; Beier, 100 Jahre Pariser Verbandsübereinkunft, 1983 GRUR Int. 339 and Henning-Bodewig, 30 IIC 166 (1999).
2. On the development of unfair competition law in Europe at the early stage cf., e.g., Schricker, Unfair Competition and Consumer Protection in Western Europe, 1 IIC 415 (1970).

the Anglo-American group. This, however, seems not to be true. On the contrary, in the period 1919 to 1925 the United Kingdom was one of the driving forces for establishing international protection against unfair competition, although there was a strong opposition to achieve this by means of a general clause like Article 1382 Code Civil (instead of very detailed legislative languages).[3]

At the Brussels Revision Conference of 1900, at least unity prevailed on a provision (now Article $10^{bis}(1)$ Paris Convention) which obliged the contracting states to grant nationals of other contracting states the same protection against unfair competition as their own citizens. This codification of the principle of national treatment for legal protection against unfair competition was a decisive step forward in cases in which a contracting state—such as France—already possessed a well-developed jurisdiction against "concurrence déloyale", yet had little effect where the contracting state concerned granted its own citizens only rudimentary protection or none at all. In order to compensate for this shortcoming, Article 10bis of the Paris Convention was therefore expanded at the Washington Revision Conference of 1911 to oblige the member states to ensure "effective protection against unfair competition", and (according to the newly inserted Article 10ter of the Paris Convention) to create appropriate legal remedies to combat it.

At the Washington Conference it was simultaneously recognized that the repression of unfair competition constitutes protected subject matter of industrial property (Article 1(2) Paris Convention), and thus in general is subject to the principle of national treatment (Arts. 2 and 3). The Paris Convention thus regards unfair competition law as belonging to industrial property, a view which for instance the European Court of Justice[4] (and also TRIPS)[5] do not share. The inclusion of unfair competition in the sphere of industrial property by the Paris Convention is understandable if one examines more closely the torts already recognized as unfair competition. They mainly concerned cases like passing off, exploitation of another's reputation, disparagement, betrayal of secrets, etc. which could indeed be regulated just as well in another context (which is now partly the case, as the expanded protection of marks in the new European trademark law illustrates).

The decisive breakthrough for international protection against unfair competition finally succeeded in 1925 at the Revision Conference in The Hague. Here it came to a remarkable international compromise between the French preference for broad general clauses and the Anglo-American adherence to enumerated torts. At the urging of France, a definition of unfair competition ("any act of competition contrary to the honest practices in industrial or commercial matters") was adopted in Article $10^{bis}(2)$ of the Paris Convention. The inclusion of the risk of confusion as one of the examples of dishonest practices complied with the legal tradition of the common-law countries, resembling the important tort of passing off in the common-law legal sphere. Finally another express prohibition against the discrediting of competitors ("dénigrement") by false allegations proved to be capable of consensus, since all the member states recognized it in one form or another. At the Lisbon Revision Conference of 1958, the example of misleading designations, which was disputed at first, also gained entry into the Paris Convention. The driving force this time was the Austrian delegation,

3. Wadlow, The International Law of Unfair Competition: the British Origins of Article 10bis of the Paris Convention for the Protection of Industrial Property, Oxford Intellectual Property Research Centre Working Paper Series No. 4 February 2003, <www.oiprc.ox.ac.uk/EJWP043.html>.
4. Chapter 3, II.
5. See under II.

which could cite a proposal of the AIPPI and a similarly worded recommendation of the International Chamber of Commerce. The tort was however deliberately drafted narrowly; the attempt also to include misleading indications of source failed, for instance, on the resistance of the American delegation, which, in view of the many foreign geographical indications of source that are regarded as generic names in the USA, feared difficulties for its national industry.

With the adoption of the example of misleading designations in 1958, the development of unfair competition in the Paris Convention was completed. Amendments have not been made since then and concrete plans are not known at this time.[6]

The present status of international competition law in the Paris Convention de lege lata may therefore be outlined as follows:

- Pursuant to Article $10^{bis}(1)$, the contracting states are obliged to ensure citizens of other contracting states "effective protection against unfair competition".
- In Article $10^{bis}(2)$ (general clause), unfair competition is defined as any act of competition which is "contrary to honest practices in industrial or commercial matters".
- Three cases are named in Article $10^{bis}(3)$ which "in particular shall be prohibited", namely creating the risk of confusion, discrediting competitors through false allegations and making misleading indications or allegations about one's own goods. This list is not enumerative, so that other competitive acts can also be covered by the general clause.
- Pursuant to Article 10ter(1) of the Paris Convention, appropriate legal remedies must be made available to the citizens of other contracting states, in order to ensure the effective repression of acts contravening Article 10bis; these must also include the power of federations and associations to take legal action (Article 10ter(2)).

2. Risk of confusion, discrediting, misleading allegations and the general clause of "honest trade practices"

In the literature, relatively scant attention has been paid until now to the international competition law anchored in Article 10bis and 10ter of the Paris Convention.[7] This is regrettable to the extent that there are definitely some interesting questions requiring clarification. Some of them are briefly considered below.

a. Risk of confusion

The distinction between Article 10bis Paris Union Convention and the other intellectual property rights is to a large extent unclarified. This is particularly true of Article $10^{bis}(3)(1)$ which prohibits acts that are liable "to create confusion by any means whatever with the establishment, the goods, or the industrial or commercial activities, of a competitor". Pursuant to the wording and history of development, there can be no doubt that in principle all modes of competition likely to create

6. But see the WIPO "Model Provisions on Protection Against Unfair Competition", which are based on Art. 10bis of the Paris Convention (Chapter 2.III.).
7. This may be attributable to the fact that most European countries already meet the standard set by Art. 10bis Paris Convention (or else have little interest in adopting a corresponding regulation).

confusion are embraced, and that the risk of confusion by marks is thereby not excluded. This, however, inevitably raises the question of demarcation to trademark law, which of course likewise concerns the risk of confusion between marks, business designations, etc. The general demarcation between IP rights and unfair competition law was already discussed above.[8] As far as the Paris Union Convention is concerned it should be kept in mind that the interpretation of the terms like confusion are to be construed autonomously in the context of the Convention. Thus not only the approach of one Member State is decisive, but rather the interpretation of all contracting States of the PC.

b. Discrediting competitors, misleading allegations

The two other examples of unfair competition mentioned in Article 10bis of the Paris Union Convention are less controversial than the risk of confusion. The prohibition on the discrediting of competitors in Article 10bis(3)(2) is probably found in all the legal systems of the contracting states, in any event in the relatively narrow area of objectively false allegations for the purposes of competition (whereby neither effective damage to another's reputation nor intent is required).

The same goes for the third expressly mentioned tort of unfair competition, the prohibition on misleading allegations, which since the enactment of the Directive on Misleading Advertising of 1984 at the latest has in any event been recognized for the EC states. Nor should it give rise to much conflict for the remaining contracting states of the Paris Convention in its (deliberately) narrow version, which relates only to misleading allegations about goods. Here, too, it should be indicated that the concept of the risk of misleading the public, which is not defined more closely, is to be construed autonomously in the context of the Directive. Thus, for instance, national peculiarities should not be decisive, but rather only a "middle" interpretation obtained by a comparison of laws should prevail.

c. "Honest practices"

There is unanimity that such acts of competition which do not fall into the groups of cases specified in para. (3) can nevertheless constitute unfair competition. The general clause in para. (2) embraces "any act of competition"—i.e., any act in a competitive relationship—that is contrary to "honest practices".[9] This concept, which was initially influenced by French legal thinking, is also to be interpreted autonomously in the context of the Convention. By "practices" ("usages") the actual practices are referred to; the qualification that these practices must be "honest" ("honnêtes") indicates a normative criterion. Since, with regard to "honest practices", there may be no universally accepted uniform standard—even within the European Union until now no real consensus has been achieved on this—, it will primarily depend upon the view of the protecting country in question, whereby in the case of international subject matter this national view must be supplemented by the possible existence of internationally accepted usage.

8. Cf. Chapter 1, II.2.
9. For more details on the interpretation of "honest practices" within the meaning of Art. 10bis PC, see Schricker, in: "Festschrift für Fikentscher" 1990, p. 990 et seq.

The question as to the perspective from which "honest practices" are determined is particularly important where the consideration of consumer interests is concerned. To the extent, for example, that "honest practices" in the relevant protecting country are also determined by consumer protection considerations, these interests are also to be taken into account—although consumer protection as such in the general perception is not covered by the Paris Union Convention. To that extent (but only to that extent) the general clause may also be assessed as an "entry gate" for consumer protection in the Paris Union Convention. If, on the other hand, in the protecting country consumer protection is separated from competitor protection and does not figure in the judgment of the fairness of an act of competition, then a definition of business ethics is adhered to that is viewed strictly from the perspective of the competitor.

II. TRIPS

Intellectual property, regulated in the TRIPS Agreement (Trade-Related Aspects of Intellectual Property Rights),[10] acceded to by 148 states at the beginning of 2005, forms (along with trade in goods and services) what is known as the third pillar of the World Trade Organization (WTO). TRIPS thereby contains very detailed and sometimes extensive regulations on copyright law and related rights (except personality rights), trademarks, geographical indications, industrial designs, patents, layout designs (topographies), trade secrets, and on the control of anti-competitive practices in contractual licenses; in addition, a detailed regulation of the "Enforcement of intellectual property rights" may be found in Part III. For conflicts between the member countries a special procedure was stipulated, the dispute prevention and settlement procedure. TRIPS also contains a most-favoured nation clause, which for the first time has been introduced into the context of international-law agreements on intellectual property and which supplements the principle of national treatment which is already familiar from the Paris and Berne Conventions. In contrast to the Paris Convention, however, it is not just a question of extending the protection granted nationally to foreigners; TRIPS also contains an independent obligation to create corresponding national law in the regulated sectors. Should a country refuse to do so, the non-fulfilment of obligations from the TRIPS Agreement can form the basis for trade policy sanctions and the withdrawal of trade privileges, indeed an effective means of pressure. Furthermore, TRIPS is directly applicable where national constitutional law permits such direct application upon ratification and where the provisions in question are sufficiently precise. As concerns the relationship to the EU, TRIPS is considered at least part of Community law.[11]

These general principles illustrate what an incomparably stronger impact could have been achieved if unfair competition law had been included in TRIPS. This did not however happen. Unfair competition law as such is not mentioned in Part II of the TRIPS Agreement, nor is there anything to be found in the wording of TRIPS which

10. On the TRIPS Agreement, cf., e.g. Chasen Ross, in: Steward (ed.), *The GATT Uruguay Round*, p. 2245 et seq., vol. 2 (Deventer, Boston 1993); Blakeney, *Trade-Related Aspects of Intellectual Property Rights: A Concise guide to the TRIPS Agreement* (London 1996); Staehlein, Das TRIPS-Abkommen (Bern 1997); Gervais, *The TRIPS Agreement: Drafting History and Analysis*, 2nd ed., 2003; Reger, *Der internationale Schutz gegen unlauteren Wettbewerb und das TRIPS-Abkommen*, 1999; Mankowski, GRUR Int. 2001, 100.
11. As to the link between TRIPS and the EU see the decision of the ECJ 16.6.1998, Case C-53/96 *Hermès* (1998) ECR I-3603 and 14.12.2000, Case C-300/98 *DIOR*.

would support the conclusion that it was to be put on an equal footing with patent, trademark, copyright and design law. Unfair competition law as such is quite plainly not the regulated subject matter of TRIPS.[12]

Yet in some places reference is indeed made to unfair competition law. Thus there are two cases in the TRIPS Agreement in which competition-law elements at least play a role. These concern the protection of trade secrets and the protection of geographic indications, neither of which can be counted as the central subject matter of unfair competition law (and which are regulated in many countries under trademark law or in special statutes), but which nevertheless exhibit clear links to unfair competition law. These ties also find expression in TRIPS.

Thus, for example, Article 22(2) of the TRIPS Agreement obliges member countries to protect geographic indications of source from the application of misleading designations and generally from any use which "constitutes an act of unfair competition within the meaning of Article 10bis of the Paris Convention". By virtue of this reference to Article 10bis of the Paris Convention, geographic origin is therefore protected against any unfair use, particularly through the creation of a risk of confusion or other such misleading indications; by virtue of the connection with Article 10bis of the Paris Convention, it is argued that the use of designations which lie in the field of similarity with geographic indications may also be covered.

And also for the protection of trade secrets—"protection of undisclosed information" according to TRIPS—blanket reference is made to Article 10bis of the Paris Convention. Thus, Article 39(1) states: "In the course of ensuring effective protection against unfair competition as provided in Article 10bis of the Paris Convention (1967), Members shall protect undisclosed information in accordance with paragraph 2 below and data submitted to governments or governmental agencies in accordance with paragraph 3 below". Further, pursuant to para. (2): "Natural and legal persons shall have the possibility of preventing information lawfully within their control from being disclosed to, acquired by, or used by others without their consent in a manner contrary to honest commercial practices".

Apart from these two special cases, which refer to Article 10bis of the Paris Convention and the provision specified there, TRIPS elsewhere also makes a general reference to the Paris Convention. Thus Art. 2(1) states that: "In respect of Parts II, III and IV of this Agreement, Members shall comply with Articles 1-12 and 19 of the Paris Convention (1967)". Whether this means that the substantive legal standard in Art. 10bis of the Paris Convention must be taken up by members of the WTO in their national legislation in favour of their own citizens is to be doubted. The reference to the Paris Convention, pursuant to the unambiguous wording of Art. 2(1) of the TRIPS Agreement, only applies to the subject matter expressly named in Parts II, III and IV. Unfair competition as such does not count among them, but only the two expressly regulated cases of trade secrets and geographic indications of source. It must also be recalled that the Paris Convention only stipulates national treatment and not the protection of a member state's own citizens in its own country. The effect of the reference in Art. 2 of the TRIPS Agreement to Art. 10bis of the Paris Convention, in my opinion, is therefore restricted in that those members of the WTO that do not already belong to the Paris Convention are henceforth obliged, with regard to the subject matter regulated in the TRIPS Agreement (in the field of competition law: trade secrets and

12. For an indepth discussion see Reger (fn. 10) and the *Havanna-Club* case, which concerned the protection of a trade name; Panel Report. US-Section 211 Omnibus Appropriations Act of 1998 of 6.8.2001 and 22.2.2002.

geographic indications), to grant foreigners at least the protection provided for under Art. 10bis of the Paris Convention, and that the failure to fulfil this obligation leads to the application of the specific sanctions provided for under the TRIPS Agreement, i.e., the dispute settlement procedures.

In summary, it may be concluded that, because of the close relationship of the law of unfair competition to intangible property rights, the TRIPS Agreement refers on several occasions to Art. 10bis of the Paris Convention and thus to specific unfair competition-law principles; these sporadic mentions of fair practices law do not, however, lend themselves to be interpreted as an international regulation of the legal protection against unfair competition.

III. WIPO MODEL PROVISIONS ON PROTECTION AGAINST UNFAIR COMPETITION

At the Stockholm Conference on the revision of the Paris Convention (1967), the Agreement to Establish a World Intellectual Property Organization (WIPO) was adopted.[13] It repeatedly proved to be the locomotive for developments in industrial property law. This also applies to unfair competition law. For this reason, it must attract special attention that WIPO has again increasingly concerned itself with unfair competition law. Decisive for this was the idea that the worldwide (and European) harmonisation of competition law has been stagnating for a long time, yet on the other hand that, especially during the past decade, many countries—e.g., the former socialist states of eastern Europe and some countries in Asia—have shown, and still show, a strong interest in the introduction of unfair competition laws. Additionally, at WIPO the opinion apparently prevails that—contrary to the view presented here—Art. 2 of the TRIPS Agreement obliges, or at least could oblige, the member countries to introduce a regulation into national law in order to satisfy Art. 10 of the Paris Convention.

In any event, all this has moved WIPO to devote itself increasingly to unfair competition law. The first step was a worldwide "stocktaking" of the "Protection Against Unfair Competition" (1994).[14] In 1996, WIPO published the "Model Provisions for Protection Against Unfair Competition".[15] According to the "Notes" on Art. 1, they should particularly serve to put at the disposal of the countries, which in future by virtue of Art. 2 of the TRIPS Agreement are for the first time obliged to observe Art. 10bis of the Paris Convention, a type of guideline to manage this difficult task. It should be unambiguously pointed out that this does not mean binding law, but merely a proposal without any legal commitment. It therefore needs no further explanation that the WIPO Model Provisions are of a quite different calibre to the Paris Convention and the TRIPS Agreement.

The WIPO Model Provisions refer to Art. 10bis of the Paris Convention. However, they are not only (as the Notes on Art. 1 might suggest) to be seen as an interpretation of the regulation in the Paris Convention, but expand the protection conferred there

13. WIPO is structured on the model of the United Nations and is an organization with its own international-law objectivity.
14. WIPO Study No. 725 (in English, French, Spanish); prepared by Henning-Bodewig and Ruijsenaars.
15. WIPO Study No. 832 (complied by Dutoit, Gielen, Keffauer and Matsu), WIPO Publication No. 832 (E).

considerably. Therefore, the primary points of interest are those in which the WIPO Model Provisions differ from Art. 10bis of the Paris Convention, or go beyond these.

At first glance, certainly the most conspicuous change is that the examples of prohibited acts are expanded from three to five: besides the risk of confusion, disparagement and misleading, mention is now made of damaging goodwill or reputation and the protection of trade secrets. Yet the field of application of the three "old" groups of prohibited acts in Art. $10^{bis}(3)$ of the Paris Convention has also been considerably expanded by virtue of the adoption of further sub-examples. On the other hand, the general clause in Art. 10bis of the Paris Convention, as the Notes on Art. 1 also ascertain, at first appears unchanged, i.e., it is still based on being "contrary to honest practices", whereby the notes emphasize that the construction of this concept should also be on the basis of international trade practices. A substantial novelty as compared with Art. $10^{bis}(2)$ of the Paris Convention exists, however, in that there no longer need be a competitive relationship between the parties. Article 1 of the WIPO Model Provisions now only mentions "any act or practice in the course of industrial or commercial activities" and the Notes emphasize that this must be interpreted broadly, and thus also embraces activities of professionals and non-profit making activities. Finally the express and repeated emphasis that the purpose of the regulation is also the protection of consumers is also new; a view which until now was always denied for Art. 10bis of the Paris Convention.

In contrast to the Paris Convention, the WIPO Model Provisions provide for a regulation of sanctions in Art. 1b. In principle, any natural or legal person that is "damaged or likely to be damaged" by a competitive act should be entitled to legal protection. The exact sanctions are still open, however; WIPO first wishes to await a corresponding study, but has announced that it intends to stay close to the provisions on the enforcement of rights in the TRIPS Agreement.

One of the most important new aspects of the WIPO Model Provisions may be found in the second paragraph of Art. 1. This concerns the demarcation of protection against unfair competition and intellectual property rights. This lays down that the protection conferred in Arts. 1-6 is independent and supplementary to any special statutory regulation in the field of patents, industrial designs, marks, copyrights "and other intellectual property subject matters". Further explanations are not given. The Notes on this paragraph are also kept brief; here the example is merely given that the inventor has the option of keeping his invention secret, treating it like a trade secret and protecting it under competition law. Further reference is made in the notes to the fact that the Model Provisions do not contain a specific provision against slavish imitation, since to this extent there are no "generally accepted conditions for such protection that would justify introducing it in addition to protection by patent law;" slavish imitation can, however, fall under the general clause. Otherwise neither from the text nor the Notes suggest how the distinction from industrial property rights and copyright is to be made in practice. In particular, it is not clear how competition-law protection relates to the specific standards of the special laws in the area of industrial property—which, for example, subject protection to formal requirements or limit its term.

Chapter 3. Protection Against Unfair Competition Law on the Community Level

I. PRIMARY AND SECONDARY COMMUNITY LAW

As stated at the beginning, there is as yet no European unfair competition law in the sense of a uniform and coherent legislative system. However, particular aspects have been approximated, above all by Directives and occasionally by Regulations, usually referred to as "secondary Community law". At the same time, there is a negative harmonisation via the fundamental freedoms of the EC Treaty, i.e. via the judicial practice of the ECJ on the basis of Arts. 28 and 49 of the Treaty ("primary Community law").[1] European unfair competition law therefore currently consists of a combination of primary and secondary Community law. In cases of doubt, primary law takes priority, i.e. European Directives etc. are in turn to be interpreted in the light of the fundamental freedoms.[2]

A further basis is in the future likely to be the European Constitution.[3] Although it does not deal expressly with unfair competition law, the Charter of Fundamental Rights lays down important basic rights for market participants. Mention is made, for instance, of the dignity of man (Art. II-61), the right to the free expression of opinion and freedom of information (Art. II-71), to entrepreneurial freedom (Art. II-76) and property (Art. II-177), to non-discrimination (Art. II-81), to the protection of health (Art. II-85) and to consumer protection (Art. II-98). Already, Art. 6 Para. 2 second sentence of the EU Treaty lays down that Community law must respect the fundamental rights—as guaranteed in the European Convention on Human Rights and as far as they correspond with the joint conviction of all Member States. Hence today, the ECJ naturally includes in its argumentation the right, for instance, to the free expression of opinion in Art.10 of the European Convention on Human Rights. In the future, the construction of secondary Community law in conformity with the EU Constitution could acquire an importance of its own, especially by balancing conflicting constitutional rights (for instance the fundamental right to entrepreneurial freedom and the freedom of opinion on the one hand and the right to a high level of consumer protection on the other hand).

1. For details, cf., e.g. Wyatt & Dashwood's, *European Union Law*, 4th Ed. 2000.
2. Established judicial practice of the ECJ, cf., for instance Case C-315/92 *Verband Sozialer Wettbewerb* v. *Clinique Laboratories and Estée Lauder* [1994] ECR I-317.
3. Draft Treaty on a European Constitution dated 20.6.2003 (CONN 820 (3)).

II. THE ROLE OF THE EUROPEAN COURT OF JUSTICE

The judicial practice of the ECJ is of particular importance for both primary and secondary Community law.[4] The ECJ monitors both the interpretation of existing directives etc. by the Member States and the compatibility of national regulations (and their interpretation) with Arts. 28 and 49 of the EC Treaty. National unfair competition law regulations can be submitted to the ECJ by a number of routes. If a court or a tribunal of a Member State considers that a decision of a question concerning these matters is necessary it may request a "preliminary ruling" of the ECJ provided there is no further judicial remedy under national law (Article 234 EC Treaty).

A preliminary ruling by the ECJ does not achieve harmonisation of competition law directly. Instead, the ECJ is limited to a finding that the provision in question (or the interpretation by the courts) is incompatible with secondary Community law (e.g. a directive) or infringes the principles of the free movement of goods or services. In fact, however, this has a substantial harmonisation effect, since as a rule it leads to an adjustment of the contested aspect of national competition law.[5] In contrast, a uniform (higher) standard of protection can only be created by means of secondary Community law.

III. NATIONAL UNFAIR COMPETITION LAW AND ARTICLES 28, 49 EC

1. Basic principles of the ECJ

a. Article 28 EC

Most ECJ decisions on unfair competition law are based on Art. 28 of the EC Treaty (formerly Article 30), which states

> *"Quantitative restrictions" on imports and all measures having equivalent effects shall be prohibited between Member States".*

According to Article 30 EC (formerly Article 36) this does not, however, preclude national prohibitions which are justified on the grounds expressly cited.

The basis for a decision in the field of unfair competition law has changed in the course of time, despite the wording remaining the same. The landmark judgments here are "Dassonville", "Cassis de Dijon" and "Keck & Mithouard".

According to the "Dassonville" decision[6] (which concerned the import of Scotch whisky into Belgium from France) all

> *"...trading rules enacted by Member States which are capable of hindering, directly or indirectly, actually or potentially, intra-Community trade are to be considered as measures having an effect equivalent to quantitative restrictions".*

4. As to the role of the ECJ in general, see Wyatt & Dashwood (fn. 1), p. 264 ff.
5. For instance, the decision of the ECJ in the *Yves Rocher* case (fn. 17) led the German legislature to repeal the provision in question (restriction of price comparisons).
6. Case 8/74 *Procureur du Roi* v. *Dassonville* [1974] ECR 837.

Since accordingly practically all regulations of national unfair competition law could constitute a restriction of trade, particular importance was attached to the grounds for justification. Article 30 of the Treaty permits, inter alia, national "prohibitions or restrictions . . . justified on rounds of public morality, public policy or public security; the protection of health . . . or the protection of industrial and commercial property" provided that these national restrictions are not "a means of arbitrary discrimination or a disguised restriction on trade . . . " Unlike the Paris Convention, the ECJ does not include unfair competition law within "intellectual property".[7] Instead, the leading decision, "Cassis de Dijon",[8] recognised the following "mandatory requirements" of Art. 28 EC:

> *8. Obstacles to movement within the Community resulting from disparities between the national laws relating to the marketing of the product in question must be accepted in so far as these provisions may be recognized as being necessary in order to satisfy mandatory requirements relating in particular to the effectiveness of fiscal supervision, the protection of public health, the fairness of commercial transactions or/and the defence of the consumer . . ..*

Subsequently, more and more questions were submitted to the ECJ, which consequently found itself obliged to impose restrictions on the cases it hears.[9] 1993, in the "Keck & Mithouard" judgment,[10] which concerned a (French) prohibition on resale at a loss, the court tried to draw the line as follows:

> *12. National legislation imposing a general prohibition on resale at a loss is not designed to regulate trade in goods between Member States.*
>
> *13. Such legislation may, admittedly, restrict the volume of sales, and hence the volume of sales of products from other member States, in so far as it deprives traders of a method of sales promotion. But the question remains whether such a possibility is sufficient to characterize the legislation in question as a measure having equivalent effect to a quantitative restriction on imports.*
>
> *14. In view of the increasing tendency of traders to involve Article 30 of the Treaty as a means of challenging any rules whose effect is to limit their commercial freedom even where such rules are not aimed at products from other member States, the court considers it necessary to re-examine and clarify its case-law on this matter.*
>
> *15. It is established by the case-law beginning with "Cassis de Dijon" (Case—120/78 Rewe-Zental* v *Bundesmonopolverwaltung fuer Branntwein [1979] ECR I-649) that, in the absence of harmonization of legislation, obstacles to free movement of goods which are the consequence of applying, to goods coming from other member Stats where they are lawfully manufactured and marketed, rules that lay down requirements to be met*

7. ECJ Case C-113/80, [1981] ECR I-01625.
8. Case C-120/78 *Rewe-Zentrale AG* v. *Bundesmonopolverwaltung für Branntwein*, [1979] ECR-649.
9. See Joliet, Droit de la concurrence déloyale et le libre circulation des merchandises. La jurisprudence de la Cour de Justice des Communautés Européennes, in: Un droit Européen de la Concurrence Déloyale en Formation, Actes du Colloque de Lausanne 1994, p. 29 ff.
10. Joined cases C-267/91-268/91, *Keck* and *Mithouard* [1993] ECR I-6097.

> *by such goods such as those relating to designation, form, size, weight, composition, presentation, labelling, packaging) constitute measures of equivalent effect prohibited by Article 30. This is so even if those rules apply without distinction to all products unless their application can be justified by a public, interest objective taking precedence over the free movement of goods.*
>
> *16. By contract, contrary to what has previously been decided, the application to products from other Member States of national provisions restricting or prohibiting certain selling arrangements is not such as to hinder directly or indirectly actually or potentially, trade e between member States within the meaning of the Dassonville judgment (Case 8/74 [1974] ECR 837), so long as those provisions apply to all relevant traders operating within the national territory and so long as they affect in the same manner, in law and in fact, the marketing of domestic products and of those from other Member States.*
>
> *17. Provided that those conditions are fulfilled, the application of such rules to the sale of products from another Member State meeting the requirements laid down by the State is not by nature such as to prevent their access to the market or to impede access any more than it impedes the access of domestic products. Such rules therefore fall outside the scope of Article 30 or the Treaty.*

In practice all national rules that lay down requirements to be met by goods (such as those relating to designation, form, size, weight, composition, presentation, labelling, packaging) constitute measures of equivalent effect still prohibited by Article 28, EC whereas "selling arrangements" (such as advertising rules) do not hinder trade between Member States provided that they apply to all relevant traders and provided that they affect in the same manner, in law and in fact, domestic and foreign products.[11]

According to the 2001 "Gourmet" decision[12] (concerning the Swedish prohibition on advertising for alcoholic drinks in the press), the above is to be interpreted as "market neutrality":[13]

> *21. Even without its being necessary to carry out a precise analysis of the facts characteristic of the Swedish situation, which it is for the national court to do, the Court is able to conclude that, in the case of products like alcoholic beverages, the consumption of which is linked to traditional social practices and to local habits and customs, a prohibition of all advertising directed at consumers in the form of advertisements in the press, on the radio and on television, the direct mailing of unsolicited material or the placing of posters on the public highway is liable to impede access to the market by products from other member States more than it impedes access by domestic products, with which consumers are instantly more familiar.*

11. Mere "selling arrangements" are, for instance, advertising restrictions and prohibitions in the field of television advertising (Case C-412/93 *Leclerc-Siples* [1995] ECR I-179), the prohibition on advertising the sale of pharmaceuticals by mail order (Case C-322/01 *Deutscher Apothekerverband* v. *Doc Morris* [2004] ECR I-0000) and the prohibition on certain announcements of bankrupt stock sales (Case *Karner* (2004) ECR I-3025).
12. Case C-405/98 *Gourmet International Products* [2001] ECR I-1795.
13. Similar, with respect to the question of market neutrality, ECJ, joined Cases C-418/93-C-332/94, [1996] ECR I-02975.

In summary, it can be stated that the ECJ examines national unfair competition regulations on the basis of Art. 28 of the EC Treaty as follows:

- Article 28 EC covers as a matter of principle all national unfair competition regulations (or their interpretation) that act like a "measure of the same effect".
- As a matter of principle, this is not the case for "selling arrangements" that affect the sale of domestic and foreign products both legally and in fact in the same way ("Keck doctrine").
- Even if there is an obstacle to the free movement of goods, this can be justified, for instance, by the protection of health (Art. 30) or by "mandatory requirements of the fairness of commercial transactions or consumer protection", provided that the principle of proportionality is maintained ("Cassis de Dijon").

b. Article 49 EC

National unfair competition law regulations (e.g. on advertising services) are also increasingly reviewed by the ECJ from the point of view of the freedom of services, Art. 49 of the EC Treaty. It is not yet clear whether the Keck doctrine will apply accordingly; however, national restrictions on the freedom of services can also be justified by mandatory requirements of the fairness of commercial transactions and consumer protection.[14]

2. Some landmark judgments of the ECJ

a. Article 28 EC

The ECJ, in an older decision, held the protection granted in the Netherlands against the slavish imitation of an imported technical device to be an obstacle to the free movement of goods but justified by "mandatory requirements of the fairness of commercial transactions".[15]

"Not justified" were national prohibitions of certain types of price comparisons in Luxembourg[16] and Germany.[17]

The national prohibition on premiums has also been the subject of a number of preliminary rulings.

– In 1980, the ECJ held that the (now repealed) prohibition of Dutch law on certain premiums could impair the sales opportunities for imported products and hence fall under Art. 30 of the EC Treaty (now Art. 28). Ultimately, however, this restriction was held to be justified from the point of view of consumer protection.[18]

– 20 years later, the ECJ came to the same conclusion. The "Familiapress" decision[19] concerned the Austrian restriction on premiums in the form of prize

14. See the ECJ decisions set out under 3, "Alpine Investment", "Baccardi" and "Loi Evin".
15. Case 6/89 *Industrie Diensten* v. *J.A. Beele* [1982] ECR 1982, p. 00707.
16. Case 362/88 *GB Immo* [1990] ECR I-00667.
17. Case C-126/91 *Yves Rocher* [1993] ECR I-2361.
18. Case C-286/81 *Oosthoek*, [1982] ECR I-04575.
19. Case C-368/95 *Vereinigte Familiapress Zeitungs- und VertriebsGmbH* v. *Heinrich Bauer Verlag* [1997] ECR I-03689.

competitions in magazines. The ECJ first held that the practice (despite the "Keck" doctrine) fell under Art. 28 of the EC Treaty, but that the Austrian prohibition was justified by the objective of media variety.

> *34. In the light of the foregoing considerations, the answer to be given to the national court's question must be that Article 30 of the EC treaty is to be interpreted as not precluding application of legislation of a Member State the effect of which is to prohibit the distribution on its territory by an undertaking established in another member State of a periodical produced in that latter State containing prize puzzles or competitions which are lawfully organized in that state, provided that that prohibition is proportionate to maintenance of press diversity and that that objective cannot be achieved by les restrictive means. This assumes, inter alia, that the newspapers offering the chance of winning a prize in games, puzzles or competitions are in competition with small newspaper publishers who are deemed to be unable to offer comparable prizes and the prospect of winning is liable to bring about a shift in demand. Furthermore, the national prohibition must not constitute an obstacle to the marketing of newspapers which, albeit containing prize games, puzzles or competitions, do not give readers residing in the Member State concerned the opportunity to win a prize. It is for the national court to determine whether those conditions are satisfied on the basis of a study of the national press market concerned.*

The already mentioned "Gourmet" decision[20] concerned a Swedish prohibition on print advertising for alcohol. Although the prohibition of itself constituted a "selling arrangement", the ECJ held that this was a measure that restricted the free movement of goods, since the effects for foreign products were not market-neutral (see above). However, the Swedish prohibition was justified

> *"... unless it is apparent that, in the circumstances of law and of fact which characterise the situation in the Member Stated concerned, the protection of public health against the harmful effect of alcohol can be ensured by measures having less effect on inter-community trade".*

b. Article 49 of the EC Treaty

The principle of the free movement of services of Art. 49 of the EC Treaty (formerly Art. 59) is playing an increasing role in unfair competition law, in particularly in the field of advertising services.

The "Alpine" decision[21] concerned unsolicited telephone calls by a financial service provider, prohibited under Dutch law. The ECJ held that this was a restriction of the free movement of services, but held it also to be necessary in order to satisfy mandatory requirements as to the fairness of commercial transactions and "imperative reason of public interest"; furthermore the "prohibition of cold calling does not appear disproportionate to the objective which it pursues".[22]

20. See fn. 12.
21. Case C-384/93 *Alpine Investments BV* [1995] ECR I-01141.
22. Para. 44, 55.

The "Loi Evin"-decision[23] concerned a French media law regulation that subjected the broadcasting of (foreign) events on (French) television to the removal of any advertising for alcoholic drinks. According to the ECJ, this regulation restricts the freedom of services:

> *26. In the first place, it must be observed that the French rules on television advertising constitute a restriction on freedom to provide services within the meaning of Article 59 of the Treaty. They entail a restriction on freedom to provide advertising services in so for as the owners of the advertising hoardings must refuse, as a preventive measure, any advertising for alcoholic beverages if the sporting event is likely to be retransmitted in France. They also impede the provision of broadcasting services for television programmes. French broadcasters must refuse all retransmission of sporting events in which hoardings bearing advertising for alcoholic beverages marketed in France may be visible. Furthermore, the organisers of sporting events taking place outside France cannot sell the retransmission rights to French broadcasters if the transmission of sporting events taking place outside France cannot sell the retransmission rights to French broadcasters if the transmission of the television programmes of such events is likely to contain indirect television advertising for those alcoholic beverages.*

However, the French regulations were considered necessary to protect public health, and on the whole not disproportionate:

> *30. Second, the French rules on television advertising pursue an objective relating to the protection of public health within the meaning of Article 56(1) of the Treaty, as the Advocate General stated in paragraph 69 of his Opinion. Measures restricting the advertising of alcoholic beverages in order to combat alcohol abuse reflect public health concerns (see Case 152/78 Commission* v *France [1980] ECR 2299, paragraph 17; Aragonesa de Publicidad Exterior and Publivia, paragraph 15; and Case C-405/98 Gourmet International Products [2001] ECR I-1795, paragraph 27).*
>
> *31. Third, the French rules on television advertising are appropriate to ensure their aim of the protection of public health. Furthermore, the do not go beyond what is necessary to achieve such an objective. They limit the situations in which hoardings advertising alcoholic beverages may be seen on television and are therefore likely to restrict the broadcasting of such advertising, thus reducing the occasions on which television viewers might be encouraged to consume alcoholic beverages.*

c. The benchmark of the "European Consumer"; the determination of deception

There are particularly numerous decisions by the ECJ on the national prohibitions against misleading practices (also to be found in legislation concerning food, cosmetics etc.). They frequently concerned the German law on misleading practices,

23. Case C-262/02 *Commission* v. *French Republic* [2004] ECR I-00000; see also Case C-429/02 *Baccardi* Case C-429/02[2004] ECR I-0000; the Baccardi-case is discussed in extcuso by Stuyck, C.M.L. Rev. 2005, 783.

which was still very strict at the time.[24] Justification via the mandatory requirements of the "fairness of commercial transactions and consumer protection" was as a rule rejected, mainly because the ECJ applied the new benchmark of the "average consumer", which had considerable influence on the judicial practice of all Member States. In connection with this benchmark, additional principles have been developed to assess deception. The following decisions are cited as examples:

– The "Clinique" decision[25] concerned the name "Clinique" for cosmetic products. The Berlin District Court submitted to the ECJ the question whether this designation could be prohibited according to German law on deception, since it created the incorrect impression of a clinical product. The ECJ examined the designation on the basis of the prohibition on deception contained in the Directive on the packaging and labelling of cosmetics.[26] This Directive in turn was to be construed in the light of the principle of the free movement of goods. The ECJ also held:

> *21. In particular, it is apparent from that information that the range of cosmetic products manufactured by the Estée Lauder company is sold in the Federal Republic of Germany exclusively in perfumeries and cosmetic departments of large stores, and therefore non of those products are available in pharmacies. It is not disputed that those products are presented as cosmetic products and not as medicinal products. It is not suggested that, apart from the name of the products, this presentation does not comply with the rules applicable to cosmetic products. Finally, according to the very wording of the question referred, those products are ordinarily marketed in other countries under the name 'Clinique' and the use of that name apparently does not mislead consumers.*
>
> *22. In the light of these facts, the prohibition of the use of that name in the Federal Republic of Germany does not appear necessary to satisfy the requirements of consumer protection and the health of humans.*
>
> *23. The clinical or medical connotations of the word 'Clinique' are not sufficient to make that word so misleading as to justify the prohibition of its use on products marketed in the aforesaid circumstances.*

The "Mars"-decision[27] concerned the question of a potential deception created by the text "Plus 10%" printed on a bar of ice cream. The ECJ rejected a justification on the grounds of mandatory requirements of consumer protection and fairness of commercial transactions. The purpose intended, the prevention of deception as to the quantity of the product, could also be achieved by other means:

> *24. Reasonably circumspect consumers may be deemed to know that there is not necessarily a link between the size of publicity markings relating to an increase in a product's quantity and the size of that increase.*

24. The ECJ-jurisdiction has led to German judicial practice becoming increasingly more liberal. In the meantime, a completely new Act against Unfair Competition has been in force since 2004; see country report Germany (Chapter 4).
25. Case C-315/92 *Verband Sozialer Wettbewerb* v. *Clinique Laboratories and Estée Lauder* [1994] ECR I-317.
26. Council Directive 76/68/EEC of 27.7.1976 on the approximation of laws of the Member States relating to cosmetic products; OJ 1976, L 262; No. 169.
27. Case C-470/93 *Mars* [1995] ECR I-1923.

The "Gut Springenheide"[28] and "Sektkellerei Kessler"[29] decisions were even clearer. The former concerned the question of a potential deception created by labelling hen's eggs as "six-grain eggs" (the types of grain mentioned only constituted 60% of the fodder mix). The headnote of this decision reads:

> *"In order to determine whether a statement or description designed to promote sales of eggs is liable to mislead the purchaser, in breach of Article 10(2)(e) of Regulation (EEC) No. 1907/90 of 26 June 1990 on certain marketing standards for eggs, the national court must take into account the presumed expectations which it evokes in an average consumer who is reasonably well informed and reasonably observant and circumspect".*

In the Clinique decision, the ECJ did not take account any national peculiarities (e.g. the pronunciation in German). Following criticism, a certain differentiation was made in the "Lifting" decision,[30] which was based on a similar constellation of facts, the question of deception through calling an anti-wrinkle cream "Lifting". Again, the ECJ first held that what mattered were

> *27. . . . the presumed expectations of an average consumer who is reasonably well informed and reasonably observant and circumspect and that this is also relevant for the interpretation of Article 6 (3) of Directive 76/68 which prohibits misleading representations of cosmetic products.*

However, according to the Court, "national specialities" must be taken into account:

> *29. . . . it must be determined whether social, cultural or linguistic factors may justify the term 'lifting' used in connection with a firming cream, meaning something different to the German consumer as opposed to consumers in other member States or whether the instructions for the use of the product are in themselves sufficient to make it quite clear that the effects are short-lived, thus neutralising any conclusion to the contrary that might be derived from the word 'lifting'.*

Mostly, the ECJ emphasises that the ultimate decision as to deception lies with the national courts. Thus, for instance, it held in the "Sechs-Korn" decision

> *However, community law does not preclude the possibility that, where the national court has particular difficulty in assessing the misleading nature of the statement or description in question, it may have recourse, under the conditions laid down by its own national law, to a consumer research poll or and expert's report as guidance for its judgment.*

These findings are to a certain extent in conflict with the "Naturrein"[31] decision, which concerned the labelling and presentation of strawberry jam as "naturally pure" (although the jam contained pectin and traces of lead, cadmium and pesticides).

28. Case C-210/96 *Gut Springenheide* [1998] ECR I-04657.
29. Case C-303/97 *Sektkellerei Kessler* [1997] ECR I-513, para. 36.
30. Case C-220/98 *Estée Lauder* and *Lancaster* [2000] ECR I-00117.
31. Case C-465/98 *Verein gegen Unwesen* in *Handel und Gewerbe* v. *Adolf d'Arbo ECR* [2000] I-02297.

Here the ECJ, referring to the model of the "average consumer", denied a deception because the food was significantly below the maximum limit permissible according to all Member State regulations.

> *1. Whilst, therefore, it is for the national court to decide, in the light of that criterion, whether, in view of the presence of this substances in Darbo jam, use of the term naturally pure is liable to mislead consumers as regards the characteristics of that foodstuff, the Court has before it the information it needs in order to expound the following considerations concerning each of the substances mentioned in the question referred to it.*

IV. SECONDARY COMMUNITY LAW: DIRECTIVES, REGULATIONS

1. Basis of secondary Community law

(Partial) harmonisation of national unfair competition law in the Member States has hitherto been effected above all by means of directives. Where national law deviates from these directives, they are to be implemented, taking into account the principles of clarity, unambiguity, etc, and as a rule apply equally to domestic and cross-border situations. Only in exceptional cases can third-party claims be based directly on directives.[32] The (less frequent) regulations, on the other hand, enjoy general and direct application, and need no implementation in national law. The ECJ is responsible for the interpretation of both (Art. 220 of the EC Treaty).

The EC Treaty does not contain a basis that directly deals with the regulation of unfair competition law. However, pursuant to Art. 2, it is the function of the Community "... by establishing a common market ... to promote throughout the Community ... a high degree of competitiveness and convergence of economic performance ..."

The Community's activity as described in Art. 3 of the Treaty involves issues of unfair competition law above all in connection with

- the prohibition of restrictions on the import and export of goods (a);
- the establishment of "a system ensuring that competition in the internal market is not distorted" (g);
- the approximation of the laws of Member States to the extent required for the functioning of the common market (h)

Most approximation measures in the field of unfair competition law are based on Art. 95 of the Treaty, which concerns the establishing or functioning of the common market. According to Para. 3 the Commission shall seek "a high level of protection", especially in matters concerning health, safety, environment and consumer protection.

2. History and present state of harmonisation

The attempts to approximate national unfair competition law by means of directives etc. can look back over a long and eventful history.[33]

32. Cf. Wyatt & Daswood's (fn. 1), p. 110 ff.
33. Cf., e.g. Schricker, Twenty-Five Years of Protection Against Unfair Competition, 26 IIC 782 [1999] Bakardjieva Engelbrekt (fn. 3 on p. 1).

Immediately after the Treaties of Rome were concluded, a start was made on approximation, which according to the "Ulmer" Expertise[34] was to cover the field of unfair competition law in a broad sense. The prospects of a successful result were relatively good, since the six Member States at the time had a very similar approach to competition law, with a strong focus on the individual rights of the competitor.

Ultimately, however, such a comprehensive harmonisation was politically unfeasible. There were a number of reasons, including

- the question whether and to what extent unfair competition law should also take account consumer interests; this question became increasingly important in the course of the consultation work, and was dealt with differently in the various Member States (see Chapter 1, I.).
- the resulting change in responsibilities on the part of the Commission; responsibility lay not only with the Directorate-General for the Internal Market but also with the consumer protection department (what was later to become GD SANCO).
- the accession of the United Kingdom and Ireland with their critical attitude towards approximation, in particular by means of general clauses.

These political difficulties led to the regulation being restricted to specific aspects in the field of unfair competition law, in particular advertising. However, a proposed directive on misleading and unfair advertising also failed.[35] Directive 84/450/EEC,[36] finally adopted in 1984, had to be restricted to misleading advertising; unfair advertising was supposed to follow "in a second stage". This did not happen; instead, it was extended in 1997 by a regulation of comparative advertising.[37] Advertising was further regulated in numerous product-specific regulations and some media-specific regulations, such as the Television Directive and the E-Commerce Directive. It was only in 2005 that a Directive on Unfair Commercial Practices was adopted.[38] This Directive is broader, insofar as it is not restricted to specific products, media or types of market behaviour (like advertising). On the other hand it is restricted to business-to-consumer practices and thus does not – like most other Directives—protect consumer and competitor alike and applies only in so far as there are no other Community law provisions regulating specific commercial practices.

As far as advertising is concerned there is now indeed extensive and detailed regulation on Community level. This regulation, however, is fragmented into several directives[39] which partly overlap, making comprehension more complicated with every new directive. The constantly repeated purpose to "increase legal certainty for both consumers and business" by eliminating "the barriers stemming from the fragmentation of the rules on unfair commercial practices . . ."[40] thus becomes somewhat

34. Ulmer (ed.), Das Recht des unlauteren Wettbewerbs in den Mitgliedstaaten der Europäischen Wirtschaftsgemeinschaft: 7 volumes; some volumes are translated into French, Italian, Spanish, Dutch.
35. OJ J, 21.3.1978, p. 1.
36. See IV.3.
37. See IV.4.
38. See IV.10.
39. Directive 84/450/EEC on misleading advertising; Directive 97/55/EC on comparative advertising; Directive 89/452/EC on television broadcasting; Directive 2000/31/EC on E-commerce; Directive 2003/33/EC on tobacco advertising; Directive 76/68/EEC concerning cosmetic products; Directive 92/28/EEC on the advertising of medical products for human use; Directive 97/112/EEC relating to the labelling, presentation and advertising of foodstuff, etc.
40. Recital 12 of the Unfair Commercial Practices Directive.

doubtful.[41] Furthermore, according to the point of view of most Member States, advertising is not the only aspect of unfair competition law nor are business-to-consumer-practices (see the country reports in Chapter 4).

The following sets out the most important directives in the field of unfair competition law. For reasons of space, apart from the directive on tobacco advertising, product-specific legislation, which frequently only contains advertising provisions on the margin, is not discussed.

3. Directive 84/450/EEC concerning misleading advertising

Council Directive 84/450/EEC of 10 September, 1984, relating to the approximation of the laws, regulations and administrative provisions of the Member States concerning misleading advertising[42] was for a long time the most important regulation in the field of unfair competition law. Its aim is to "set out minimum objective criteria that can be used to determine whether advertising is misleading". The Directive grants a minimum level of protection (Art. 7), so that the Member States can retain and adopt stricter regulations. Since some Member States had already achieved the minimum level of protection the Directive has not been implemented expressly in all Member States.

a. Scope of application and purpose of protection

Initially the purpose of the Directive was "to protect consumers, persons carrying on a trade or business or practising a craft or profession and the interests of the public in general against misleading advertising and the unfair consequences thereof". However, according to the Unfair Commercial Practices Directive[43] of 2005, misleading advertising in the relationship between business and consumers now falls exclusively within the scope of application of this Directive. The purpose of Directive 84/450/ECC has been restricted "... to protect traders against misleading advertising and the unfair consequences thereof ...". 'Trader' is defined in Article 1(d)(2)(d) as "any natural or legal person who is acting for purposes relating to his trade, craft, business or profession". It is at present difficult to say what the practical effects of this restriction on protection will be, especially since the relevant standards seem to be the same.

In substantive terms, the scope of application of Directive 84/450/EEC is determined by the concept of "advertising". According to Article 2(1) "advertising is defined as

> *"... the making of a representation in any form in connection with a trade, business, craft or profession in order to promote the supply of goods or services, including immovable property, rights and obligations".*

Thus the "representation" must not only be objectively capable of promoting sales, the advertiser must also intend such effect.[44] It does not cover advertising effects that result

41. The "frame work" Directive 2005/29/EC does not repeal any of the existing directives but rather adds to the fragmentation by, for instance, splitting Directive 84/450/EC so that there are now two sets of regulation for misleading advertising.
42. OJ L 250, 19.9.1984, p. 17.
43. Discussed under 10.
44. The definition of advertising is different in the Tobacco Directive and in the TV-Directive see under 6 and 5.

as a mere side-effect of an act taken for other reasons. This applies above all to the media (press, broadcasting) or consumer associations. Their activity is only regarded as advertising in exceptional cases. Unlike in the Television Directive, there is no indication of when the decisive subjective intention is to be assumed; the Directive leaves the determination of this point to the Member States.

The concept of advertising is otherwise broad. It does not require the intended promotion of sales to be actually achieved, nor is it relevant whether the promotion relates to the advertiser's own or another's sales. The term also includes persons who professionally (e.g. advertising agencies) or occasionally (e.g. a celebrity who promotes a product in return for a fee) intend to promote the sales of a third party.

However, there must be a "representation" (in German "Äusserung", in French "communication"). This covers every kind of communication, both express and implied, whether by word or by image. Sales promotion measures as such, however, are not included,[45] the same is probably true for merely indirect image promotion measures such as sponsoring and public relations. Nor is what is known as suggestive advertising included. As follows from the list of the possible subject matters of deception in Art. 3 in conjunction with the provision concerning the burden of proof, only rationally perceivable representations that contain an objectively verifiable factual core can be regarded as misleading advertising.

The concept of "representation" requires a positive act as a matter of principle. Silence alone is not sufficient, but omission of relevant facts can be. However, there must be some kind of "representation" on which the case can be based; this may be an (incomplete) advertising, the designation of a product or even its putting into circulation without comment.[46]

b. The concept of misleading

Article 3 as the central provision contains the prohibition on misleading advertising. What is understood by "misleading" follows from the definition in Article 2(2):

> *"'Misleading advertising' means any advertising which in any way, including its presentation, deceives or is likely to deceive the persons to whom it is addressed or whom it reaches and which, by reason of its deceptive nature, is likely to affect their economic behaviour or which, for those reasons, injures or is likely to injure a competitor".*

Thus all kinds of representations are covered, irrespective of the medium and the specific means of communication. The express emphasis on the irrelevance of the presentation permits the conclusion that deception as to the commercial nature of a representation also falls within the Directive.[47]

In the subsequent text (sub-paragraphs a-c), the subject matter of deception is explained on the basis of three major points of reference—product/service, price and advertiser. As the initial "in particular" makes it clear, this is not an exhaustive catalogue but only a list of examples, so that other constellations can also be covered.

45. The concept of "commercial communication" is broader, as used for instance in the E-Commerce Directive (see under 8).
46. See, e.g., the "Nissan" case (fn. 53).
47. This is also supported by the fact that camouflage is regulated as a case of misleading in Directive 2005/29/EC on unfair commercial practices (see under 10).

Thus as a rule there is no need to distinguish the subject matters of deception from each other in detail. However, it may be noteworthy that Art. 3(c) expressly refers to the "identity of the advertiser" as a subject matter of deception. This indicates that the creation of confusion between trademarks, company names and other business designations is also included. On the other hand, it is not intended to undermine the specific principles of trademark law in the core field of this law, the likelihood of confusion.[48]

In most cases, Art. 3 will only apply if the advertising claim is objectively inaccurate. However, the wording of Art. 3 expressly names misleading advertising, which also includes true but misunderstood advertising. Nor does it depend on whether the advertiser knows, or even ought to know, of the capacity to deceive, and even an advertising statement made in good faith can be misleading; the often used expression deceptive "advertising" does not imply that there must be intent on the part of the advertiser. Obvious exaggerations (puffing) that are a priori not taken seriously (and which frequently already lack the status of a representation) do not cause deception.[49]

As made clear by Art. 2(2), the deception must be capable of influencing the economic behaviour of the addressee of the advertising, and deception that does not have this effect is not covered by the prohibition. The Directive thus does not serve to provide theoretical protection against misinformation ("truth for the sake of truth") but rather protection against undesired commercial effects.

It is not entirely clear whether the Directive covers misleading advertising that has some effect on economic behaviour, but that does not lead to a commercial transaction, for instance because the addressee discovers the deception or obtains corrective information at the point of sale. In some countries of Europe, it is sufficient for the misleading statement to cause the addressee to consider an offer that he normally would not have considered.[50] In other Member States, more consideration is given to whether wrong decisions are in fact made.[51] This leads, for instance, to a differing assessment of look-alikes (i.e. imitation products that have an identical get-up but different trademarks).[52]

As yet, the ECJ has only addressed this issue once, although somewhat contradictorily and without detailed justification. The "Nissan" decision[53] concerned advertising published in France for cars licensed (but not yet driven) in Belgium that had a lower standard of equipment than the models licensed in France. On the question whether the failure to indicate the lower standard of equipment constituted deception within the meaning of the Directive, the ECJ held:

> *16. On the second point, concerning the claim that the cars are cheaper, such a claim can only be held misleading if it is established that the decision to buy on the part of a significant number of consumers to whom the advertising in*

48. On the differentiation, see Chapter 1, II.2.
49. The threshold held to be decisive for "puffing" varies from country to country. While some member states (Germany, Austria, Denmark, Sweden) traditionally apply a strict standard, the frequent comment in Great Britain is that much advertisement is recognized by the public as hyperbole (see the respective country reports in Chapter 4).
50. Cf. for instance the country reports Germany, Austria, France, Italy (Chapter 4).
51. Cf, for instance the country report Great Britain (Chapter 4).
52. Hill, Own label products and the "look-alike" phenomenon: A lack of trade dress and unfair competition?, 3 EIPR 116 (1995).
53. Case C-373/90 *Nissan* [1992] ECR I-00131; see also Case C-220/98 *Estée Lauder and Lancaster* [2000] ECR I-00117.

> *question is addressed was made in ignorance of the fact that the lower price of the vehicles was matched by a smaller number of accessories on the cars sold by the parallel importer.*

The need for showing actual purchases is, however, incompatible with the wording of the Directive, which expressly lays down that a capacity to affect the economic behaviour or to injure a competitor is sufficient. The ECJ also applied this to another aspect (first licensing in Belgium):

> *15. It is for the national court, however, to ascertain in the circumstances of the particular case and bearing in mind the consumer to which the advertising is addressed, whether the latter could be misleading in so far as, on the one hand, it seeks to conceal the fact that the cars advertised as new were registered before importation and, on the other hand, that fact would have deterred a significant number of consumers from making a purchase, had they known it.*

c. *Criteria to determine the capacity to mislead*

The Directive only provides few indications concerning the core issue of the criteria to be used to determine deception. Article 3 only lays down that "in determining whether advertising is misleading, account shall be taken of all its features, and in particular of any information it contains . . . ". It remains to be seen to what extent the (more detailed) provisions in Article 6 and 7 of the Directive 2005/29/EC,[54] which only apply to the relationship between business and consumers, will lead to more legal certainty. At first glance it essentially reflects what has already been developed by judicial practice and legal literature to give specific meaning to Directive 84/450/EEC.

In any event, pursuant to Article 2(2), the decisive factor is the point of view of the persons to whom the advertising is directed (addressees) or whom it reaches (spill-over). Since the Directive is now restricted to "traders", it is the opinion of these circles that matters. Here too, however, there are graduations. What may be clear to computer experts may be capable of causing misconceptions amongst fashion dealers, for instance.

The Directive does not state the intellectual, cognitive and analytical skills to be ascribed to the addressee of the advertising. As far as concerns consumers, the ECJ (as also in decisions on primary Community law) has developed the European benchmark of the "reasonably well informed and reasonably observant and circumspect average consumer".[55] This case law will apply mutatis mutandis to traders. The decisive factor is thus the average entrepreneur of the relevant target group.

Another question is how the interpretation of a statement in its factual context by such an average addressee is to be determined. In a number of Member States, deception is dealt with as a question of fact, and deception is frequently proven by means of opinion polls. In other Member States, the courts decide on the basis of a grammatical and systematic construction of the advertising in question. The ECJ[56]

54. See under 10.
55. For details, see above, III.2.c.
56. See the "Lifting"-decision; discussed under III.2.c.

has held both to be compatible with the Directive, with the result that the Member States retain considerable scope:

> *28. In the absence of any provisions of community law on this matter, it is for the national court—which may consider it necessary to commission an expert opinion or a survey of public opinion in order to clarify whether or not a promotional description or statement is misleading—to determine, in the light of its own national law, the percentage of consumers misled by the description or statement which would appear to it sufficiently significant to justify prohibiting its use.*

According to the "Nissan" decision[57] it is necessary that the "fact would have deterred a significant number of consumers from making a purchase . . ." This is in any event more than a "not insignificant part of the target public", as was previously sufficient under German and Austrian judicial practice.[58] However, it is a matter for the Member State to determine the exact percentage that must be achieved in the individual case.[59]

d. Enforcement

Article 4 regulates the capacity to sue, the remedies and the proceedings. Only a minimum harmonization was possible in the light of the differences in the Member States' laws in this field in particular. The basic rule is stated in Article 4(1):

> *"Member States shall ensure that adequate and effective means exist for the control of misleading advertising in the interests of consumers as well as competitors and the general public. Such means shall include legal provisions under which persons or organizations regarded under national law as having a legitimate interest in prohibiting misleading advertising may*
> *(a) take legal action against such advertising; and/or*
> *(b) bring such advertising before an administration authority . . ."*

Thus the Member States have considerable scope. Since the capacity to file an action expressly refers to the legitimate interest "under national law", the latter can for instance permit class actions or grant the individual consumer a right of action. However, there is no obligation to do so.

The Directive allows the Member States to chose between judicial proceedings (civil or penal law) and the intervention of an administrative authority. Pursuant to Art. 4(3), the administrative authority must be impartial, have adequate powers and give reasons for its decisions. If a country provides legal protection against misleading advertising exclusively by means of an administrative authority, it must also be possible for its rulings to be the subject of judicial review (Art. 4(3)(c)).

Article 4(2) lays down that a necessary remedy must be the termination of the misleading advertising (injunction) and—if it has not yet been published—the possibility of preventing future publications (preventive injunction). Both must be irrespective of the occurrence of an actual loss or of fault. In addition, injunctive measures must

57. See fn. 53.
58. This practice has since changed; see the country reports Germany and Austria (Chapter 4).
59. Held expressly by the ECJ in the "Lifting"-decision para. 29-31 (fn. 30).

also be available in summary proceedings, it being left to the individual Member State to determine whether these summary proceedings are with interim or with final effect. Other sanctions such as corrective advertising, publication of the decision and damages are left to the discretion of the Member States.

Article 5 emphasises the supplementary function of self-regulation, which plays a major role in some Member States. (The Unfair Commercial Practices Directive of 2005 also refers to the importance of codes of conduct.) However, as follows from Art. 4, a self-regulatory system cannot replace state control.[60]

Article 6 regulates the reversal of the burden of proof. There is no binding obligation on the Member States to reverse the burden of proof with respect to the allegations of fact contained in the advertising. However, Member States shall confer upon the courts or administrative authorities powers enabling them in the civil or administrative proceedings:

(a) to require the advertiser to furnish evidence as to the accuracy of factual claims in advertising if, taking into account the legitimate interests of the advertiser and any other party to the proceedings, such a requirement appears appropriate on the basis of the circumstances of the particular case; and
(b) to consider factual claims as inaccurate if the evidence demanded in accordance with (a) is not furnished or is deemed insufficient by the court or administrative authority.

4. Directive 97/55/EC concerning comparative advertising

a. Full harmonisation

Directive 97/55/EC of the European Parliament and of the Council of 6 October 1997 amending Directive 84/450/EEC concerning misleading advertising so as to include comparative advertising[61] was integrated in Directive 84/450/EEC in 1997. This Directive now covers two fields: misleading advertising (see under 3) and comparative advertising. However, in terms of the manner of regulation, there was a priori a difference between the two aspects. While the regulation of misleading advertising merely creates a Community-wide minimum prohibition standard (Art. 7), the conditions for lawful comparative advertising are listed exhaustively in Art. 3 a. Accordingly, the Member States are neither permitted to prohibit comparative advertising that satisfies these requirements, nor permitted to allow comparative advertising that does not satisfy the requirements. Exceptions are only permitted for specific products and for the liberal professions.

Directive 97/55/EC has been implemented in the national legislation of most Member States, in part word for word.

b. Scope of application and purpose of protection

According to Article 1 the purpose of the Directive is "to lay down the conditions under which comparative advertising is permitted". Since Directive 2005/29/EC did

60. This implied a need for change above all in Great Britain, see country report Great Britain (Chapter 4).
61. OJ L 290, 23.10.1997, p. 10.

not change Article 1 in respect to comparative advertising,[62] this part of Directive 84/450/EEC is still covered by the original three-fold purpose of protection (consumers, business and the general public).

The scope of protection is furthermore determined through the term "comparative advertising", namely any advertising "... which explicitly or by implication identifies a competitor or goods or services offered by a competitor". (Article 2(2)(a)).

According to the 6th Recital of Directive 97/55/EC, the concept of comparative advertising was deliberately given a broad wording in order to cover all manifestations. This is also assumed by the ECJ.[63] There is no doubt that the Directive therefore covers criticising comparative advertising ("X is better than Y") and advertising by association ("X is just as good as Y"). In contrast, it is not entirely clear whether this also applies to personal advertising and whether there is always a need for a "comparison". The legal definition in Art. 2(2)(a) lacks this requirement. Admittedly, it might be concluded from the overall context, the repeated use of the term "comparative advertising" and the reference to "competitors" that there must be a comparison of competing enterprises, goods or services, which would exclude from the scope of regulation one-sided criticism, in particular disparagement ("X charges excessive prices").

On the other hand, the Toshiba decision of the ECJ[64] seems to be in favour of the possibility of comparative advertising without a comparison. The decision concerned advertising by Katun, a producer of spare parts, which had referred in its advertising to the trademark and the Article number of the Toshiba devices for which the spare parts were intended. To begin with, the ECJ held, referring to the deliberately broad wording:

> *30. In order for there to be comparative advertising within the meaning of Article 2(2a) of Directive 84/450 as amended, it is therefore sufficient for a representation to be made in any form which refers, even by implication, to a competitor or to the goods or services which he offers. It does not matter that there is a comparison between the goods and services offered by the advertiser und those of a competitor.*

In spite of this, there is an attempt to construe a "comparison":

> *38. In a situation such as that in the main proceedings, specification of the product numbers of the equipment manufacturer alongside a competing supplier's product numbers enables the public to identify precisely the products of the equipment manufacturer to which that supplier's product correspond.*
>
> *39. Such an indication does however constitute a positive statement that the two products have equivalent technical features, that is to say, a comparison of material, relevant, verifiable and representative features of the products within the meaning of Article 3a(1)(c) of Directive 84/450 as amended.*

62. Unlike for misleading advertising (see under 3); the Directive 2005/29/EC has brought few changes in the field of comparative advertising. Misleading and confusing comparative advertising in a "B2C" relationship is now judged according to the new Directive; for the rest, only the numbering has changed.
63. Case C-112/99 *Toshiba Europe* [2001] ECR I-7945; Case C-44/01 *Pippig* [2003] ECR I-03095.
64. See above.

In practice, the problem is less important, since most references, indications etc that appear one-sided at first sight contain indirect claims of equivalence. According to the meaning and purpose of the regulation, the decisive factor should be whether the addressee of the advertising is presented with purchase alternatives. According to the Second Recital of the objectives of the Directive, comparative advertising must help demonstrate objectively the merits of the various comparable products. This is not the case if a known product is for instance primarily used as an attention-grabber, but is the case for an "invitation to compare" or a reference to the suitability of the advertiser's own product as spare part, accessory, etc.[65]

In the Toshiba decision, the ECJ also distinguished the Directive on comparative advertising from the Trademark Directive. Both directives were to be reconciled in the light of their meaning and purpose:

> *33. It follows from a comparison of Article 2(2a) of Directive 84/450 as amended, on the one hand, and Article 3a of that directive, on the other, that, on a literal interpretation, they would render unlawful any reference enabling a competitor, ort he goods or services which he offers, to be identified in a representation which did not contain a comparison within the meaning of Article 3a. That would have to be the case where there were mere mention of the trade mark of the manufacturer of the original models or of the reference numbers of models for which the spare parts and consumable items are manufactured. In the main proceedings, Toshiba Europe does not contest Katun's use of such marks or reference numbers.*
>
> *34. However, it is apparent from Article 6(1)(c) of First Council Directive 89/104/EEC of 21 December 1988 to approximate that laws of the member states relating to trade marks (OJ 1989 L 40, p. 1) and the case-law of the Court (Case C-63/97 BMW [1999] ECR I-905, paragraphs 58 to 60) that the use of another person's trade mark may be legitimate where it is necessary to inform the public of the nature of the products or the intended purpose of the services offered.*
>
> *35. A literal interpretation of Directive 84/450 as amended results in a contradiction with Directive 89/104 and cannot therefore be accepted.*
>
> *36. In those circumstances, it is necessary to take account of the objectives of Directive 84/459 as amended. According to the second recital of the preamble to Directive 97/55, comparative advertising will help demonstrate objectively the merits of the various comparable products and thus stimulate competition between suppliers of goods and services to the consumer's advantage.*
>
> *37. For those reasons, the conditions required of comparative advertising must be interpreted in the sense most favourable to it.*

c. The reference to a competitor

The direct or indirect reference to one or more competitors, his products or services as required in Art. 2(2)(a) is an indispensable part of comparative advertising. There is a

65. See, for instance, the decisions of the German Federal Supreme Court, GRUR Int. 1999, 453—"Vergleichen Sie"; GRUR 2001, 350—OP-Lampen and GRUR 2005, 1110—Aluminiumräder.

direct reference if the competitor, his products, services or trademark are mentioned directly. There may be an indirect reference if the reference to specific competitors etc. is obvious in the light of the circumstances (from the point of view of the target group). In this, the overall arrangement of the advertising (e.g. a more or less clear reference to the competitor's trademark or his famous advertising) plays just as much a role as the market conditions. The closer the situation is to an oligopoly, the easier it will be for the public to identify a specific competitor even without the express mention of his name or trademark.

It is a matter for the Member States to determine the requirements to be made of "identifiable"; the ECJ has not yet decided on this point. In Italy, for instance, the question whether a comparison not identifying individual competitors was also to be included was initially disputed (it is rejected today by the Autorità Garante).[66] In Germany the courts initially assumed a rather broad interpretation, but later decisions emphasised that "not every far-fetched possibility of identification" is sufficient.[67] No doubt in all countries, a mere comparison of system or type of product where no individual supplier is identifiable will not be regarded as comparative advertising within the meaning of Directive 97/55/EC, but will be measured directly against the prohibitions on deception and disparagement.

According to the definition in Art. 2(2)(a), the comparison must relate to a "competitor" or his "products and services". The concept of "competitor" causes difficulties in those countries whose unfair competition laws no longer require a competitive relationship, but instead are based on criteria like "seller".[68] A competitor is anyone whose products or services are, from the point of view of the target public, identical, the same or at least substitutable. The requirements made of substitutability are not set too high, and in particular it is sufficient if such a substitutability is created by the advertising itself.

d. Misleading comparisons

Pursuant to Art. 3a(1)(a), the comparison must not be misleading. In the relationship between business and consumer, the question of deception has now to be answered on the basis of Articles 6 and 7 of Directive 2005/29/EC;[69] in the business to business relationship it continues to be dealt with on the basis of Art. 2(2) of Directive 84/450/EEC. It remains to be seen whether there are any differences, and what these might be.

The prohibition on misleading comparisons is actually self-evident, since it applies to all types of advertising (see above). However, there may be specific problems with comparative advertising. In particular, the question arises whether a comparison that does not list all relevant aspects is misleading for this reason. The answer must as a matter of principle be in the negative. There is fundamentally no obligation to be complete, as follows inter alia by reverse conclusion from Art. 3a(1)(c), according to which the characteristics compared must be "representative". Only in exceptional cases can the selection of characteristics be so arbitrary that the overall impression is misleading.

66. See the country report Italy (Chapter 4).
67. See country report Germany (Chapter 4).
68. See for instance the country report Belgium (Chapter 4).
69. Discussed under 10.

This and the question of misleading comparative advertising in general was addressed in particular by the "*Pippig* v. *Hartlauer*" decision of the ECJ[70] in 2003.

The decision concerned a comparison by the Austrian retailer Hartlauer between the prices for its own spectacles and the prices for those supplied by traditional opticians. The comparison related to "branded spectacles" marketed by the specialist optical store, Pippig, fitted with lenses of the famous Zeiss brand (while Hartlauer's parallel import spectacle frames used lenses from the unknown Optimed brand). The Hartlauer television advertisements also showed the Pippig store and the company logo.

The ECJ first held that the Member States were not entitled to apply stricter criteria to misleading comparative advertising than the Directive, since according to Art. 7(2), the "minimum standard clause" of the Directive 84/450/EEC does not apply to comparative advertising. This is true of all three parts of the comparison, namely the statements about the advertiser's own product, the statements about the competing product and the statements about the relationship between these two:

> *44. It follows that Directive 84/450 carried out an exhaustive harmonisation of the conditions under which comparative advertising in Member States might be lawful. Such a harmonisation implies by it nature that the lawfulness of comparative advertising throughout the community is to be assessed solely in the light of the criteria laid down by the community legislature. Therefore, stricter national provisions on protection against misleading advertising cannot be applied to comparative advertising as regards the form and content of the comparison.*

The ECJ also addressed the question whether and under what circumstances the identification of the competitor's product—or even its non-identification!—constitutes deception:

> *56. Article 3a(1)(a) of Directive 84/450 must be interpreted as meaning that, whereas the advertiser is in principle free to state or not to state the brand name of rival products in comparative advertising, it is for the national court to verify whether, in particular circumstances, characterised by the importance of the brand in the buyer's choice and by a major difference between the respective brand names of the compared products in terms of how well known they are, omission of the better-known brand name is capable of being misleading.*

In contrast, it was not considered misleading to omit a reference to the fact that the branded spectacle frames used by the advertiser were parallel imports.[71] Nor is it unfair to determine comparative prices by means of test purchases[72] and for the advertiser only to include certain products in its range on the basis of such test purchases[73] or to chose a rival product where the price difference (or quality difference) is particularly large. Insofar the ECJ stated:

> *81. The choice as to the number of comparisons which the advertiser wishes to make between the products which he is offering and those offered by his*

70. Case C-444/01 *Pippig* [2003] ECR I-03095.
71. Para. 59.
72. Para. 67.
73. Para. 68.

> *competitors falls within the exercise of his economic freedom. Any obligation to restrict each price comparison to the average prices of the producers offered by the advertiser and those of rival product would be contrary to the objectives of the Community legislature.*
>
> *82. In the words of the second recital in the preamble to Directive 97/55, comparative advertising must help demonstrate objectively the merits of the various comparable products. Such objectivity implies that the persons to whom the advertising is addressed are capable of knowing the actual price differences between the products compared and not merely the average difference between the advertiser's prices and those of its competitors.*

e. Comparison of products for the same needs or purpose

According to Article 3a(1)(b) a comparison shall (only) be permitted if "it compares goods or services meeting the same needs or intended for the same purpose". Accordingly it must be at least a substitution product (from the point of view of the target group). In contrast, the comparison need not necessarily concern identical products.[74]

f. Objective comparison of material, relevant, verifiable and representative features

According to Article 3a(1)(c), comparative advertising shall (only) be permitted if "it objectively compares one or more material, relevant, verifiable and representative features of those goods or services, which may include price".

As mentioned above, "objectivity" does not necessarily mean completeness. It has not yet been decided whether a comparison of purely subjective preferences ("I prefer X to Y") is prohibited. Strictly speaking, such a comparison is neither objective nor verifiable. However, a prohibition would lead to the curious result that the Directive, which aims at the liberalisation of comparative advertising, would be stricter than the previous national law of almost all the Member States, which had at least tolerated such subjective preference comparisons.[75]

In addition, the comparison must concern the features of goods or services (or their price). According to this, personal comparative advertising ("X is a foreigner, I am not") is no doubt prohibited. The term "features of goods or services", if construed literally, would also not include company-related details such as turnover, the product's fame or the media's audience penetration. Possibly, their inclusion could be justified by the broad interpretation of the concept of comparative advertising in the ECJ Toshiba decision and the information needs of the addressee, to whom such advertising can also present alternatives.

Closely related to the requirement of objectivity is the need for verifiability. Verifiability means first of all that the comparison involves allegations of fact, since only these can be checked for objective justification. The decisive factor is that the

74. For this reason, the provision in France restricting price comparisons to identical products had to be repealed; see country report France (Chapter 4).
75. Thus for instance the German Federal Supreme Court GRUR 1987, 49—"Cola-Test" with comment by Sack and in Belgian Cour d'appel de Bruxelles 7.6.1983, JT 1983, 117; confirmed by Cass. 21.3.1985, Arr. Cass. 1985, 1001.

addressee can verify such claims, i.e. the addressee of the advertising must at least with reasonable effort himself be able to check the features compared.

The features compared must also be "material, relevant and representative". This ultimately amounts to the same thing, the aim being to prevent the creation of a distorted overall impression by selecting irrelevant secondary features that are as a rule of no relevance for the purchase. What is decisive for the purchase and hence "material" etc. depends strongly on the type of product. While for instance the packaging of most products is of secondary importance, it may for certain products (perfume, sweets) indeed also be a material, relevant or representative feature.

g. Comparisons creating confusion

Article 3a(1)(h) prohibits any comparison that "creates confusion among traders, between the advertiser and a competitor or between the advertiser's trademarks, trade names, other distinguishing marks, goods or services and those of a competitor". Comparative advertising that creates such a risk of confusion towards consumers, is now prohibited by Article 6(2)(a) of the Directive 2005/29/EC so that insofar two different sets of regulation apply. Whether this will also lead to a difference in interpretation remains to be seen.

Insofar as a risk of confusion arises, trademark claims may also be possible in many cases. As the ECJ held in the Toshiba decision, the rules on comparative advertising are to be construed such that they take account of the purpose of trademark law (and vice versa). It is generally assumed that terms that are used identically in both directives—for instance the likelihood of confusion—are to be interpreted on the basis of the same principles (such that in 3a(1)(h), as in trademark law, the abstract likelihood of confusion is sufficient and there is no need for there to have been actual confusion). In addition, the underlying benchmark of the "reasonably informed and reasonably observant and circumspect average consumer" is identical.[76]

h. Discrediting or denigrating comparisons

According to Article 3a(1)(d), comparative advertising "shall not discredit or denigrate the trademarks, trade names, other distinguishing marks, goods, services, activities or circumstances of a competitor".

Discrediting is a milder form of denigration, and since both are covered there is no need for further distinction. System-immanent discrediting does not constitute discrediting within the meaning of Art. 3a(1)(e), since any critical comparative advertising involves a certain discrediting of the competitor or his products. If this were prohibited, the intended liberalisation of comparative advertising would not be achieved. What is therefore meant is only "unnecessarily" discrediting comparative advertising. This occurs, in particular, if the comparative advertising does not primarily emphasise the benefits of the advertiser's own achievement—which is always permissible, even if this logically means showing the disadvantages of the rival product—but rather focuses on the negative aspects of the competitor or his product. Discrediting can also result from an inappropriate and aggressive tone, an unobjective representation or valuation or even a unspecific, global disqualification.

76. See fn. 20 on page 5.

In the *Hartlauer* v. *Pippig* decision, the ECJ[77] based its conclusion on the meaning and purpose of the Directive, in particular the public's interest in information. According to this, neither the selection of one of a number of the competitor's products (e.g. the one with the greatest price or quality difference) nor the pictorial representation of the competitor's store and trademark is of itself disparaging. It also follows from the interaction between the Comparative Advertising Directive and the Trademark Directive that as a rule this will not involve a trademark infringement either:

> *83. Having regard to the above considerations, the answer to the fourth question must be, first, that a price comparison does not entail the discrediting of a competitor, within the meaning of Article 3a(1)(e) of Directive 84/450 either on the grounds that the difference in price between the products compared is greater than the average price difference or by reasons of the number of comparison made. Secondly, Article 3a(1)(e) of Directive 84/450 does not prevent comparative advertising, in addition to citing the competitor's name, from reproducing its logo and a picture of its shop front, if that advertising complies with the conditions for lawfulness laid down by community law.*
>
> *As for the second part of the question, concerning the reproduction in the advertising message of the competitor's logo and a picture of its shop front, it is important to note that, according to the 15th recital in the preamble to Directive 97/55, use of another's trade mark, trade name or other distinguishing marks does not breach that exclusive right in cases where it complies with the conditions laid down by the directive.*

Nevertheless, the question of discrediting remains one of the aspects where the interpretation of the Member States diverge most. While the courts of some states apply a relatively strict standard, others have hitherto shown themselves to be rather tolerant.[78]

i. Comparisons exploiting a competitor's reputation

According to Article 3a(1)(f), comparative advertising shall not "take unfair advantage of the reputation of a trademark, trade name or other distinguishing marks of a competitor or of the designation of origin of competing products". Here, too, as with discrediting, there are problems in drawing a distinction to trademark law and it should be noted here, too, that the "attachment" to another's reputation that is necessarily associated with comparative advertising ("X is just as good as Y") must be permitted, since otherwise derivative comparative advertising would per se be forbidden. The wording of subparagraph f. (unlike for discrediting comparative advertising) makes this clear in that the advantage must be "unfair". Thus the reference must be accompanied by "particular circumstances" for the transfer of the reputation of a sign to another to be regarded as unfair, for instance an excessive emphasis of the well-known rival product. However, it is not an unfair exploitation of another's reputation to claim expressly or implicitly that an inexpensive ("no name") product is equivalent to a prestigious brand product.[79]

77. See fn. 63.
78. For the different views, see for instance the country reports France and Belgium on the one hand and Great Britain on the other hand (Chapter 4).
79. As held by the ECJ in the "Pippig" decision (fn. 63).

j. Designations of origin, imitations, special offers

Article 3a(1)(e) restricts comparisons for products with designation of origin to products with the same designation. According to this "Champagne clause" (included at the request of France), products bearing designations of origin cannot be compared with products without designations of origin (thus Champagne cannot be compared with sparkling wine, instead comparisons can only be made between various Champagne brands). It is doubtful whether this restriction results already from Art. 13 of Regulation 2081/92/EC on the Protection of Geographical Designations.

According to Article 3a(1)(g), comparative advertising shall not "present goods or services as imitations or replicas of goods or services bearing a protected trademark or trade name". This provision provides a certain degree of protection against comparison for the manufacturers of original goods (e.g. pharmaceuticals, perfumes) who, often after expiry of the industrial property rights, cannot take action against imitations as such. Thus, for instance, the perfume or a pharmaceutical may not be described as being identical with an original perfume or pharmaceutical.

According to Article 3a(2) of the original version of the Directive 84/450/EEC comparisons referring to a special offer had to meet certain transparency requirements. This paragraph seems to have been repealed through Directive 2005/29/EC. In any event the information about any restrictions applying to special offers, in particular the indication of possible restricted stocks, can already be seen from the point of view of deception (see the Directive on Unfair Commercial Practices) and is subject to additional regulations in the field of the Internet (E-Commerce Directive). These information requirements apply irrespective of whether the advertising in question is a comparison or not.

5. Directive 89/452/EC on Television Broadcasting Activities

Council Directive 89/452/EC of 10 October 1989 on the Coordination of Certain Provisions laid down by Law, Regulation or Administrative Action in Member States concerning the Pursuit of Television Broadcasting Activities, as amended by Directive 97/36/EC of 30 June 1997 ("Television Directive")[80] was implemented word for word in almost all Member States. It contains amongst other things regulations on (television) advertising, sponsoring etc which, in the view of most Member States, concern aspects of unfair competition law.

a. Scope of application

The Directive applies to all aspects of television activity—but not radio—that originate within the EU. According to Article 2(3)(i) it does not, however, apply to broadcasts "intended exclusively for reception in states other than Member States, and which are not received directly or indirectly in one or more Member States".

Article 1(a) defines "television broadcasting" as

> *"...the initial transmission by wire or over the air, including that by satellite, in unencoded or encoded form, of television programmes intended for*

80. OJ 1989 L 298, p. 23.

reception by the public. It includes the communication of programmes between undertakings with a view to their being relayed do the public",

with the exception of

"... communication services providing items of information or other messages on individual demand such as telecopying, electronic data banks and other similar services".

b. Regulation of TV advertising

Television advertising is defined in Article 1(a) of the Directive as

"... any form of announcement broadcast whether in return for payment or for similar consideration or broadcast for self-promoting purposes by a public or private undertaking in connection with a trade, business, craft or profession in order to promote the supply of goods or services, including immovable property, or rights and obligations, in return for payment".

According to a recent decision of the ECJ,[81] this does not include "indirect" television advertising, for instance resulting from the fact that advertising hoardings are broadcast during the transmission of a sports event. As the ECJ stated in the "Baccardi"-decision:

27. In this case, for the reasons set out by the Advocate General in paragraphs 48 to 52 of his Opinion, the indirect television advertising for alcoholic beverages resulting from hoardings visible on screen during the retransmission of sporting events does not constitute a separate announcement broadcast in order to promote goods or services. For obvious reasons, it is impossible to show such advertising only during the intervals between the different parts of the television broadcast concerned. The images on the advertising hoardings which appear in the background of the pictures broadcast, in a random and unpredictable fashion according to the requirements of the retransmission, do not have any distinct character in that context.

28. Such indirect television advertising cannot, therefore, be regarded as television advertising within the meaning of Directive 89/552, and accordingly the directive is not applicable to it.

Article 10 contains the general principles for distinguishing between advertising and programmes. Television advertising shall be "readily recognizable as such and kept quite separate from other parts of the programme service by optical and/or acoustic means". Subliminal techniques and surreptitious advertising are expressly forbidden. Surreptitious advertising is defined in Article 1(c) as:

"... the representation in words or pictures of goods, services, the name, the trade mark or the activities of a producer of goods or a provider of services in programmes when such representation is intended by the broadcaster to serve

81. Case C-429/92 *Baccardi*, [2004] ECR I-0000; see also under 26.

> *advertising and might mislead the public as to its nature. Such representation is considered to be intentional in particular if it is done in return for payment or for similar consideration".*

This includes techniques such as product placement, in which the television broadcaster requests or receives money for the placing of brands etc.

In order to avoid the impression of an unlawful combination with the programme, Art. 10(2) also lays down that "isolated spots shall remain the exception". With respect to the placing of advertising generally, Art. 11 contains the basic rule that

> *"...advertisements and teleshopping spots shall be inserted between programmes. Provided the conditions contained in paragraphs 2 to 5 of this Article are fulfilled, advertisements may also be inserted during programmes in such a way that the integrity and value of the programme, taking into account natural breaks in and the duration and nature of the programme, and the rights of the rights holders are not prejudiced".*

The transmission of feature films and films made for television (excluding series, light entertainment programmes etc) may be interrupted once by advertising if the programmed duration is more than 45 minutes. A further interruption is permissible if their programmed duration is at least 20 minutes longer than two or more complete periods of 45 minutes. In any event, a period of at least 20 minutes should elapse between the interruptions. The term "programmed duration" is interpreted by the ECJ[82] in accordance with what is known as the "gross principle"—i.e. the block of advertising within the programme may be included. Certain programmes (religious services, news and current affairs programmes, children's programmes with a programmed duration of less than 30 minutes) shall not be interrupted at all by advertising. Article 18 lays down the maximum advertising time per day.

The Television Directive also contains prohibitions or restrictions on the advertising of potentially dangerous products. Television advertising for cigarettes and other tobacco products (Art. 13) and for medicinal products and medical treatment available only on prescription (Art. 14) is completely prohibited. Article 15 imposes restrictions on advertising for alcoholic beverages that largely correspond with the Codes of Conduct of the International Chamber of Commerce.

Article 16 deals with the protection of children and minors against television advertising. Television advertising 'shall not cause moral or physical detriment to minors' and shall therefore 'not directly exhort minors to buy a product or a service by exploiting their inexperience or credulity,' nor directly encourage minors to persuade their parents to buy the goods being advertised, exploit the special trust in parents and teachers or unreasonably show minors in dangerous situations.

In addition, Art. 12 contains general requirements applicable to the content of all television advertising. According to this, television advertising shall not

- prejudice respect for human dignity;
- discriminate on grounds of race, sex, nationality;
- be offensive to religious or political beliefs;
- encourage behaviour prejudicial to the protection of the environment.

82. Case C-6/98 *ARD* v. *PRO* 7 [1999] ECR-06 599.

c. Regulation of sponsoring

Article 1 (d), defines sponsoring as

> *"...a contribution made by a public or private undertaking not engaged in television broadcasting activities or in the production of audio-visual works, to the financing of television programmes with a view to promoting its name, its trademark, its image, its activities or its products".*

Accordingly, this does not include "events sponsoring", the sponsoring of events that are then transmitted by television, although in practice there is often no clear-cut dividing line.[83]

Pursuant to Art. 17(a) and (c), (programme) sponsoring is permissible if the responsibility for the programme remains with the broadcaster and if the public is not unduely influenced by the content of the programme:

> *"(a) The content and scheduling of sponsored programmes may in no circumstances be influenced by the sponsor in such a way as to affect the responsibility and editorial independence of the broadcaster in respect of programmes.*
>
> *(c) They must not encourage the purchase or rental of the products or services of the sponsor or a third party, in particular by making special promotional references to those products or services".*

News and current affairs programmes must not be sponsored. Article 17(3) furthermore prohibits any "sponsoring not permitted by legal or natural persons whose principal activity is the manufacture or sale of products, or the provision of services, the advertising of which is prohibited by Article 13 or 14".

According to Article 17(b), sponsored programmes must be clearly identified as such by the name and/or logo of the sponsor at the beginning and/or the end of the programme. The reference to the sponsor can also be repeated during the programme, provided that the sponsored programme does not "encourage a purchase" as a result.[84]

d. Minimum standard and country-of-origin principle

The advertising regulations contained in the Directive merely constitute a minimum standard. According to Article 3(1)

> *"Member States remain free to require television broadcasters under their jurisdiction to lay down more detailed or stricter rules in the areas covered by this Directive".*

Whether a broadcaster is subject to the legal sovereignty of a country is determined according to the place of broadcast.[85] According to Art. 2(1) and (3), the decisive

83. For instance, the event sponsor can be identical with the programme sponsor.
84. It is not entirely clear to which extent the sponsored programme as such may be in the interest of the sponsor.
85. Case C-222/94 *Commission* v. *United Kingdom* [1996] ECR I-4025.

factor is the focus of activity, which is determined on the basis of a number of criteria such as the registered office of the headquarters.

However, excessively strict national regulations on television advertising may infringe Art. 49 EC. The ECJ tends to see television broadcasting, including advertising, as a service[86] (see Chapter III.2.b.). Nevertheless, such national regulations may be justified pursuant to Art. 46 para. 1 in conjunction with Art. 55 of the EC Treaty. For instance, the ECJ held the French prohibition on the transmission of foreign alcohol advertising as being justified by the objective of the protection of health, and as being within the limits of proportionality.[87]

The Television Directive also lays down a country-of-origin principle. According to Art. 3(2)

> *"Member States' shall, by appropriate means, ensure, within the framework for their legislation, that television broadcasters under their jurisdiction comply with the provisions of this Directive".*

This means that all Member States are obliged by Art. 3 para. 2 to make available "adequate means" to ensure that third parties directly affected, including the nationals of other Member States, can address the judicial authorities or other agencies in order to obtain the actual application of the national provisions to the broadcast.

Art. 3 lays down the principle of reciprocal recognition:

> *"Member States shall ensure freedom of reception and shall not restrict retransmission on their territory of television broadcasts from other Member States which fall with the field coordinated by this Directive".*

The receiving Member States no longer have as a matter of principle any powers of examination in the areas coordinated by the Directive. The only exceptions are subject to very close limits, namely if the broadcast received obviously, seriously and grievously infringe Arts. 22 and 22 a (protection of minors).

The country-of-origin principle, however, only applies within the "coordinated field" of the Directive. According to the 1997 "de Agostini" decision of the ECJ,[88] this only covers the areas directly harmonised by the Directive.

The de Agostini decision concerned television advertising broadcast from Great Britain to Sweden in Swedish. It was contested by the Swedish consumer ombudsman as being an infringement of the deception provisions of the Marketing Act and the Broadcasting Act (prohibition of television advertising directed at children under 12).

The ECJ emphasised that the Television Directive only achieved partial coordination with respect to television advertising and sponsoring, for instance on advertising directed at children, which for this reason cannot be reviewed again by the receiving country. In contrast, misleading advertising is not coordinated by the Television Directive, with the result that the receiving country remains entitled to apply controls.

86. See Case C-412/93 *Leclerc Siples* [1995] ECR I-179 (French prohibition on TV advertising for certain traders); see also the Baccardi-case.
87. See the Baccardi and Loi Evin decisions, set out above.
88. See fn. 57 on page 13.

33. Although the Directive provides that the Member States are to ensure freedom of reception and are not to impede retransmission on their territory of television broadcasts coming from other Member States on grounds relating to television advertising and sponsorship, it does not have the effect of excluding completely and automatically the application of rules other than those specifically concerning the broadcasting and distribution of programmes.

34. Thus the Directive does not in principle preclude application of national rules with the general aim of consumer protection provided that they do not involve secondary control of television broadcast in addition to the control which the broadcasting Member State must carry out.

37. In response to that objection, it is sufficient to observe that Council Directive 84/450/EEC of 10 September 1984 relating to the approximation of the laws, regulations and administrative provisions of the Member States concerning misleading advertising (OJ 1984 L 250, p. 17), which provides in particular in Article 4(1) that Member States are to ensure that adequate and effective means exist for the control of misleading advertising in the interests of consumes as well as competitors and the general public, could be robbed of its substance in the field of television advertising if the receiving member state were deprived of all possibility of adopting measures against and advertiser and that his would be in contradiction with the express intention of the community legislature (see, to this effect, the judgment of the Court of the European Free Trade Association of 16 June 1996 in Joined Cases E-8/904 and E-9/94 Forbrukerombudet v Mattel Scandinavia and Lego Norge, Report of the EFTA Court, 1 January 1994—30 June 1995, 113, paragraphs 54 to 56 and paragraph 58).

38. It follows from the foregoing that the Directive does not preclude a Member State from taking, pursuant to general legislation on protection of consumers against misleading advertising, measures against an advertiser in relation to television advertising broadcast from another member State, provided that those measures do not prevent the retransmission, as such, in its territory of television broadcast coming from that other Member State.

6. Directive 2003/33/EC on Tobacco Advertising

Directive 2003/33/EC of the European Parliament and the Council of 26 May 2003 on the approximation of the laws, regulations and the administrative provisions of the Member States relating to the advertising and sponsorship of tobacco products[89] goes back to Directive 98/43/EC[90] which was annulled by the ECJ.[91] It extends the prohibition on television advertising and sponsoring of tobacco products to printed media and information society (Article 3), radio advertising and sponsorship (Article 4) and sponsorship of events (Art. 5).

The concept of advertising is defined broadly in Art. 2(b)

89. OJ L 152, 20.6.2003, p. 0016. The Directive must be transferred into national law by 31.7.2005.
90. OJ Nr. L 213 30.7.1998, p. 0009.
91. Case C-376/98 *Federal Republic of Germany* v. *European Parliament and Counsel* and Case C-74/99. The *Queen* v. *Secretary for Health ex parte Imperial tobacco Limited* (2000) ECR I-8599.

". . . : any form of commercial communications with the aim or direct or indirect effect of promoting a tobacco product".

Thus, unlike the Directive 84/450/EEC on misleading and comparative advertising, the mere effect is sufficient, the intent to promote the products not necessary.

In other respects, however, the Directive 2003/33/EC is considerably less rigid than the annulled Directive 98/43/EC. The original version of Art. 2 included a prohibition on "advertising, while not specifically mentioning the tobacco products, tries to circumvent the advertising ban by using band names, trademarks, emblems or other distinctive features of tobacco products". As Recital 12 now states "other forms of advertising, such as indirect advertising, as well as the sponsorship of events or activities without cross border effects, fall outside the scope of this Directive". This includes the former Article 3(a) which prohibited the use of tobacco trademarks for non-tobacco products.

Furthermore, Article 5(2) limits the former prohibitions of any free distribution having the purpose or the direct or indirect effect of promoting a tobacco product to promotions "in the context of the sponsorship of the events". Whether Member States are permitted to impose more extensive and stricter regulations (as was provided for in the former Art. 5) is unclear. The Directive also contains an "internal market clause".

7. Directive 97/7/EC on Distance Contracts

Directive 97/7/EC of the European Parliament and of the Council of 20 May 1997 on the Protection of Consumers in respect of Distance Contracts[92] primarily regulates the civil-law consumer protection for contracts concluded in distance sales, in particular the right to withdraw. However, it also contains some regulations that belong to the field of direct marketing. Directive 97/7/EC must be seen in connection with Directives 2000/31/EC and 2002/58/EC (discussed below) which partly extant, partly repeat the regulation in the Distance Contract Directive.

Article 9 forbids the supply of goods or services to a consumer without their being ordered by the consumer beforehand where a demand for payment is involved. According to Article 10(1) direct marketing via telephone calls by automatic calling machines and faxes to consumers require prior consent (opt-in). All other means of distant communication are only permitted if there is "no clear objection from the consumer" (Article 10(2)).

Since according to Art. 14 this is a minimum standard, Member States may adopt or retain stricter regulations. An "opt-in" solution for individual commercial communications by telephone would thus be permissible (for e-mails it is now prohibited by Direction 2002/58/EC).

8. Directive 2000/31/EC on Electronic Commerce

a. Scope of application, purpose of protection

Directive 2000/31/EC on Certain Legal Aspects of Information Society Services, in particular Electronic Commerce, in the Internal Market of 8 January 2000

92. OJ L 144, 4.6.1997, p. 19.

(E-Commerce Directive)[93] deals with three topics—contracts concluded by electronic means, liability of intermediary service providers and the regulation of "commercial communication".

According to Article 1(1), the Directive "seeks to contribute to the proper functioning of the internal market by ensuring the free movement of information society services between the Member States". Although the goal is to increase consumer confidence, the Directive is not restricted to the protection of consumers but aims at ensuring legal certainty for competitors and business as well.

b. Commercial communications

The Directive applies to all "commercial communications" in electronic commerce. The concept of commercial communication, first launched in the Green Paper on Consumer Protection,[94] is broader than that of advertising; includes also, for example sales promotion and sponsoring. According to Art. 2(f), it covers

> *"... any form of communication designed to promote, directly or indirectly, the goods, services or image of a company, organisation or person pursuing a commercial, industrial or craft activity or exercising a regulated profession".*

However, the following do not in themselves constitute commercial communications:

- information allowing direct access to the activity of the company, organisation or person, in particular a domain name or an electronic-mail address,
- communications relating to the goods, services or image of the company, organisation or person compiled in an independent manner, particularly when this is without financial consideration.

Pursuant to Article 7(1) all commercial communication must at least be clearly identifiable as such. Furthermore, the natural or legal person on whose behalf the commercial communication is made shall be clearly identifiable; promotional offers and promotional competition or games must be clearly identifiable as such and the condition for participation etc. must be presented clearly and unambiguously.

Article 7 deals with unsolicited commercial communication by electronic mail. Commercial emails shall be clearly and unambiguously identifiable as such, and without prejudice to Directive 97/7/EC and Directive 97/66/EC—which allow Member States to set up an "opt-in" system for e-mail advertising and certain forms of telephone advertising—opt-out registers in which natural persons not wishing to receive such commercial communications can register themselves, must be consulted regularly and respected.

According to Article 8 Member States shall ensure that commercial communications by "regulated professions" (called liberal professions in other Directives) are permitted "subject to compliance with the professional rules regarding, in particular, the independence, dignity and honour of the profession ...".

93. OJ L 178, 17.7.2000, p. 1.
94. COM (2001) 531 final.

c. Country-of-origin principle

With the exception of unsolicited commercial e-mails, the E-Commerce Directive subjects the regulation of commercial communications to the country-of-origin principle. According to Article 3(1) each Member state

> *"... shall ensure that the information society services provided by a service provider established on its territory comply with the national provisions applicable in the Member State in question which fall within the coordinated field".*

On the other hand Member States

> *"... may not, for reasons falling within the coordinated field, restrict the freedom to provide information society services form another Member State".*

According to Art. 3(3), exceptions to this principle apply to the fields specified in the annex, including copyright, neighbouring rights, rights referred to in Directive 87/54/EC and Directive 96/9/EC as well as industrial property rights; the freedom of the parties to choose the law applicable to their contract; contractual obligations concerning consumer contents; the permissibility of unsolicited commercial communications by electronic mail. Furthermore, Member States may derogate from Paragraph 2 under certain conditions, especially where public policy, public health or security or the protection of consumers are involved.

As already discussed in Chapter 1, VI.2.b., the country-of-origin principle laid down in Art. 3 is very broad. This is due to the definition of the "coordinated field" in Art. 2:

> *"Requirements laid down in Member State's legal system applicable to information society service providers or information society services, regardless of whether they are of a general nature or specifically designed for them".*

This covers all national requirements applicable to advertising, marketing, sponsoring, sales promotions etc. (but not to goods or the delivery of goods as such).

9. Directive 2002/58/EC on Privacy in Electronic Communications

Directive 2002/58/EC of 12 July 2002 concerning the Processing of Personal Data and the Protection of Privacy in the Electronic Communication Sector[95] primarily deals with aspects of data protection. However, advertising by fax, telephone or electronic mail is once more regulated. Article 13(1) states

> *"The use of automated calling systems without human intervention (automatic calling machine), facsimile machines (fax) or electronic mail for the purposes of direct marketing may only be allowed in respect of subscribers who have given their prior consent".*

As a result, the protection already granted by the Distance Contracts Directive ("opt-in" for advertising via voice mail systems and fax) is extended to advertising by e-mail and sms. For these means of communication "opt-in" has become mandatory.

95. OJ L 201, 31.7.2002, p. 37.

However, according to Art. 13(2), an exception applies for specific cases in connection with previous online contracts:

> *"Notwithstanding paragraph 1, where a natural or legal person obtains from its customers their electronic contact details for electronic mail, in the context of the sale of a product or a service, in accordance with Directive 95/46/EC, the same natural or legal person may use these electronic contact details for direct marketing of its own similar products or services provided that customers clearly and distinctly are given the opportunity to object, free of charge and in an easy manner, to such use of electronic contact details when they are collected and on the occasion of each message in case the customer has not initially refused such use".*

For all other types of direct marketing via telephone, fax and electronic means, either the Distance Sales Directive and the Directive 2005/29/EC on unfair commercial practices (annex 1, No. 26) apply directly or the Member States are free to choose between opt-in and opt-out. In any event, account must be taken of the requirements for transparency (see also the Directive on E-Commerce), and an address must be given in order to terminate future e-mails (Art. 13(4)).

10. Directive 2005/29/EC on Unfair Commercial Practices

a. Relationship to other Directives and to national unfair competition law

Directive 2005/29/EC of the European Parliament and of the Council concerning unfair commercial practices in the internal market and amending Council Directive 84/450/EEC, Directives 97/7/EC, 98/27/EC and 2002/65/EC[96] seeks to contribute to the proper functioning of the internal market and to achieve a high level of consumer protection (Article 1). To this purpose, the Directive contains a general clause (prohibition on unfair commercial practices) and regulates two of these practices in detail (deception and aggressive practices); in addition, the annex contains a blacklist of practices that must be prohibited in all cases.[97]

Although the aim is complete harmonisation, the Directive in itself does not create a general framework for unfair commercial practices. Firstly, it is restricted to business-to-consumer practices ("B2C"), and therefore, according to the understanding of some Member States, does not cover the entire field of unfair competition.[98] In addition, according to Art. 3(4), "all other Community rules governing specific aspects of unfair commercial practices will prevail". Directive 84/450/EEC on misleading and comparative advertising, for instance, has not been repealed but only partly amended: With two exceptions, comparative advertising continues to be governed by Directive 84/450/EC for competitors and consumers alike[99] while the regulation on misleading advertising previously protecting both consumers and competitors

96. OJ No. L 149 of 11.6.2005, p. 22.
97. On the draft Directive, see for instance Micklitz, in: Collins (ed.) (fn. 38 on p. 9); Henning-Bodewig; GRUR Int. 2004, 183; Gamerith, WRP 2005, 391; Stuyck/Terryn/Van Dyck, *La proposition de directive "practiques commerciales déloyales"; quel marché unique pour le consommateur*; Rev. Eur. Dr. Consomm. 2003, 239; Leistner, *Unfair Competition or Consumer Protection*?, in: Bell/Kilpatrik (ed.) The Cambridge Yearbook of European Law Studies, Vol. 6, 2003, p. 141.
98. Recital 8 of the Directive acknowledges this indirectly.
99. See in this chapter under 4.

is split into two regulatory texts: the 2005 Directive applies to B2C advertising, while Directive 84/450/EC continues to apply to B2B advertising. Aggressive commercial practices such as telephone marketing etc. are (at least partly) regulated in Directives 97/7/EC, 2002/58/EC, 2000/31/EC; and the important field of sales promotions, is to be reserved to a proposed EC-Regulation etc.

The directive on Unfair Commercial Practices was published on 11 June 2005 so that the implementation period expires on 12 June 2007. It is currently not possible to predict how the Directive will affect the national law in the Member States.[100] The Directive neither hinders Member States to uphold legal requirements concerning B2B-practices nor provisions "related to taste and decency which vary widely among Member States" (Recital 7).

b. Scope of application and purpose of protection

Pursuant to Art. 1, the Directive is aimed at preventing business practices that "harm consumers' economic interests". Consumer is defined as "any natural person who, in commercial practices covered by this Directive, is acting for purposes which are outside his trade, business or profession". (Article 2(a)). As Recital 8 makes it clear, the Directive "directly protects consumers economic interests from unfair business-to-consumer commercial practices. "Legitimate business" is only protected indirectly from competitors "who do not play by the rules in this Directive". The Directive "thus guarantees fair competition in fields coordinated by it".[101]

As stated above, the specific regulations concerning unfair practices take priority over the Directive. In addition, Art. 32(2) excludes for instance consumer contract protection, being "without prejudice to the rules on the validity, formation or effect of a contract".

In material terms, the scope of application is determined by the concept of "commercial practice". According to Article 2(e) this means

> *"...any act, omission, course of conduct or representation, commercial communication including advertising and marketing, by a trader, directly connected with the promotion, sale or supply of a product to consumers".*

Accordingly, the concept of "commercial practice" is in part narrower and in part broader than the term "competitive act" used in many Member States. In any event it is broader than the concept of "advertising" (which requires a representation) but narrower than the concept of commercial communications in the E-Commerce Directive. It can be concluded from the word "direct" that indirect advertising (public relations, sponsoring, etc) is not covered. As far as the Directive refers to "advertising", this term is to be interpreted within the meaning of Directive 84/450/EEC, which emphases the intent to promote goods or services (see under 3.a.).

c. General clause

The core of the Directive is the general clause in Art. 5(1); less in terms of its direct application—which will probably be relatively small—than its role as the basis for the

100. See fn. 97
101. This shows that the restriction to consumer protection is probably less due to objective reasons than to limits on the powers of the Directorate-General responsible.

two examples regulated in detail (aggressive and misleading commercial practices) and the "blacklist".[102] Whether the general clause implies a new interpretation to the notion of "unfairness" has already been discussed in detail in Chapter 1.VI.

The general clause in Article 5(1)lays down very briefly:

> *"Unfair commercial practices shall be prohibited".*

More explicit is Article 5(2), which establishes a two-step-criterion for determining unfairness. A commercial practice shall be regarded as unfair if:

- it is contrary to the requirements of professional diligence and
- it materially distorts or is likely to materially distort the economic behaviour with regard to the product of the average consumer whom it reaches or to whom it is addressed, or of the average member of the group when a commercial practice is directed to a particular group of consumers.

Thus in a first stage it must be determined whether the commercial practice corresponds with professional diligence. According to Article 2(h), 'professional diligence' means

> *". . . the standard of special skill and care which a trader may reasonably be expected to exercise towards consumers, commensurate with honest market practices and/or the general principle of good faith in the trader's field of activity".*

The terms "honest market practices" and "good faith" were only included during the consultations in the European Parliament. The concept of "honest practices" is obviously based on Art. 10bis of the Paris Convention.[103] By providing the alternative basis of good faith or honest practices, it is made clear that the actual business conduct may be corrected by extra-legal criteria; this brings the general clauses in line with the laws of those Member States which use terms like "honest practices", "good faith" etc. (as to the determination of these terms see Chapter 1.IV).

In a second step, it must be determined whether the business practice is capable of materially influencing the economic behaviour of the consumer. Article 2(2) speaks of the average consumer and Recital 18 states:

> *"This Directive takes as a benchmark the average consumer, who is reasonably well-informed and reasonably observant und circumspect, as interpreted by the Court of Justice, and taking into account social, cultural and linguistic factors".*

At the same time however, it emphasises:

> *"but also contains provisions aimed at preventing the exploitation of consumers where characteristics make them particularly vulnerable to unfair commercial practices".*

102. The general clause is discussed by Micklitz, Henning-Bodewig, Gamerith, see fn. 100.
103. Discussed in Chapter 2.I.

> *"Where a commercial practice is specifically aimed at a particular group of consumers, such as children, it is desirable that the impact of the commercial practice be assessed from the perspective of the average member of that group".*

This corresponds largely with the interpretation already give to Directive 84/450/EEC (see above, 3) and the legal view in all Member States (see Chapter 4).

d. Misleading commercial practices

1. Scope of application
Deception is regulated as one of the two examples where unfairness is to be assumed "in particular". This feature is divided into "misleading actions and misleading omissions". Deceptions as against persons who are not consumers within the meaning of Art. 2(a) continue to be determined according to Directive 84/450/EEC. There are at first sight no apparent material differences in the assessment, since Art. 6 and 7 essentially codify the judicial practice of the ECJ, which is also decisive for the interpretation of Directive 84/450/EEC.

2. Misleading actions
Article 6 deals with "misleading actions". A commercial practice is misleading if it "in any way, including overall presentation, causes or is likely to cause the average consumer to take a transactional decision that he would not have taken otherwise because it deceives or is likely to deceive him . . .". As discussed above, "average consumer" means the consumer who is reasonably well-informed and reasonably observant and circumspect.

Article 6(1) subparagraphs a-g list points of reference (intended apparently as exhaustive) for misleading actions, namely the existence or nature of the product (a); the main characteristics of the product (b); the extent of the trader's commitments and the motives for the commercial practice etc. (c); the price (d); the need for a service or repair (e); the nature, attributes or rights of the trader (f); or the consumer's rights or the risks he may face (g). They can largely also be subsumed under the "references" already known from Directive 84/450/EEC, particularly since the latter does not contain an exhaustive list (see above).

Article 6(2) regulates specific forms of deception. These involve the additional restriction that the assessment must be made "in its factual context, taking account of all its features and circumstances" (whether this is intended to differ from the similar wording used in para. 1 remains uncertain). In (a), any marketing of a product, including comparative advertising, which creates confusion with any product, trade names . . . of a competitor is prohibited, while (b) prohibits "non-compliance by the trader with commitments obtained in codes of contact" if the latter satisfy certain requirements.

3. Misleading omissions
Article 7 regulates misleading omissions.

> *"A commercial practice shall be regarded as misleading which, in its factual context, taking account of all its features and circumstances, omits material information that the average consumer needs, according to the context, to take*

> *an informed transactional decision and thereby cause or is likely to cause the average consumer to take a transactional decision that the would not have taken otherwise".*

According to Article 7(2) it shall also be regarded as a misleading omission "when a trader hides or provides in an unclear, unintelligible, ambiguous or untimely manner such material information or fails to identify the commercial intent of the commercial practice". If there is an 'invitation to purchase' (defined in Article 2(i)) this includes the main characteristics of the product (a), the geographical address and the identity of the trader (b), the price including taxes etc. (c), the arrangements for payment, delivery etc. (d); the right of withdrawal or cancellation (e).

While these requirements mainly correspond to these already known under Directive 84/450/EEC—which has been interpreted by the ECJ as also covering the omission of material information[104]—the link established in Art. 7(5) to all other transparency requirements in Community law that "shall be regarded as material" may possibly lead to a broader interpretation.

Since this can also lead to an information overload, Article 7(3) provides that "where the medium used . . . imposes limitations of space or time, these limitations and any measures taken by a trader to make the information available to consumers by other means shall be taken into account in deciding whether information has been omitted".

4. "Blacklist" of misleading practices

Annex 1 lists 21 misleading commercial practices which, according to Art. 5(5) "are in all circumstances considered unfair". By this is obviously meant that no additional examination should take place whether the practice in question is capable of influencing the consumer's economic behaviour or not. The individual practices are set out word for word here because of their importance for the Member States, which must implement them. Account must be taken of the fact that the terms used in the individual examples themselves in part require interpretation, rendering absolute application more difficult. Misleading commercial practices are:

(1) Claiming to be a signatory to a code of conduct when the trader is not.
(2) Displaying a trust mark, quality mark or equivalent without having obtained the necessary authorisation.
(3) Claiming that a code of conduct has an endorsement from a public or other body which it does not have.
(4) Claiming that a trader (including his commercial practices) or a product has been approved, endorsed or authorised by a public or private body when he/it has not or making such a claim without complying with the terms of the approval, endorsement or authorisation.
(5) Making an invitation to purchase at a specified price without disclosing the existence of any reasonable grounds the trader may have for believing that he will not be able to offer for supply or to procure another trader to supply, those products or equivalent products at that price for a period that is, and in quantities that are, reasonable having regard to the product, the scale of advertising of the product and the price offered (bait advertising).

104. See, for instance, the Nissan decision of the ECJ (fn. 53 on p. 38).

(6) Making an invitation to purchase products at a specified price and then:
   (a) refusing to show the advertised item to consumers, or
   (b) refusing to take orders for it or deliver it within a reasonable time, or
   (c) demonstrating a defective sample of it,

with the intention of promoting a different product (bait and switch).

(7) Falsely stating that the product will only be available for a very limited time, or that it will only be available on particular terms for a very limited time, in order to elicit an immediate decision and deprive consumers of sufficient opportunity or time to make an informed choice.

(8) Undertaking to provide after-sales service to consumers with whom the trader has communicated prior to a transaction in a language which is not an official language of the Member State where the trader is located and then making such service available only in another language without clearly disclosing this to the consumer before the consumer is committed to the transaction.

(9) Stating or otherwise creating the impression that a product can legally be sold when it cannot.

(10) Presenting rights given to consumers in law as a distinctive feature of the trader's offer.

(11) Using editorial content in the media to promote a product where a trader has paid for the promotion without making that clear in the content or by images or sounds clearly identifiable by the consumers (advertorial). This is without prejudice to Council Directive 89/552/EEC.

(12) Making a materially inaccurate claim concerning the nature and extent of the risk to the personal security of the consumer or his family if the consumer does not purchase the product.

(13) Promoting a product similar to a product made by a particular manufacturer in such a manner as deliberately to mislead the consumer into believing that the product is made by that same manufacturer when it is not.

(14) Establishing, operating or promoting a pyramid promotional scheme where a consumer gives consideration for the opportunity to receive compensation that is derived primarily from the introduction of other consumers into the scheme rather than form the sale or consumption of products.

(15) Claiming that the trader is about to cease trading or move premises when he is not.

(16) Claiming that products are able to facilitate winning in games of chance.

(17) Falsely claiming that a product is able to cure illness, dysfunction or malformations.

(18) Passing on materially inaccurate information on market conditions or on the possibility of finding the product with the intention of inducing the consumer to acquire the product at conditions less favourable than normal market conditions.

(19) Claiming in a commercial practice to offer a competition or prize promotion without awarding the prizes described or a reasonable equivalent.

(20) Describing a product as "gratis", "free", "without charge" or similar if the consumer has to pay anything other than the unavoidable cost of responding to the commercial practice and collecting or paying for delivery of the item.

(21) Including in marketing material an invoice or similar document seeking payment which gives the consumer the impression that he has already ordered the marketed product when he has not.

e. Aggressive commercial practices

1. Harassment, coercion, undue influence
Article 8 regulates "aggressive commercial practices". A commercial practice shall be regarded as aggressive if

> *"in its factual context, taking account of all its features and circumstances, by harassment, coercion or undue influence, including the use of physical force, it significantly impairs or is likely to significantly impair the average consumer's freedom of choice or conduct with regard to the product and thereby causes him or is likely to cause him to take a transactional decision that he would not have taken otherwise".*

Article 2(j) only defines "undue influence" (as "exploitation a position of power in relation to the consumer to apply pressure, even without using or threatening to use physical forced, in a way that significantly limits the consumer's ability to make an informed decision").

Harassment and coercion are not defined but are (only) to be determined according to Article 19:

> *"In determining whether a commercial practice uses harassment, coercion or undue influence account shall be taken of*
> *(a) its timing, nature or persistence;*
> *(b) the use of threatening or abusive language or behaviour;*
> *(c) the use by the trader of any specific misfortune or circumstance of such gravity as to impair the consumer's judgment, of which the trader is aware, to influence the consumer's decision with regard to the product;*
> *(d) any onerous or disproportionate non-contractual barriers established by the trader where a consumer wishes to exercise rights under the contract, including rights to terminate a contract or to switch to another product or another trader;*
> *(e) any threat to take any action that cannot legally be taken".*

2. "Blacklist" of aggressive commercial practices
Pursuant to Art. 5(5) these commercial practices named in annex 1 are considered "in all circumstances unfair":

(22) Falsely claiming or creating the impression that the trader is not acting for purposes relating to his trade, business, craft or profession, or falsely representing oneself as a consumer.
(23) Creating the false impression that after-sales services in relation to a product is available in a Member State other than the on in which the product is sold.
(24) Creating the impression that the consumer cannot leave the premises until a contract is formed.
(25) Conducting personal visits to the consumer's home ignoring the consumer's request to leave or not to return except in circumstances and to the extent justified, under national law, to enforce a contractual obligation.

(26) Making persistent and unwanted solicitations by telephone, fax, e-mail or other remote media except in circumstances and to the extent justified under national law to enforce a contractual obligation. This is without prejudice to Article 10 of Directive 97/7/EC and Directives 95/46/EC and 2002/58/EC.

(27) Requiring a consumer who wishes to claim on an insurance policy to produce documents which could not reasonably be considered relevant as to whether the claim was valid, or falling systematically to respond to pertinent correspondence, in order to dissuade the consumer from exercising his contractual rights.

(28) Including in an advertisement a direct exhortation to children to buy advertised products or persuade their parents or other adults to buy advertised products for them. This provision is without prejudice to Article 16 of Directive 89/552/EEC on television broadcasting.

(29) Demanding immediate or different payment for or the return of safekeeping of products supplied by the trader, but not solicited by the consumer except where the product is a substitute supplied in conformity with Article 7(3) of Directive 97/7/EC (inertia selling).

(30) Explicitly informing a consumer that if he does not buy the product or service, the trader's job or livelihood will be in jeopardy.

(31) Creating the impression that the consumer has already won, will win, or will on doing a particular act win, a prize or other equivalent benefit, when in fact either:
   - there is no prize or other equivalent benefit, or
   - taking any action in relation to claiming the prize or other equivalent benefit is subject to the consumer paying money or incurring a cost.

f. Enforcement

The Directive contains a rudimentary regulation of sanctions which mainly corresponds to those of Directive 84/450/EEC. According to Article 11(1) "Member states shall ensure that adequate and effective means exist to combat unfair commercial practices and for the compliance with the provisions of this Directive in the interest of consumers". Such means shall include legal provisions under which persons or organisations regarded under national law as having a legitimate interest in combating unfair trade practices, including competitors, may take legal actions or bring the matter before an administrative authority. A mere system of self-control is not considered sufficient (nor is a system of codes of conduct expressly mentioned in Article 10), but Member States may require "prior recourse to other established means of dealing with complaints".

Article 12 regulates questions of evidence. According to this, the Member States must grant the courts or the administrative authorities the power to demand evidence for allegations of fact related to a commercial practice in appropriate cases and where necessary to regard allegations of fact as incorrect.

Pursuant to Art. 13, the Member States are also obliged "to lay down penalties for infringements of national provisions adopted in application of this Directive". These include in any event the action for an injunction (including preventive) and the interlocutory protection based thereon.

g. Internal market clause

According to Article 4

> *"Member States shall neither restrict the freedom to provide services nor restrict the free movement of goods for reasons falling within the field approximated by this Directive".*

The country-of-origin principle contained in the original proposal for Art. 4 para. 1 and the principle of control at source were abandoned on the occasion of the EU Council on Competitive Activity. It is as yet not certain how the internal market clause of Art. 4 is to be construed (see in detail Chapter 1, VI.2.).

11. The Consumer Protection Cooperation Regulation

The Regulation of the European Parliament and Council on Cooperation between the National Authorities Responsible for Enforcing Consumer Protection Legislation (Consumer Protection Cooperation Regulation)[105] complements the Directive on Unfair Commercial Practices. Its aim is to improve the cooperation between the authorities responsible for enforcing consumer protection in the case of infringements within the Community. At the same time, according to Recital 3a, the "smooth operation of the internal market, the quality and the coherence of the enforcement of consumer protection legislation and the monitoring of the protection of the consumer's economic interests should be improved".

Alongside the exchange of information, the Regulation provides above all for administrative assistance. Upon application by a competent authority of another Member State, the competent authority must ensure that infringements within the Community are immediately terminated and prevented. Pursuant to Art. 1, the Regulation sets out the modalities according to which the competent authorities in the Member States must collaborate with each other and with the Commission in order to ensure compliance with the legislation listed in the annex and to guarantee the smooth operation of the internal market.

From this it follows indirectly that the Member States that as yet do not have an authority responsible for enforcement[106] must establish one. However, the competent authority can, pursuant to Art. 4, designate other authorities and other agencies that pursuant to Art. 8 Para. 2a have a legitimate interest in the termination of infringements within the Community. The powers stated in Para. 2 can, in accordance with national legislation, be exercised either under the authority's own responsibility or by means of an application to the courts that are responsible for issuing the necessary decisions.

The powers enjoyed by the authority include the right to inspect relevant documents, to require anyone to provide relevant information about infringements within the Community, to conduct the necessary investigations on site, and demand that the activity in question is terminated. If a decision is ignored, the authority can demand that the losing defendant pay a certain amount into a specified fund.

105. Regulation 2006/2004/EC of 27 October 2004, OJ 2004 L 364/1 of 9.12.2004.
106. Austria, Germany, the Netherlands and in part Luxemburg.

12. The proposed Regulation on Sales Promotion

In 2001, the Commission proposed a Regulation concerning Sales Promotion in the Internal Market[107] covering discounts, free gifts, premiums and promotional contests or games (Art. 2(b)). In 2005 the proposal was put "on hold" so that its fate remains unclear.

The Proposal is not applicable to seasonal, clearance or closing down sales, sales below costs, sales promotions of tobacco products, alcoholic beverages, medicinal products, sales promotion of legal services; promotional contents and games in the editorial contents of a media or where a media is the promoter, nor does it cover national regulations relating to health or safety aspects.

The main provisions can be found in Article 3, which prohibits Member States from imposing

- a general prohibition on the use or commercial communication of a sale promotion unless required by Community law,
- a limitation on the value of a sales promotion, except for books, sheet music and press products, or
- a requirement to obtain prior authorisation, or any requirement having equivalent effect, for the use or commercial communication of a discount, a free gift or a premium.

Instead, Article 5 requires Member States to ensure that mandatory information requirements set out in the Annex of the Regulation are fulfilled. The Annex contains a detailed list of information for each form of sales promotion. In addition, Article 7 requires promotional games not to be linked to the purchase of the product promoted. Article 8 prohibits any enticement to hatred on grounds of race, sex, religion etc., while Article 6 deals with the protection of children.

The Proposal contains a county-of-origin-clause.

107. COM (2002) 585.

12. The proposed Regulation on Sales Promotion

[illegible]

Chapter 4. Unfair Competition Law in the Member States

I. AUSTRIA

Selected Literature: Ackermann, *Nachahmen und Übernahme fremder Leistung im Wettbewerb*, ÖBl 1999, 3; Ackermann, *Zur Wettbewerbswidrigkeit* "gefühlsbetonter Werbung", WBl 1998, 474; Aicher, *Das Recht der Werbung*, 1984; Artmann, *Wettbewerbsrecht und Umweltschutz*, 1997; Bultmann/Schuhmacher, *Austria*, in: Micklitz/Keßler (ed.), Marketing Practices Regulation and Consumer Protection in the EC Member States and the US, 2002, p. 1; Enzinger/Spiring, *Der Handy-Boom und die Preisschlacht der Mobilfunkanbieter*, ecolex, 2001, 243.; Essl, *E-Commerce-Richtlinie und Wettbewerbsrecht: Eine kritische Anmerkung*, ÖBl 2000, 156; Farnleitner/Straberger, *Nahversorgungsgesetz*, 1978; Fitz/Gamerith, *Handelsrecht-Wettbewerbsrecht: Unlauterer Wettbewerb und Kartelle*, 4th ed. 2003; Gamerith, *Vergleichende Werbung, Auswirkungen der Richtlinie 97/55/EG auf das österreichische Wettbewerbsrecht*, ÖBl 1998, 114; Gruber, *Wettbewerbsrechtlicher Nachahmungsschutz gegen kompatible Produkte?*, WBL 2000, 145; Gumpoldsberger, *UWG*, 2003; Hanreich, *Das neue österreichische Wettbewerbs- und Preisrecht*, ÖZW 1994, 33; Hauser/Thomasser, *Wettbewerb- und Immaterialgüterrecht, Österreich*, 1998; Hödl, *Die Folgen des EuGH-Urteils* "Familiapress" für § 9a UWG, WBl 1997, 324; Höhne, *Zum Stand der Domain-Judikatur des OGH*, MR 2000, 356; Kapferer, *Das österreichische Zugaberecht*, 1996; Kapferer/Pahl, *Kennzeichenschutz für Internet-Adressen ("domains")* ÖBl 1998, 275; Koppensteiner, *Zugaben de lege ferenda*, ÖBl 2000, S. 195; Koppensteiner, *Österreichisches und europäisches Wettbewerbsrecht*, 3rd ed. 1997; Kusco, *Österreichisches und europäisches Wettbewerbs-, Marken-, Muster- und Patentrecht*, 1995; Kusco, *Geistiges Eigentum*, 2003; Laga, *Das österreichische Spam-Verbot, Ein rechtlich bedenkliches Kuriosum*, ÖBl 2000, 243; Pöch, Austria, in: Campbell (ed.), *Unfair Trade Practices*, 1996, 1; Prunbauer, *Zur Zulässigkeit von Gewinnspielen nach den UWG-Novellen 1992 und 1993*, MR 1993, 137; Prunbauer/Seidelberger, *Die Wettbewerbsfibel*, 2003; Rüffler, *Österreichisches und europäisches Wirtschaftsprivatrecht*, Teil VI/2, Wettbewerbsrecht—UWG, 1998; Rüffler, *Umweltwerbung und Wettbewerbsrecht*, ÖBl 1999, 267; Schönherr/Wiltschek, *UWG. Kommentierte Gesetzesausgabe*, 2000; Schuhmacher (ed.), *Verbraucherschutz in Österreich und der EG*, 1992; Schutzverband gegen unlauteren Wettbewerb (ed.), *Aktuelle Fragen des Lauterkeitsrechts*, 2004; Tahedl, *Zur Kennzeichnungspflicht für Radio- und Fernsehwerbung, ecolex* 1997, 583; Walter, *"JUSLINE"—"Domain-Grabbing" im Internet*, MR 1998, 106; Wamprechtshamer, *Die Neuordnung der vergleichenden Werbung*, ÖBl 2000, 147; Wiltschek, *UWG*; 7th ed. 2003; Wiltschek, *Neues im Irrgarten des UWG, ecolex 1999*, 635; Winternitz/Steinmair, *Das Wettbewerbsrecht in Österreich*, in: Heidelberger Kommentar, 2nd ed. 2005, p. 918; Zweng, *Die wettbewerbsrechtliche Beurteilung der Werbung mit Gewinnspielen*, 1993.

1. Sources of law

Gesetz gegen den unlauteren Wettbewerb (Act against Unfair Competition) from 1984 (UWG)

2. Austrian competition law in a nutshell

Austrian unfair competition law is largely based on the Gesetz gegen den unlauteren Wettbewerb from 1984 (UWG),[1] which is supplemented by the co-called "Local Supply Act".[2]

In terms of approach and content, the Austrian UWG is similar to the German UWG in its 1909 version. It is dominated by a general clause in § 1 UWG prohibiting all competitive practices that are against "gute Sitten" ("bones mores"). The general clause in § 1 UWG is supplemented by a "small general clause" against misleading advertising in § 2 UWG. Furthermore, there is some detailed legislation, for instance, on disparagement (defamation), premiums, risk of confusion, price indications, bribery of employees and agents, disclosure of company secrets, misuse of designs and patterns. In addition, § 27 et seq. UWG deals with certain types of marketing practices (sweepstakes, bankruptcy assets, usurpation of distinction and privileges, labeling, clearance sales, sectional sales, special sales).

The UWG requires in its most important provisions, especially the general clause(s), a business activity for the purpose of competition as well as a competitive relationship.[3] The subjective intent to promote one's own sales is assumed if there is an objective capability to promote competition.[4] The UWG serves a threshold purpose: it protects competitors, consumers and the public at large.

Austrian courts have developed extensive case law of different causes of action (canvassing, exploitation, breach of law, etc.) especially regarding the general clause in § 1 UWG and the "small general clause" in § 2 UWG (misleading indications).[5] Its interpretation often shows parallels to the German jurisdiction.

The interpretation of the general clause(s) also takes into account the purpose of the Anti-trust law[6] and (especially where danger of confusion, disparagement etc. is involved) of the respective laws to protect intellectual property;[7] in consumer matters

1. For an extensive discussion of Austrian unfair competition law see, for instance, Koppensteiner, Schönherr/Wiltschek und Fitz/Gamerith as well as the concise but comprehensive "Wettbewerbsfibel" of Prunbauer/Seidelberger. Regarding current development in competition and trademark law, the annual overviews from the WRP (Wiltschek) can be consulted. Decisions and the current version of all federal laws can be found free of charge at the law information system RIS at www.ris.bka.gv.at.
2. Law from 29.6.1977 regarding the improvement of the local supply and the competition conditions. See Gamerith, *Renaissance des Nahversorgungsgesetzes?*; in: Schutzverband (ed), p. 35.
3. The term competitive relationship is interpreted broadly, cf., e.g. OGH 9.3.1999, MR 1989, 186—"Talfahrt der A". It can also be established ad hoc, i.e. it can develop from the act of competition itself, cf. OGH 24.2.1998, ÖBl. 1998, 229—"Nintendo".
4. With regards to parties other than the competitor an act of competition is only assumed if there is a "typical action" furthering another's competition (e.g. advertising agencies or newspapers as far as the publishing of advertising is concerned); OGH 18.5.1999, ÖBl. 2000, 109—"Bezirkstelefonbuch"; if not, the burden of proof is on the plaintiff.
5. Cf., for instance, the commentary Koppensteiner, which cites abundant decisions of the Supreme Court (OHG).
6. Available under the address cited in fn. 1.
7. An introduction to the Austrian IP laws is given by Kusco; as to trade mark law see also Koppensteiner, p. 781 ff.

the Consumer Protection Act is of some importance.[8] The self-regulation Code of the Austrian advertising industry[9] also has at least an indirect effect on the interpretation of the general clause.

3. Regulation of advertising

a. Misleading advertising

§ 2 UWG prohibits misleading statements regarding commercial aspects. Any statement—regardless of the means of communication—that contains a provable fact falls under this category. Exaggerations, for example superlative claims, are only considered harmless "puffing" in exceptional cases.[10] Omissions of fact can fall under § 2 UWG if the omission leads to a misleading general impression.[11]

Whether an advertisement will be considered misleading depends on the perception of the target group. Under influence of the ECJ, the Austrian Supreme Court (OGH) uses the benchmark of the reasonably informed, observant and circumspect average consumer.[12] However, this does not exclude the possibility that the consumer—especially in case of special products and certain circumstances—relies on a rather general overall impression.[13] In cases of ambiguous statements, the advertiser must consider all reasonable interpretation by the public (ambiguity rule),[14] and may not rely on the most favorable for him.

The misleading advertising must be capable of influencing the commercial behavior of a substantial part of the target group (which is assumed in most cases). A clarification or correction before the actual conclusion of the contract does not necessarily prevent the finding of deception.[15]

Misleading advertising can relate to all business aspects; the list of reference points in § 2 UWG is not exclusive. In practice, cases often deal with misleading advertising regarding the price, which is handled rather strictly by the courts.[16] An advertiser is expected to have enough goods in stock to meet the usual demand[17]

8. Cf. Schumacher (ed.), Verbraucherschutz in Österreich und der EG, 1992.
9. Available under www.werberat.at.
10. In principle, the public acts on the assumption of a serious claim of facts. "Puffing" was denied for example to claims such as "leading advertising agency" (OGH 18.2.1986, ÖBl. 1987, 47), "Austria's purest beer" (OGH ÖBl. 1989, 141); "most qualified ski instructors" (OGH ÖBl., 2001, 76). Puffing was granted for "Best beer in Austria" (OGH ÖBl., 2001, 76), "the best magazine" or statements such as "the weekly magazine with the best quality". (OGH ÖBl. 2000, 429)
11. An offer for a cell phone combined with a subscription for a newspaper was ruled misleading, because it was not mentioned that the cell phone required a one year contract with a cell phone service provider. OGH ÖBl. 1998, 465—"Kombinationsangebot"; see Wiltschek, WRP 1999, 709, 720. This may be different if the information is considered general knowledge; OGH ÖBl. 2000, 165—"Amtstag eines Notars".
12. Cf., e.g. OHG ÖBl. 2001, 18—"Lego-Klemmbausteine"; Wiltschek, WRP 2002, 763, 765. As to the influence of European law in general see Ackermann, ÖBl. 1997, 10.
13. Cf. OGH 22.3.2001, ÖBl. 2002, 71—"Kombucha Teegetränk".
14. Cf. OGH 17.11.1987, ÖBl. 1989, 46—"Handelsregister"; OGH 3.12.1991, WBl. 1992, 241—"Kfz-Angebote"; OGH 20.10.1998, ÖBl. 1999, 22—"Stockerauer Salat-Erdäpfel".
15. See Wiltschek, WRP 1998, 698, 706.
16. See, e.g., the decisions cited at Koppensteiner, No. 507 et seq. and Prunbauer/Seidelberger, p. 58 et seq.
17. OGH 15.1.1980, ÖBl. 1980, 43—"Schallplatten-Sonderpreis". As to bait- and switch-offers OGH 23.11.1971, ÖBl. 1972, 36—"Niedrigpreis-Werbung".

when advertising special offers. In case of price reductions, the previous price must have been actually demanded for an appropriate amount of time.[18] Price guarantees are permitted if the prices for comparative goods were in fact asked, the advertiser watches these prices and adjusts his own prices accordingly.[19] Another main focus is misleading advertising regarding the characteristics of products[20] and indications of origin.[21] Environmental advertising[22] is judged especially strictly, as well as claims of superiority etc.,[23] unless they constitute an exceptional advertising exaggeration (see above, No. 6).

According to § 2 para. 5 UWG, the advertiser has the burden of proof for the truthfulness of the factual claim if the court considers this appropriate, for instance in cases of comparative advertising.[24]

b. Comparative advertising

Pursuant to the misleading advertising clause of § 2(2) UWG, comparative advertising is permitted if it is neither misleading nor a violation of §§ 1, 7 and 9 para. 1-3 UWG. This regulation was supplemented in 1999 by § 2 para. 3. UWG, which states that comparisons of goods with indications of origin must refer to the same indications, and that special offers must meet certain information requirements. The Austrian law thereby did not transpose Directive 97/55/EC almost word-by-word (like most of the other member states), but rather incorporated it into the general system of the UWG.[25]

Comparative advertising is rather strictly judged, especially under the aspects of misleading and disparagement.[25a] Unspecific, vague comparisons are, for instance, rarely allowed.[26] The competitor and its product must not be disparaged or mocked beyond what is absolutely necessary.[27] Although the comparison does not necessarily have to be complete, it may not create an incorrect overall impression by omitting

18. OGH 12.1.1988, WBl. 1988, 232—"Großer Schuhverkauf"; OGH 26.11.1996, ÖBl. 1997, 70—"B-Tiefpreishammer"; OGH 25.6.1996, ÖBl. 1997, 10—"EU-Tiefpreis"; OGH 25.9.1979; ÖBl. 1980, 76—"Computer-Preissturz"; OGH 13.9.2000, ÖBl. 2001, 121—"Konzernpreise".
19. Prunbauer/Seidelberger, p. 61 ff.
20. See the decisions cited at Prunbauer/Seidelberger, p. 67 et seq.
21. For example, Austrian salami using ribbons in the Hungarian national colors without a disclaimer was considered misleading (OGH ÖBl. 1972, 12—"Ungarische Salami III"); the indication "Fashion for Austria" for Italian loden products, which had labels in similar colors to Austrian province colors, did not provide sufficient information for clarification (OGH ÖBl. 2000, S. 139—"Tiroler Loden").
22. See especially Artmann and Rütter, ÖBl. 1999, 267 ff.
23. The claim for superiority applies to all aspects that could be considered significant and constant (OGH 20.11.1990; ÖBl. 1991, 75—"Das beste Wasser"; OGH 16.1.2001, ÖBl. 2001, 2623—"NetLine").
24. See OGH 20.8.2002, RdW 2003, 20—"Frischmilch"; Prunbauer/Seidelberger, p. 56.
25. A good overview on comparative advertising can be found by Gamerith, ÖBl. 1998, p. 114 ff.; Wamprechtshammer, ÖBl. 2000, 147.

25a. Cf. Seidelberger, *Vergleichende Werbung in Überblick*, in: Schutzverband (ed), p. 219. The Austrian jurisdiction will probably become more liberal due to the Pippig/Hartlauer decision of the ECJ (discussed in Chapters 3, 4).

26. Cf., for instance, OGH 24.10.2000, ÖBl. 2002, 19—"Heisser Streit"; OGH 9.4.2002, ÖBl. 2002, 173—"Mehr darf der Spaß nicht kosten!"; OGH 10.11.1998, ÖBl. 1999, 13—"Kleiner Bruder"; OGH 3.4.1990, MR 1990, S. 48—. "Bank-Pfandverkauf". The statement, "Before purchasing oriental carpets, please compare our prices and quality with those offered by stores which are members of the Austrian Oriental Carpet Association and then decide" was not permitted.
27. For example a sad "smiley face" sign was prohibited when shown in conjunction with a competitor's distinguishing mark. OGH 13.4.1999, MR 1999, 186—"Negative Smile".

relevant or not so favorable aspects.[28] In cases of comparative advertising the advertiser has the burden of proof (see above).

The requirement of objectivity also applies to comparisons as to systems and procedures, in which individual competitors are not identifiable. Such comparisons, too, must be accurate objective and may not contain any avoidable disparagement or aggressive wording.[29] Comparative advertising of personal facts is always prohibited.[30]

c. Concealed advertising

Concealed advertising violates (irrespective of the way of communication) the general clause of § 1 UWG. This applies to commercial mail that is presented as personal mail, concealed advertising in newspapers or magazines, and product placement on television.[31] Media-specific regulations exist for the press, broadcasters and the internet providers. (See under e) According to § 28a UWG, offers for an inclusion in directories or the like, must unmistakably disclose that they aim at the conclusion of a contract.[32]

d. Aggressive advertising

Harassing, intrusive or aggressive advertising may in principle be subsumed under the "bones mores"—clause of § 1 UWG. In practice these aspects mostly play a role to cases of direct marketing, see under 4.

e. Product- and media-specific advertising regulations

Food advertising is regulated in the Act from 1 January 1975 (Lebensmittelgesetz = LMG).[33] § 9 para. 1 LMG contains an extensive prohibition of health-related statements, which is strictly enforced.[34] In part, advertising for cosmetics and alcohol falls under this as well.[35]

28. OGH 13.11.2001, ÖBl. 2002, 13—"Freiminuten".
29. OGH 28.9.1999, ÖBl. 2000, 20—"LKW-Entfernung"; OGH 19.11.1999, WBl. 2002, 117—"Eternit"; OGH 17.2.2001, ecolex 2002, 110—"Flori"; OGH 19.8.2003, ÖBl-LS 2003, 147—"ob-Werbung".
30. Prunbauer/Seidelberger, p. 78 et seq.
31. Prunbauer/Seidelberger, p. 19; see especially OGH 21.11.1995, ÖBl. 1996, 120—"Offener Brief" (misleading as to references)
32. OGH 11.10.1988, ÖBl. 1989, 74—"Erfolgscheinwerbung III". For an indepth discussion see Feuchtinger, in: Schutzverband, (ed), p. 9.
33. Available on the internet. (see fn. 1).
34. The advertising claim "beautiful skin, beautiful hair" on the packaging and in print and radio advertising for a product made of yeast, millet and wheat was (despite the buzzword character) considered a illegitimate statement regarding physiological and pharmacological effects, OGH ÖBl. 1992, 114—"Prioflor".
35. Here the prohibition of health-related statements is, however, moderated according to §§ 9 para.1, 26 para. 2 LMG. According to the exception of § 26 para. 2., references such as "bacteria-repressing", "astringent" and others are permitted. However, the name "kario-med" for a toothpaste was not permitted as it created the impression that cavities can either be prevented or cured. (vgl. OGH ÖBl. 1983, 39—"kario-med"; see also Gladt, Zulässige "gesundheitsbezogene Angaben" für kosmetische Mittel, ÖJZ 1991, S. 51). Also recommendation at the end of an advertisement for cosmetics to "ask a doctor" or "With X you can protect yourself from gum disease" was prohibited (OLG WBL 1993, S. 58—"Sensodyne F").

Advertising-specific regulations for pharmaceutical products can be found in the Pharmaceutics Act from 3 February 1983.[36] In addition to a general prohibition of misleading advertising, it restricts advertising for certain types of pharmaceutical products. Advertising for tobacco products is regulated by § 11 Tobacco Act; media specific regulations (TV) apply to advertising of drugs, alcohol and tobacco.

The Media Law from 6 December 1981[37] requires a distinct separation of content and advertising for the press; in cases of doubt advertising must be declared as such. § 3 UWG contains a special regulation for misleading advertising. Television advertising is mainly restricted through § 5 para. 3 of the Broadcasting Act,[38] which transposed the Television directive; radio broadcasting is regulated through regional radio laws. Internet advertising is regulated through the transposition of Directive 2000/31/EC in the Telecommunication Law.[39]

f. Other advertising regulations

Advertising exploiting sentiments of fear, shocking advertising, discriminating or "emotional" advertising, for instance advertising combined with social sponsoring,[40] can at least theoretically be subsumed under § 1 UWG.

4. Direct marketing

Sending of unsolicited goods can be considered a violation of § 1 UWG.[41] Unrequested home visits are permitted if they do avoid any harassment.[42] The same applies to approaching people in public areas.[43]

Austrian courts have traditionally considered unsolicited telephone-, fax- and e-mail advertising without prior consent as unfair competition ("opt-in").[44] This applies also to business to business-calls if the permission can not at least be assumed.[45] This case law was also incorporated into the Telecommunication Act of 1 August 1997. It is not allowed only to ask permission for further telephone advertising;[46] exceptions are exclusively made for commercial calls within an existing contract relationships.

36. Available on the internet at the address stated in fn. 1.
37. Available on the internet (Fn 1). Regarding media law c.f. Foregger/Litzka, Mediengesetz, 3rd ed. 1999; Foregger (ed.), Mediengesetz, 4th ed. 2000: especially as to surreptious advertising in the press Wünsch, in: Festschrift für Fritz Schönherr, p. 97 ff.
38. Available at the internet address stated in fn. 1; see also Funk, Rechtsprobleme der Rundfunkwerbung, in: Aicher, Das Recht der Werbung, 1984.
39. BGBl. I 100/1997 (available through the Internet, see fn. 1); cf. Bultmann/Schuhmacher, p. 6.
40. For example, advertising for coffee with the claim that parts of the profit were used for a good cause, was considered as being against "bones mores" (OLG Wien 25.2.1993, ecolex 1993, 537—"Danke"; see also OGH 26.4.1998, ÖBl. 1998, 339—"Opferlicht"; Ackermann, ÖBl. 1998, 427).
41. OGH 19.9.1994, ÖBl. 1995, S. 64—"Fachbuchverlag"; Bultmann/Schuhmacher, p. 9.
42. Restrictions for certain products exist in the Commercial Code; cf. Bultmann/Schuhmacher, p. 9.
43. OGH 29.1.1980, ÖBl. 1980, 92—"Buchgemeinschaftswerbung".
44. As to advertising per fax see OGH 28.10.1997, GRUR Int. 1998, 726; a general overview can be found at Kusco, ecolex, 1990, 39; for E-mail-advertising various regulations apply; cf. Laga, ÖBl. 2000, 243; and Laga, *E-Mail Werbung 2004*, in Schutzverband (ed.), p. 159.
45. OGH 8.11.1983, ÖBl. 1984, 13—"Telefonwerbung I".
46. OGH 18.4.1999, ÖBl. 1999, 429—"Telefonwerbung III".

Commercial mail which is concealed as private mail is considered against "bones mores" as it violates privacy.[47] The conclusion of a contract in pyramid schemes and any type of gambling used to promote the sales of goods is prohibited by § 27 UWG,[48] which also contains extensive regulations to protect consumers.

5. Sales promotion

After the abolishment of the rebate law (1992), price reductions and rebates are permitted insofar as they are not misleading (§ 2 UWG) or a disguised premium.[49] A prohibition of a sale at a loss only exists in anti-trust law for companies with a market power.

On the other hand, premiums, regulated in § 9a UWG, are in principle prohibited unless one of the exceptions in § 9a para. 2 UWG (common accessories, product samples, small advertising items, items of minor value) applies.[50] If they are not linked to the purchase of the main product, the article is considered an advertising gift and is generally permitted. However, an obligation to purchase is assumed if the impression is created that one must conclude a contract in order to get the promotional gift ("psychological pressure to buy").

The option to participate in sweepstakes is also considered a premium. There are, however, exceptions for "small sweepstakes", which do not exceed a certain value, but which do not apply to sweepstakes in periodicals.[51]

§§ 33a-f UWG regulates announcements for clearance sales.[52] After the 1992 Deregulation Law, end of season sales, seasonal clearance sales, and inventory sales do not fall under the UWG.

6. Risk of confusion

§ 9 UWG grants extensive and comprehensive protection against the risk of confusion.[53] This includes company trade marks and special business terms, brand names and accessories, either protected by IP-laws or not. Domain names also fall under § 9 UWG if they contain an element that characterizes the company name; the newer

47. OGH 14.3.2000, ÖBl. 2000, 337—"Black Jack".
48. Regarding the demarcation to the (permitted) MLM-systems see Bultmann/Schuhmacher, p. 7 f.
49. Bodewig/Henning-Bodewig, WRP 2000, 1341, 1358. As to rebates in distribution systems see Hanreich/Nauer, in: Schutzverband (ed.), p. 87.
50. Regarding the regulation of premiums cf., e.g. Koppensteiner, in ÖBl. 2000, 195 und 2001, 3 as well as Kapferer (1996); Prunbauer/Seidelberger, p. 97 ff.; Bodewig/Henning-Bodewig, WRP 2000, 1358 ff. Martin Prünbauer, Zugabeverbot und Gutscheinwerbung in: Schutzverband (ed.) p. 207. The prohibition of premiums has led to extensive case law with numerous subcategories. It is enforced relatively strictly also in cases of transactions made for the purpose of evading the law. For example, a fictitious price is, according to current case law, measured at 10-15% of the market value of the free gift. (Prunbauer/Seidelberger, p. 104); see OGH 16.7.2002, MR 2002, 242—"Autobahnvignetten IV"; OGH 12.11.1997, ÖBl. 1999, 29—"Jahresabonnement-Kombiangebot" (regarding the burden of proof for fictitious prices).
51. The permissibility of this strict prohibition for the press was approved by the ECJ in the "Familiapress"—decision, see in this book Chapter 3.III.2.a. As to sweepstakes in general see Hödl, WBl. 1997, 200 and Koppensteiner, ÖBL. 2000, 195 and 2001, 3; Zweng (1993); Prunbauer, MR 1993, 137.
52. Prunbauer/Seidelberger, p. 119 et seq.
53. The importance of this regulation has lessened since the 1999 amendment of trademark law which introduced civil law sanctions (injunctive relief) for trade mark infringements.

party is obliged to add a significant disclaimer in his domain.[54] Exceptions exist for the parties with the same name (balancing of interests).[55]

7. Disparagement, defamation

Defamation is regulated in § 7 UWG. This law largely corresponds to § 14 of the German UWG from 1909. It applies to truthful statements that can not be proven. Value judgments and true disparaging claims are judged on the basis of the general clause of § 1 UWG.[56]

8. Misappropriation, imitation

The use of a competitor's name, mark, etc. for one's own goods constitutes can be an unfair exploitation of reputation which is considered as being against "bones mores" in the sense of § 1 UWG. § 1 UWG is also applicable in cases using addendums such as "appropriate for"[57] or when exploiting a renowned name for a completely different type of business.[58]

The imitation of a competitor's commercial achievements (not otherwise statutorily protected) that does not lead to a danger of confusion or an exploitation of reputation is only considered unfair competition if there are "special circumstances".[59] Such circumstances can exist when another's achievements are taken over by using modern copying techniques, when there is intent, or a systematic copying of a whole range of products.[60] In any event, it is required that the imitated product has sufficiently significant characteristics, which can also be shown through popularity of the product.[61]

9. Impediment of competitors

The impediment of competitors is considered a violation of the general clause of § 1 UWG if it aims to oust a competitor.[62] Examples are cases of boycott, refusal to do business, discrimination, the act of "tapping", the obstruction of distribution,

54. OGH 13.7.1999, ÖBl 2000, 39—"Sattler.at"; OGH 29.1.2002, ÖBl 2002, 331—"Graz 2003.at"; OGH 25.9.2001, ÖBl 2002, 142—"bundesheer.at II". As to impidement by Domains, Metatags etc. see Prunbauer/Seidelberger, 23; more general the contributions by Essl, Kapferer, Pahl, Stomper, Walter.
55. OGH 29.4.2002, ÖBl. 2002, 182—"dillinger.at"; Kusco, in Schutzverband (ed.), p. 145.
56. See Prunbauer/Seidelberger, p. 1 ff.; OGH 15.2.1994, ÖBl. 1994, 11—"Götz-Zitat".
57. OGH 12.2.2002, ÖBl. 2002, 221—"Geberit".
58. OGH 21.3.2000, ecolex 2000, S. 657 (name "Rolling Stone" for a café); OGH 17.9.1996, ÖBl 1997, 83—"Football Association" (Emblem of the national soccer team on T-Shirts).
59. Ciresa, *Der wettbewerbsrechtliche Leistungsschutz*, in: Schutzverband (ed.), p. 1.; as to "compatible products" see Gruber, WBl. 2000, 145.
60. See OGH 4.3.1980, ÖBL 1980, 97—"Österreichisches Lebensmitttelbuch"; OGH 27.7.1993, ÖBl. 1993, 156—"Loctite"; OGH 1999, 176—"Alternative zu Kreditkartenunternehmungen"; OGH 15.2.2000, ÖBl. 2001, 22;—"Jobservice"; OGH 19.12.2000, ÖBl. 2001, 111—"Online-Stellenmarkt".
61. See OGH 3.10.2000, ÖBl. 2001, S. 116—"Norweger Pullover"; OGH 22.3.2001, ÖBl. 2002, S. 87—"Studioline". A mere advertising idea or idea for a new form of sales cannot be protected (OGH 8.3.1994, ÖBl. 1995, 14—"Hello Pizza").
62. See OGH 19.10.1993, ÖBl. 1994, 60—"Indikationszeugnis"; in externo Koppensteiner, p. 575.

advertising or supplying, and certain types of price wars. A new type of obstruction is related to domains, meta tags and links.[63]

10. Breach of the law

Newer case law differentiates as to whether the violated norm outside of the UWG was violated intentionally to gain an advantage over law-abiding competitors.[64] This is not the case if the violator has relied on a reasonable interpretation of the law.[65]

11. Enforcement

The main sanction is the action for injunctive relief, which is independent of fault, but requires and assumes danger of repetition.[66] A preventative injunction is also possible as well as an interim injunction or an action for a temporary restraining order (a special requirement for competition: § 24 UWG). The claim for an injunction contains in it the claim for abatement (§ 15).

All parties directly affected by the competitive act (§§ 14, 34 para. 3 UWG), associations to promote economic interests of companies (§§ 14, 34 para. 3 UWG), as well in some regulations the federal chamber of commerce and consumer associations have standing to sue. A consumer, who, for example, consults a lawyer in conjunction with sweepstakes, can bring in a claim for damages to get reimbursed for his legal fees.[67]

II. BELGIUM

Selected Literature: Ballon, *Verglijkende reclame na de wet van 25 mei 1999*, DCCR 1999, 230; Ballon/Stuyck (ed.), *Verkoop op afstand en telematica*, 1997; Ballon/de Vroede, *Handelspraktijken & consumenten bescherming*, 1994; Buydens, *Produktpiraterie und unlauterer Wettbewerb, GRUR Int.* 1995, 15; Daele, *Vergelijkende reclame: een eerste overzicht van rechtspraak na 2 jaar toepassing van de nieuwe wetgeving*, RDCB 2002, 247; De Bauw, *Pratiques du commerce & concurrence*, Annuaire 2003; De Caluwé/Delcorde/Leurquin, *Les pratiques du commerce*, 2002; De Brouwer/De Vroede (ed.), *Handelpraktijken. Het nieuwe in de wet van 14 juli 1991 betreffende de handelspraktijken en de voorlichting en bescherming van de consument*, Die Keure, 1992; De Brouwer, *Le droit des promotions commerciales*, 2nd ed. 1997; Francq, *La publicité comparative: est-elle autorisée en Belgique?*, JT 2001, 497; Francq, *Le décloisonnement progressif du droit rélatif à la concurrence déloyale environment Belgique, GRUR Int.* 1996, 448; Gillardin/Putzeys (ed.), *Les pratiques du commerce. Autour et alentour*, 1997; Henning-Bodewig, Belgien, in: Schricker (ed.), *Recht der Werbung in Europa*, 1995; Kocks, Werberecht in Belgien, in: Schotthöfer

63. Prunbauer/Seidelberger, p. 33; Walter, MR 1998, p. 106.
64. See the decisions cited at Wiltschek, UWG, § 1, E 481 et. seq.
65. Especially in cases of unclear legal situation, see OGH 5.12.1995, ÖBl. 1996, 18—"Gleitschirmschule"; OGH 22.6.1999, ÖBl. 2000, 64—"Viagra"; OGH 21.3.2000, ÖBl 2001, 63—"Teppichknoten"; Wiltschek, UWG; § 1, E 497; Korn, in: Schutzverband (ed.), p. 135.
66. In extenso Koppensteiner, p. 33 et seq. Critical as regards the danger of repetition Pöch/Achleitner, in: Schutzverband (ed.), p. 171.
67. OGH 24.8.1998, GRUR Int. 1999, 181—"Erster Hauptpreis".

(ed.), *Handbuch des Werberechts in den EU-Staaten*, 2nd ed. 1997, p. 113; Puttemans, *Droits intellectuels et concurrence déloyale*, 2000; Schricker/Francq/Wunderlich, *La répression de la concurrence déloyale*, tome II/1, Belgique, Luxembourg, 1974; Straetmans/Stuyck/Wyttinck (ed.), *Recente wetswijzingen inzake handelspraktijken*, 2000; Straetmans, *De markt en de consument*, 1998; Straetmans, *De vernieuwde wet op de handelspraktijken*, RW 2000, 689; Stuyck/Wyttinck (ed.), *De nieuwe wet handelspraktijken*, 1992; Stuyck (ed.), *Handelspraktijken* anno 1996, 1996; Stuyck/van Dyck/Radeideh, *Belgium*, in: Micklitz/Kessler (ed.), *Market Practices Regulation and Consumer Protection in the EC Member States and the US*, 2002, p. 20; Stuyck, *Handelspraktijken*, in: Beginsel van Belgisch Privaatrecht, 2nd ed. 2004 Van den Bergh, *Das neue belgische Gesetz Über die Handelspraktiken und die Information und den Schutz des Verbrauchers, GRUR Int.* 1992, 803.

1. Sources of law

Loi sur les Pratiques du Commerce et sur l'Information et la Protection du Consommateur (Act on Commercial Practices and Consumer Information and Protection) of 14 July 1991 (LPC).

2. Belgian unfair competition law in a nutshell

The main basis of Belgian unfair competition law is found in the "Act on Commercial Practices and Consumer Information and Protection" (LPC) of 14 July 1991.[68] The LPC, which is essentially part of the civil law, has the objective of incorporating business and consumer protection into one single act. It applies to all commercial practices, aiming at a detailed comprehensive regulation. The rules themselves are correspondingly broad. They range from traditional actions for "concurrence déloyale" to consumer protection and information, also of a contractual nature (for example, standard form contracts). Subject to the law are for instance:

- consumer information (prices, amounts, labeling)
- designations of origin[69]
- advertising (misleading, comparative, distorted, bait and switch tactics)
- specific commercial practices (sales at a loss, price reductions, joined offers, vouchers or coupons, sweepstakes)
- special events (sales, close-outs, public sales or auctions)

These rules are related by two almost identical general clauses. Article 93 of the LPC prohibits (as does Section 10bis Paris Convention) any act contrary to honest practices ("usages hônnetes") whereby a seller damages or may damage another seller's economic interests. The second general clause in Art. 94 LPC, newly introduced in 1991, differs only insofar as it protects the interests of consumers. This so-called "consumer general clause" already applies if the consumer is "manipulated"; even the

68. Moniteur Belge 28.8.1991: German translation in GRUR Int. 1992, 623. The LPC has been amended several times; the most recent version is (in French) available at the Homepage of the Ministry for Economy: <mineco.fgov.be.>
69. As to designations of origin (which are left out here) see Schricker/Franq/Wunderlich, p. 74 et seq.

least attentive consumer's interest is redressed.[70] The relationship of the two general clauses to the specific provisions of the LPC is disputed; the Supreme Court (Cour de Cassation) applies the general clause(s) also to cases, which are explicitly dealt with by specific provisions of the Act.[71]

The LPC does not require any competitive relationship or any acts of a competitive purpose.[72] It rather applies to all acts of a "seller" which, under Art. 1 No. 6 of the LPC, are all natural or legal persons, who or which offer for sale or sell products or services in the course of their professional activities. Included are public enterprises and associations which conduct economic activities on a nonprofit basis. However, the law is not applicable to liberal professions (Art. 1 No. 2 LPC) for which a special law applies since 1992[73] as well as to transactions in real estate, securities and intangible assets. Some provisions apply exclusively to "consumers" that is a natural or legal person, who acts exclusively for nonprofessional purposes. As mentioned above, the purpose of the law takes into account the interests of the "seller" as well as of the "consumers". At least indirectly the interests of the public in the functioning of competition and those of small and middle size enterprises are also protected.

The rules of the LPC (and their interpretation) which primarily serve to protect other sellers, have originated from tort law; traditionally they are also related to the rules on intellectual property.[74] The relationship of LPC/IP rights is complicated.[75] Essentially, specific laws take precedence in regulating the areas subject to their rules. The Benelux Trademark Law as well as the Benelux Industrial Design Law contains blocking provisions which deny the mark, design or model capable of protection, any protection other than through trademark or design law. In a mirror image, Art. 96(1) LPC prohibits the application of the LPC on infringing acts ("contrefaçon") that could be sanctioned by the laws of patent, trade mark, industrial designs or copyright. This has been declared partly (as regards trade mark law) invalid by the Cour d'arbitrage in 2002. Anyhow, in cases in which the plaintiff objects to more than a "contrefaçon", protection on the basis of unfair competition is rarely denied (see also under 7).

The rules of the LPC which are more concerned with consumer protection can coincide with contract law regulated by the civil code although consumer contract law is not within the scope of the LPC.[76] The applicable provisions on special sales,

70. Cour de Cassation 17.10.1997 RCJB 1998, 441—"Movitex" with note Stuyck; in the same direction Cour de Cassation 12.10.2000, RDCB 2001, 669—"Saint-Brice" with note Straetmans. (≪ le consommateur le moins averti, qui, sans esprit critique vis-à-vis de ce que lui est présenté avec habillé, ne peut déceler les pièges, les outrances ou les silences trompeurs de la publicité ≫).
71. In the "Motivex"—decision (fn. 70) the Cour de Cassation has judged a sweepstake-action, that could have been also subsumed under Art. 23 No. 10 LPC on the basis of the general clause. Legal literature (cf. the note of Stuyck) is more in favour of a subsidiary appliance.
72. As to the scope of the LPC, esp. the complicated notion of "seller" see Denef/Straetmans, RW 1999-2000, 137; Wyttinck, in: Stuyck (ed.), Handelspraktijken anno 1996, p. 1; Cour de cassation 11.4.2001, RDCB 2001, 692 with note Straetmans; Cour d'appel Bruxelles 23.5.2003, RDCB 2003, 787 (insurance offer of the sickness funds). As to Belgian International Private Law Pertegas Sender, RDCB 1999, 394; Hof van Beroep te Brussel 22.12.1999, RDCB 2001, 244 with note Pertegas Sender.
73. The current Act is of August 2nd, 2002 (HB 20.12.2002); it regulates misleading and comparative advertising by the liberal professions.
74. As to the Benelux Trade Mark Law see the leading commentary of Braun, Précis du Droit de Marques, 2nd ed. 2004. As to the copyright law, e.g. Berenboom, Le nouveau droit d'auteur.
75. Francq, GRUR Int. 1996, 448; Puttemans, Droits intellectuels et concurrence déloyale, 2000.
76. Cf. Stuyck, JT 2000, 20; Straetmans, De Markt en de Consument, 1998; as to the question whether the breach of a contract violates Art. 93 LPC, see Cour de cassation, RDCB 1994, 610 with note Stuyck/Pauwels.

sales at a loss, et al which, among others, protect against strong market competitors, are in turn to be seen in relation to the Antitrust Law of 5 August 1991.[77]

3. Regulation of advertising

a. Misleading advertising

Misleading advertising is regulated in various sections of the LPC. Article 23 No. 1 deals with misleading advertising of products, No. 2 of services, No. 3 of the seller's identity, No. 4 with omissions. In addition, the following supplement these provisions: Art. 25 (advertising of prepackaged products), Art. 26 (price information), Art. 23 No. 9 (ban on bait and switch tactics) and No. 10 (sweepstakes). Since, as a result, all forms of misleading advertising are covered, the courts often refrain from naming or specifying concrete, listed legal grounds.

The term "advertising" defined in Art. 22(1) LPC is essentially the same as the term in Directive 84/450/EC, that is, the subjective aim to promote directly or indirectly the supply of goods or services is decisive.

The deception can occur through any statement, fact or representation, which contains a verifiable item, irrespective of the form of communication. Decisive is the view of the public to which the advertising is directed. Even objectively accurate statements can be misleading if they are misunderstood; this, however, is rarely assured by the courts. As a rule, the Belgian case law starts from the position of an average consumer who is reasonably attentive and sceptical and acts with a minimum of "common sense". The concrete circumstances and the importance of the information for the target group can, however, lead to differences. As to the "consumer general-clause" of Art. 94 LPC, case law emphasizes the picture of a less attentive, uncritical consumer who is particularly in need of protection against the tricks used by marketing and advertising (see above). How these two different models of consumer behavior coincident in the case of misleading advertising is not yet clarified.[78]

If an advertising slogan, often in the form of a superlative statement, is openly excessive ("gigantic, the best, the most beautiful", et al), it is treated as a harmless market hawking. If it is, however, mixed with provable facts, such as particular price information or sensitive questions such as the environmentally friendly aspects of a product, it is normally taken seriously.[79]

Article 23 No. 1-3 LPC deal with the reference points of the statements. In practice, the main factors which play a role are the characteristics of the product or the seller, the price and the environmental effects.

Article 23, No. 4 LPC bans advertising which omits essential facts with the aim of misleading the consumer. Pursuant to Art. 30 LPC, the seller must provide the consumers with all appropriate or expected information at the latest at the time of

77. See the version of 1.7.1999, Moniteur Belge 1.10.1999. The relationship LPC cartel law was dealt with in the decision Cour de cassation 7.1.2000, RCJB 2001 with note Stuyck.
78. The Cour de cassation has stressed in the "Saint Brice"—decision (fn. 70) that Art. 94 LPC is not a transposition of community law.
79. For instance, the ad of a furniture shop "Toujour le moins cher! Nous vous apportons les preuves. Venez!" was considered a normal statement as to the price. On the other hand, the claim of paper diapers "Even wet they are dry" passed as pure puffing, Pres. Tribunal de commerce Verviers 16.3.2001, JT 2001, 1316.

the conclusion of the sale. Article 23, 1 LPC[80] is applied in all other cases where an overall impression is deceptive—often through the highlighting of advantages and the leaving out of negative aspects.

The misleading statement must be capable of influencing the economic behavior of the addressee, which is in practice often implicitly assumed. This, as well as the fact of the misleading itself, is normally decided by the courts themselves. Surveys etc., although permissible, are rarely used.

A reversal of the burden of proof is provided for only in the case of warning notice procedures brought by the economic ministry (see under 9). As to the proper defendant, a so-called "cascade-liability" applies. Article 24(3) of the LPC governs the legal consequences of the misleading statements with regard to contracts made with consumers, which are construed from the actual details of the advertising.[81]

b. Comparative advertising

According to Art. 23bis, No. 1 LPC, comparative advertising is basically permitted, to the extent that the requirements of No. 1-8 are fulfilled. As until 1999 there was a strict legal prohibition against such advertising, this represents a substantial change in Belgian law. However, still today, comparative advertising is strongly scrutinized.[82]

With some smaller adaptations, the Belgian law transposed the text of Directive 57/55/EC. This leads to certain problems, as since 1991, the LPC is directed to "sellers" while the Directive uses the term "competitor". The term "competitor" is therefore interpreted as sellers of products, which are substitutable in the eye of the addressee.[83]

The competitor must at least be identifiable. The case law to date has interpreted this broadly[84] (for example, the advertisement. "To act without intermediaries is a good thing" was seen as a comparison to travel agencies).[85] If the identity cannot be ascertained or the character as a "competitor" is uncertain, Art. 23, No. 6 (disparaging information) and No. 7 (misleading, disparaging comparisons) are applied. Whether the non-approved display of "metatags" on one's own website is a comparative advertising is unclear; it is in any event "unfair" in the sense of the general clause (and is also treated, as a rule, as trademark infringement).[86]

Comparative advertising must concern goods or services that meet the same needs or are intended for the same purpose.[87] Furthermore, it must compare material, relevant, representative and verifiable characteristics. Often, overall comparisons are

80. Cf. Boeck, De informatieverplichting van de professioneel t.a.v. de consument, in: Consumentenrecht, 1998, 1. It is not entirely clear whether this is solely a repetition of general contract law principles.
81. Van den Bergh, GRUR Int. 1992, 803.
82. According to Daele, RDCB 2002, 247 in the first two years after the introduction of Art. 23bis LPC 26 out of 32 cases on comparative advertising were forbidden—15 on the grounds of denigrating, 6 on the grounds of misleading.
83. See the court decisions cited at Daele, p. 248 f.
84. Daele, p. 249 fn. 5.
85. Voorz. Rechtbank van koophandel te Gent 23.10.2000, cited at Daele, p. 249. Also a price sticker on books, which showed the actual and the recommended price was considered comparative advertising. Cour d'appel de Bruxelles 5.9.2001 (cited at Daele, p. 249 f.).
86. According to the Hof van beroep te Antwerpen this is neither a commercial representation nor a statement nor a comparison, see Hof van Beroep Antwerpen 9.10.2000, RDCB 2000, 408 with note Evrard.
87. A comparison between a generic and a well-known drug that are not prescribed for exactly the same indication does not meet the requirement, Voorz. Rechtbank van koophandel te Brussel 27.4.1999, DCCR, 44.

seen as being not objective, i.e., the advertising claim of a telecom provider, that one can phone for "double so long" or that customers are "discontent" with the quality of a competing offer.[88] These cases can also be seen as misleading, e.g. when certain information is omitted, for example, additional costs or limitations of an offer. A totally representative comparison, taking into account all factors of the competitive products, is not required but, for example, a price comparison with only one product out of hundreds can impart a misleading overall impression, e.g. indicate that all other products of the advertiser are also less expensive.

Belgian case law particularly aims at suppressing disparaging or exploitative comparisons. Advertising slogans such as "Whoever wants to pay more" (in connection with the trade mark of the competitor), were seen, for example, as an unnecessary disparagement.[89] Comparison with well-known trade marks are not prohibited but can easily qualify as taking unfair advantage of another's reputation (particularly if the well-known mark is unnecessarily emphasized).[90]

According to Art. 3, subparagraph 12 of the LPC, every reference to tests carried out by consumer organizations is prohibited.

c. Aggressive advertising

The LPC contains no special ban on aggressive, harassing or intrusive advertising.[91] The aspects of annoyance, harassment, etc. however, play a role in various fact patterns of unfair competition (see, for instance, under 4).

d. Concealed advertising

Article 23 No. 5 LPC prohibits advertising which, in consideration of its overall impression including its presentation, can not unmistakably be recognized as advertising. In cases of doubt, it must be clearly marked as "advertisement". Although this provision is primarily directed to the press, it is understood as applying to all media and thus also to the Internet and television.[92]

e. Advertising rules for specific media and products

Advertising in television is governed by various regulations (for the Flamish and the French communities); in them are the TV directive's bans on hidden or surreptious

88. See Voorz. Rechtbank van koophandel te Brussel 24.9.2001—"Telenet./. Belcom" and 7.6.2000—"Mobistar"./. KPN Orange Belgium (cited at Daele, p. 254).
89. Voorz. Rechtbank van koophandel te Brussel 4.9.2000—"Toyota./. Daewoo" (see Daele, p. 257). See also the decision "Belgakom./. Telenet" (comparison of services via cable and telephone), in which certain services of the competitor where (ironically) described as "delayed" etc.; this was prohibited as denigrating. Only the claim "Often a telephone line is necessary ... Without such a line it can be difficult" was permitted; see Voorz. Rechtbank van koophandelt te Brussel 5.1.2001—"Belgakom./. Telenet" (referred to at Daele, fn. 61).
90. See Voorz. Rechtbank van koophandelt Brussel 28.5.2001—"The Beecham Group Plc./. Eurogenerics NV (cited at Daele, p. 260). Even the remark in a newspaper interview, the own production of sweets was inspired by (the famous mark) Leonidas was considered an exploitation of reputation.
91. In theory (there is no case law) the general clause of Art. 94 LCP may apply, esp. since the courts have already addressed cases of "manipulation" on this basis; see the Movitex-case (fn. 70).
92. Stuyck/van Dyck/Radeideh, p. 27.

advertising, product placement, etc.[93] A draft law is intended to adopt the E-commerce directive.[94]

For certain products-in particular food, alcohol, drugs-detailed advertising provisions apply.[95] For tobacco there is a broad advertising ban, which includes indirect advertising. According to Art. 23, No. 13 LPC it is prohibited to assert in advertising that the health of consumers will be improved through products or appliances, which are not medications or health products.

4. Special sales methods, direct marketing

Article 77 et seq. LPC regulate distant sales.[96] Without prejudice to special (stricter) regulation, offers by mail, telephone, fax, teleshopping, and internet are permissible only if the consumer raises no apparent objections (Art. 82 Sec. 2(2) LPC). Moreover, there are comprehensive information obligations which the seller must meet and for which he has to verify. (Art. 78).

In addition to this basic rule, there are stricter provisions for individual distribution methods. According to Art. 76 LPC, the unsolicited delivery of products is prohibited even if the recipient does not have any obligation to return the goods. For door to door sales, Art. 88 provides broad protection for consumers.[97] The law of 25 July 1993 on such trade contains a basic ban on sales in the home of the consumer (Art. 4), for which, however, generous exceptions exist. Pyramid sale schemes are, according to Art. 84 LPC,[98] in principle prohibited.

Unsolicited advertising by fax and phone advertising using an automatic calling machine (voicemail) is, according to Art. 82 Sec. 2 LPC, not permitted without the prior consent of the consumer ("opt-in").[99] In all other cases the general "opt-out" rule of Art. 82 Sec. 2(2) LPC, the information obligation of Art. 78 Sec. 1 LPC and Art. 23 No. 5 LPC apply.

5. Sales promotion

All types of sales promotion can be judged on the basis of the general clauses of Art. 93, 94 LPC. The Cour de cassation explicitly accords on the basis of Art. 94 LPC protection against "manipulation" of consumers through marketing practices which are not sufficiently transparent.[100]

In addition to this, discounts, which are basically permissible, must conform to the detailed provisions on price announcements (Art. 42 et seq LPC).[101] The former price

93. Henning-Bodewig, No. 268 ff.
94. Stuyck/van Dyck/Radeideh, p. 27 f.
95. See, for instance the Foodstuff Act of 24.1.1977; the Consumer Credit Act of 12.12.1991. As to advertisement for drugs and tobacco cf. Stuyck/van Dyck/Radeideh, p. 38 f.
96. Van den Bergh, GRUR Int. 1992, 803.
97. Stuyck/van Dyck/Radeideh, p. 29.
98. Stuyck/van Dyck/Radeideh, p. 31, Cour d'appel de Bruxelles 16.9.1998, Ann. Prat. Comm, 1998, 354 with note Stuyck.
99. Stuyck/van Dyck/Radeideh, p. 26 ff.
100. See the decisions of the Cour de cassation, especially the "Movitex-case", in which a mail order company urged consumers to require which prizes they had won; the prizes were of a very low value (fn. 70).
101. The indication of the new price next to the "old" price is permitted but not claims as "Every thing at half price", etc., Van den Bergh, GRUR Int. 1992, 803.

must have been taken a full month prior to the time of the sale; the reduced price must apply for at least one day (Art. 43). For advertising of special offers, the seller must, under Art, 23 No. 9 LPC, have available sufficient supplies of the product advertised.[102] Finally, the price reduction may not lead to a loss (Art. 40 LPC). Value coupons ("bons de valeur") are subject to comprehensive information obligations (and form the basis of a redemption obligation of the advertiser, according to Art. 63 et seq. LPC).

Not only premiums, but all tie-in offers are generally prohibited in offers made to consumers (Art. 54 LPC).[103] Exceptions exist in particular for product and service packages,[104] for identical products, for minimal advantages and delayed gifts (loyalty cards, discount products, etc). Again, these exceptions do not apply for certain products.

Advertising that creates the hope that the consumer might win something by chance, such as sweepstakes, is prohibited (Art. 23 No. 10 LPC). As a result of the broad interpretation of the term advertising in Art. 22 LPC, this leads to a general ban on all promotional contests based on chance.[105] Promotional games where the winning depends upon the skill or knowledge of the participant, are in principle permitted.[106]

6. Discrediting, denigration

The LPC provides wide-reaching protection against discrediting and denigration disparagement. Both are not only expressly forbidden in comparative advertising but also in Art. 23 No. 7 LPC which deals more generally with misleading, disparaging comparisons (also of systems etc.). In addition, the general clause of Article 93 LPC applies.[107] Disparagement is always present if no objective reason for criticism that harms another's economic interests is recognizable or if the way and means the criticism is expressed is not necessary.

7. Misappropriation, slavish imitation, passing off

The exploitation of another seller's reputation is strictly judged on the basis of the general clause of Art. 93 LPC.[108]

Article 23 No. 8 LPC prohibits advertising whereby the risk of confusion with another's trade mark, product etc. could arise. Outside of the advertising area, the general clause of Art. 93 LPC applies to the copying or imitation of another's commercial achievements. However, there must be more than a "contrefaçon" (that is, an infringement of IP-rights), otherwise the restrictive provision of Art. 96 LPC is invoked.[109] Special circumstances that allow for the application of the LPC are seen in particular in the case of an unnecessary a risk of confusion as to the origin. However,

102. Cour de cassation 12.9.1996, RDCB 1997, 21 (exception: ≪force majeure≫).
103. See De Brouwer, p. 69 ff.; Stuyck/vanDyck/Radeideh, p. 37.
104. Cour de cassation 25.10.2001, RW 2001-2002, 1173 with note Steenot.
105. Heremans/Ongena, RDCB 2001, 663 ff.; van den Berg, GRUR Int. 1992, 803 ff. The Cour de cassation (s. fn. 3) has judged "sweepstake"—practices also on the basis of the general clause of Art. 94 LCP ("manipulation").
106. As to the demarcation see Hof van beroep te Gent 8.2.2001, RDCB 2001, 700 with note de Brouwer.
107. Cf., e.g. De Caluwé/Delcorde/Leurquin, . . .; Ballon/de Vroede.
108. Schricker/Francq/Wunderlich, p. 351 et seq.
109. As to trademark law the decision of the Cour d'Arbitrage has opened the path for a cumulative application; see above No. 2.

aspects as the "slavishness" of the imitation or not yet amortized investment of the competitor can also play a role.[110]

8. Breach of the law

Irrespective of the purpose of protection, any infringement of any other legal rule by a seller in the course of his business, that may harm the interests of other sellers or consumers is seen as an act contrary to honest practices in the sense of Art. 93, 94 LPC. Thus, even the breach of tax law, social security requirements and other provisions can be sanctioned under the theory of "illegal competition".[111]

9. Enforcement

The main sanction of the LPC is the action for injunctive relief ("action en cessation"), which must be filed in a special proceeding ("référé") to the president of the commercial court (Rechtbank van koophandel/Tribunal de commerce). The "référé"—proceeding is a sort of preliminary proceeding, but leads to a final judgment and is immediately enforceable. It does not require proof of particular urgency. The commercial court president has wide reaching powers and can also order the publication of the judgment (Art. 99 LPC). An action for damages can only be based on Art. 1382 of the Civil Code.

According to Art. 98 LPC, all "interested parties" (in theory also the individual consumer) have standing to sue, including the economic ministry, professional and intermediary associations as well as consumer organizations. The proper defendant is the person who actually breached the LPC. Only in the advertising area, there is a limited so-called cascade liability (Art. 27 LPC), that is, persons other than the advertiser, may be held liable only secondarily.[112]

Certain provisions of the LPC provide for penal sanctions. Administrative sanctions fall largely to the economic minister. The ministry may not only bring an action for injunctive relief, but can also, under Art. 101 LPC file "warning notice" proceedings, which allows a settlement by the dismissal of a suit against the payment of a certain monetary fine (Art. 115 LPC). The court costs in Belgium are, as a rule, to be paid by the losing party; the attorneys fees are normally paid by each party.

III. CZECH REPUBLIC

Selected Literature: Císařová, *Křest'anová, Zákon o regulaci reklamy*, Prague 2002; Dietz, *Die Einführung von Gesetzen gegen den unlauteren Wettbewerb in ehemals sozialistischen Staaten Mittel—und Osteuropas, GRUR Int.* 1994, 649; Hajn, *Soutěžni chování a právo proti nekalé soutezi, Brünn*, 2000; Eliás/Hajn, *Kurs obchodního práva—obecná ĉást, soutezni právo*, Prague 2002; Knap, in: Beier/Bastian/Kur (ed.), *Wettbewerbsrecht und Verbraucherschutz in Mittel- und Osteuropa*, 1992, 55; Macek, *Rozhodnutí ve věcech obchodního jména a nekalé souteze*, Prague 2002; Munková, *Právo proti nekalé soutěž*, Prague 2001; Opltova, *Das Recht des unlauteren*

110. Puttemans (fn. 75); Buydens, GRUR Int. 1995, 15 and Leroy/Mouffe (copying of advertising).
111. Pres. Tribunal de commerce de Bruxelles, GRUR Int. 1982, 177—≪Sozialausgaben≫.
112. Henning-Bodewig, note. 93 ff.

Wettbewerbs in der Tschechischen Republik, GRUR Int. 1994, 710; Vecerkova, *Nekalé Soutěž a Reklama*, Brno 2004; Winter, *Reklama a právo*, 2001.

1. Sources of law

Obchodní zákoník č. 513/1991 Sb. (Commercial Code) (C.C.) §§ 41-54; Zákon o regulae, reklamy (Law No. 40/1995 regarding the regulation of advertising) from 1 April 1995 (Advertising Law).

2. Czech unfair competition law in a nutshell

The current basis for protection against unfair competition in the Czech Republic can be found in the §§ 41 et seq. C.C.[113] and the Advertising Law from 1995.[114]

The regulation against unfair competition is thus part of the Commercial Code (C.C.). It is derived from a corresponding regulation of the former ČSFR.[115] When the Czech Republic was founded, the C.C. and its unfair competition regulations were incorporated into Czech civil law. In the meantime, however, the C.C. has been reformed several times, especially through the extensive reform of 2000.[116]

The fact that the provisions concerning unfair competition were implemented into the C.C. is based more on political than on legal reasons (originally a regulation in conjunction with the anti-trust law was planned.[117]) In any case, the implementation in the C.C. does not mean that the regulations concerning unfair competition are only applicable in cases of trade relations. Pursuant to § 44 C.C. it is sufficient that there is an action in economic competition;[118] a competitive relationship between plaintiff and defendant is not required.

As long as there is no mutual obligation from international contracts, the application of Czech law depends on an effect on the Czech market. Foreign companies are treated the same as Czech companies.

According to §§ 44(1), 54(2) C.C. the regulation in the C.C. aims at the protection of competitors and consumers alike; the general public's interest in a functioning of competition is partly protected as well (for example in § 41 C.C.).

The most important part of the regulation is the general clause in § 44(1) C.C. It declares any action in economic competition which is in conflict with the "bones mores" of competition and capable of affecting other competitors or consumer as unfair competition—and thereby, at the same time, an illegal exploitation of the freedom of commercial activity guaranteed by § 41 C.C. The term "bones mores" is interpreted objectively, that is, independent of intent etc. The deciding factor is whether the action is capable of having an impact on the functions of commercial competition and

113. Sbírka zákonu c. 98/1991, strana 2474. The C.C. has been reformed several times, most recently through law No. 432/2004.
114. Sbírka zákonu 1995, Vol. 8, No. 40, p. 467; cf. also Aktuelle Informationen, GRUR Int. 1995, 742.
115. See Knap, p. 55 et seq. The C.C. of the former ČSFR is published in German in Beier/Bastian/Kur, p. 213.
116. Aktuelle Informationen, GRUR Int. 2001, 273.
117. In the former CSFR, such a uniform regulation failed mostly because the anti-trust laws were considered more urgent and thus were enacted sooner. Whether the future Czech civil law code will contain the unfair competition regulations or if they are going to be separated and incorporated in its own law, is still unclear.
118. This was decided by the Supreme Court in a decision from 23.10.2003.

thereby limits or effects the positive effects of competition.[119] The general clause is applicable independently or in addition to the other provisions in the C.C. regulating particular actions of unfair competition.

These specific causes of action can mainly be found in §§ 45-52 C.C. which concern competitive actions that are "especially" considered unfair competition:[120] misleading advertising (§ 45), misleading labeling of goods or services (§ 46), causing danger of confusion (§ 47); parasitic exploitation of another's reputation (§ 48); bribery (§ 49); denigration (§ 50); unauthorized comparative advertising (§ 50a); violation of company secrets (§ 51); and endangering health and environment (§ 52). The remaining regulations (§ 53 and 54) deal with (civil law) sanctions.

In addition to the regulation in the Commercial Code, the Advertising Law of 1995 applies. It defines the term "advertising" and lists several requirements which advertising must fulfill in order to be legal. § 2(3) Advertising Law also contains a general clause that prohibits any advertising that is against "bones mores". The term of bones mores is, however, interpreted differently than in the C.C.; it is understood more in the sense of a general requirement of ethical behavior. The Advertising Law also contains regulations to protect minors as well as extensive product-specific advertising regulations, see §§ 20 et seq., which also serve the public interest. In principle, the regulations in §§ 41 et seq. C.C. and in the Advertising Law can be applied in a parallel fashion; they often refer to each other.

The regulations regarding unfair competition in the C.C. do have some connection with the anti-trust law[121] especially as regards causes of action like boycott, obstruction, undercutting, but also with the intellectual property laws, (Patent Law No. 527/1990 Sb., Design Law No. 207/2000 Sb., Copyright Law No. 121/2000 Sb. and the Trademark Law No. 441/2003 Sb.).[122] The regulations in the Advertising Law also show a conjunction with the other regulations regarding consumer protection, especially the Consumer Protection Act No. 634/1992, which has been amended several times. They are supplemented by self regulation in the Code of Ethics edited by the "Council for Advertising".

Like in all new Member States, relatively few case law material is available as of yet.[123]

3. Regulation of advertising

a. Misleading advertising

Misleading advertising is regulated in § 45 C.C. to which § 2(2) Advertising Law refers to. Both regulations are thus to be interpreted by consistent criteria. It can be assumed that in cases of doubt the interpretation of Directive 84/450/EEC by the ECJ will be followed.[124]

119. See Opltova, p. 712.
120. They are discussed in the Czech legal literature by Hajn, Vercerkovà.
121. Law from 4.4.2001. Regarding the scope of application see GRUR Int. 2001, 803.
122. An introduction to the law of industrial property in the Czech Republic can be found (in English) in "Manual Industrial Property"; Vol. 2 (2003) and in World trade executive Intellectual Property law in the European Community, p. 87 (2004). The copyright law of the former CSFR can be found (in German) in Möring/Schulze/Ulmer/Zweigert (ed.), Quellen des Urheberechts, Vol. 5.
123. An overview regarding more recent cases in Czech can be found in Macek.
124. Discussed in this book in Chapter 3. 3 Czech courts are well aware of the impact of community law on the interpretation. For instance, on 11.11.2003 the Supreme Court in Bruenn had a seminar "The case law of the ECJ and its effects to the Czech Law".

§ 45 C.C. covers all statements about one's own or another party's company, goods, services, etc., that are capable of creating a false impressions and thereby may give a competition advantage to one company at the disadvantage to another company. According to para. 2 the means of dissemination is irrelevant. Para. 3 also covers true statements if they can be misunderstood by the target group of the advertisement.

§ 46 C.C. prohibits misleading information about geographic origin. It is considered an act of unfair competition if the assumption is created by using a specific indication of the goods or services that the goods originate from a certain country, area or place or have distinctive characteristics. Here again, true statements are covered if they can be misunderstood. For example, "Koelnisch Wasser" must come from the city of Cologne ("Koeln") by the Rhine river, not Koeln near Prague.[125] In para. 2, descriptions using addendums such as "type", "category", and "kind" are prohibited if they create a false impression regarding the origin and nature of the item. § 46 C.C. also includes false statements regarding the commercial origin from a certain manufacturer.

In all formations of cases of misleading advertising, the impression of the target group is decisive. The European benchmark of the reasonably informed, observant and circumspect average consumer is recognized. Czech literature, however, also emphasizes the fact that certain consumer groups (for example youth) are more gullible than others and that some Czech consumers are still less experienced with "tricks" in advertising. Advertising exaggerations are only tolerated if they can be clearly recognized as such (for example "Pilsen—the capital of beer").[126]

According to §§ 44(1), 45 C.C. the action must be capable of harming the economic interests of competitors or consumers. As the courts themselves decide if a statement is misleading or not, this requirement is hardly ever described in more detail.

b. Comparative advertising

Comparative advertising in the former law of the ČSFR was not explicitly prohibited, but it was considered unfair competition.[127] The reformation in 2000 of the Czech Commercial Code added a regulation in § 50 C.C. which is almost identical to Directive 97/55/EC.[128] According to the regulation, comparative advertising is permitted if it does not mislead, if it compares relevant criteria objectively, etc. Furthermore, comparative advertising may not be denigrating or exploit the reputation of a competitor. As to the interpretation of these requirements, Directive 97/55/EC and its interpretation by the ECJ play in important role.

c. Concealed advertising

§ 2(1)(b) Advertising Law prohibits advertising that targets the subconscious, (lit. d.) prohibits concealed advertising. For television advertising, a special prohibition of surreptitious advertising exists, see under f.

125. See the examples given by Hajn.
126. See Hajn, p. 266.
127. Court of appeals Prague R 3 CNMO 803/95.
128. Discussed in this book in Chapter 3, IV.4.

d. Aggressive advertising

§ 2(1)(e) Advertising Law prohibits any unrequested advertising that has a harassing effect on the addressee or leads to a financial disadvantage.

e. Product and media specific advertising regulations

Tobacco advertising is totally forbidden in television and in radio between 6 a.m. and 10 p.m. (§ 3 Advertising Law and § 48(1) Television Law). In any event, tobacco advertising may not encourage excessive smoking or persuade youth to start smoking. The same applies for alcohol advertising (§ 4 Advertising Law and § 52 Television Law), although it is generally permitted in radio.

Pharmaceutical products may only be advertised if they are permitted in the Czech Republic (§§ 2a, 5 to 5c Advertising Law). For prescription medication and potentially addictive medication, a complete prohibition exists. Advertising for foodstuffs and baby food is regulated by §§ 5d—f Advertising Law; it may not be misleading as regards health and other effects of the product. Advertising for weapons and ammunition is strongly limited under § 6 Advertising Law.

Law No. 231/2001 Sb. from 17 May 2001 regarding radio and television broadcasting contains, in transposition of the Television Directive, a requirement of separation of advertising and program as well as a prohibition of surreptitious advertising. Law No. 610/2003 on electronic communications contains the transparency requirements of the E-Commerce Directive.

f. Other regulations of advertising

The Advertising Law furthermore forbids advertising for goods and services that cannot be sold legally. For example, since § 52 C.C. forbids offering of products that may be harmful to the health or the environment, a corresponding prohibition on advertisement also exists.

Advertising may not be against honest trade principles, harm national or religious feelings, attack political beliefs, violate human dignity, exalt violence or exploit sentiments of fear (§ 2(3) Advertising Law). Special importance is given to the protection of children and minor according to § 2c Advertising Law.

4. Direct marketing

Direct marketing is mainly judged on the basis of § 2(1)(e) Advertising Law, but also on the basis of the general clause in § 2(3) Advertising Law and § 44(1) C.C.

5. Sales promotion

Sales promotion activities are mainly measured by the prohibition of misleading advertising. For special sales, certain transparency requirements have to be met, § 50(a)(3) C.C.

6. Risk of confusion

According to § 47 and § 44(2) C.C., causing a risk of confusion is considered unfair competition. A risk of confusion is assumed in one of the following cases:

(a) The unauthorized use of the name of a company that has prior rights to this name;
(b) the unauthorized use of special designations or the get up of products, services, or business records that are considered characteristic of a certain company, for example, the identification of packaging of printed materials, catalogs, or advertisements;
(c) the unauthorized imitation of another's products, packaging or get up etc. in a way that causes danger of confusion as regards the company, trade name, or a special mark; unless it is a functional, technical or aesthetical element, and the imitator has used all reasonable means of avoiding or limiting the danger of confusion.

The imitation of the competitors achievements are thus only illegal if there is a concrete danger of confusion. This is deemed to exist when the imitation causes mistaken beliefs regarding the relationship of competitors and their achievements. In general, judgment under Art. 47 C.C. leads to the same results as the danger of confusion under trademark law.

7. Denigration, exploitation of reputation

Denigration is regulated in § 50 C.C. It is unlawful to make or spread false statements regarding relationships, products or services of a competitor if this could have a negative effect on competitors or consumers. The same applies to true statements, according to para. 2, if they are capable of impairment (for example, if the tone is inappropriately harsh, rude or aggressive or goes beyond what is necessary), and the person making the statement is "not forced into such an act by the circumstances". The exception for justifiable defense only applies to true statements. Generally, the claimant has the burden of proof as to the untruth of the statements; a reversal of the burden of proof does not occur.

According to § 48 C.C., the misappropriation of reputation is unlawful, if it "aims at gaining advantages which the competitor might otherwise not achieve". Exploitation of reputation that does not aim to gain a competitive edge as well as all other forms of parasitic exploitation of another party's achievements can be judged on the basis of the general clause of § 44 C.C.

These regulations of denigration and exploitation of reputation are to be interpreted restrictively in cases of comparative advertising: A comparative advertisement that meets the requirements of § 50a C.C. can not be prohibited on the basis of §§ 48, 50 C.C. As concerns the demarcation from trademark law, that protects trademarks against denigration and dilution etc., the regulations in the C.C. start from another point of reference and therefore can be applied parallel to trademark law.[129]

129. See, for instance, Court of Appeals Prague of 1994 (R 3 Cmo 1446/94) which prohibited the denomination "CEZ—České energeticke závody" (Czeck Enterprise); see also *Macek*, p. 78.

8. Misappropriation, imitation

As already explained in No. 26, the exploitation of a competitor's achievements, especially by means of imitation is prohibited if it leads to a danger of confusion or misappropriation of reputation. In all other cases, the general clause of § 44 C.C. applies.

9. Impediment of competitors

Bribery is, according to § 49 C.C., considered unfair competition. The same applies for the disclosure of trade secrets under § 51. A "trade secret" is any kind of information that has current or potential economic value, is not easily obtainable in that area of trade, and that the business wishes to keep secret (§ 17 C.C.) A "harm" exists if the person with knowledge of the trade secret makes it available to third parties or abuses it for his own or another's gain. The person must have been given the knowledge in secrecy based on an employment relationship or some other relationship, or have gained the knowledge through an unlawful act by himself or another.

10. Breach of law

The violation of norms other than those in §§ 45 et seq. C.C. can be considered a violation of "bones mores" in the meaning of the general clause if it leads to a competitive advantage.[130] In the case of a violation of the Advertising Law, this is assumed.

11. Other forms of unfair competition

Unfair competition exists when one distorts the conditions of competition by producing or distributing goods or services that harm the legally protected interests of the environment or endanger health in order to gain an advantage for himself or another (to the disadvantage of competitors or consumers).

This applies independently of whether an actual damage occurs, or even whether the advertiser was aware of it. The gaining of an advantage or the creation of a disadvantage for a competitor or consumer is usually assumed if there is actual danger.

12. Enforcement

The regulations against unfair competition in the Commercial Code are sanctioned by civil law. § 53 C.C. names as possible sanctions injunction, removal, compensatory damages, the restitution of unjustified profit, and the "appropriate satisfaction, which can also be granted financially". The latter is a kind of compensation for pain and

130. For example, the court held that such an advantage existed where a driving school did not follow purlic requirements regarding education of the driving instructors. The claim of another driving school was rejected in the first instance with the reasoning that the control over driving schools is given to the administrative authorities. This was nullified by the Appeals Court of Prague CR3 (no. 253/91) and the claim was upheld based on § 44 para. 2 C.C. The driving school gained a commercial advantage by not training the drivers as per regulations; see *March*, p. 98.

suffering, although it is based on a non-monetary damage. The competitor is first in line for standing to sue, although a competitive relationship is not required. For a violation of §§ 48-51 C.C. legal persons that are authorized to represent the interests of the competitor or the consumers also have standing to sue. The situation in which multiple claimants or defendants are parties to the suit is regulated in § 90 et seq. Code of Civil Procedure. The ordering of interim measures is possible and common if there is a certain probability of the claim being successful according to § 74 et seq. and 102 Code of Civil Procedure.

The Advertising Law provides for administrative sanctions (through monetary sanctions), but also allows suits for injunctions and removal. The organs named in § 7 of the Advertising Law have enforcements powers, for example, the Council for Radio and Television, the Minister of Health, and the local commercial ministry where the company does business.

IV. CYPRUS

1. Sources of law

Regulation relating to the control of misleading and comparative advertising (2000).

2. Cypriot unfair competition law in a nutshell

Unfair Competition law in Cyprus is not uniformly regulated. Some laws address specific aspects of unfair commercial practices, for instance, misleading advertising, but do not aim at a coherent and systematic regulation. Further regulations are being prepared in order to be on par with the directives of the European Union. Overall, the law of Cyprus is still largely shaped by that of Great Britain. As in England, self-control mechanisms ("Codes of Conduct") play a large role although they are not legally binding.

How the different regulations are interpreted in practice is difficult to determine given the lack of applicable precedents. Where the transposition of European Union Directives is at issue, however, the guidelines given by the ECJ (and the interpretation by other member states, especially Great Britain and Greece) can provide an indication.

3. Misleading and comparative advertising

In the area of advertising, the 2002 "Regulation relating to the control of misleading and comparative advertising"[131] transposed Council Directive 84/450/EEC (in its current version, modified by Directive 97/55/EC) into Cypriot law. The purpose of the law is to protect the consumer, the trader, and the general public from misleading advertising, as well as to specify the requirements for allowable comparative advertising. The Director of the "Competition and Consumer Protection Division" of the "Ministry of Commerce, Industry and Tourism" has a mandate to investigate complaints, which are submitted to him or his office. He then must determine whether a

131. Law No. 92 I/2000, available (in Greek) on the Website of the Cypress Consumer Association <www.cyprusconsumers.org.cy>.

current or soon-to-be published advertisement is misleading or is an improper comparison under Cypriot law. If the director believes it to be necessary, he can request a cease-and-desist-order from the court. The court must take the interests of all parties as well as the interest of the general public into consideration when making its decision.

Persons[132] and organizations that can prove a legal interest in the issue have standing to sue as well. However, consumer groups such as the "Cyprus Consumer Association" do not have standing, and are instead limited to submitting complaints to the "General Director". The proper defendant is every natural or legal person who is responsible for the advertisement in question. For a cease-and-desist order, neither proof of damages nor of fault of the respondent is necessary.

4. Otherwise regulated advertising measures

The "Law regarding Contract Conclusion via Long Distance Sales" (No. 14(I)/2000) implements the EC Directives 97/7/EC and 85/577/EC. It prohibits the sending of unordered goods when payment is required. The "Law regarding the conclusion of contracts outside of business offices" also regulates sales promotions tied to excursions by bus, door-to-door sales, and advertising at the workplace. Information must be provided to consumers regarding consumer credit ("Consumer credit and consumer protection" law from 2002).[133]

5. Advertising in the telecommunications area

Radio, television, fax and email advertising is, it seems, not yet statutorily regulated. Rather, they fall under the jurisdiction of the "Telecommunications regulator". The Telecommunications regulator is an independent organ not related to the state to which individual consumers can submit complaints regarding these forms of advertising. A statutory regulation of direct marketing seems to be imminent.

6. Impediment of competitors

The "Commission for the Protection of Competition" is responsible for the question of obstructive competitive practices and market disruption (discrimination, dumping prices, free distribution of newspapers, etc.), and makes its decision on the basis of antitrust law.[134]

7. Misappropriation, imitation, risk of confusion

The exploitation of reputation, the imitation of another's trademark, etc., which involves a danger of confusion can lead to a trade mark infringement per Sec. 6(1) of the Trade Mark Act, Chapter 268 (most recent change through the act No. 206/90

132. I.e. competitors and individual consumers who can prove a legal interest in the issue.
133. As to the content of the three laws see the website address in fn. 131.
134. Act No. 207/1989; available (in English) on the website <www.competition.gov.cy/competition/competition.nsf/legislation_en/legislation_en?OpenDocument>.

law)[135] Common law remedies, especially passing off, are possible in cases of imitation of brand names, trademarks, get up and labels of third parties; the danger of confusion is a necessary element. The prerequisites and the application of the tort of passing off are similar to the British common law remedy.[136]

V. DENMARK

Selected Literature: Dahl, *Antitrust, Unfair Competition, Marketing Practices and Consumer Law*, in: Gammeltoft-Hansen/Gomard/Philip (ed.), *Danish Law*, 1982, p. 297; Eckhardt-Hansen, *Werberecht in Dänemark*, in: Schotthöfer (ed.), *Handbuch des Werberechts in den EU-Staaten*, 2nd ed. 1997, p. 148; Keyßner, *Täuschung durch Unterlassen—Informationspflichten in der Werbung*, 1986; Keßler/Bruun-Nilsen, *Denmark* in: Micklitz/Keßler (ed.), *Marketing Practices Regulation and Consumer Protection in the EC-Member States and the US*, 2002, p. 44; Koktvedgaard, *Lærebog i konkurrenceret*, 5th ed. 2003; Kur/Schovsbo, *Dänemark*, in: Schricker (ed.), *Recht der Werbung in Europa*, 1998; Madsen, *Markedsret*, Part 2, 4th ed. 2000.

1. Sources of law

Lov om markedsføring (Marketing Practices Act) of 1 June 1994.

2. Danish unfair competition law in a nutshell

The Danish unfair competition law is based upon the Marketing Practices Act ("Lov om markedsføring") of 1994 in the version of the reform law of 2003.[137] Its objective is to regulate all business activities in a broad sense. Of essential significance is the general clause of Sec. 1 whereby each business activity must conform with "good marketing practices" ("god markeds foringeskik"). The interpretation of the general clause by the courts and legal literature encompasses different aspects such as manipulation of consumers, misappropriation or distribution of dangerous products.[138] In Sec. 2 an almost equally broad ban on misleading or disparaging market behavior can be found. This is followed by some provisions regulating specific market behavior: Sec. 2(a) deals with comparative advertising, Sec. 3 with instructions, Sec. 4 guarantees, Sec. 5 distinctive business marks, Sec. 6 collateral gifts, Sec. 6(a) unsolicited calls, Sec. 7 quantitative restrictions, Sec. 8 trading stamps, Sec. 9 lotteries and prize competition, Sec. 10 trade secrets and Sec. 11 labeling and packaging. These specific regulations are always supplemented by the general clause in Sec. 1 which acts as a "safety net".

135. All IP-Statutes can be found (in English) under <clea.wipo.int>; see also (in English) Manual Industry Property, Vol. 2 (2002)

136. See *Chrysostomides*, Trade Marks in Cyprus, 1990, p. 17, who refers to the decisions "*Hadjikyriakos Co.* v. *United Biscuits* (1979) 1 C.L.R. 689" und "*Universal Advertising and Publishing Agency and others* v. *Vouros XIX C.L.R. 87*"; see also "Manual Industrial Property", Vol. 2, Republic of Cyprus, p. 26.

137. The latest version of the Marketing Practices Act in Danish (and sometimes also in English) can be found on the Website of the Consumer Ombudsman <forbrugerstyrelsen.dk>. The Marketing Practices Act is, for instance, discussed (in Danish) by Madsen and Koktvetgaart, in English by Keßler/Bruun-Nielsen and Dahl, and in German by Kur/Schovsbo.

138. See Alsted, p. 677 f.

The field of application of the Marketing Practices Act is very broad. It includes business conduct before and after the conclusion of a contract and applies to private persons, public legal entities and independent professions equally. A competitive relationship, an action with a competition purpose or an intention to make a profit are not a prerequisite. Since 2000, however, exceptions are finance transactions to the extent that the Minister of Business and Industry has enacted special fairness provisions.

Despite the clear emphasis on consumer protection, the Marketing Practices Act is not solely a consumer protection law. Rather, protection of the consumer, business and the public at large are placed on an equal footing.

The second part of the Marketing Practices Act contains provisions on sanctions and procedure. The Marketing Practices Act is sanctioned predominantly through civil law, although enforcement is also, but not exclusively, the responsibility of a Consumer Agency which is headed by the Consumer Ombudsman. As in all Scandinavian countries, the Danish Consumer Ombudsman plays an essential role in the combat of unfair competition.[139] The Ombudsman possesses wide reaching and broad powers: He can file a suit for an injunction, conduct individual negotiations with specific companies, issue cease and desist orders and pass guidelines for specific advertising and distribution practices.[140] The latter, although not directly binding, are normally taken into account in interpreting the Marketing Practices Act. The strong position of the Ombudsman may be one of the reasons that in Denmark there are relatively few court judgments in the field of unfair competition law.

The Marketing Practices Act, especially Sec. 1, supplements in some respect the Competition Law of 1997,[141] but there are also some points in common with the regulations on Intellectual Property, in particular Trademark Law[142] (see under 6) and with the various regulations for the Protection of the Consumer,[143] for instance the Price Marketing and Display Act.[144] Furthermore, there is frequent reference to the Code of Conduct of the International Chamber of Commerce (ICC-Codex).

3. Regulation of advertising

a. Misleading advertising

Section 2(1) of the Marketing Practices Act prohibits false, misleading or "unreasonably incomplete" indications or statements which are likely to affect the demand for or supply of goods or services. The term indication or statement is understood broadly and includes any expression of a direct or indirect nature. As Sec. 2(3) extends the prohibition to "misleading practices", a precise demarcation between advertising and marketing practices seems superfluous.

139. As to the function of the Consumer Agency see the website of the Consumer Ombudsman (fn. 137).
140. The guidelines can be found (often also in English) on the website of the Consumer Ombudsman (fn. 137).
141. Act No. 384 of 10.6.1997 in the version of Act No. 416 of 31.10.2000 and No. 426 of 6.6.2002; the Danish Cartel Law see Koktvedgaard. Sec. 1 of the Marketing Practices Act can, for instance, be applied to facts below the threshold of Cartel law, see Keßler/Bruun-Nielsen, p. 58.
142. Koktvetgaard, Lærebog i immaterialret, 6th ed. 2002.
143. See Keßler/Bruun-Nielsen, p. 44.
144. Danish Price Marketing and Display Act (No. 209 of 28.3.2000), available under <www.fr.dk/uk/acts/ukpml.htm>.

The question whether there is an inaccurate or misleading statement is decided from the perspective of the target group. Although the Danish courts apply EJC's benchmark of the "reasonably observant and circumspect average consumer" they impose unmistakably strict requirements on advertisers.[145] For instance, advertising exaggerations are seldom seen as harmless puffing etc.

The prohibition of Sec. 2(1) includes not only false and misleading, but also "unreasonably incomplete" statements. Although the entrepreneur in principle is not required to disclose negative aspects of his product, any positive statement may not leave out relevant aspects so as to create an inadequate picture of the actual features of the product.[146] Which aspects must be disclosed depends upon the kind of product and the degree of the possible disadvantage in the case of undisclosure. Generally all relevant information or instructions have to be disclosed at the latest by the time of the making of an offer or by the conclusion of a contract (Sec. 3 Marketing Practices Act).

Section 2(5) contains a reversal of the burden of proof. In a civil proceeding, the correctness of all factual elements has to be proven by the advertiser. Furthermore, the Consumer Ombudsman may request the presentation of all relevant documents under Sec. 15(2) of the Marketing Practices Act. In the rare instance of criminal proceedings, however, the burden of proof remains with the state attorney.

In practice, most cases concern what is misleading as to price, the calculation of the price, the amount, et al; these aspects are also regulated by the specific provisions on price information, etc.[147] Case law in this area is predominantly strict.[148] It refers frequently to the "Guidelines on Price Marketing"[149] enacted by the Ombudsman in 1997, which regulate marketing and advertising with price in detail. Price guarantees are, for example, tied to especially strict requirements. Special sales (which are otherwise not regulated) may refer only to those goods that the shop carried at the beginning of the sale, et al. Also strictly judged is advertising with environmental arguments, which must meet not only the requirements of the Act on the Protection of the Environment,[150] but also the guidelines of the Nordic Consumer Ombudsmen on environmental protection of 1997.[151]

b. Comparative advertising

Although comparative advertising was never prohibited under Danish law, the Danish legislature in 2000 adopted Directive 97/55/EC almost literally in a newly introduced Sec. 2(a) Marketing Practices Act. According to the (still relevant) case law till then, comparative advertising is strictly judged primarily from the viewpoint of deception. The reference to personal circumstances is already forbidden according to Sec. 2(2) as this is an "irrelevant matter". The same is true for denigrations or exploitations of a competitor's reputation, which are also expressly forbidden (are under 6).

145. See, for instance, the decisions of the Maritime and Commercial Court, cited at Kur/Schovsbo, No. 32, or the "McDonald/McAllen"—decision GRUR Int 1996, 834.
146. As to this information duty see Keyßner; Kur/Schovsbo, No. 38.
147. See the cases cited by Kepler/Bruun-Nielsen.
148. Cf. for instance, the decisions of the Maritime and Commercial Court cited by Kur/Schovsbo, No. 44.
149. Available in English on the website of the Consumer Ombudsman (fn. 137).
150. Act of 6.9.1991; s. Keßler/Bruun-Nielsen, p. 57.
151. Available on the website of the Consumer Ombudsmann (fn. 137).

c. Concealed advertising

Under Danish law, the concealment of the commercial character is seen as being against "good marketing practices" in the sense of the general clause; often a reference to Article 12 ICC-Codex is made.[152] A contractual offer which was concealed as an invoice was thus prohibited as a violation of Sec. 1. With newspaper advertising, the advertiser may not conceal his location by the use of a P.O. Box.[153] Advertising in television and electronic commerce is submitted to additional regulations (see under e).

d. Aggressive advertising

It is considered as being against "good marketing practice" in the sense of Sec. 1 Marketing Practices Act, to manipulate, to annoy or to harass other market participants or to invade their private sphere.[154] In practice, these issues play a role primarily in the area of direct marketing (see under 4).

e. Advertising regulations for specific product and media

TV advertising is regulated in the Radio and TV Act of 1989 and in the respective "advertising notices",[155] which also implement Directive 89/452/EC (for example, the requirement to separate advertising and programming). In practice, the Guidelines of the Nordic Ombudsman for TV advertising of August 1991[156] must also be observed; they contain detailed provisions on surreptious advertising, the protection of children and youth and generally emphasize the social responsibility of all TV advertising. The Nordic Consumer Ombudsmen have also provided detailed guidelines for Internet advertising.[157]

Detailed provisions also exist for advertising specific products.[158] For example, tobacco advertising is regulated in the Tobacco Law; which is supplemented by a self restriction agreement between the Health Minister and the Tobacco Industry.[159] For alcohol advertising there are guidelines of the Consumer Ombudsman, whose violation in practice is seen as a breach against the duty of "social responsibility" in the sense of the general clause of Sec. 1.[160] Drinks with an alcohol content of more than 2.8% may not be advertised on radio or TV, etc.

f. Other advertising regulations

As mentioned before (see No. 1), Danish unfair competition law emphasizes the social responsibility for advertising and marketing. Failure to comply with this responsibility

152. SH, UfR 1980, p. 342.
153. Kur/Schovsbo, No. 104.
154. Keßler/Bruun-Nielsen, p. 47.
155. Kur/Schovsbo, No. 154.
156. Which can be found on the Website of the Consumer Ombudsman (fn. 137).
157. "Position Statement of the Nordic Consumer Ombudsmen on e-commerce and marketing on the Internet", 2002, see the Website of the Consumer Ombudsman (fn. 137).
158. Kur/Schovsbo, No. 182 ff.
159. Keßler/Bruun-Nielsen, p. 56.
160. Keßler/Bruun-Nielsen, p. 56.

is considered as a direct breach of "good marketing behavior" in the sense of the general clause in Sec. 1 of the Marketing Practices Act.

In particular, children and youth are to be protected from the harmful influence of advertising and marketing, for instance in connection with potentially dangerous products or conduct. The same applies, at least in principle, for violence, sentiments of fear or injury to religious feelings[161] or "shocking advertising".[162] Also "sexually or racially discriminating" advertising breaches the duty of social responsibility, in particular if women are presented in a degrading way.[163]

Section 5 regulates in detail advertising on guarantees.[164]

4. Direct marketing

Unsolicited door to door sales and commercial calls to a consumer in his house, place of work, club or school are basically already prohibited according to Sec. 2, 6 of the Consumer Contract Law.[165] To implement the EU provisions, a prohibition was also enacted in the Market Practice Act in 2002. Pursuant to Sec. 6 a, any unsolicited commercial contact with the consumer by email, automatic answering machine or fax is prohibited ("opt-in").[166] With respect to individual telephone calls to consumers, a reference is made to the Consumer Contract Law which, in other words, means a prohibition. For email advertising, Sec. 6(a)(2) provides a modification (implementation of the Privacy and Electronic Communications Directive[167]) so that following an electronic sale, similar products may be offered, provided the customer does not forbid it ("soft opt-in"). To reinforce and further define all these provisions, there are additional guidelines from the Nordic Consumer Ombudsman.[168]

For all other cases, the "opt-out" solution of Sec. 6(a)(3) applies. Pursuant thereto, the advertiser must respect the known wishes of a natural person not to be bothered as well as persons entered on a list. To the extent that a contact is permitted at all, the commercial purpose of the contact must be explained immediately and the possibility to decline must be given under Sec. 6 a(5). According to Sec. 6(a)(6), no costs can be imposed. The sending of non-ordered products can infringe the general clause in Sec. 1, for example, if—against the provisions of the Consumer Contract Law—the impression is given of an obligation to pay or to store a product. Pyramid and snowball schemes similarly infringe Sec. 1 and 2 of the Marketing Practices Act if they are joined with a duty to recruit friends or family members, if they address a particularly

161. A violation of Section 1 was denied, however, in the case of an advertising with the Pope, GRUR Int. 1993, 553 with note Kur (which was, however, a criminal preceding; in a civil law case the standard might have been stricter).
162. The Consumer Ombudsman did not pursue the Benetton-advertising because he did not want to add to the publictiy, Kur/Schovsbo, No. 113.
163. Kur, WRP 1995, 790 and Kur/Schovsbo, No. 114 ff. There is also a Guideline of the Ombudsman (see Kur/Schovsbo, Annex).
164. See the Guideline of the Consumer Ombudsman of 1978; available on the website of the Consumer Ombudsman (see fn. 137).
165. Law No. 886 of 29.12.1987, in the version of the reform act of 31.5.2000; see Keßler/Bruun-Nielsen, p. 48.
166. In January 2004, the Maritime and Commercial Court in Copenhagen sentenced a Danish company that had sent more than 15.000 unsolicited commercial faxes to a fine of 66.700 Euro.
167. Discussed in this book in Chapter 3, III.
168. See fn. 137.

gullible public, if they make unrealistic and unproven earning promises or if it is shown that they do not possess a sufficient distribution network.[169]

5. Sales promotion

Discounts are neither prohibited nor is there a ban on sales at a loss. However, according to Sec. 8 Marketing Practices Act, discounts and other services through the use of coupons which are given out before the purchase are prohibited; this includes coupons in newspapers which entitle to a price reduction.[170] (See also the Notice of the Consumer Ombudsman of 1994).[171] For the rest, price reductions are seen primarily under the aspect of misleading.

On the other hand, collateral gifts or similar inducements which are conditional to a purchase are prohibited with respect to end users (Sec. 6(1)). If an item is announced as "gratis" together with a purchase, this is seen as synonymous for a premium. If the price for the additional product is not fictitious it is treated as a tie-in. Such tie-in offers are permitted if the products are combinable in a natural way, the normal sales price for each product is clearly given, and the consumer can also acquire both products separately. Furthermore, there are exceptions to the prohibition of premiums in Sec. 6(2) for identical products ("three for the price of two"), for items of a "negligible value"[172] and according to Sec. 6(3) for so-called airline mileage programs.[173] Stricter prohibitions on premiums and free gifts exist for potentially dangerous products, for instance pharmaceuticals, alcohol and tobacco. For customer loyalty programs, the Nordic Consumer Ombudsmen have published special guidelines ("Loyalty programs in marketing") which supplement and define Sec. 6 of the Marketing Practices Act.[174]

Drawing of lots and promotional games, whose result depends upon chance, and where the participation is conditional upon purchase, are essentially prohibited (Sec. 9). There are exceptions for the publishers of periodical magazines and for promotional games with a maximum price limitation, which is established by the Minister of Business and Industry.[175] In contrast, promotional games which depend upon the skill or knowledge of the participant are generally permitted, even if they are linked to a purchase.[176]

6. Disparagement and denigration

Although Art. 4(2) Trademark Act provides for trademark law protection against disparagement and denigration,[177] additional protection under the Marketing Practices Act is often claimed because of the more flexible legal remedies. Issues of determining which law to apply apparently do not exist.

169. See Keßler/Bruun-Nielsen, p. 51.
170. Cf. the Maritime and Commercial Court Copenhagen, UfR 1993, 631, has prohibited Coupons in a newspaper that entitled to gifts with a value of 15 DKK or to cash of 5 DKK.
171. On the website of the Consumer Ombudsman (fn. 137).
172. According to the Maritime and Commercial Court Copenhagen (UfR 1991, p. 250)
173. The exception applies also to the offering of premiums provided for by third parties, like free trips, hotels or cars, if they are part of an airline mileage program. Other premiums in connection with airmileage programs are submitted to an information duty to the Ombudsman (para. 4).
174. See the Website of the Danish Consumer Ombudsman (fn. 137).
175. Keßler/Bruun-Nielsen, p. 54.
176. Keßler/Bruun-Nielsen, p. 54
177. See fn. 142.

Apart from the area of comparative advertising (see under No. 11), Sec. 2(2) of the Marketing Practices Act prohibits all statements which, "because of their form and reference to irrelevant matters, are improper in relation to other persons carrying on a trade or business or to consumers". In this category are personal circumstances and all commercial communications which inappropriately criticize or make fun of a competitor, his trademark or product.[178]

The exploitation of another businessman's reputation is covered by the general clause in Sec. 1 Marketing Practices Act. For example, the name of a snack stand as "McAllen" was forbidden because of the exploitation of the famous name "McDonalds" (and because of the misleading consumers over possible business relationships).[179]

Also the exploitation of the name or popularity of natural or legal persons can be regarded as being against "good marketing practices" in the sense of Sec. 1. The details are specified through Guidelines passed by the Consumer Ombudsman of 1997.[180]

7. Misappropriation, risk of confusion, imitation

Sec. 5 Marketing Practices Act prohibits the use of confusingly similar trade marks or other distinctive business marks of another trader. The necessary distinctiveness can be acquired also through extensive use, but the interest of competitors in the free availability of colors, numbers etc. are also taken into account.[181]

Protection against imitation of products and services is granted on the basis of the general clause in Sec. 1 Marketing Practices Act. This requires that a product or service has a certain distinctiveness and that there is, as a rule, a risk of confusion. In particular factual situations, the general clause can apply even without the risk of confusion. For example, the distribution of play blocks which were compatible with the well known Lego blocks was prohibited as unfair competition.[182]

8. Impediment of competitors

Section 10 Marketing Practices Act protects business and trade secrets as well as technical drawings against misappropriation and unlawful use.

9. Breach of the law

The breach of provisions outside the Marketing Practices Act can constitute a violation of "good marketing practices" in the sense of the general clause of Sec. 1 Marketing Practices Act. However, the breached regulation must equally aim at the regulation of the market in the interest of consumers and traders.[183]

178. See Kur/Schovsbo, No. 86.
179. GRUR Int. 1996, 136.
180. Kur/Schovsbo, No. 125. See also the "Shit op Chanel"—decision, GRUR Int. 1982, 456. (which was, however, rendered before the reform of the Trademark Act).
181. For instance, the use of a certain shade of blue for construction elements was not considered an infringement of Sec. 5 Marketing Practices Act although a competitor already sold blue construction elements under the name "The blue . . ."; see Kur/Schovsbo, No. 125.
182. CF. UfR 1995, p. 92.
183. See Keßler/Bruun-Nielsen, p. 58.

10. Enforcement

The Danish Marketing Practices Act is in the first place sanctioned by civil law, but also characterized by the central function of an administrative authority, headed by the Consumer Ombudsman (see above, No. 4) who has broad powers and may, for instance, also issue interlocutory injunctions (Sec. 21).

According to Sec. 13 civil law remedies are mainly injunctions and complaint for damages. The courts also may order restoration of the conditions prior to the illegal act, including destruction or withdrawal of products and publication of information or correction of indications or statements. Locus standi is granted to any person who can assert a "legal interest", in theory also individual consumers (Sec. 19). According to Sec. 20, if several consumers have uniform claims for damages, the Consumer Ombudsman may, upon request, recover the claims collectively. In the first instance, the Maritime and Commercial Court of Copenhagen is competent for disputes of issucs based on market behavior; the highest court is competent for appeals (Sec. 14 of the Marketing Practices Act).

VI. ESTONIA[184]

Selected Literature: Dietz, *Die Einführung von Gesetzen gegen den unlauteren Wettbewerb in ehemals sozialistischen Staaten Mittel- und Osteuropas, GRUR Int.* 1994, 649; Koitel, *USSR und Estland*, in: Beier/Bastian/Kur (ed.), *Wettbewerbsrecht und Verbraucherschutz in den Länder Mittel- und Osteuropas*, 1992, p. 60; Koitel, WiRO 1993, p. 443; Pisuke, Consumer Protection in Estonia, in: Alexiev et al., *Consumer Protection in Bulgaria, Czech Republic, Estonia, Hungary, Latvia, Lithuania and Romania*, CICPP No. 4; Pisuke, The Influence of Social Reforms and the Information Society on Consumers in a Transition Economy, in: Wilhelmsson/Tuominen/Tuomola, *Consumer Law in the Information Society*, 2001, p. 31.

1. Sources of law

Konkurentsiseadus (Competition Act) of 2001 (KS); Reclaamiseadus (Advertising Act) of 1997 (RS); Tarbijakaitseadus (Consumer Protection Act) of 2004 (TKS).[185]

2. Estonian unfair competition law in a nutshell

The legal protection against unfair competition is in Estonia treated as part of competition law in a broad sense. The Competition Act of 2001[186] pursues the twofold objective of promoting freedom of competition and the fairness of commercial transactions.

The rules against unfair competition are to be found in Chapter 7 KS. Prominent place occupies the general clause of Art. 50 KS, which is oriented around the concept

184. This report was authored by Dr. Antonina Bakardjieva-Engelbrekt of the University of Stockholm. The author wishes to thank Addi Rull (LL.M., Stockholm) and Teddi Rull (LL.M., Stockholm) for valuable comments on an earlier draft.
185. The TKS of 2004 replaced the earlier Consumer Protection Act of 1993.
186. Estonian legislative acts can be retrieved in English from: <www.legaltext.ee/indexen.htm>.

"dishonest trading practices". As "dishonest" the law defines acts which are contrary to good morals and practices (Art. 50(1) KS). Several factual situations are specifically identified as constituting acts of unfair competition. Enforcement is left to the affected parties and falls under the jurisdiction of ordinary courts (Art. 53 KS).[187]

A parallel, consumer-oriented duty to trade fairly is stipulated in Art. 12 Consumer Protection Act of 2004. Of relevance for advertising is the Advertising Act of 1997.

3. Regulation of advertising

The RS represents an attempt at a comprehensive legislative treatment of the area of advertising. Many of the rules and principles in RS originate from European directives. Article 2 RS defines advertising as: "information which is made public for the purpose of increasing the sale of products or services, promoting an event or idea, or achieving other desired results in other areas and which an advertiser disseminates for a fee or other consideration".[188] Despite the ambitious scope of RS, one finds additional rules on advertising also in KS and TKS.

a. Misleading advertising

Misleading advertising is prohibited (Art. 4 RS). The definition of misleading advertising is taken from Directive 84/450/EEC, omitting however the requirement that the advertising shall influence the economic behavior of consumers (Art. 4(1) RS).[189]

The publication of misleading information is furthermore prohibited as an act of unfair competition under KS (Art. 50(1) Nr. 1 and Art. 51 KS).[190] According to Art. 50(3) KS when misleading information is used in advertising the rules of RS apply. Finally, pursuant to Art. 12(3) TKS sellers are prohibited to influence consumers through misleading advertising.

b. Comparative advertising

Comparative advertising is regulated exclusively in RS (Art. 4(1) RS). The rules follow closely Directive 84/450/EEC as amended by Directive 97/55/EC but with some modifications. Article 4(1) RS defines comparative advertising as advertising that directly or indirectly identifies a competitor operating in the same market, or goods or services offered by a competitor, which meet the same needs or are intended for the same purpose as the advertised goods or services. Thus one of the conditions

187. Under the preceding Competition Acts of 1993 and of 1998 enforcement was vested in the Competition Council (Konkurentsiamet, KSt). The Competition Act as well as decisions and other documents of the KSt are available at the site of the KSt: <www.konkurentsiamet.ee/>.
188. If interpreted literally this definition does not seem to require any commercial purpose and would encompass even information campaigns by non-profit organizations. At the same time, the definition appears narrower in that it does not cover all kinds of representations.
189. The features that have to be considered when establishing whether advertising is misleading include the environmental and health-related qualities of a product (Art. 4(2) Nr. 1, 8 RS).
190. Misleading information is defined in KS as incorrect information which, given ordinary attention on the part of the buyer, may lead to receiving misleading impression of an offer or which harms or may harm the reputation or economic activities of another undertaking. See decision of the KSt in the case "Pärnu", Annual Report of the KSt for 1999, p. 12.

for permitting comparative advertising in the Directive (cf. Art. 3a(1)(b) Directive 84/450) is incorporated in the definition, which may narrow the scope of the rules.

c. Concealed advertising

Advertising shall be presented so that it is recognizable as such, given ordinary attention by the public (Art. 3 RS).[191] Surreptitious advertising is prohibited (Art. 8 RS).

d. Product- and media-specific advertising regulation

Chapter 3 of the RS contains a detailed list of restrictions and special conditions for advertising of particular products and services. Article 10 RS stipulates a total ban of tobacco advertising. The advertising of alcoholic beverages promoting initiation of the use of alcohol, or containing appeal to purchase such drinks, or directed to persons under the age of 21 is prohibited. Strong alcoholic beverages (with an alcohol content of more than 22 percent per volume) are subject to more severe restrictions than low-alcohol beverages (Art. 12 RS). Further conditions and limitations are set out for health-related or morally objectionable products and services.[192]

Advertising in radio and television broadcasting is subject to the rules of Chapter 3 of the Broadcasting Act of 1995, which largely correspond to Directive 89/552/EC as amended.

e. Other regulations on advertising

Article 5 RS prohibits offensive advertising. The latter is defined as advertising contrary to good morals and customs, which calls on people to act unlawfully or to violate prevailing standards of decency.[193] Prohibited is also advertising containing presentations of a sexual act, inappropriate nudity and socially unacceptable sexual behavior (Art. 5(2) Nr. 5 RS).

Advertising directed at children shall not exploit their natural credulity or lack of experience and shall fulfill other stringent requirements (Art. 9 RS).

4. Information duties

The TKS proclaims it a fundamental right of consumers to obtain necessary and truthful information for making a conscious choice, as well as timely information on any risks relating to the goods or services (Art. 3 (2) TKS).[194] Advertising shall contain clearly distinguishable information concerning the advertiser (Art. 3(2) RS).

191. Cf. Art. 12(1) TKS, according to which the commercial purpose of an offer shall be clear to consumers.
192. E.g. medicinal products (Art. 14 RS), medical services (Art. 14^1 RS), financial services (Art. 15 RS), dangerous products (Art. 16 RS), biocidal products (Art. 16^1RS), foodstuffs (Art. 20 RS), weapons and ammunitions (Art. 18 RS), gambling (Art. 19 RS). Advertising of narcotic drugs and psychotropic substances is prohibited (Art. 17 RS), as is the advertising of prostitution (Art. 20 RS).
193. Examples of offensive advertising are adverts that are discriminatory on grounds of nationality, race, color, sex, age, religion, and even financial or social status (Art. 5(2) Nr. 1 RS).
194. This right is further specified through long catalogues of information and labeling requirements in Arts. 4-8 TKS, including provisions on indication of prices.

5. Direct marketing, specific marketing techniques

The requirements of the EC directives on distance selling (Directive 97/7/EC) and on contracts negotiated away from business premises (Directive 85/577/EEC) are incorporated in Chapter 2, Divisions 3 and 4 of the Law of Obligations of 2001 (Võlaõigusseadus = VS) as well as in Arts. 12-14 TKS. Art. 60 VS provides for an "opt-in" principle for unsolicited commercial communication by facsimile, telephone answering machine or electronic mail. Other means of communication may be used only if the consumer has not expressly forbidden such use ("opt-out").[195]

6. Disparagement

Pursuant to Art. 50 KS disparagement of a competitor or the goods of a competitor is prohibited as an act of unfair competition.[196] Art. 6 RS stipulates a ban on advertisement which denigrates (directly or by implication) a person, activity, product or service. In addition, Art. 1047 VS stipulates liability for damages caused by interference with the economic or professional activities of a person by way of disclosure of incorrect information (1), or disclosure of facts which may adversely affect the economic situation of a person (2).

7. Passing off, imitation

The KS does not contain an explicit rule on product imitations or on confusing use of commercial signs. However, the provision on misleading information in Art. 50(1) Nr.1 KS has been interpreted to include confusing use of trade marks.[197]

8. Impediment of competitors

The use of confidential information concerning a competitor is prohibited if it is obtained illegally. The same applies to the misuse of an employee or representative of a competitor, if influence is exerted over the employee to act in the interests of the influencing party or a third party (cf. Arts. 50(1) Nr. 2 and 52 KS). Following Art. 1049 Law on Obligations it is unlawful to cause a complete or partial halt in the economic or professional activities of another person for a significant period if the halt is caused by interfering in the activities by means of an unlawful threat or a prohibited boycott, demonstration or strike, or in another manner aimed specifically at halting the economic or professional activities of the person.

9. Enforcement

According to Art. 53 KS the existence or absence of unfair competition shall be ascertained in a dispute between the parties pursuant to the rules of civil procedure. Standing to sue is apparently granted only to the negatively affected competitor.

195. Estonian law does not have special rules on pyramid sales. In grave cases the rules on fraud in the Penal Code can be invoked. See Fazekas, Some Facts about Pyramidal Sales in Central and East European Countries, CLJ 1998, 495, referring to the cases "AS Gering" and "AS Sire".
196. See the case "OÜ Kirjastus Avita", Annual Report of the KSt for 1999, p. 13.
197. See Annual report of the KSt for 1998, p. 12, cases "Klubitakso/Klubi Takso"; "Canon Kabushiki Kaisha/Canon-Control". The decisions have been confirmed by the court.

The RS is designed as an administrative law statute. Different supervisory authorities are assigned the task to monitor the market and to ensure compliance with the standards set forth in RS by way chiefly of administrative penalties (Chapter 5 RS).

The TKS sets forth administrative and criminal law penalties for infringements upon the rights of consumers (see Arts. 43-47 TKS), but also stipulates a general consumer right to protection (Art. 21 TKS). The Consumer Protection Board, together with other public bodies, monitors the market and is entitled to impose fines and prescriptive orders for termination of the infringements of the law (Art. 38 TKS). The TKS of 2004 envisages the setting up of a Consumer Complaints Committee as an independent institution for out-of-court settlement of consumer complaints (Arts. 22-37 TKS). Consumers have the right to submit a complaint to the trader, to the Committee (via the Consumer Protection Board), or directly to the court (Art. 21 TKS).[198] Consumer associations have the right to represent consumers in court as well as in extra-judicial proceedings (Art. 15(2) TKS). Under certain circumstances the Consumer Protection Board can file an action with a county or city court as representative of the consumer if the dispute is of principal importance or affects the general interests of consumers (Art. 37(4) TKS).

Compensation for damages caused by acts of unfair competition or by unlawful advertising can be sought on the basis of the general rules of non-contractual liability (see Chapter 53, Division 1, Arts. 1043 ff. VS).

VII. FINLAND

Selected Literature: Fallund/Salmi, *Finnland*, in: Schotthöfer (ed.), *Handbuch des Werberechts in den EU-Staaten*, 2nd ed. 1997, p. 217; Kaulamo, *Finnland*, in: Schricker (ed.), *Recht der Werbung in Europa*, 2002; Keßler/Wilhelmsson, *Finnland*, in: Micklitz/Kessler (ed.), *Marketing Practices Regulation and Consumer Protection in the EC Member States and the US*, 2002, p. 60; Koivuhovi, *Das Wettbewerbsrecht in Finnland*, in: Heidelberger Kommentar zum Wettbewerbsrecht, 2000, p. 705; Kur, *Das Recht des unlauteren Wettbewerbs in Finnland, Norwegen und Schweden, GRUR Int.* 1996, 38; Wilhelmsson, *Konsumentskyddet i Finland*, 1989; Wilhelmsson., *Kuluttajansuoja*, in: Kirsti Rissanen (ed.), *Yritysoikeus*, 1999, 723.

1. Sources of law

Laki sopimattomasta menettelystä elinkeinotoiminnassa (Unfair Trade Practices Act) of 22 December 1978 (SopMenL); Kuluttajansuojalaki (Consumer Protection Act) of 1 January 1978 (KSL).

2. Finnish unfair competition law in a nutshell

Finnish unfair competition law is based upon two laws. The relationship between competitors is regulated in the Unfair Trade Practices Act ("Laki sopimattomasta

198. The remedies that consumers may claim before the court are not specified but they should include compensation for damages on the basis of VS. On the integration of consumer protection law in general civil law see Pisuke, 2001, p. 35.

menettelystä elinkeinotoiminnassa" = SopMenL).[199] For the relationship between business and end user or consumer, the second chapter of the Consumer Protection Act ("Kuluttajansuujalaki" = KSL) applies.[200]

Despite this division of the laws according to the purpose of protection, the content, scope and interpretation of the SopMenL and KSL is quite similar.[201] In both sets of laws, the scope of application is very broad, including each marketing practice with regard to consumer goods (Sec. 1 KSL) or each business practice (Sec.1 SopMenL). Moreover, both laws contain an almost identical general clause, which is supplemented by specific provisions regulating particular cases of unfair market behavior. The KSL, for instance, regulates false or misleading advertising, comparative advertising, special forms of price advertising, the sending of unsolicited goods, premiums, tie-in offers, other tie-in transactions, and promotional games. The SopMenL is concerned with untruthful or misleading statements, irrelevant or improper expressions, comparative advertising, promotional games based on chance, and the protection of trade secrets.[202]

Of major significance in both laws are the general clause(s). Sec. 1 SopMenL prohibits every business practice which breaches "good market practices" or is "otherwise unfair towards other traders". Sec. 1(1) KSL prohibits marketing practices which are contrary to good market practices or "otherwise unfair with respect to consumers". According to Sec. 1(2) KSL marketing practices are always seen as improper if they do not convey the information, which is necessary for the health or economic security of the consumer.

Despite existing differences—the main criterion of unfairness is seen in the KSL from the perspective of the consumer, in the SopMenL from the perspective of other traders—both general clauses are interpreted to be in agreement with each other to a great extent.[203] The ICC-Codex of the International Chamber of Commerce, the extensive guidelines of the Consumer Ombudsman[204] and the decisions of the Market Court are of major importance for interpreting these laws. The courts usually aim at a fair balance between the interests of all market participants and the functioning of market competition but, as all Scandinavian laws, emphasize also the social responsibility of advertising and marketing.[205]

Enforcement of the SopMenL is left to private party complaints; enforcement of the KSL is handled primarily by the Consumer Ombudsman. In both cases, the Market Court has (exclusive) jurisdiction. As in all Scandinavian countries, the level of protection is high; the provisions of the SopMenL and the KSL are strictly enforced. The burden of proof for all actual statements lies with the advertiser.

The regulation of marketing practices with respect to the end user or consumer in Chapter 2 of the KSL has a close relationship to the regulations in other chapters in this Act that deal, for instance, with consumer contracts, credit contracts, timesharing

199. Act No. 1061 of 22.12.1978; German translation in GRUR Int. 1979, 556. The SopMenL was amended through Act No. 461 of 5.6.2002.
200. Act No. 38 of 1.1.1978. The KSL was last amended through Act No. 741 of 15.8.2003.
201. As to the similarities see Kaulamo (2002).
202. As to the protection of trade secrets see Koivuhori, p. 707 f.
203. See Kaulamo, No. 51.
204. The Finish Consumer Ombudsman often passes guidelines together with the other "Nordic Ombudsmen". See the Website of the Consumer Ombudsman <www.kuluttajavirasto.fi>.
205. See Kessler/Wilhelmsson, p. 61.

etc. The regulations in the SopMenL, in turn, must at least partly be considered in connection with the protection of intellectual property.[206]

3. Regulation of advertising

a. Misleading advertising

According to Chapter 2, Sec. 2 KSL, no false or misleading statement may be made with regard to marketing. Inaccurate or misleading statements are also forbidden by Sec. 2 SopMenL if they are made with reference to one's own business activity or that of another and if they are capable of creating demand or offers of the goods or of resulting in damage to a business. Independent of these specific provisions, the general clauses of the SopMenL and the KSL are applicable in case of misleading advertising statements.[207] Since misleading statements are considered improper irrespective whether it is directed towards consumers or traders, it is in practice not necessary to draw a sharp line between the two laws.

Both laws prohibit inaccurate as well as misleading statements. Advertising exaggerations are considered irrelevant only in exceptional cases.[208] The question of misleading is decided from the perspective of the relevant target group; for the KSL the European benchmark of the average consumer who is reasonably informed and observant is applied.[209] However, if the advertising is directed to a particularly sensitive consumer group, case law emphasizes stricter standards. In particular, advertising aimed at children and minors must avoid any overly emotional or suggestive influence.[210]

Finnish law presumes that the average consumer observes mass advertising in a rather superficial way, and in any event does not read it word for word. An overall impression which is misleading, can therefore only be counterbalanced through disclaimer in exceptional cases.

Advertisers are obligated under Sec. 4 KSL (criminal penalty) to make available to the Consumer Ombudsman all necessary documents. It is generally seen as "improper" within the meaning of the general clause to assert facts of which the correctness cannot be proven.[211] Since the ban on misleading can be based not only on the specific provisions in Sec. 2 KSL but also on the general clause in Sec. 1 KSL, as a result, the advertiser has the burden of proof for the correct content of the advertisement.[212] The greater the degree to which a specific target group can be influenced, the higher the level of substantiation is for the advertiser. Advertising aimed at health issues must, for example, be comprehensively substantiated.[213]

206. For an discussion in English see Bruun, Intellectual Property in Finland, 2002.
207. In practice, misleading advertising is often judged on the basis of the general clause, see Kaulamo, No. 53.
208. Kaulamo, No. 52.
209. See the jurisprudence of the ECJ in this book, Chapter 3, II. Demoscopic surveys are rarely used, see Kaulamo, No. 56.
210. This is strictly enforced. The Consumer Ombudsman has given a . . ., see Kaulamo, No. 61.
211. See Kaulamo, No. 67.
212. For instance, the advertising claim "the lightest running shoes in the world" was considered as contrary to the general clause of Section 1 KSL because the advertiser could not prove the accuracy of the statement; MT 1980:2.
213. See Kaulamo, No. 74.

The largest group of case law exists in the field of misleading or deficient advertising on the price. Price discount advertising (comparison with one's own previously claimed prices) is regulated in Chapter 2, Sec. 3 KSL. Also to be observed is the Price Information Regulation of 1999[214] and a Marketing Guideline of the Consumer Ombudsman which regulates certain forms of announcements on price or special sales (for example references to recommended retail prices, market prices, wholesale prices, subscription prices, liquidation sale prices, factory prices, etc.).[215] Another Marketing Guideline of the Consumer Ombudsman deals with "abuse of terminology". As to the use of the term "price guarantee", particularly strict requirements are imposed: "Lowest price guarantees" constitutes, for instance, a statement that is taken literally. It may only be used if the advertiser constantly observes the prices of his competitors and can prove his statement through objective comparisons.[216]

Also with regard to the use of test results, there is a Marketing Guideline of the Consumer Ombudsman,[217] as well as with regard to advertising with environmental arguments to which a far reaching duty to substantiate any claim is imposed on the advertiser.[218] Vague statements are often taken literally, for example, a TV commercial for a car with the background song "What a wonderful world" (to which a car drives through the country) and the claim "Each kilometer economize. For a cleaner world" was forbidden because the advertiser could not prove superior environmental effects.[219]

b. Comparative advertising

With effect as of 1 March 2001, the Finnish legislature adopted a regulation on comparative advertising (Chapter 2, Sec. 4 KSL),[220] which corresponds in substantial part to the Directive 97/55/EC. The SopMenL refers to this regulation, so that irrespective of whether the addressee is a consumer or another trader, the assessment of comparative advertising is identical (Sec. 2(3) SopMenL).[221] In practice disputes in this area are frequently framed as competitor disputes on the basis of the SopMenL.

The term comparative advertising is broadly interpreted and includes (at least according to the opinion of the legislature)[222] the comparison of systems. With regard to interpretation, it is to be expected that the strict former case law will be continued. Superlative advertising ("the most beneficial", "the most practical", "better for the teeth") can be regarded as comparative advertising so that the advertiser must be prepared to prove the correctness of the claim. Moreover, the advertiser must refrain from any sweeping conclusions as to the results of the comparison.

214. Published in Kaulamo, Annex.
215. Also terms like "guarantee", see Kaulamo, No. 88.
216. Market Court 2002:6; see Kocher, GRUR Int. 2002, 707.
217. Kaulamo, No. 108.
218. See Kaulamo, No. 102. As to the availability of this guideline see fn. 204.
219. Market Court MT 1992:26, see Kaulamo, No. 109.
220. See Kaulamo, No. 150 ff. The regulation is in the tradition of Finnish law that always had considered comparative advertising as legal.
221. Not transposed were the provision on geographical indications because they are already regulated in Art. 13 of the Decree No. 2081/92. Article 3(a)(2) of the Directive—information requirements for special offers—has been implemented in Chapter 2 § 4 KSL (premiums).
222. See HE 79/2000, S. 21.

c. Concealed advertising

Concealment of the commercial character of sales measures breaches not only the general clause of the SopMenL but also the general clause of the KSL. The Market Court imposes relatively strict requirements in this regard, particularly if advertising is not easily differentiable from other forms of information.[223] For television there is in implementation of the TV Directive an obligation to separate advertising from programming and a prohibition on surreptious and subliminal advertising. In addition, commercials must not only be technically distinguished from programming but also in terms of its contents.[224] For the Internet there are transparency requirements (in implementation of the E-Commerce Directive), see Chapter 2, Sec. 1a KSL and Sec. 1(2) SopMenL.

d. Aggressive advertising

Annoying or intrusive marketing methods, including advertising, are contrary to the general clause of Chapter 2, Sec. 2a KSL, if they constitute an improper influence over the freedom of decision. In practice, this applies mostly to cases of direct marketing, see under 5.

e. Advertising regulations for specific products

According to Sec. 6 of the Foodstuffs Act,[225] advertising for food must not only be correct but must also provide adequate information on the foodstuff. Prohibited are all indications which imply a medicinal or therapeutic effect such as "milk helps against osteoporosis".[226]

Advertising for medicines is subject to the Pharmaceutical Products Act,[227] and must comply with an additional regulation of the Pharmaceutical Government Office of Marketing of Medicines dated 26 September 1997.

According to the Alcohol Act of 1 January 1995[228] advertising of drinks with more than 22% alcohol content is permitted only in special magazines and specific sales shops. The strict advertising restrictions apply also to indirect advertising.[229] Advertising with regard to minors is completely forbidden. A Special Governmental Authority supervises the enforcement of additional marketing directives for individual drinks and marketing practices.[230]

The advertising of tobacco products is, according to the Tobacco Act,[231] generally prohibited outside of the point of sale. According to Sec. 8(1) of the Tobacco Act, this

223. The standard is especially strict if the advertising is aimed at children and minors; see Kaulamo, No. 179.
224. See Kaulamo, No. 183; Kur, GRUR Int. 1989, 368.
225. Act No. 361/1995, published at Kaulamo, Annex, and No. 264 ff.
226. See Kaulamo.
227. Act No. 395/1987; published at Kaulamo, Annex; see also under No. 26 ff.
228. Act No. 1143/1994; Kaulamo, Annex; No. 286 ff.
229. See Kaulamo, No. 292.
230. Kaulamo, No. 287 f.
231. Act No. 693/1976, published at Kaulamo, Annex, see also under No. 297 ff.

also applies to indirect advertising and all sales promotion measures, for example, the advertising of shoes under the trademark "Camel Boots".[232]

Particular advertising provisions exist also, for example, for securities, investments and credit, package trips and real estate.[233]

f. Other Regulations on Advertising

According to Chapter 2, Sec. 1 KSL, every act of improper marketing with respect to the consumer is unfair. The term "improper" includes not only undue influence on the consumer‘s decision, but also the breach of generally recognized social values (for example protection of children and youth). The presentation of violence[234] for the purpose of promoting sales is always seen as unfair even when it is presented in a humorous form of advertising. According to the opinion of the Market Court the general clause is also applicable to advertising which is discriminating, in particular, sexually discriminating because women are presented in a denigrating way as sexual objects or as attention getter.[235] The assessment of the so-called shocking advertising is disputed. For example, the Market Court was of the opinion that there was no unfair exploitation of fear of war or violence with regard to a war picture.[236]

4. Information duties

According to Chapter 2, Sec. 2 KSL, it is deemed unfair if the marketing does not convey information that is necessary for the health or economic security of the consumer. Independent of any misleading, there exists a duty to provide "information" as to health and economic security issues. Basically, all information must be given which the average consumer with regard to a specific product and under the specific circumstances would not think of himself. The scope and clarity of such information depend upon the degree of potential damage which may occur without providing it.[237]

5. Direct marketing[238]

According the Chapter 2, Sec. 2 KSL, the sending of unsolicited goods is prohibited if it gives the impression that the consumer must pay for them, send them back or in any way deal with them. Advertising material may be sent, but it must be recognizable from the outside as such and may not illicit the curiosity or attention of children (for example through comics).

232. Market Court MT 1988:1—"Camel Boots"; Kaulamo, No. 299.
233. Kaulamo, No. 301 ff.
234. Cf. Market Court MT 1998:18—"Gone with the Winchester" (TV-commercial for ice cream in which soldiers attack a farm house see Kaulomo, No. 190.
235. Market Court MT 1994:7—"Danu" (Advertisement for paint with a denigrating presentation of a woman); see also Kaulamo, No. 193; Kur, WRP 1995, 790.
236. GRUR Int. 1996, 251.
237. For instance, it was considered unfair not to point out clearly that a travel agent is not the contract partner as regards the airlines, see Market Court MT 1988:4. As to the information duties see also Kaulamo, No. 112.
238. See Keßler/Wilhelmssen, p. 65 ff.

Advertising through telecommunications, including email advertising, is regulated by the Protection of Privacy Act of 1999.[239] Accordingly, advertising via an automatic system with regard to the consumer requires a prior consent. For all other forms of communication the Act imposes the "opt-out" solution. This does, however, not necessarily mean that these communications are ultimately legal. Email advertising, advertising per phone and fax are also judged on the basis of the general clause. It can be improper market behavior if the consumer is harassed, if the advertisement is too intensive, if it blocks equipment or incurs costs.[240] Of significance for the interpretation are also the guidelines of the Nordic Ombudsmen on e-commerce of 2000, which, for example, impose strict requirements on email advertising with regard to children and youth.[241]

Door-to-door sales are generally permitted according the Chapter 6 KSL. The same applies for addressing consumers in public places. The permissibility of pyramid schemes is decided upon on the basis of the general clause. They are considered unfair if the participants have no refund guarantee with regard to the products they acquire.[242]

6. Sales promotion

Rebates, discounts etc, are not subject to any general restrictions.[243] However, it must be kept in mind that the ban on misleading advertising is handled strictly, especially in matters of price reductions (see above, 3a). This is supplemented by the guideline of the Consumer Ombudsman with regard to sales and special sales. According to Sec. 2(3) KSL, the price reduction of a consumer good may not exceed the price difference between the actually lowered price and the price previously offered by the business concerned.

Tie-in offers and premiums are generally permissible (as a result of the Reform Act 1072/2000 which took effect on 1 March 2001). According to Chapter 2, Sec. 4b KSL and Sec. 3(2) SopMenL, the former ban on premiums was replaced by extensive information duties. The content and value of the offer must be clearly disclosed; tie-in offers must indicate separate prices (unless the price of a consumer good is less than €10). The Consumer Ombudsman has passed guidelines on the use of terms such as "gratis". There are also guidelines of all Scandinavian Ombudsmen with regard to customer loyalty systems.[244]

Lotteries and promotional games based on chance are generally prohibited according to Chapter 2, Sec. 5 KSL if they are tied to the acquisition of goods. Exceptions apply the typical prize quizzes and puzzles in newspapers and magazines. Prize quizzes in which winning does not occur entirely or partially by chance seem to be permitted even if linked to the purchase of products.[245] In any event, the conditions must be given clear and specific (Chapter 2, Sec. 4 KSL and Sec. 3(3) SopMenL).

Liquidation sales and closing sales are not regulated by special laws. Their permissibility is determined on the basis of the provision on misleading indications and

239. Laki yksityisyyden suojasta televiestinnässa ja teletoiminnan (Act No. 1991/565).
240. For instance, the Market Court (MT 1997:20) has forbidden unrequested advertising on a cell phone.
241. Available on the Website (see fn. 204).
242. See Keßler/Wilhelmsson, 66.
243. See Bodewig/Henning-Bodewig, WRP 2000, 1348 f.
244. See Bodewig/Henning-Bodewig, WRP 2000, 1348.
245. Kessler/Wilhelmsson, p. 69; different Kur, GRUR Int. 1996, 38.

the general clause, which is also interpreted according to the guidelines of the Consumer Ombudsman on Special Sales.[246]

7. Disparagement and denigration

According to Sec. 2(2) SopMenL disparaging or (because of the manner of presentation or form) improper business assertions are prohibited. In spite of this express prohibition, in practice most suits regarding disparagement are made on the basis of the general clause. They often concern statements in comparisons of systems etc. or statements which blame another for illegal conduct.[247] Similarly, the exploitation of another's reputation is determined on the basis of the general clause.

8. Misappropriation, imitation

The SopMenL contains no special provisions on risk of confusion. The imitation of a distinctive business symbol, mark etc. can, however, be prohibited as improper conduct in commerce according to the general clause in Sec. 1 SopMenL.[248] The Market Court, for instance, considered it unfair to sell an imitation of the world renowned "Cabbage Patch Kids" which were distributed under the name "Kaalimaan Vekarat" (the literal translation in Finnish). The imitation of the get up of products ("look alike"—cases) is also often viewed a breach of Sec. 1 of the SopMenL.[249] If there is no danger of confusion, the exploitation of the goodwill and commercial achievements of another trader can at least in theory also be judged on the basis of Sec. 1 SopMenL (even though this seldom arises in practice).[250]

9. Breach of the law

The breach of provisions designed to protect consumers are deemed as unfair marketing behavior in the sense of the general clause of Sec. 2, Chapter 1 KSL.

10. Enforcement[251]

The central remedy of the SopMenL is the preliminary or permanent cease- and desist-order by the Market Court. Correcting measures and publication of judgments are also possible. Entitled to sue are traders. Claims for damages may be asserted under general tort law principles but require fault. Certain intentional or grossly negligent breaches are also subject to criminal penalties.

The enforcement of the KSL is the responsibility of the Consumer Ombudsman. He may file a suit with the Market Court but may also on his own behalf render a provisional or permanent ban. If the KSL as well as the SopMenL is applicable, according to Sec. 7a of the Market Court Act, the Consumer Ombudsman has priority.

246. See fn. 204.
247. See Kaulamo, No. 165; Kur, GRUR Int. 1996, 38.
248. MT 1985:2—"Cabbage Patch Kids"; see Kaulamo, No. 218.
249. See the decisions discussed by Kaulamo, No. 219. The SopMenL can be applied parallel to trade mark law.
250. See Kaulamo, No. 220.
251. See Kaulamo, No. 309.

As the Market Court is exclusively competent for both laws, the court will decide on the legality of specific market behavior in the same proceeding on suits filed by a competitor and the Consumer Ombudsman.

VIII. FRANCE

Selected Literature: Arn, *La publicité choquante*, 2001; Biolay, *Publicité comparative*, in: J.Cl., Conc., Cons., Fasc. 902 (2003) Blaise, *Droit des Affaires, Commerçants, Commerce, Distribution*, 1999; Calais-Auloy/Steinmetz, *Droit de la Consommation*, 6th ed., Dalloz 2003; Delbarre, in: J.Cl., Conc., Cons., Fasc.:300: *Ventes avec primes*; Dreier/v. Lewinski, *Frankreich*, in: Schricker (ed.), *Recht der Werbung in Europa*, 1995; Greffe/Greffe, *La publicité et la loi*, 9th ed. Paris 2000; Kamperman Sanders, *Unfair competition law*, 1997; Kraßer, *France*, in: Ulmer (ed.), *La répression de la concurrence déloyale dans les Etats members de la Communauté Economique Européen*, 1967; Lamy, *Droit économique—Concurrence, Distribution, Consommation*, 2004; Laurent, *La publicité comparative harmonisée, Contrats-Conc.-Cons.* 2001, p. 6; Lecourt, *Protection des consommateurs. Les loteries publicitaires. La déception a-t-elle un prix?*, JCP 1999, I, 155; Le Tourneau, Parasitisme—Concurrence parasitaire et agissements parasitaires, *J.-Cl., Conc., Cons., Fasc.* 227 (2002); Picot, *L'obligation de communication préalable à l'épreuve de la directive sur la publicité comparative*, Dalloz 2001, 914; Radeideh/Franck, *France*, in: Micklitz/Kessler, *Marketing Practices Regulation and Consumer Protection in the EC Member States and the US*, 2002, p. 75; Ranke, *Werberecht in Frankreich*, in: Schotthöfer (ed.), *Handbuch des Werberechts in den EU-Staaten*, 2nd ed. 1997, p. 245; Raymond, *Promotion des ventes par une action directe sur les prix*, J. Cl. Conc.-Cons. Fasc. 280 (2002); Serra, *Concurrence déloyale, Rép. Com. Dalloz*, No. 116; Serra, *Concurrence interdite et concurrence déloyale*, Dalloz 2003, 900 (Jurisprudence—Somm. commentés); Serra (ed.), *Concurrence déloyale*, Dalloz, Thèmes et commentaires, 2001; Stadelmann, *Die Entwicklung der kritisierenden vergleichenden Werbung in Deutschland und in Frankreich*, 1999; Thiébart, *France*, in: Campbell (ed.), *Unfair Trade Practices—The Comparative Law Yearbook of International Business*, 1996, p. 91; Varet, *Le cadre juridique du spam: état des lieux*, Communication Commerce électronique 2002, 14; Vogel, *Französiches Wettbewerbs- und Kartellrecht*, 2003.

1. Sources of law

Article 1382, 1383 Code Civil (CC); Art. L.121 et seq. Code de la Consommation (C.Cons.)

2. French unfair competition law in a nutshell

Although the unfair competition law of most continental European states was influenced by French doctrine, France itself has no coherent regulation against unfair trade practices.[252] Since the 19th century, however, case law has developed extensive civil

252. For the development and main features of French unfair competition law see (in English) Kamperman Sanders, p. 24; (in French) Kraßer, p. 1; Greffe/Greffe, p. 223; Serra, Rapport introductif, p. 1; (in German) Vogel, p. 32 and Dreier/v. Lewinski.

law protection against "concurrence déloyale"[253] on the basis of the general tort law clause of Art. 1382 CC. In addition to this, various laws, regulations and decrees have been put into effect that protect especially consumers against concurrence déloyale in a broader sense. They are predominantly criminal and administrative laws and can be found in the Code de la consommation. Overall, the protection against unfair competition, although sometimes difficult to access, is seen as efficient (and rather strict).

Article 1382 CC requires those who cause damages to others to give compensation. The tort of "concurrence déloyale", which was developed by the courts on this basis, in principle requires a competitive relationship between the parties, an incorrect behavior by the defendant ("faute"), damages ("prejucide") and causality between "faute" and damages ("lien de causalité").

In practice, however, the key element is almost always the "faute",[254] which is defined as violation of the "usages honnêtes du commerce". In the extensive case law, the following offenses were developed:[255]

- Defamation ("dénigrement")
- Causing of confusion ("confusion")
- Individual obstruction ("desorganisation")
- Parasitic exploitation of other parties' commercial achievements ("parasitisme")
- Misleading ("tromperie")

In addition to this "traditional" civil law approach there are multiple—mainly criminal and administrative—regulations that deal with advertising and marketing. As of 1993, they have been incorporated in the "Code de la Consommation" (C. Cons)[256]. In Title 1 ("Consumer Information") and Title 2 ("Commercial Practices"), the following are among the issues regulated:

- misleading advertising
- comparative advertising
- premiums/package deals
- lotteries
- pyramid schemes
- indications of geographic origin
- sales at a loss

The civil law protection against "concurrence déloyale" and the protections effected though the various regulations in the C.Cons. have different protective aims. Article 1382 CC provides for protection of the individual (competitor) who is injured

253. As to the difference between "concurrence déloyale" and "concurrence illicite"—acts of competition that violate legal provisions—see e.g. De Ferrier, in: Serra, Dalloz, p. 47.

254. The "faute" does not necessarily require intent; See Cour de cassation 11 March 2003 Sicabam/Tropic. The other requirements are handled rather flexibly. A competitive relationship is not always necessary (see under 8); damages are generally assumed to exist in cases of unfair competition and the courts often bypass the difficulties of establishing the exact damage by granting symbolic damages (see under 11).

255. The classification tends to vary somewhat, cf. Arn, p. 191. Roubier, *le droit de la propriété industrielle*, 1952, No. 110 distinguished between denigrement, imitation, desorganisation and parasitisme.

256. Despite the fact that this was not bound to any substantive alignment and overlaps still occur, the incorporation in the C.Cons. has made access much easier.

by a fault. This strictly individualistic approach is in certain aspects similar to that of the intellectual property laws which can be found in the "Code de la Propriété Intellectuelle".[257] The various regulations in the "Code de la Consommation", on the other hand, serve the public interest by protecting consumers, competitors, the general public and often small and midsize business against certain harmful business practices. A close relationship exists between these laws and other public policy laws, especially some regulations composed in the Code de commerce[258] which also includes the cartel law.[259] Finally, the Ordonnance No. 2001-741 is of importance; it transposed seven European Directives into French law.[260] Self-regulation is provided for through the "Bureau de la Vérification de Publicité" (BVP).[261]

In spite of this demarcation, certain interconnection exists between the regulations, decrees etc. of the C.Cons. on the one hand and Art. 1382 C.C. on the other hand, especially issues of procedure, such as the possibility of an "action civile" (see under 11).

3. Regulation of advertising

a. Misleading advertising

In principle, competitors can bring a civil law suit for misleading advertising on the basis of Art. 1382 CC. In practice, however, this occurs relatively seldom. Rather, civil claims are pursued by means of the "partie civil" in criminal suits under Art. L.121-1 C.Cons. (see under 11).

The main focus in the fight against misleading advertising today is clearly Art. L. 121-1 et seq. C.Cons.,[262] which provides for criminal sanctions. This statute has the following elements:

- It must concern an advertisement
- The advertisement must contain a false or misleading statement,
- The statement must refer to one of the enumerated elements,
- The advertiser must be at fault (which is in practice assumed).

257. As to French IP-Law see e.g. Chavanne/Burst, Droit de la Propriété Industrielle, 3rd. ed.1990; Schmidt-Salewski/Pierre, Le droit de la propriété industrielle, 2nd ed. 2001; Dreyfus/Thomas, Marques, Dessin et Modèles, Encyclopédie Delmas 2002.
258. E.g. price fixing ("prix imposes"), discriminatory practices and breach of contract ("rupture brutale des relations commerciales"), selective distribution systems, etc. The regulations in the Code de commerce are comprised of various laws, especially the former Ordonannce of 1.12.1986 and the former laws of 1.7.1996 and 15.5.2001.
259. Sec. L 420-443 Code de Commerce.
260. JCP G 2001, III, 20543. Among others, the Directives on comparative advertising, distance contracts and standard form contracts.
261. Greffe/Greffe, No. 26; Bonis, Gaz.Pal 1996. Members of the BVP can ask for a (voluntary) control of their advertisement; at the request of television broadcasters, the BVP submits TV-commercials to a (mandatory) pre-control.
262. An English translation of Article L.121-1 et seq.—the former Art. 44 Loi Royer—can be found at Tiébart, p. 98; an intensive discussion (in French) of all relevant decisions in Greffe/Greffe, No. 15 et seq. Suits regarding misleading advertising that borders on deceit can also be brought under other laws. Article 405 Code pénal, however, requires that false names are used or that deceitful mechanisms are employed; Art. L.113-1 C.Cons. is restricted to deceit in connection with contracts and is therefore only applicable for commercial statements that directly influence a contract.

The term "advertising" ("publicité"), which is not defined statutorily, is understood as every statement before the conclusion of a contract with the general goal of promoting sales.[263] The means of conveyance does not matter;[264] it can be oral, visual, and through any medium (even printed on napkins[265]). Indirect statements are also included. For example, an advertisement for a drink that did not contain orange juice but had the image of oranges and orange leaves in the background, was considered as misleading. The scope of application is (at least expressly) not limited to statements made to the end user. The statement must only be addressed to a larger group of people.

Article L.121-1 C.Cons. requires in principle a positive behavior. However, the omission of certain information ("half-truths") can lead to an overall deceptive impression.[266]

The statement must be either objectively incorrect or (alternatively) capable of misleading. In practice, the capability for misleading is always tested even if the untruth is undisputed. This is done in order to avoid the criminal pursuit of statements that are objectively incorrect but not really taken seriously, i.e. clear exaggerations ("publicité hyperbolique"). Case law on this is relatively liberal.[267]

Whether an advertisement in a concrete situations will be taken seriously and/or is misleading depends on the view of the target group. Case law on the issue especially takes into account the precise target group of the advertisement and the type of the advertised product.[268] The benchmark traditionally is the "bon père de famille", who is well informed and rather circumspect of advertisements.[269]

As the danger of misleading is generally determined by the court through its own knowledge without the assistance of public opinion research, questions such as the relevant rate of the deceived addressees or the impact of the misleading statement on their commercial behaviour are seldom expounded upon.[270] However, it is stressed

263. See Greffe/Greffe, No. 972; Cass.crim. 27.3.1996, BRDA No. 1996, No. 13, p. 15. It is not entirely clear whether members of the liberal professions are included in this definition; denied, for instance, for attorneys by Trib.corr. Lyon 9.4.1980, Gaz.Pal. 1980, 2. Jur. 526; see also *Dreier/v. Lewinski*, No. 45.
264. Neither is it decisive whether the statement is recognized as "publicité" by the public. Thus, an article that was written by the company but appeared to the public as a normal newspaper article was held to be advertising, see the cases citied at Greffe/Greffe, No. 976.
265. As to advertisements on labels see the decisions cited at Geffe/Greffe, No. 972, especially Cass.crim. 25.6.1984, D. 1985, p. 80 with note Fourgoux.
266. See for instance the French decision that led to the Nissan-decision of the ECJ (discussed in Chapter 3, IV.2).
267. For example, a television commercial that "demonstrated" the durability of a suitcase by having a bulldozer drive over it was allowed, although the suitcase could not actually have stood up to such treatment. Advertising for diet pills, hair growth items, etc. are often held to be harmless "publicité hyperbolique". See, e.g., Cass.crim. 21.4.1984, D. 1985, Jur. 105 with note Marguery; CA Paris 6.4.1998, Rs. Crim. 1999, p. 116 with note Giudicelli; Trib.corr. Paris 13.4.1983, Gaz.Pal. 1983, 1 Jur. 343 with note March; and the decisions cited at Greffe/Greffe, No. 917.
268. See, e.g., CA Bordeaux 29.4.1981, Gaz.Pal. 1981, Jur. 392 ("The purchase of contact lenses can not be compared to every day's grocery shopping . . .").
269. It is often emphasized that is it not for the courts "pour proteger les faibles d'esprit".; see, e.g., the decisions cited at Greffe/Greffe, No. 995 et seq. In some cases, however, it was also assumed that the model of a "bon père de famille" is unrealistic in modern business; for instance in CA Bourges 5.10.1998, Gaz.Pal. 1999 (Greffe/Greffe, No. 1004). Such decisions, however, generally concern a consumer group that is in need of particular protection or a product that the consumer views as important for his health, safety, or the environment.
270. But see the "Nissan"—decision of the ECJ Chapter 3, III.3.

frequently that disclaimers in small print do not always cancel out a misleading overall impression and that an advertisement may be misleading based on eye-catching statements.[271]

The misleading statement must concern one of the reference points enumerated in Art. L.121-1 C.Cons. Although this list is exhaustive, the terms are interpreted so broadly that all cases of false statements are included. In practice, the main issue is often deception as to product characteristics. The misleading must be "substantial", i.e. in the view of the targeted consumer, the characteristic in question must have some importance.[272] Statements as to the environmental friendliness of products fall under product characteristics.[273] Case law as to the composition ("composition") and origin ("espèce et origine") is extensive too. The term "origin" is interpreted broadly and includes operational origin (ostensible factory outlets, etc.[274]) commercial and geographical origin.[275]

A further emphasis is on advertising with the price, such as with loss-leader pricing.[276] Jurisprudence is especially strict when the consumer is lead to believe that a price advantage exists that doesn't actually exist,[277] or when the terms upon which a consumer can receive the lower price are not clearly und unambiguously laid out.[278]

As a criminal provision, Art. L.121-5(1) C.Cons. presupposes fault, e.g. at least negligence. In practice, however, fault is assumed and the advertiser can seldom provide the necessary exculpatory evidence.[279]

The proper defendant is the "annonceur" (Art. L.121-5(1) C.Cons.). This means not only the advertiser but also the advertising agency and in particular cases even the franchise owner or an agent of the company.[280]

271. For example, the name "contonelle" for paper towels was considered misleading despite the disclaimer in small print that the item was not actually made of cotton. Trib.com. Rouen, Gaz.Pal. 1997, 1; cited at Greffe/Greffe, No. 1038, see also fn. 278.
272. According to a decision of the Cour de cassation from 1996 (discussed at Greffe/Greffe, No. 105) replacing natural ingredients ("pin des landes") with chemical scents in a cleaning agent is not a "qualité substantielle", since the general public does not consider such aspects when purchasing such a product.
273. A product must not be absolutely environmentally friendly (which is hardly ever the case) but rather must be considerably more so than comparative products.
274. See the decisions cited at Greffe/Greffe, No. 1071 et seq. For example, the labelling of a sweater with 40-70% wool as "Shetland" was held to be misleading.
275. Indications of origin are also protected through Art. L.115-1 et seq. und L.217-6 et seq. C.Cons. without there being a clear demarcation between the respective provisions.
276. Raymond, J. Cl. Conc., Cons., Fasc. 900, No. 66.
277. See the cases cited at Greffe/Greffe, No. 1094.
278. For example, it is misleading to advertise "free credits" without clearly disclosing that they are only awarded once a certain sum is reached. TGI Lyon 26.4.1984, Gaz. Pal. 1984, 1, Somm. 116; see also Trib.corr. Paris 22.11.1984, Gaz.Pal. 1985, 1, p. 42 with note Marchi; for further decisions Greffe/Greffe, No. 1275.
279. The advertiser must do "everything necessary" to prove the truth of his claim, and is responsible also for the actions of certain third parties, such as his advertising agency. Exculpatory evidence is sometimes recognized in cases of special offers where the difficulties of delivery were unforeseeable, or when the BVP (see fn. 261) has given its preliminary approval; see Raymond, No. 66; Greffe/Greffe, No. 37.
280. If the criminally liable defendant is a legal person, the sanctions are aimed at the CEO ("dirigeant"), that is, the person who is actually responsible for the advertisement in question. Other people can be liable under the general provisions of the Code penal (Art. 60-3) as a participant, instigator and accessory.

b. Comparative advertising

In 1992, the French legislature began regulating comparative advertising, and later incorporated these regulations, without changes, into the Code de la Consommation. A formal transposition and adaptation of Directive 97/55/EC did not occur until August 2001.[281] The main basis for comparative advertisement can today be found in Article L. 121-8 et seq. C.Cons. However, it must be kept in mind that comparative advertising is traditionally also considered a subcategory of disparagement and thus represents "concurrence déloyale" in the sense of Art. 1382 CC.[282] Both regulations are intertwined insofar, as a practice that is allowed under Art. 121-8 C.Cons. cannot be forbidden under Art. 1382 CC.

The scope of application of Art. L.121-8 C.Cons. is not restricted to consumers but includes comparative advertising in "B2B" relationships as well.[283] After the adoption of the Directive 97/55/EC, the comparison may occur also through reference to a third party's test results, but there are still some restrictions for comparisons on the packaging, on receipts, on train tickets, methods of payment, or tickets for events occurring in public areas (Art. 121-11 C.Cons.).[284]

In order to be allowed, comparative advertising must be "fair, correct and not misleading or disparaging". Since misleading comparisons are already prohibited under Art. L.121-1 C.Cons. (see above 2), the focus is generally on the notion of "loyalité". A "loyal" comparison is above all a comparison that is not disparaging.[285] Forbidden is thus every comparison that criticizes beyond what is absolutely necessary, as well as a comparision that has a harsh or aggressive tone, devalues, mocks or is in another form harmful. However, disparagement cannot be assumed simply because the advertiser has picked out one product of many products; there is no duty to compare all items or all wares (no general requirement of completeness).

According to Art. L.121-9 C.Cons., a comparison may not be made for the primary purpose of exploiting the reputation of the band compared ("nororiété"). When making comparisons to renowned brand names, exploitation cannot be presumed.[286]

The comparison must also be objective and refer to material, significant and verifiable characteristics. A comparison of general beliefs or value statements is thus not sufficient even when this is done through a survey or examination (by the advertiser

281. Through the Ordonnnance of 23.8.2001. With the transposition of Directive 97/55/EC, Art. L. 121-8 to 14 C.Cons. were changed or adapted; certain articles were completely taken out, such as the duty to inform the competitor of the comparison (the former Art. L.121-12); see Laurent, Contracts-Conc.-Cons 2001, p. 6; Wilhem/Dubarry, Revue Lamy Droit des Affaires 2002. As to the legal situation till 2001 see Greffe/Greffe, No. 731 and the references to judicial practice and literature; as to the current situation Biolay. J.Cl. Concurr, Cons. Fasc. 902 and Cass. 21.3.2001, Gaz. Pal. 2001, Somm. 2089.
282. This is emphasized through Art. L.121-14 C.Cons, which explicitly refers to Art. 1382 CC.
283. This was confirmed several times by the courts; see for instance, CA Versailles 11.4.2000, Gaz.Pal. 2000, 2, Somm. 273. As to the scope of application in general see Biolay, No. 15-20 und Greffe/Greffe, No. 742.
284. See CA Aix-en-Provence 21.12.2001, Contrats-Conc.-Cons. 2002, No. 83.
285. Since 2001, disparagement is explicitly named in Art. L.121-9(2). In the past, most prohibitions were based on the aspect of disparagement; see the decisions cited at Greffe/Greffe, No. 777; furthermore Biolay, No. 45.
286. A motion to change the law to allow only comparisons of brands with about the same level of reputation was rejected in 1990.

or a third party).[287] According to Art. L-121-12 C.Cons., the advertiser bears the burden of proving the truth of factual assertions.[288] The characteristics being compared must be material ("essentielle"), relevant ("significative"), permanent and inherent in the product.[289] Finally, the comparison must refer to items that are actually available on the market and which are of the same nature ("de meme nature"); this requires at least the possibility of substitution.

Originally, the regulations regarding price comparisons in Art. L.121-8 C.Cons. required identity of the compared products. This requirement was given up in 2001 because of a possible conflict with the Directive 97/55/EC. Then as now, however, special attention to the requirement of "fairness" is given in price comparisons. It is, for instance, considered "unfair" to compare prices when no comparable sales conditions exist, especially when sales methods are different.[290] Also, the timeframe for a quoted price must be clearly and unmistakably given.

The earlier requirement found in Art. L.121-12(2) C.Cons. of notification of the intended comparison to the affected competitor has been omitted in the new 2001 regulations.[291]

Article L.121-8 et seq. C.Cons. is only applicable if the competitor is at least identifiable.[292] A comparison as to systems and procedures or comparison of kinds of wares, that does not identify an individual business is dealt with under Art. 1382 CC (see under 6).

An illegal comparative advertising, according to Art. L.121-14, triggers primarily criminal sanctions according to the Code penal. Competitors can, however, also file civil suits under Art. 1382 CC (see under 2).

c. Concealed advertising

Whether disguised advertising falls under the notion of misleading is doubtful.[293] According to Art. 10(2) of the press law from 1986, content with definite advertising character must be marked as "publicité" or "communiqué" if it can be mistaken for an editorial article. Surreptitious advertising on television is explicitly prohibited (see under 3e).[294]

287. Advertising slogans such as "70% of all consumers questioned prefer product x over product y" are thus problematic. The car manufacturer Renault was not allowed to advertise as follows: "Renault sells twice as many cars in Germany as VW in France". TGI Paris Réf. 23.9.1991, Gaz.Pal. 1991, 2. Jurisprudence 576.
288. With the 2001 adaption to the EC Directive, the advertiser must now prove the accuracy of his statements "within a short period of time".
289. According to the parliamentary history, comparisons that are based on aspects that do not play a role in normal use should be prevented.
290. A price comparison between a large supermarket and small grocery stores was thus forbidden. How far further conditions of sales (terms of payment, policy of refunds or exchanges, customer service, etc.) must be comparable, has not been decided yet.
291. Laurent, p. 8 and Picod; see also CA Paris 18.1.2002, D. 2002 AJ, p. 1345 (no retrospective effect of the new Art. L.121-12 C.Cons.).
292. The identification can occur through any indirect method (without naming the competitor or its brand name), for example when only one competitor exists on the market or when the slogan of the competitor is used. CA Versailles 18.2.1999, JCP E 1999, No. 44, 1753; Cass. 27.3.2001, Gaz.Pal. Nov. 2001, p. 57.
293. The aspect of disguise is not included in the list of reference points in Art. L-121-1 C.Cons.
294. Regarding the internet, s. under 3e.

d. Other advertising regulations

As a result of the rather inflexible interpretation of "concurrence déloyale" (see the "case groups" of Art. 1382 CC, discussed under 2) and the criminal, non-analogy permitting character of the regulations in the C. Cons., new forms of advertising are hard to bring suit against. This applies, for instance, for advertisements which are intrusive, harassing, offensive, shocking[295] or gender discriminating, for advertising, combined with "social sponsoring" or advertising directed towards children, etc. The monitoring of these forms of adverting is mainly left to self-regulation.

Law No. 94/665 from 8 April 1994 requires that the French language be used in advertising.[296] Exceptions do exist, such as for the names of typical products and specialties or for registered trademarks that are used in foreign expressions. Apart from this, the regulation is rather rigid.

e. Regulations for specific media and products

French law contains several product-specific advertising regulations.[297] Advertising on television is regulated by law No. 86/1067 from 30 September 1986 in its 1998 version.[298] For example, TV-advertising for alcoholic beverages with more than 1.2% alcohol content is prohibited. According to the ECJ the so-called "Loi Evin" that regulates advertising for alcohol is not against Art. 49 EC even though it leads to an obstacle of the free movement of services.[299] As for the press, the law of 1986 applies;[300] as to the Internet, see under.

4. Direct marketing

According to Art. L. 121-21-33 C.Cons., door-to-door sales are only restricted for certain products (for example, health products).[301] The delivery of unrequested goods[302] is prohibited per Art. L. 122-2 C.Cons, if the impression of any kind of obligation is given. Direct advertising using letters, catalogues and leaflets is permitted, according to Art. L. 121-21 C.Cons., if the necessary trade-specific disclosures are made. The executive decree No. 91-638 from 9 July 1991, however, prohibits sending any kind of advertising material to consumers that have been on the so-called "Liste Safran" for more than 2 months.

295. See Arn, p. 225 et seq.
296. See Radeideh/Franck, p. 93.
297. See for instance Greffe/Greffe, No. 1470 et seq.
298. See Radeideh/Franck, p. 93; Biolay, J.Cl. Cons., Cons., Droit de la concurrence en matière audiovisuelle, Fasc. 140 (2002). Teleshopping decree No. 92-99 of 1.9.1992, amended through decree No. 95-477 of 25.1.1995.
299. See the decisions "Baccardi" and "Loi Evin" of the ECJ (discussed in Chapter 3, III, 2).
300. Dreier/v. Lewinski, No. 211.
301. The Cour de cassation defines the term door-to-door sales broadly: Cass. 9.7.2003. Furthermore, contract-specific regulations need to be followed. According to Art. L.122-8 et seq., contracts for payments in installments are generally prohibited if the inexperience of consumers is thereby exploited; see Radeideh/Franck, p. 84.
302. This also includes the delivery of tickets (in conjunction with invoices), already filled-out order forms etc. Product samples or vouchers to obtain goods, however, are permitted.

As of 2001, Art. L.121-20-5 C.Cons.[303] prohibits telephone advertising using automated calling systems and fax advertising without the prior consent of the consumer ("opt-in"). In all other cases, the "opt-out" solution applies. The recommendations of the self regulation (BVP) are more extensive, they require a "reasonable interest" of the trader. In any case, the commercial purpose must be clearly stated, and children may not be addressed. The situation regarding unrequested internet advertising ("spamming") is currently unclear;[304] BVP guidelines exist and an "Internet law" is expected.[305]

Pyramid schemes are prohibited by law in accordance to Art. L.122-6 C.Cons.[306]

5. Sales promotion

Rebates to consumers are in general permitted, but may not lead to a sale below costs (Art. L. 442-1-8 C.Cons) or to a deception (see above, under 3a).[307] Further regulations regarding price indications can be found in Art. L. 113-1, Art. L.121-35 and Art. L. 142-2 C.Cons, supplemented by edict No. 77-105/P from 2 September 1997 (announcement of price reductions). Rebates to dealers are measured by the general antitrust law prohibition of discrimination.

Premiums to consumers are generally prohibited[308] when they have more than just an insignificant value ("faible valeur").[309] The prohibition of premiums in Art. L. 121-35 C.Cons is further supplemented by Art. 23-25 of the Decree No. 86-309 from 29 December 1986. Additional prohibitions exist for pharmaceutical products, tobacco products and alcohol.

The regulation of premiums applies only if there is an incidental relation between the purchased item and the premium.[310] Promotional gifts that are free of any charge and are not linked to a purchase are permitted.[311] However, it must be kept in mind that all exceptions to the prohibition of premiums are interpreted restrictively.[312]

303. The EC-Directive on Distance Contracts, discussed in Chapter 3.II., was transposed almost word forward.
304. See Varet, Communication-Commerce électronique 2002, p. 14.
305. This text, known as LEN ("Confiance dans l'economie numerique") and representing the first step of the program "RESO 2007", contains among other things measures against cyber crime and unsolicited advertisement; see <www.assemblee-nat.fr>. Till the enactment the existing general regulations are applicable to advertising on the internet. CA Rennes 31.3.2000, RJDA 2000, Nr. 3, Nr. 378; especially concerning the practice of spamming" TGI Paris, réf. v. 15.1.2002, Dictionnaire permanent du droit des affaires, Bull. Nr. 582, p. 7542; Lamy Droit économique, 2004, No. 2703. See also Verbiest, *La Protection juridique du Cyber consommateur, Publicité*, Contrats et contentieux, 2002.
306. See Desurvire, *Controverse autour des réseaux de vente multi-niveaux*, Contrats-Conc.-Cons. Juin 1995, 6.
307. See Raymond, *Promotion des ventes par une action directe sur les prix*, J. Cl., Conc., Cons. Fasc. 280 ff.
308. See Raymond, Fasc. 281 and Delbarre, Fasc. 300.
309. This is strictly interpreted by the jurisdiction, see for instance Cass. 11.3.2003, cited in J.Cl. Fasc. 281.
310. Which also exists if the "free gift" imposes a psychological pressure to buy, CA Paris 6.6.1990, JCP 1990, ed. E, I. 20228 ("free" baguettes in a supermarket).
311. Practices like "prime autopayante" or the "couponage croisé", in which granting advantages occurs through a different person than the one that closes the main deal, seem to be permitted. Delbarre, No. 24 et seq.
312. In accordance with Art. L. 121-35 C.Cons. exceptions exist for identical goods and services (i.e. offers such as "three for the price of two"), low-value objects, "loyalty cards" (if repeated purchases qualify for larger gifts), samples with advertisements on them, as well as accessories and customer

According to Art. 1 of the law of 21 May 1836 regarding lotteries in its 1992 version, lotteries that are not approved by the state are prohibited as a violation of criminal law.[313] Included in this are all types of events in which participants, in return for payment ("participation onereuse") have a chance of winning a prize based on luck ("voie du sort"). Sweepstakes that require a participant to answer questions that are extremely simple for the average person are also considered to depend on chance.[314]

On the other hand, the so-called "loterie publicitaire", in which all participants win (Art. L. 121-36 C.Cons) are permitted,[315] as are lotteries where the prize is already determined or where it is clearly stated that participation requires no financial contribution.[316] Linking participation with the purchase of goods or services is generally regarded as a "financial contributions".[317] According to L.121-36 § 2 C.Cons, permissible sweepstakes (for example in mail-order business) must be clearly differentiated from a purchase order, may not be mistakable for official money, and the prize that can be won must be clearly described (including the value of the prize).

Promotional games based on skill are permitted even when linked to a sales.[318]

6. Disparagement

Protection against disparagement ("dénigrement") is granted to competitors under Art. 1382 CC (see above, 2).[319] Any statement, true or false, will suffice if it harms the commercial reputation of a competitor, its company or its product. For truthful statements, however, the defaming character of the advertisement must be shown by additional circumstances such as the unnecessary aggressive choice of words or a mocking tone. Advertising such as "A biscuit a day is more harmful than passive smoking",[320] package labels like "Buy a quality product cheaper" or the (implicit) claim that other products are obsolete[321] are considered collective disparagement ("dénigrement collectif"). As to disparagement in comparative advertising see under 3b.

services, parking and parking fee reimbursements. Raymond, Fasc. 281, No. 20 et seq.; Biolay, Fasc. 907, No. 95 et seq.; Bodewig/Henning-Bodewig, WRP 2000, 1348.

313. See Lecourt, JCP 1999, I, p. 155; Greffe/Greffe, No. 1211 et seq.; Thiébart, p. 97; Radeideh/Franck, p. 88.
314. See Raymond, Fasc. 281, No. 20 et seq.; Biolay, Fas. 907, No. 95 et seq.
315. See the decision cited at Biolay, Fasc. 907, No. 114 et seq.; furthermore J.O. 3012.1986, p. 15775.
316. Lecourt, JCP 1999, I, 155; Greffe/Greffe, No. 1211 ff., Thiebart, p. 97; Radeideh/Franck, p. 88.
317. For instance, a sales promotion at a grocery store for mineral water where random customers that had either three bottles of Evian at the cashier or could show three labels of Evian bottles (which were available for free inside the store) received an amount of money was prohibited. The decision is cited at Greffe/Greffe, No. 1217. See also CA Paris 176.11.1999, BRDA 2000, No. 3, 10 and Radeideh/Franck, p. 88. Normal telephone fees and the costs of a stamp, however, do not count as an illegal linking.
318. See Biolay, Fasc. 907, No. 135.
319. Vogel, p. 47; Malaurie-Vigual, Dénigrement, J.Cl. Conc., Cons. Fasc. 210 (1996), No. 13.
320. CA Paris 24.9.1996, Dalloz Affaires, 1996, 1189; see also CA Bordeaux 3.7.1991, Gaz.Pal. 1971, 2, 398 and TGI Paris réf, 16.6.1987, JCPed. G, II, 20900 with note Viandier (collective dénigrement of small grocery stores through big department chains.).
321. CA Paris 21.6.1984, Gaz.Pal. 1985, 2, Somm. 296.

7. Danger of confusion

Risk of confusion[322] is considered as one of the traditional case groups of "concurrence déloyale" (see above, 2). It requires that the target group could mistake the products or services in question for that of a competitor's. If this happens by using similar or identical marks, a delineation between risk of confusion and trademark infringement becomes necessary.[323] The difference is usually seen in the fact that the concurrence déloyale claim requires no infringement of a property right ("contrefaçon") but rather an action that violates the "usages honnêtes in commerce".[324]

8. Misappropriation, imitation

Protection against exploitation of reputation, also one of the case groups of "concurrence déloyale" (see above, 2) often plays a role in protection against illegal comparative advertising (see above, 3b). It is, however, also of relevance in cases of imitation, comparisons of systems or procedures, and geographical indications of origin.[325]

Based on Art. 1382 C.C., a suit can always be brought against imitation of another party's products and services which involves a danger of confusion.[326] That requires the imitated products or services to be sufficiently original.[327] The imitation of functional characteristics is in most cases not objectionable.

Even without danger of confusion, the exploitation of another parties' commercial achievements can be prohibited as "concurrence parasitaire" if there is an exploitation of reputation. Apart from confusion or exploitation of reputation, imitations can be prohibited if a sufficiently original product which is considered an innovation or was created with significant investments is exploited to save on one's own expenditures.[328] The suit against parasitic competition does not necessarily require a direct competitive relationship.[329]

Suits regarding exploitation of another parties' achievements often contain elements of "confusion" as well as "parasitisme" and obstruction("desorganisation").[330]

322. See Thiébart, p. 106 f.; Vogel, p. 54.
323. See Blaise, No. 682 f.; Passa, Domaine de l'action en concurrence déloyale, in: J.C.conc., Cons. Fasc. 240, No. 32 (1998); Mingam/Vilmart/Sigrist, *Le droit de la concurrence déloyale peut-il compléter on se substituer á la protection specifique conférée á la propriété intellectuelle?* Report for the Ligne Internationale du Droit de la Concurrence, Ghent, 2005.
324. A suit under "concurrence déloyale" can thus be brought in if no absolute right exists, as long as it concerns a sufficiently distinctive service or characteristic.
325. See the decision cited in footnote 290, 329; further Vogel, p. 63.
326. See Kraßer, p. 147 ff.; Serra, Rep. Dalloz, 329 114; Kamperman Sanders, p. 24.
327. Cass.com. 15.6.1983, Bull.civ. IV Nr. 174; Cass. 22.2003: Buydens, Produktpiraterie und unlauterer Wettbewerb, GRUR Int. 1995, 14. As to the imitation of get-up, see CA Versailles 8.11.2001, discussed at Dorandeu, in: Serra, Dalloz 2003, p. 1032.
328. The concept of "concurrence parasitaire" was—despite criticism in the legal literature—explicitly confirmed by the Cour de cassation. 30.1.2001, D 2001 Jur. 1939 with note Le Tourneau. Cf. further Mingam Vilmart/Sigrist (fn. 323).
329. See the case of a French flower shop that was using the advertising slogan of the Dutch department for milk products—"La Hollande, l'autre pays du fromage"—in a modified form—"La Côte d'Azur, l'autre pays de la tulipe". Cass. 30.1.1996, Dalloz 1997, Jur. p. 232 with note Serra
330. For example, if a commercial logo of a computer program is merged into the own sources and thus leads to opening up the absorber's website; see CA Paris 3.4.1998, Dalloz 1999, Somm. S. 95 with note Izorda; CA Paris 13.3.2002, discussed by Auguet, in: Serra, Concurrence interdite, Dalloz 2003, p. 1030.

9. Impediment of competitors

Multiple acts that can be summarized as "impediment" fall into the category of "désorganisation",[331] one of the traditional case groups of "concurrence déloyale" under Art. 1382 CC. Poaching of employees ("débauchage") in general is permitted, as long as there is no involvement in a breach of contract.[332] The same applies to blocking sales ("détournement de clientèle"), as long as no "special circumstances"[333] apply. Selective distribution systems[334] are regulated by the Code de commerce; Parallel imports in general are permitted.[335]

The breach of an agreement to keep know-how, company and business secrets confidential can likewise be considered as "concurrence déloyale".[336] Because Art. 1382 CC in principle requires a competitive relationship (see above, 2), an action against the betraying employee can generally only be based on contract law. According to Article L 152-7 Code du travail, the violation of a restraint on competition (even post-contract) is considered a crime.[337]

10. Breach of law

The violation of any law can be a "faute" in terms of Art. 1382 CC (and thus "concurrence déloyale"), if the violation is at the same time against the principle of the "usages honnêtes in commerce".

11. Enforcement

The French system to combat unfair competition is distinguished by a confusing multiplicity of partially intersecting options for sanctions.[338]

Affected competitors and trade associations can claim the civil law "action en concurrence déloyale" based on Art. 1382 CC (see above, 2). Claims for compensation,

331. Blaise, No. 684.; Thiébart, p. 110; Vogel, p. 80.
332. In regards to the possible liability of a third party for the breach of an employment-contract related prohibition of competition, French case law is becoming stricter. The obligations of the employer have been tightened; an employer now is not only obliged to require whether such a prohibition exists, but also must check the behavior of its employees. It can be unfair competition to poach all employees of a competitor at once (not, however, to employ a competitor's work force that has already been terminated). CA Versailles 29.6.2000, Dalloz 2001, Jurisprudence 134 with note Picod; as to "tierce complicieté" Cass. 18.12.2001, discussed by Picod, in: Serra, Concurrence interdite, Dalloz 2003, Nr. 15, 1029. CA Paris 3.4.2002, D.1031 with note Robin.
333. As to the so-called "couponage éléctronique", whereby an automated card reader at the cashier shows cheaper competitor's products and prints out vouchers for the customer, Cass.18.11.1997, JCP 1998, 10026 with note Gautier; furthermore Blaise, No. 686 ff.
334. See Cass. 25.4.2001, D.2001 Jur. 1946 with note Chevrier
335. Although French courts acknowledge parallel imports they also emphasize the principle of fair competition; see the four decisions of the Cour de Cassation of 27.10.1992, Dalloz 1992, Jur., p. 404 with note v. Bénebent; furthermore Cass. 11.3.1994, Dalloz 1995, Somm. p. 211. As to parallel imports in general see also Dutoit, Concurrence déloyale et droit comparé, in: Serra, p. 68.
336. The company Chantelle was awarded a compensation of 75.000.000 Million Francs because of a violation of its "savoir faire" by a former employee, see CA Paris 27.9.2000, Dalloz 2001, Jurisprudence 1309 with note Auguet.
337. Cass. 12.6.1974, Annales de la Prop. Indus. 1975, p. 98.
338. See Thiébart, p. 119 ff.; Vogel, p. 35.

forbearance and removal can be asserted at the Tribunal de commerce.[339] The claim for damages is—because of the difficulty of estimation the actual damage—often granted in the form of a symbolic compensation of one Franc. Interim legal protection can be claimed according to Art. 809 in conjunction with Art. 873 of the New Code of Civil Procedure if there is a threat of immediate damages and the violation of the law is obvious.

The regulations in the "Code de la Consommation" are sanctioned by criminal and administrative law, but the courts may also render injunctions or corrective statements or in some cases even compensation. Normally, a State Agency ("Direction General de la Concurrence et de la Repression des Frauds") conducts the investigation, which is in practice often triggered by tips given by a third party. If there is a justified suspicion of a violation of the law, the agency passes the case on to the state prosecutor. The affected competitor, individual consumers and consumer groups[340] can assert claims by means of an adhesive procedure ("partie civile") and thereby also start the criminal proceedings.[341]

IX. GERMANY

Selected Literature: Baumbach/Hefermehl, edited by Köhler and Bornkamm, *Wettbewerbsrecht*, 23rd ed. 2004; Beater, *Unlauterer Wettbewerb*, 2002; Berlit, *Wettbewerbsrecht*, 5th ed. 2004; Berlit, *Das neue Gesetz gegen den unlauteren Wettbewerb: von den guten Sitten zum unlauteren Verfälschen*, WRP 2003, 563; Bornkamm, *Markenrecht und wettbewerbsrechtlicher Kennzeichenschutz*, GRUR 2005, 97; Fezer (ed.), *Kommentar zum UWG*, 2004; Eckey/Klippel/Kotthoff/Meckel/Plaß, *Heidelberger Kommentar zum Wettbewerbsrecht*, 2nd ed. 2005; Emmerich, *Unlauterer Wettbewerb*, 7th ed. 2004; Harte-Bavendamm/Henning-Bodewig (ed.) *UWG*, 2004; Herrmann, *Die Erheblichkeitsschwelle in § 3 UWG*, GRUR 2004, 94; Henning-Bodewig, *UWG-Reform und Richtlinienvorschlag, GRUR Int.* 2004, 183; Henning-Bodewig, *A New Act Against Unfair Competition in Germany*, 36 11C 421 (2005); Henning-Bodewig/Schricker, *New Initatives for the Harmonisation of Unfair Competition Law in Europe*, 24 EIPR 271 (2002); Gloy/Loschelder, *Handbuch des Wettbewerbsrechts*, 3rd ed. 2005; Keßler/Micklitz, *Reform des Lauterkeitsrechts*, 2003; Köhler, *Das neue UWG*, NJW 2004, 2121; Köhler, *Zur Konkurrenz lauterkeitsrechtlicher und kartellrechtlicher Normen*, WRP 2005, 645; Köhler, *Die "Bagatellklausel" in § 3 UWG*, GRUR 2005, 1; Ohly, *Das neue UWG. Mehr Freiheit für den Wettbewerb?*, GRUR 2004, 889; Ohly/Spence, The Law of Comparative Advertising. *Directive 97/55/EC in the United Kingdom and Germany*, 2000; Lettl, *Der Schutz der Verbraucher nach der UWG-Reform*, WRP 2004, 449; Lettl, *Das*

339. The jurisdiction can also follow the "qualité" of the parties and the kind of the suit. For example, the Tribunaux de grande instance have exclusive jurisdiction if parallel to the "action en concurrence déloyale" an infringement of industrial property rights is claimed.
340. In general, recognized consumer groups can not only claim the direct or indirect damages that were caused to the collective interest of the consumers, but also their own damages; this can lead to a confiscation of profit. They can also request the forbearance and a cease- and-desist-order of any act that illegally violates the interests of consumers.
341. However, switching between civil law suits at will is not permitted. Once a public criminal claim is brought to court, an attached civil suit is put on hold until a decision is made by the criminal court. The civil court is bound to the relevant findings of facts by the criminal court; see Thiébart, p. 119 ff.

neue UWG, 2004; Omsels, *Kritische Anmerkung zur Bestimmung der Irreführungsgefahr*, GRUR 2005, 548; Sack, *Die Haftung für unbegründete Schutzrechtsverwarnungen*, WRP 2005, 252; Sack, *Folgeverträge unlauteren Wettbewerbs*, GRUR 2004, 625; Sack; *Gesetzeswidrige Wettbewerbshandlungen nach der UWG-Novelle*, WRP 2004, 1307; Sack, *Personen- und unternehmensbezogene Werbehinweise auf Mitbewerber als vergleichende Werbung nach § 6 UWG*, WRP 2004, 817; Sack, *Die relevante Irreführung im Wettbewerbsrecht*, WRP 2004, 521; Scherer, *Abschied vom psychologischen Kaufzwang*, WRP 2005, 672; Schünemann, *"Unlauterkeit" in den Generalklauseln und Interessenabwägung nach neuem UWG*, WRP 2004, 925; Sosnitza, *German Law of Unfair Competition*: Toward Liberal Standards, 36 11C 525 (2005); Steinbeck, *Übertriebenes Anlocken, psychischer Kaufzwang etc., GRUR Int.* 2005, 540; Steingass/Tework, *Stellung und Reichweite des Transparenzangebots im neuen UWG*, WRP 2005, 676; Teplitzky, *Wettbewerbsrechtliche Ansprüche und Verfahren*, 8th ed. 2002; Wagner/Ruess, *Neues zur wettbewerbsrechtlichen Beurteilung sog. Kopplungsangebote*, WRP 2005, 24; Wimmer-Leonhard, *UWG-Reform und Gewinnabschöpfungsanspruch*, GRUR 2004, 12.

1. Sources of law

Gesetz gegen den unlauteren Wettbewerb (Act against Unfair Competition) of 3 July 2004 (UWG).

2. German unfair competition law in a nutshell

The primary basis for the German unfair competition law is the "Act against Unfair Competition" of 3 July 2004 ("Gesetz gegen den unlauteren Wettbewerb" = UWG) which entered into effect on 8 July 2004.[342] Just as the previous regulation (UWG of 1909), the new law provides a coherent, uniform regulation of all unfair competitive practices in the interest of consumers and competitors. It is almost exclusively enforced through civil law remedies with the decisions of the courts playing a major role in defining the legal rules.[343]

For a long time, German unfair competition law was considered to be extremely strict.[344] During the last 10 years, however, jurisprudence and legal literature have become increasingly liberal, and in 2001 the German legislature repealed all regulations on rebates, premiums etc. The UWG of 2004 continues this liberalisation, while remaining an important area of German economic law.[345] The high number of suits mainly by competitors and their associations[346] must be seen in view of the background

342. BGBl. (Federal Gazette) 2004, p. 1414; GRUR 2004, 660; the "Referentenentwurf" including an Explanatory Memorandum is published in GRUR 2003, 298.
343. An overview can be found in German in Henning-Bodewig, GRUR 2004, 713 and Köhler, NJW 2004, 2121; in English in: Henning-Bodewig, 36 IIC 421 (2005).
344. For details of the history of unfair competition law in Germany; see Schricker, IIC 77 (1973) Henning-Bodewig (fn. 343).
345. As regards the reasons for the new Act, see in detail Keller, in: Harte-Bavendamm/Henning-Bodewig (ed.), Einl. A and the literature cited in fn. 343.
346. Considerable de facto regulatory activity is carried out by the "Center for Competition" ("Wettbewerbszentrale"), an association of a great number of companies. The Center, frequently at the request of third parties, issues warnings against infringements of unfair competition law which in most cases settle the issue and (as an association entitled to file an action) brings an action for an interlocutory injunction if agreement is not reached.

that these are predominantly claims for injunctions in preliminary proceedings, which settle most disputes in a fast and relatively inexpensive way.[347] Self-regulation does exist but plays no major role in unfair competition law.[348]

The UWG of 2004 is construed similar to the "modern" unfair competition laws of other European states.[349] It is headed by a clause stating the purpose of the Act (Sec. 1), followed by a catalogue of definitions (Sec. 2) and a general clause (Sec. 3) forbidding all "unfair activities for the purpose of competition". The general clause is explained through eleven examples of commercial behaviour that are seen as particularly unfair (Sec. 4), and three specific causes of action: misleading advertising (Sec. 5), comparative advertising (Sec. 6) and intrusive, harassing advertising (Sec. 7). The legal consequence of unfair competitive practices (injunctive relief, removal, damages and confiscation of profits) as well as the right of action are regulated in Sec. 8-10 UWG; the rules on procedure (including the so-called "warning procedure") can be found in Sec. 12-15 UWG. Criminal sanctions for certain forms of unfair competition (deceptive advertising, betrayal, know how etc.) are regulated by Sec. 16-19 UWG.

Section 1 UWG deals with the purpose of protection. Similar to Directive 84/450/EEC, the UWG of 2004 serves a threefold objective: the protection of the competitor (as defined in Sec. 2 No. 3 UWG), the consumer[350] and of the general public.[351] The protected interests of the general public are, however, restricted to the interest in well-functioning competition; aspects as consumer health in general, the protection of the environment or against discrimination are not subject matter of the UWG.[352]

The scope of application is restricted to activities for the purpose of competition. Pursuant to Sec. 2 No. 1 UWG, which is construed similar to Sec. 1 of the Directive 84/450/EEC, these are all activities with the goal of promoting the sale (or the procurement) of goods or services for the benefit of one's own or somebody else's enterprise.[353] Private actions, journalistic or editorial comments, the work of consumer

347. The majority of all preliminary injunctions is accepted by the parties or forms the basis for a settlement.
348. Self-monitoring by the "Advertising Council"("Werberat") is not comparable to self-regulation systems in the Netherlands, Italy or Great Britain. In any event, the objections the "Werberat" raises (e.g. in the Benetton cases) are not always respected.
349. One of the objectives of the reform of 2004 was to bring the German UWG in line with modern drafting and terminology. The laws of other European states as well as the EC-Directives, especially Directive 84/450/EEC, were taken as examples; see the extensive comparative study by Henning-Bodewig/Schricker on behalf of the German Ministry of Justice (WRP 2001. 1367; short version in English in 24 EIPR 271 (2002)).
350. The definition in Sec. 2(2) UWG refers to that of the Civil Code.
351. Already under the UWG of 1909, jurisdiction and legal literature had held that the UWG not only serves the interests of competitors (as it was intended in the beginning) but also that of consumers and the public at large. The interests of competitors and consumers are seen as inseparably intertwined in most unfair competition cases. The "B2C"—restriction of Directive 2005/29/EC on unfair commercial practices (discussed in this book in Chapter 3, IV.10) was therefore met with some scepticism; see, for instance, Köhler/Lettl, WRP 2003, 1019; Keßler/Micklitz, BB 2003, 2073; Henning-Bodewig, GRUR Int. 2003, 926; Veelken, WRO 2004, 1.
352. See Schünemann, in: Harte-Bavendamm/Henning-Bodewig, § 1 UWG No. 52.
353. An action for the purpose of competition is assumed in "normal" cases where the respondent is a business person who objectively benefits from the action, see in details Keller, in Harte-Bavendamm/Henning-Bodewig, § 2 UWG No. 41; Köhler, in: Baumbach/Hefermehl, § 2 UWG, No. 31. If third parties, especially the media are involved, this assumption is restricted to cases where the respondent typically serves the economic interest of an enterprise (e.g. an advertising agency, or a newspaper publisher as regards the publication of ads). Due to constitutional reasons, the defendant has to prove the intent in all other cases. If this is not possible, the action in question is judged on the basis of Sec. 823 et seq. Civil code; see for instance, BGH GRUR 1986, 812—Gastrokritik; OLG Hamburg, GRUR-RR 2005, 20—Marktpreis.

associations, etc. are only within the scope of application, if they can exceptionally be qualified as acts for the purpose of competition.[354] On the other hand, a concrete competitive relationship is not required for the application of the UWG; this is considered as a matter of the right of action (see under No. 10).

As under the previous UWG of 1909, the general clause in Sec. 3 UWG continues to be at the core of German unfair competition law. The direct application of the general clause, however, has declined considerably as most unfair commercial activities are now expressly regulated by means of "examples" (Sec. 4-7 UWG).[355] Only if a competitive activity cannot be subsumed under Sec. 4 et seq. UWG is is dealt with on the basis of the general clause; in this case it must meet the requirement of "unfairness" in the sense of the Sec. 3 UWG and be roughly in line with the expressly regulated causes of action.[356]

In contrast to the previous UWG of 1909, the general clause in Sec. 3 UWG does not speak of "bones mores" ("gute Sitten") but more neutrally of "unfair competitive practices". The UWG 2004 itself refrains deliberately from defining the notion of "unfair" but leaves this to the courts and legal literature.[357] The previous interpretation of "gute Sitten"—which referred to the actual practices of the trade in question corrected by ethical standards—is now not more than a starting point.[358] In view of the purpose-of-protection-clause in Sec. 1 UWG, which expressly refers to the functioning of the market, a more "functional" assessment is expected. The economic aspects rather than the ethical aspects are considered decisive; the goal is the protection of the market participants freedom of economic action and decision,[359] subjective elements play no role. Insofar the interpretation of "unfairness" corresponds to that of the Directive on unfair commercial practices.[360]

The general clause furthermore contains a de minimis criterion.[361] Even if a competitive action is unfair, it can only be prohibited if it is "capable of impairing

354. See for instance BGH GRUR 1998, 164—Modenschau (concerning the press) or BGH GRUR 1999—Werbung im Programm (concerning a broadcasting company).
355. As to the factual situations that still justify to a direct application of the general clause, see Sack, WRP 2005, 531.
356. As to the new function of the general clause see Schünemann, WRP 2004, 925; Köhler, in: Baumbach/Hefermehl, § 3 UWG; Berlit, WRP 2003, 563; Sack WRP 2005, 531.
357. During the discussion for the 2004 reform in the "expert group" established by the Ministry of Justice, it had become apparent that all considered definitions themselves required further definitions. A reference to "honest practices" (Art. 10bis of the Paris Convention) is in truth merely an empty formula, since the crucial question of what is "honest" remains undefined. "Gute Sitten" or "Treu und Glauben—two terms that are more or less interchangeable—must also be interpreted according to the special requirements of fairness in the respective trade. The concept of competition based on own's own merit ("Leistungswettbewerb") that dominated the earlier theory of German competition law was ultimately also rejected. Although it can explain many causes of action, it has become increasingly vague.
358. The interpretation was originally in line with that of Art. 10bis PC. Later on it also took into consideration the economic interests of consumers and the public at large by aiming at a fair balance of interests; see for instance, BGH GRUR 2001, 1181—Telefonwerbung für Blindenware.
359. For details see Schünemann, in: Harte-Bavendamm/Henning-Bodewig (ed.), §§ 1 and 3 UWG.
360. Discussed in this book in Chapter 3, IV.10. See, in particular, Glöckner/Henning-Bodewig, WRP 2005, 1311.
361. Previous reforms of the UWG already had restricted the right of action of competitors and their associations, which were obliged to provide evidence of a substantial impediment on the relevant market. This "de minimis clause" is now to be found in all substantive torts in the new UWG. In addition, Sec. 8(4) UWG prohibits the abusive filing of an action, i.e. where the action is filed primarily for the purpose of obtaining a refund of costs.

competition to a not insubstantial extent".[362] Due to the system of references, the de minimis criterion of the general clause also applies to Sec. 4 to 7 UWG.

The UWG of 2004 aims at a horizontal regulation with the main goal being to prepare a level playing field for marketing activities in the interest of all market participants and the functioning of competition. Although the law directly protects consumers (see Sec. 1 UWG) it is not predominantly concerned with the protection of the individual consumer.[363] The consumer interests protected by the UWG are seen in a collective, abstract sense, e.g. the prevention of practices that hinder a free economic decision making, prohibition of intrusive advertising, while the interests of the individual consumer are taken care of by contract law or other regulations in the Civil Code ("Bürgerliches Gesetzbuch").[364] In spite of this, there are overlapping areas, for instance as regards the influence of misleading advertising on a contract.[365]

Other provisions, such as impediment of competitors, misappropriation or denigration are primarily concerned with the protection of business, although they often also indirectly harm consumers interest; at the least their interest in well-functioning competition. They can be related to intellectual property rights, especially the Trademark Act of 25 October 1994.[366] The UWG is also closely related to the Kartellgesetz whose basic principles are—as can be seen in the purpose-of-protection clause of Sec. 1 UWG -of special importance for the interpretation of the UWG provisions;[367] the prohibition of unfair commercial behaviour should not restrict competition more than absolutely necessary.

3. Regulation of advertising

a. Misleading advertising

Misleading advertising is regulated in Sec. 5 UWG. Paragraph 1 contains the basic prohibition of misleading advertising as "unfair" competition within the meaning of the general clause (with the consequence that the "de minimis criterion"—see above—applies here too). Similar to Directive 84/450/EEC, Sec. 5 para. 2 UWG states the reference points of the misleading statement as well as the special case of misleading through omission. Para. 3 deals with misleading comparative advertising, para. 4 with special offers and para. 5 with bait & switch tactics.

362. In assessing this, all market factors but also aspects such as the intensity of the unfair action, subjective elements as the intent, the time and the effect on other competitors (who might be under the pressure to behave likewise) are taken into consideration; see Heermann, GRUR 2004, 94; Köhler, GRUR 2005, 1.
363. As regards the protection of consumers in the new Act see, for instance, Lettl, GRUR 2004, 449.
364. Köhler, GRUR 2004, 265; critical Fezer, in: Fezer § 1 UWG No. 6, 25, 38.
365. According to Sec. 434 of the Civil Code, for instance, misleading advertising statements can lead to a contractual warranty; as regards the validity of contracts based on unfair competition, see Sack, GRUR 2004, 625.
366. Although Sec. 2 Trademark Act explicitly allows for additional unfair competition protection, the more specific trademark rules prevail in those areas that are considered "genuine" trademark law; see BGH GRUR1999, 161—MACDog and the leading commentary of Ingerl/Rohnke, Trademark Law, 3rd ed. 2004. The exact demarcation is disputed; see for instance Ingerl, WRP 2004, 809 and Bornkamm, GRUR 2005, 97.
367. UWG and Kartellgesetz are considered as the two basis laws on competition. Although they have different objectives—the Kartellgesetz is concerned with the freedom, the UWG with the fairness of competition—modern legal thinking stresses the common basis which lies in the well-functioning of competition; see Köhler, WRP 2005, 645. Glöckner/Henning-Bodewig, WRP 2005, 1311.

The German legislature has refrained from regulating any further principles as to the assessment of misleading which mainly correspond to the guidelines given by the jurisdiction of the ECJ. According to the relevant case law in this area,[368] the statement is to be seen from the perspective of the average addressee of the target group who is reasonably informed, observant and circumspect but whose attentiveness may also vary according to the concrete situation.[369] It is assumed that the reasonably observant, average consumer views everyday mass-media advertisement rather superfluously, relying especially on its overall impression and key elements. Disclaimers can counterbalance a misunderstanding caused by headlines etc. but must be unambiguous and clear.[370] Pursuant to Sec. 4 No.2 UWG, the assessment of a statement can be different if it is directed to a particularly vulnerable target group, especially if it is capable of exploiting the business inexperience of, for instance children, youth, older consumers or emigrants.

A statement ("Angabe") in the meaning of § 5 UWG requires a positive communication containing verifiable facts.[371] Mere opinions or subjective impressions or especially "suggestive" presentations are not enough. On the other hand, an advertisement that appears "vague" or subjective at first sight can contain verifiable facts at its core.

Clearly recognizable exaggerations are considered as harmless "puffing". The older jurisdiction has been rather reluctant in assuming this and often considered superiority claims as a normal "Angabe".[372]

Silence as such is not an "Angabe" and the advertiser, in principle, is neither required to reveal negative aspects of his offer nor to provide consumer with information necessary to make a rational or "informed" decision. It is different, however, if a commercial statement omits relevant information and thus leads to an overall deceptive perception. Sec. 5(2) UWG expressly states that the court has to take into account the significance of the omission in the conclusion of the agreement "according to general opinion" as well as the suitability of the omission to influence the decision of the addressee.[373] Case law has considered as misleading, for instance, advertising for technical devices[374] and sports equipment[375] without disclosing that they are no longer produced because consumers are interested in getting spare parts without problems or just having the "latest state of the art".

Misleading advertising must have an impact on the economic behaviour of the addressee; inaccurate information that does not influence the decision making is considered irrelevant. However, it is sufficient that the misleading statement attracts consumers to an offer that he or she would not have taken into consideration otherwise.

368. See the detailed discussion of § 5 UWG in the leading commentaries by Harte-Bavendamm/Henning-Bodewig and Baumbach-Hefermehl and Fezer.
369. BGH GRUR 2002, 715—Scanner Werbung; BGH WRP 2000, 517—Orient-Teppichmuster.
370. BGH GRUR 2002, 1259—Kopplungsgeschäfte II.
371. The means of communication are irrelevant. The statement can be direct or indirect; it must not necessarily be directed towards a greater number of people.
372. Jurisdiction under the previous Act was rather strict on this point. It was assumed that in principle all advertising claims are taken seriously also superiority claims like "the best" etc.; see the decision cited by Bornkamm, in: Baumbach/Hefermehl, § 5 UWG. In recent years the courts have become more liberal. For instance, the advertising for a cereal with "the best every morning" was not considered a serious claim to superiority but a mere subjective assessment (BGH GRUR 2002, 182—Das Beste jeden Morgen).
373. This was already the point of view of the jurisdiction under the Act of 1909.
374. BGH GRUR 2000, 616—Auslaufmodelle III.
375. BGH GRUR 1982, 374—Auslaufmodelle.

A correction of the incorrect fact before the conclusion of the contract thus does not always prevent the finding of deception; the enticing effect ("anlockende Wirkung") is considered sufficient in most cases.[376]

Which exact percentage of the average addressees of the target group has to be misled, is left open in recent case law. Following the "Nissan" decision of the ECJ,[377] the courts mainly speak of a "significant number".[378] While in normal cases this will tend towards 30 to 50%, a lower rate may be sufficient if the advertisement is directed towards a vulnerable target group or concerns aspects (safety, health, etc.) that are crucial to the decision making of the consumer.[379] Since the question of deception is predominantly treated as a question of fact[380] which has to be proven by the plaintiff, the necessary quota is often proven with the help of public opinion surveys etc.

Section 5(4) UWG deals with special offers. Deception will be assumed if the advertisement refers to a price that was only charged for an unreasonably short period of time. In a dispute, the advertiser bears the burden of proof that the period of time was "reasonable". According to Sec. 5(5) UWG it is also considered as deception if the expected demand cannot be satisfied appropriately; an "inappropriate" stock of goods will be assumed if the demand cannot be covered for at least two days. Apart from this, the UWG contains no general reversal of the burden of proof in the field of deception, although the courts may adapt the rules on evidence in cases where it is impossible or difficult for the plaintiff to gather the necessary evidence (for instance, in cases of superiority claims and in advertisements referring to expert opinions).[381]

b. Comparative advertising

The provision concerning comparative advertising in Sec. 6 UWG has essentially been adopted from Directive 97/55/EC. It should merely be noted that for systematic reasons the Directive's regulation concerning deception was integrated in the provisions on misleading advertising (Sec. 5 para. 3 UWG).[382]

Section 6 UWG requires that a competitor or his product can at least be identified through a reasonably attentive addressee of the target group. In its first decisions,[383] the Supreme Court has assumed recognisability rather generously while in more recent decisions it was implied that the competitor must come to mind naturally.[384] One

376. See, for instance, Bornkamm, in: Baumbach/Hefermehl, § 5 UWG No. 2.190. But see also BGH WRP 2000, 1992—Last Minute Reisen, where the enticing affect was denied.
377. Discussed in this book in Chapter 3, IV.2.; see the similar decision of the BGH in GRUR 1999, 1222—EG-Neuwagen.
378. See for instance BGH WRP 2003, 640—Gemeinnützige Wohnungsgesellschaft; BGH GRUR 2003, 361—Sparvorwahl; BGH GRUR 2001, 78—Falsche Herstellerpreisempfehlung; BGH GRUR 2002, 715—Scanner
379. See BGH/GRUR 2002, 715-Scanner.
380. This is not undisputed. A decision by the BGH in 2000 (Orient-Teppichmuster) is partly seen as a change towards a normative assessment; in this sense Dreyer, in: Harte-Bavendamm/Henning-Bodewig, (ed.), commentary to see 5; critical Omsels, GRUR 2005, 548.
381. See BGH GRUR 2004, 246-Mondpreise.
382. Sec. 6 UWG corresponds to the regulation in Sec. 2 of the Act of 1909. As to its content see the commentaries in the leading treatises and (in English) the overview given by Bastian, IIC 151 (2000).
383. See for instance BGH GRUR 1998, 824—TestpreisAngebot.
384. See GRUR 1999, 1100—Generika-Werbung; GRUR 2002, 75—Sooo billig!

sided criticism not involving any real comparison is not covered by Sec. 6 UWG; a "comparison" requires the presentation of economic alternatives.[385] On the other hand, even before the "Toshiba"-decision of the ECJ, the German Supreme Court has considered references of spare part manufacturers to original equipment[386]—or suggestions to compare the own offer with that of a competitor[387]—as (indirect) comparisons.

Case law judges comparative advertising strictly if aspects of deception[388] or denigration are involved. The overall impression must be correct and the competitor's product may not be criticized more than (objectively) necessary: the claim "we won't subject you to a quality like this" was, for instance, considered denigrating.[389] In contrast, the advertiser is always free to name the (well-known) mark of a competitor[390] or to (truthfully) highlight the positive aspects of his own offer even if this indirectly points to negative aspects of the competitor's products.

c. Concealed advertising

Pursuant to Sec. 4 No. 3 UWG the concealment of the commercial nature of a competitive practice is "unfair" within the meaning of the general clause in Sec. 3 UWG.

This general rule is irrespective of the question if a medium is involved or not.[391] In practice, case law regarding surreptitious advertising often involves the press (and sometimes also TV and the Internet).[392] The laws for the press as well as for broadcasters and internet providers require a clear separation of advertisement from any editorial content or programme and prohibit surreptitious advertising. If these rules are infringed, they can also be sanctioned as unfair competition under the aspect of breach of the law (see under 9). The concealment of the commercial character thus can be unfair competition under two aspects: as a direct violation of the general principle in Sec. 4 No. 3 UWG and (if the press, TV or Internet are involved) as a violation of the "breach of law-principle" in Sec. 4 No. 11 UWG.

385. BGH GRUR 2005, 163—Aluminiumräder (The ad of a producer of car-wheels with a prominently displayed Porsche sporting these wheels was not considered as comparative advertising although the producer and Porsche (who also sells spare wheels) were considered competitors. In addition, the BGH denied an unjustified exploitation of reputation.
386. BGH GRUR 2001, 350—OP-Lampen; see also Sack, GRUR 2004, 720.
387. BGH GRUR 1999, 501—Vergleichen Sie.
388. See Sack, GRUR 2004, 89; Ohly, GRUR 2003, 641.
389. BGH GRUR 1998, 824—Testpreis-Angebot (different—no denigration—BGH GRUR 2002, 72—Peisgegenüberstellung im Schaufenster).
390. BGH GRUR 2003, 444—Ersetzt.
391. For instance, a marketing practice that was disguised as a consumer survey was considered unfair competition, see BGH GRUR 1973, 268—Verbraucher-Briefumfrage. The same applies to advertising disguised as a scientific statement, BGH GRUR 2002, 633—Hormonersatz-Therapie.
392. As regards the press, see for instance, BGH GRUR 1979, 562—Produktinformation I; BGH GRUR 1988, 4932—Unbestimmter Unterlassungsantrag III. As regards TV see BGH GRUR 1990, 611—Werbung im Programm; as to movie-films: BGH GRUR 1995, 744—Feuer, Eis & Dynamit. The crucial question is usually whether there is a "competitive action" on behalf of the medium (see. fn. 353).

d. Aggressive advertising

According to Sec. 7(1) UWG, advertising or market practices that are unreasonably annoying, harassing or intrusive ("belästigend")[393] are deemed unfair competition in the meaning of the general clause of Sec. 3 UWG.

Section 7 para. 2 UWG defines the crucial term "unreasonable". The general principle can be found in para. 2 No. 1: It is, in particular, unreasonable to direct marketing or advertising towards a market participant against his or her express (at least recognisable) wish. This basic "opt-out"—rule is modified for particular forms of communication. According to Sec. 7(2) No. 2 UWG, telephone advertising to end consumers requires express or implied prior consent while assumed consent is sufficient for calls to trades people.[394] Pursuant to Sec. 7(2) (3) UWG, "opt-in" also applies to all advertising using automatic calling machines, fax machines and electronic mail, with an exception corresponding to Directive 2002/58/EC in Sec. 7(3) for electronic mail.

e. Advertising regulation for special products etc.

Advertising for foodstuff etc. is regulated in a special law ("Lebensmittel- und Bedarfsgegenstände Gesetz = LMBG); for pharmaceuticals the "Heilmittelwerbegesetz". (HWG) applies.[395]

In the Treaty on Broadcasting ("Rundfunkstaatsvertrag")[396] the advertising provisions of the Directive 89/452/EC were transposed; advertising in the press is regulated by the "Landespressegesetze".[397] The transparency requirements for commercial communications via the internet can be found in the "Teledienstegesetz".[398]

f. Other forms of advertising

The exploitation of feelings of fear, superstition etc. can be unfair competition if it is capable of impairing the decision making of the addressee, Sec. 4 No. 1 UWG. Whether "shocking advertising" is unfair competition was disputed under the UWG of 1909; according to a landmark judgment of the Constitutional Court, the freedom of speech (Art. 5 Grundgesetz) prevails in most cases.[399] The same applies to advertising

393. The German word "belästigend" is difficult to translate; it involves elements of harassment, annoyance and intrusion.
394. The prohibition of unsolicited telephone calls is in line with the established jurisdiction of the Supreme Court under the previous Act; see for instance BGH WRP 2000, 722—Telefonwerbung VI. Liberalisation was discussed but finally rejected.
395. Both laws contain provisions on misleading advertising; the HMG also on sales promotions which are restricted for drugs.
396. The regulation of broadcasting activities is within the exclusive competence of the German States ("Länder") so that an uniform regulation could only be reached via a treaty. As to the provisions on advertising in the Rundfunkstaatsvertrag, see the leading commentary Hartstein/Ring/Kreile/Dörr/Stettner, Rundfunkstaatsvertrag.
397. The "Landespressegesetze" of the States have not been unified. They all contain, however, a provision requiring the clear separation of ads and editorial content; in cases of doubt, a publication has to be declared as "Anzeige" (advertising). For details, see the leading treatise Löffler/Richter, Handbuch des Presserechts, 5th ed. 2005.
398. They correspond to Directive 2000/31/EC (discussed in this book in Chapter 3, IV.).
399. Decision of the Federal Constitutional Court, GRUR 2001, 170—Schockwerbung.

combined with "social sponsoring" which is allowed so long as it is not misleading and meets basic transparency requirements.[400]

4. Direct marketing

Door-to-door sales are not prohibited as such but are submitted to the "opt-out" rule of Sec. 7(2) UWG (see under 3d); they must, for instance, respect a note on the front door not to be bothered. The same applies for unsolicited advertising material, brochures etc. The sending of unsolicited goods is prohibited, unless it is made quite clear that the consumer has no obligation to pay for it, return it or to keep it (Sec. 241 a Civil Code).

The addressing of private people in public areas can be prohibited on the basis of Sec. 7 No. 1 UWG especially if the commercial purpose is concealed.[401] Unsolicited telephone calls to consumers require express or implied prior consent (see, under 3d), while assumed consent is sufficient for B2B-calls. Pursuant to Sec. 7(2)(3) UWG, this "opt-in"-rule also applies to all commercial communication via automatic calling machines, fax machines, and e-mails. Snowball techniques are forbidden according to Sec. 16(2) UWG.

5. Sales promotion

After the repeal of the "Zugabe-Verordnung" and "Rabattgesetz" in 2001, sales promotion practices like price reductions, premiums, tie-ins, promotional games etc., are not prohibited as such. They must, however, fulfil certain transparency requirements laid down in Sec. 4 No. 4-6 UWG and be in accordance with the general provisions of the UWG, especially the regulations on misleading advertising (Sec. 5 UWG) and impairment of the decision making (Sec. 4 No. 1 UWG).[402]

In particular, sales promotion measures may neither contain false or misleading statements, nor lead to an incorrect overall-impression. If the misleading is seen in the omission of information, it coincidences with the transparency requirements set out in Sec. 4 No. 5-6 UWG. Pursuant to Sec. 4 No. 4 UWG, all conditions for taking advantage of sales promotions must be "clearly and unambiguously" provided. The addressee must be capable of assessing the real value of the offer. This sometimes, but not necessarily, requires information as to the actual value of the premium, the gift, etc. The scope of the transparency requirements depends on the product, the target group, the concrete conditions of the sale, etc.

The second (general) barrier for sales promotion measures lies in Sec. 4 No. 1 UWG which prohibits competitive practices capable of impairing the freedom of decision of consumers or other market participant. Jurisprudence under the previous UWG from 1909 had frequently assumed the unfairness of expensive premiums, prizes, etc., under the aspect of "excessive enticement" and/or "psychological pressure to buy".

400. Decision of the Federal Constitutional Court, GRUR 2002, 455—Tier- und Artenhaltung. But see also Court of appeals Hamm GRUR 2003, 975—Regenwald (deceptive advertising because of a vague promise to save the rain forest).

401. BGH GRUR 2004, 699—Ansprechen in der Öffentlichkeit.

402. For a recent overview see Wagner/Ruess, WRP 2005, 24; for a detailed discussion Köhler, in Baumbach/Hefermehl, § 4 No. 1.42; Stuckel/Omsels, in: Harte-Bavendamm/Henning-Bodewig, § 4 No. 1 UWG.

These aspects no longer justify a prohibition. On the contrary, recent case law[403] has stressed that Sec. 4 No. 1 UWG only applies in situations where the enticement makes a rational decision "nearly impossible". According to the landmark judgment "Kopplungsgeschäfte I and II" of the Supreme Court,[404] the reasonably attentive, observant average consumer is normally not influenced to such a degree, so that sales promotions are only submitted to a kind of "misuse"-control, especially under the aspect of misleading and transparency. The legal assessment, however, can be different if sales promotions are directed to a particular gullible target group (children, youth, old people, immigrants etc.) and thus exploit the business inexperience or gullibility of these groups (Sec. 4 No. 2 UWG).[405]

In addition to these general requirements, there are special requirements for certain sales promotion measures. Price reductions that are advertised as "special offers" are subject to a reversal of the burden of proof as to the practicing of a lower price during an "appropriate" time (see above, 3a). Promotional games—irrespective of whether they depend on chance or skill—may not be tied to the purchase of goods or the use of services;[406] exceptions apply for promotional contents or games that are inherently tied to the goods or services (like in magazines). For certain products, especially health products, but also alcohol and tobacco, premiums and free gifts are forbidden or at least strictly regulated.

Liquidation sales and end-of season sales are no longer regulated.[407] Their permissibility is determined mainly on the basis of the provision on misleading advertising.

6. Disparagement and denigration

Most cases of disparagement and trade libel take place within the framework of comparative advertising (regulated in Sec. 6 UWG), or are dealt with under trademark law. However, disparaging allegations of facts outside comparative advertising and trademark law that cannot be proven true are prohibited (Sec. 4 No. 8 UWG). The same applies to depreciative comments and value judgments (Sec. 4 No. 7 UWG).[408]

7. Risk of confusion; misappropriation

Under the headline of "supplementary protection of achievement", Sec. 4 No. 9 UWG regulates the three most important cases of misappropriation through imitation. Avoidable deception as to the commercial origin,[409] exploitation of reputation and obtaining

403. See for instance, BGH GRUR 2004, 1359—500 DM-Gutschein für Autkoauf:
404. GRUR 2002, 976 and 979—Kopplungsgeschäfte I and II.
405. See for instance Court of Appeals Nürnberg, GRUR-RR 2003, 315—Werbeschreiben an Jugendliche.
406. Sec. 4 No. 6 UWG.
407. The provisions in the Act of 1909 were repealed.
408. As to the difference between "allegations of act" and "value judgments", see BGH WRP 2003, 384—Feldenkrais. The demarcation is important because of the different regulation of the burden of proof.
409. Most cases of imitation are handled under the aspect of deception as to the commercial origin. Jurisdiction requires a certain distinctiveness of the copied product ("wettbewerbliche Eigenart") and the imitation of features that are not merely technical. See for details Sambuc, in: Harte-Bavendamm/Henning-Bodewig, § 4 No. 9 UWG.

know-how under false pretences are expressly forbidden as unfair competition. This does not mean that all other imitations are ultimately legal. It is not excluded that, for instance, slavish imitation leading to an impediment of a competitor is subsumed under Sec. 4 No. 10 UWG, while the so-called "parasitic exploitation of another's achievements" (without confusion of origin) can in exceptional cases be dealt with on the basis of the general clause in Sec. 3 UWG (but requires greater efforts in the justification.).[410]

8. Impediment of competitors

Section 4 No. 10 UWG prohibits the impediment of individual competitors; it requires a "deliberate" competitive action directed towards a competitor. This is intended to cover cases such as calls for boycotts, unjustified proprietary right warnings, etc.

"General market disturbance", e.g., the blocking of the market resulting from the massive distribution of original products as gifts, was deliberately not included. This cause of action is now at best to be dealt with on the basis of the general clause in Sec. 3 UWG, although the courts have already shown substantial reluctance to do so.[411]

As previously, the new Act also contains specific torts for the protection of business and trade secrets (Sec. 17-19 IWG). Infringements are (also) subject to criminal penalties.[412]

9. Breach of the law

According to Sec. 4 No. 11 UWG, the infringement of provisions outside of the UWG can be considered as unfair competition if the infringed regulation is (also) intended to regulate market conduct in the interest of market participants. In addition, the "de minimis clause" of Sec. 3 UWG applies, with the result that the infringement must also be capable of impairing competition to a not insignificant extent.[413]

Section 4 No. 11 UWG expressly refers to the infringement of regulations governing market conduct, and not to regulations governing access to the market.[414]

10. Enforcement

Section 12 et seq. UWG regulates the civil law sanctions of unfair competition—removal, injunctions, damages, confiscation of profit. The focus is on the claim for an injunction (Sec. 8 UWG), which is, in practice, the most important remedy. It is usually started with a so-called warning procedure, now regulated in Sec. 12(1)

410. Under the Act of 1909, the courts had granted protection against the offer of compatible products for established series of products; BGH GRUR 1992, 619—Klemmbausteine II; Recent jurisdiction shows some reluctance to uphold this doctrine, see BGH GRUR 2000, 521—Modul-Gerüst.
411. Federal Supreme Court, 35 IIC 1063 (2004)—20 Minuten Köln (distribution of a "free" newspaper).
412. For details see Harte-Bavendamm, in Harte-Bavendamm/Henning-Bodewig, § 17 UWG.
413. Already under the UWG of 1909, the Supreme Court had given up the former division between "neutral" and "ethical" provisions; see BGH GRUR 2002, 1076—Abgasemmissionen; BGH GRUR 2003, 164—Altautoverwertung. For a detailed discussion see Sack, GRUR 2004, 1307.
414. This restriction gave rise to considerable criticism in the legislative proceeding, since it will make it more difficult to use unfair competition law to take action against private business activity on the part of local government authorities, see the decisions cited in fn. 413.

2nd sentence UWG[415]. In addition, the right of action (for injunctions and removal) is regulated under Sec. 8(3) UWG. Locus standi is granted to all competitors who have a competitive relationship with the defendant, their associations and consumer associations as well as the Chamber of commerce.

In Sec. 10, the UWG of 2004 introduced a new sanction—confiscation of profits which mainly serves the (collective) interests of consumers. It is intended to ensure that "diffuse" damages which in each individual case may be below the "de minimis"-level (but which can amount to considerable profits), are deducted. The remedy is restricted to deliberate infringements and profits being made to the detriment of a large number of purchasers. The amount confiscated is paid to state funds, although the state itself does not enjoy the status of plaintiff. Consequently, there is probably little incentive for associations, which alone have power of action, to take steps. Nevertheless, the preventive effect of such a provision could be considerable.[416]

In unfair competition matters, the commercial courts have exclusive competence in the first instance (with the Oberlandesgerichte as the court of appeals and the "Bundesgerichtshof" in the 3rd instance). The majority of all unfair competition law suits concerns injunctions, often in preliminary proceedings, regulated in the Code of Civil Proceedure.

The loosing party has to bear not only the costs of the court but also the cost of the (winning) party's attorney.

X. GREAT BRITAIN

Selected Literature: Borrie, *The Development of Consumer Law and Policy*, 1984; Bradgate/Brownsword/Twigg-Flessner, *The Impact of Adopting a Duty to Trade Fairly*, (Report für DTI) Juli 2003; Brett, *Unfair Competition—Not Merely an Academic Issue?* [1979] 11 EIPR 295; Burns, *Unfair Competition a Compelling Need Unmet* [1981] 11 EIPR 311; Carty, *An Analysis of the Economic Torts*, 2001; Cornish/Llewelyn, *Intellectual Property*, 5th ed. 2003; Dworkin, *Unfair Competition: Is the Common Law Developing a New Tort?* [1979] 9 EIPR 241; Dworkin, *Passing Off and Unfair Competition: An Opportunity Missed* [1981] 44 MLR 564; Harvey/Parry, *The Law of Consumer Protection and Fair Trading*, 6th ed. 2000; Howells/Weatherill, *Consumer Protection Law*, 1995; Howells/Voigt, United Kingdom, in: Micklitz/Kessler (ed.), *Marketing Practices Regulation and Consumer Protection in the EC Member States and the US*, 2002, p. 361; Huntley, United Kingdom, in: Campbell (ed.), *Unfair Trade Practices—The Comparative Law Yearbook of International Business*, 1996, p. 313; Kamperman Sanders, *Unfair Competition Law*, 1997; Lowe/Woodroffe, *Consumer Law and Practice*, 6th ed. 2003; Mills, *Own Label Products and the "Lookalike" Phenomenon: A Lack of Trade Dress and Unfair Competition Protection?* [1995] 3 EIPR 116; Ohly, *Richterrecht und Generalklausel im Recht des unlauteren Wettbewerbs*, 1995; Ohly, Vereinigtes Königreich von Großbritannien und Nordirland, in: Schricker (ed.), *Recht der Werbung in Europa*, 1995 (Schricker/Ohly); Ohly/Spence: *The Law of Comparative Advertising: Directive 97/55/EC in the United Kingdom and Germany*,

415. The plaintiff is not obliged to "warn" the wrongdoer via a cease-and-desist letter. However, in a suit for an injunction the immediate acception by the defendant can lead to a negative decision on the costs for the plaintiff.
416. For details, cf. Goldmann, in: Harte-Bavendamm/Henning-Bodewig (ed.), § 12 UWG.

2000; Palomba, *The Use of Celebrities in Advertising—How the Position Has Changed*, Communications Law 2002, S. 223; Ramsay, *Consumer Protection*, 1989; Ulmer/v. Westerholt, *Das Recht des unlauteren Wettbewerbs in den Mitgliedstaaten der EWG*, Band VI: Vereinigtes Königreich von Großbritannien und Nordirland, 1981; v. Westerholt, *Die Passing off-Klage im englischen Recht*, 1976; Wadlow, *The Law of Passing-off. Unfair Competition by Misrepresentation*, 3rd ed. 2004; *Department of Trade and Industry* and *Office of Fair Trading*, various reports and publications.

1. Sources of law

Common law: passing off, injurious or malicious falsehood, defamation; Statutes and Regulations: Trade Description Act 1968, Consumer Protection Act 1987, Control of Misleading Advertising Regulations 1988 (with amendments); Self Regulation: British Code of Advertising, Sales Promotion and Direct Marketing 11. ed.; ITC Code of Advertising Standards and Practice 2002 (TV); RA Advertising and Sponsorship Code (Radio).

2. English unfair competition law in a nutshell

English law[417] has neither a comprehensive statutory regulation directed against unfair trade practices nor a specific common law tort of unfair competition;[418] the notion of "unfair competition law" is regarded as a continental European specialty. Rather, various elements of common law and statutes can be applied to certain aspects of unfair trade behavior.[419] Added to that—with state approval, support and recognition—are standards of self-regulation promulgated by the industry that play a major role in combating unfair competition.[420]

The passing-off suit is the most important common law remedy.[421] Because of it's broadly defined elements (and if extensively construed) it could be the most likely candidate for fulfilling the function of a general clause against unfair competition. It was originally aimed at the deceitful use of distinctive signs or markings of a third party, for example when a supplier passes off its own products as that of a third party. Protection is not aimed at the marking itself, but rather at the goodwill embodied in that mark. What constitutes a marking is therefore interpreted broadly, and includes, for example, packaging or advertising slogans. This tort also forbids false statements

417. The term "English Law" instead of British Law is used deliberately in order to stress that the following remarks are restricted to England and Wales; the laws of Scotland and Northern Ireland some differences that could only be touched upon from time to time. S. Huntley, p. 317 ff.
418. Kamperman Sanders, p. 53 ff. There has been some discussion lately to introduce a general duty "to trade fairly", s. in the study by Bradgate/Brownsword/Twigg-Flessner, The Impact of Adopting a Duty to Trade Fairly, <www.dti.gov.uk/ccp/topics1/pdf1/unfairreport.pdf>. S. also Dworkin, [1979] 9 EIPR 241; Brett, [1979] 11 EIPR 295; Dworkin, [1981] 44 MLR 564; Burns, [1981] 11 EIPR 311. As regards the possible changes indicated by the Directive 2005/29/EC (Chap. 3, 10) see Twigg-Flesner Report for the DTI (2005).
419. A helpful survey of the protection of consumers in the UK can be found in the report of the Department of Trade and Industry (DTI) under <www.dti.gov.uk/ccp/topics1/pdf1/benchuk.pdf>.
420. This is emphasised by Britain's efforts to have self-regulation recognized as an adequate control mechanism in the EC-Directive.
421. Wadlow, 3d ed. 2004; Carty, 2001; Cornish/Llewelyn, 16-01 ff.

regarding the composition of a product or offering used products as new. The requirements of a passing-off suit are: a goodwill of the plaintiff; misrepresentation by the defendant, which lead to a risk of confusion, and the probability of damages.[422] Intent to deceive is not required.[423]

The demarcation of cases of passing-off and claims under the Trade Marks Act has recently caused some problems, especially when so called "look alikes" were concerned.[424] They involve products where there is no risk of confusion relating to the affixed marks but their get up and/or the advertising for them has such strong similarities to an older established product of a competitor that confusion or deception could be caused or that at least associations with the "original" products or their manufacturer can be evoked. Since after the Sabèl/Puma decision of the ECJ also in the UK the evocation of an association with an older trade mark is to be seen merely as a sub-category of likelihood of confusion[425] it is an obvious step to try those cases under a passing off theory. Following the "Pub Squash"-decision of the Privy Council most courts have, however, denied likelihood of confusion when clearly distinguishable trade marks had been used. It does not suffice that for the respective trade circles merely an association with the established product is evoked.[426]

The suit of "injurious falsehood" covers false statements, that harm the plaintiff—even without impairment to his reputation.[427] The false statement must pertain to circumstances in the plaintiff's domain.[428] It requires malice rather than mere negligence. The plaintiff must prove the falsehood of the statement. These rather strict elements of the tort and the burden of proof limit the practical relevance of such a claim.

With a suit of defamation, according to English law,[429] the plaintiff can bring a suit against statements which impair his/her personal honor and are meant to openly disparage the plaintiff. Defamation is split into written form ("libel") and oral form ("slander"). The difference between the two is that slander requires damage to the plaintiff, while slander does not. Fault is not required. The defendant has the burden

422. The damage to the goodwill has not be to concrete, *Irvine* v. *Talksport Ltd*, [2002] 1 W.L.R. 2355.
423. *Reckitt & Coleman* v. *Borden*, [1990] 1 W.L.R. 491; [1990] 1 All E.R. 873; [1990] R.P.C. 341 and *Erven Warnink* v. *Townend*, [1979] 3 W.L.R. 68; [1979] 2 All E.R. 927; [1980] R.P.C. 31.
424. Hills, [1995] 3 EIPR 116.
425. [1998] R.P.C. 199. S. Cornish/Llewelyn, 16-39; 17-94 ff.
426. *Cadbury-Schweppes* v. *Pub Squash* [1981] R.P.C. 429, PC. It involved the imitation of the style and the themes of a sucessful advertising campaign. Examples of later decisions are *Scott* v. *Nice-Pak* [1989] F.S.R. 14 (blue containers for baby wipes); *Financial Times* v. *Evening Standard* [1991] F.S.R. 17 (pink pages in newspapers); *United Biscuits* v. *Burtons Biscuits* [1992] F.S.R. 14 (packaging). But see *Reckitt & Colman* v. *Borden*, note 7, where the use of a bottle in the form of a lemon by a competitor was supposed to cause likelihood of confusion despite clearly non-confusing marks because the public was used so much to the notion that lemon-shaped bottles come from their first user that they would overlook or disregard the different markings. Cornish/Llewelyn, 16-39 summarize the position of the courts: "The judges are not, however, prepared to allow any wholesale abandonment of the need to show confusion of customers leading to damage in favour of some loosely defined wrong covering cases where all that can be said is that a defendant derives some tangential advantage from imprecise recollection and association".
427. Cornish/Llewelyn, 16-48 ff. Scottish Law does not know this suit; respective cases can be drawn under the suit of verbal injury, see Country Report Great Britain, Question 140, AIPPI, Yearbook 1998/IV, S. 97
428. False statements concerning plaintiff's own products etc. are not covered.
429. Cornish/Llewelyn, 16-52; Scottish Law is slightly different, see Country Report Great Britain, Question 140, AIPPI, Yearbook 1998/IV, S. 97; Schricker/Ohly, no. 74.

of proof regarding the truthfulness of the statement. Such suits can be brought when products have been criticized.

A host of other causes of action that in specific cases also may combat unfair competition exist:[430] "Inducement to breach of contract, "intimidation" or "unlawful threat", "conspiracy", "breach of statutory duties", and "breach of confidence".

The Trade Description Act of 1968[431] contains regulations regarding the false description of goods and services (Sec. 1 et seq., 14). Explicit and implicit false or misleading information about the company, its goods or services are prohibited. A violation can also exist for goods when the false information was given unintentionally, but for services only when the supplier acted recklessly or intentionally regarding the falsehood.[432] The person who attaches the incorrect description of the goods, provides the goods, or delivers the goods is considered a perpetrator. These regulations are subject to penalty and enforced by the "Local Trading Standards Authorities".

The Consumer Protection Act of 1987 regulates misleading pricing or price comparisons of goods, services, real estate, etc. as to the consumers (Sec. 20 et seq.).[433] According to Section 25, a Code of Practice for Traders on Price Indications[434] was issued, that, although not binding on the courts, serves as guiding principles when interpreting the law. One becomes liable only when making untrue statements about his/her own business.[435] These regulations are also enforced by the Local Trading Standards Authorities.

The Control of Misleading Advertisements Regulations of 1988[436] implement the EC-Directive on misleading and comparative advertising.[437] Although the EC Directive obliges Member States to control misleading advertising either through the courts or an independent administrative authority whose decision must be controllable through the courts, Great Britain in practice succeeded in maintaining the role of self regulation of the industry. The regulations are now enforced on the government side mainly through the Office of Fair Trading (OFT). OFT generally intervenes only if the protection through the local governmental institutions and self regulation bodies fails and if it is in the best interests of the general public.[438] Accordingly, the right to complain to the local and self regulatory authorities must first be exhausted. Once the OFT takes on a case, it generally tries to settle the case with the advertiser before bringing a suit for a cease and desist order.[439] Consequently such suits are rare.

430. Cornish/Llewelyn, 2-12 ff. S. also Ohly, Richterrecht, p. 34 ff.
431. British statutes and regulations can be found on the website of the Office of Public Sector Information (OPSI) (formerly Her Majesty's Stationary Office (HMSO)) (<www.opsi.gov.uk/>).
432. The courts interpret this rather narrow language more as leaning to simple negligence, see Schricker/Ohly, no. 43.
433. See under 3.
434. Website of the Department of Trade and Industry: <www.dti.gov.uk/ccp/topics1/guide/ misleading-price.pdf>.
435. Employees, except directors and chief executive officers, Sec. 40(2), are therefore not liable, *Warwickshire County Council* v. *Johnson* [1993] 1 All E.R. 299.
436. SI 1988/915 (amended through the Control of Misleading Advertisements (Amendment) Regulations 2000—SI 2000/914).
437. Directives 84/450/EEC and 97/55/EC.
438. *Director General of Fair Trading* v. *Tobyward Ltd*, [1989] 2 All ER 266.
439. See for instance the Barclay's Bank-case, which concerned a clearly deceptive advertising for a credit card with "0% interest for ever"; Press release OFT PN149/03, 18.11.2003.

An array of further laws and regulations[440] pertain to misleading advertising for consumer credit, land and buildings, foodstuffs, pharmaceutical products, items made of precious metal, all-inclusive vacations, etc.

The most important self-regulation standard[441] is the "British Code of Advertising, Sales Promotion and Direct Marketing" of the Committee on Advertising Practice (CAP),[442] that, however, does not encompass radio and television advertising.[443] The "Advertising Standards Authority" (ASA)[444] enforces the Code. Where a marketing practice has violated statutory law, but ASA does not or cannot provide appropriate protection, the route to OFT is open.[445]

The regulatory authority for radio and television is the Office of Communications (OFCOM).[446] OFCOM has the administrative responsibility of regulating the communications industry; it is responsible for advertising and thus for the implementation of Standards and the Council Directives.[447] To fulfill this responsibility, the ITC already promulgated the Advertising Standards Code, the Code of Program Sponsoring, and the Rules on Amount and Scheduling of Advertising.[448] Under the Communications Act 2003, OFCOM was encouraged towards contracting-out functions and to a co-regulatory partnership with effective self-regulation. After public consultation and parliamentary approval, OFCOM has authorized the Committee of Advertising Practice's Broadcast Committee (BCAP) to take responsibility for maintaining, reviewing and updating the Code. BCAP has amended the ITC code to reflect these regulatory changes but did not change the substance.[449] Complaints about apparent breaches of the Code will be considered by the Advertising Standards Authority, through its broadcasting arm ASA(B).

To get licensed the stations must prove that they can secure adherence to these regulations. Further, they can, through the Broadcast Advertising Clearance Center (BACC), undertake a "pre-transmission advertising checking and approval".[450] The BACC publishes Notes of Guidance, which explain its practice and the application of the ITC Code.[451] The similar radio version of the television code is the Advertising and

440. Consumer Credit Act 1974 (Sec. 43-46) und Consumer Credit (Advertisements) Regulations 1989 (SI 1989/1125); Property Misdescription Act 1991 (Sec. 1(1) with Property Misdescriptions (Specified Matters) Order 1992; Food Safety Act 1990 (Sec. 15); Medicines Act 1968 (Sec. 92 ff.); Tobacco Advertising and Promoting Act 2002; Hallmarking Act 1973 (amended 1999); Food Labeling Regulations 1984; Package Travel, Package Holidays and Package Tours Regulations 1992; Trading Stamps Act 1964 (which was repealed on 6.4.2005, trading stamps schemes are now covered by general consumer protection laws, <www.dti.gov.uk/ccp/topics1/pdf1/tradstampsguide.pdf>)
441. Since 2001 there is a voluntary approval procedure for all codes at the OFT, now regulated in Sec. 8 Enterprise Act 2002.
442. The 11. edition of 4.3.2003 is currently in force, see the web site of the Committee of Advertising Practice (CAP): <www.cap.org.uk/>. For a comprehensive list of activities covered s. Rule 1.1. There are special regulations for certain products and services in Rules 46-55.
443. For a detailed list of all activities that are not included s. Rule 1.2 ASA/CAP Code.
444. An independent organisation consisting of members from all branches concerned and from the most important groups of society.
445. S. for instance *Office of Fair Trading* v. *Tobyward Ltd*, [1989] 1 WLP 517, in which ASA could not reach a settlement.
446. The Independent Television Commission (ITV) and the Radio Authority (RA) have been abolished through the Communications Act of 2003. OFCOM has taken over there competences and functions.
447. Section 9 Broadcasting Act 1990, amended 1996 for regulations concerning radio and TV in digitalized form and the Communications Act 2003.
448. <www.ofcom.org.uk/tv/ifi/codes/>.
449. <www.cap.org.uk/cap/about/cap_broadcast/>
450. See Associated Advertising Guidance Notes, ibd.
451. <www.bacc.org.uk/bacc/notes_of_guidance/>

Sponsorship Code first promulgated by the RA and now also taken over by BCAP.[452] Further standards exist for various other industries, for example for direct marketing[453] and the financing business.[454]

The purpose of protection varies according to the legal basis of the suit or regulation involved. The goal of the common law suits is to protect the injured party, in unfair competition law cases, therefore, most often the competitor.[455] The protection of consumers, on the other hand, is the primary goal of criminal and administrative laws and regulations, although they protect the honest businessmen indirectly as well. Self-regulation of the industry tends to protect the consumers and competitors. Inasmuch as the protection of medium-size companies is considered at all to be a goal of competition policy, it is dealt with mainly in cartel/anti-trust laws rather than fair trade laws.

3. Advertisement

There is no general civil law forbidding misleading advertising. Of the common law remedies, the passing-off suit has the broadest applicability.[456] It has, for example, successfully been used by celebrities against the unauthorized commercial use of their persona.[457] The benchmark is in general the rational, reasonably attentive and circumspect consumer.[458] In special cases the injurious (malicious) falsehood or defamation suits[459] can also be successful against misleading advertising.

The fight against misleading advertising is based on the Regulations on Misleading Advertising 1988, which implemented the respective EU Council Directive.[460] The enforcement on the government side occurs through the OFT, although it is mainly subsidiary. If an amicable settlement cannot be reached—which in practice rarely happens—the court can render a cease and desist order. Separate regulations exist for misleading statements of price.[461]

The British Code of Advertising, Sales Promotion, and Direct Marketing[462] is the most important standard of the self-regulation of the industry. It contains in Rule 2.1 the general requirement that "All marketing communications should be legal, decent, honest and truthful". This is supplemented through definitions of the terms, for example of truthfulness.[463] Clearly recognizable untruths and exaggerations are allowed

452. <www.cap.org.uk/cap/about/cap_broadcast/>
453. Discussed below under
454. <www.fsa.gov.uk/who/>. Information for the practice can be found in a handbook <fsahandbook.info/FSA/handbook.jsp?doc=/handbook/COB>. Chap. 3 contains detailed rules for "financial promotion".
455. Consumers are protected only indirectly in as far as e.g. likelihood of confusion is a necessary element for a sucessful passing off suit.
456. See above, 2.
457. *Irvine* v. *Talksport Ltd.*, [2002] 1 W.L.R. 2355. For a detailed discussion and for the problems of "look alikes" or "sound alikes" s. Palomba, Communications Law 2002, p. 223.
458. With slightly different wording see e.g. *British Airways* v. *Ryan Air*, [2001] FSR 541 and *Irvine* v. *Talksport Ltd*, [2002] 1 W.L.R. 2355; *Arsenal Football Club* v. *Reed* [2001] R.P.C. 622.
459. As to the respective requirements s. above.
460. See above.
461. Code of Practice for Traders on Price Indications des Department of Trade and Industry, <www.dti.gov.uk/ccp/>; ITC Advertising Standards Code for TV Advertising, Sec. 5.3.
462. <www.asa.org.uk/asa/codes/>
463. Rule 7.1: "No marketing communication should mislead, or be likely to mislead, by inaccuracy, ambiguity, exaggeration, omission or otherwise".

(Rule 3.4). Statements of fact must be able to be substantiated (Rule 3.1), and mere opinions must be clearly identifiable as such (Rule 8.1). These general rules are further defined for specific areas of advertising, such as for "testimonials and endorsements" by celebrities or other people (Rule 14). For advertising in television the Advertising Standards Codes[464] establishes a prohibition of misleading statements.[465] Special consideration is given to the use of the term "free" (Sec. 5.2.4). For radio advertising the Radio Advertising Code[466] refers to the Regulations on Misleading Advertising and paraphrases its wording.[467] It gives special mention to superlative claims; the truth of the statement must be proved when it is not clear puffery.[468]

Comparative advertising traditionally is handled liberally in Great Britain.[469] Only in very specific situations the common law remedies of injurious falsehood (in cases of deceit) and defamation (in cases of denigration) can be considered.[470] Since the transposition of the EC Directive on comparative advertising on 23 April 2000, a statutory regulation can be found in the Control of Misleading Advertising Regulations 1988.[471] Regulations for certain kinds of comparative advertising are also found sporadically in consumer safety norms such as the Consumer Protection Act of 1987 (price comparison)[472] or the Consumer Credits (Advertisements) Regulations 1989 (credits).

According to Sec. 10(6) of the current Trademark Act 1994, it is now[473] permissible to use another party's brand name even without authorization of the owner to identify the services or products of the owner or his licensee, as long as it is done in a way that follows "honest practices in industrial and commercial matters". Truthful, non-disparaging comparisons do not violate this requirement. Substantial deceit in comparative advertising,[474] however, is considered being against "honest practices".[475]

More extensive is the general regulation of comparative advertising in the ASA/CAP Code.[476] There and in television advertising[477], any comparison may not be misleading.[478] Furthermore, advertising in general may not discredit goods or services of other parties or attack them in an unfair manner. The definition of comparative advertising in the television broadcasting code is extensive and includes—as opposed to the Council Directive—comparisons that do not identify individual competitors

464. <www.asa.org.uk/asa/codes/>.
465. Section 5.1. For advertising directed at children also Sec. 7.1 applies (exploitation of the credulity etc.).
466. <www.asa.org.uk/asa/codes/>.
467. See Section 2 Nr. 3.
468. Section 2 Nr. 4.
469. For a detailed discussion see Ohly/Spence, 2000:
470. For an unsuccessful attempt of British Airways to stop a comparative (denigrating) ad by its competitor *Ryan Air s. British Airways* v. *Ryan Air*, [2001] F.S.R. 541.
471. S. above.
472. As regulated in detail in the Code of Practice for Traders on Price Indications, <www.dti.gov.uk/ccp/>, which applies to price comparisons with own and third parties prices.
473. Section 4(1)(b) of the Trade Mark Act 1938 forbade any reference to registered marks of third parties.
474. S. the leading case *Barclays Bank* v. *RBS Advanta* [1996] R.P.C. 307; *Vodafone Group* v. *Orange Personal Communications Services Ltd* [1997] F.S.R. 34; *British Telecommunications* v. *AT&T Communications (UK) Limited* [1997] 5 EIPR D-134, *Cable & Wireless* v. *British Telecommunications* [1998] F.S.R. 383].
475. S. the summary of the legal situation (before the implementation of the *Directive in Cable & Wireless* v. *British Telecommunications* [1998] F.S.R. 383.
476. Rules 18-20.
477. <www.asa.org.uk/asa/codes/>
478. Television Advertising Standards Code Sec. 5.4.6.

such as comparative advertising as to procedures or systems. The code regulating advertising on the radio, however, does not follow this broader interpretation, but is limited to repeating the laws in the Council Directive and the Regulations.[479]

A general legal prohibition of disguised advertising does not exist. The ASA/CAP Code, however, bans concealed advertising (Rule 22.1) and incorporates the principle of separation of advertising and content.[480] This also applies to radio and television advertising.[481] The Code also specifically prohibits subliminal advertising in television.[482]

Sponsoring of broadcasts is regulated in detail for television and radio in the relevant Codes.[483] Product Placement is not permitted in television and radio.[484] Equipment items can be acquired "under price" only under special circumstances.[485] The undue prominence of certain products or services is also prohibited unless there is a certain level of relation to the content.[486]

There is no general legal regulation or common law remedy for harassing or annoying advertising.[487] However, in recent years, extensive regulations were put into place regarding unsolicited phone calls, faxes, emails and text messages.[488] In theory, disparaging, offensive and defamatory advertising can be brought to court as defamation or injurious falsehood under common law. However, the latter seems to offer only limited protection, if the alleged defamation occurred together with truthful, non-misleading comparative advertising.[489] Comparisons may not discredit or denigrate characteristics, products, activities or the relations of a competitor.[490] This was incorporated into the ASA/CAP Code[491] and extended to all types of marketing communication.[492] Shocking advertising with controversial pictures has been the topic of several of ASA's decisions. The demarcation between what is allowable and what is not is not clearly defined and has been called hardly comprehensible.[493]

Media-specific regulation of advertising in commercial radio broadcasting has already been addressed. BBC is not permitted to broadcast advertising or shows that

479. Radio Advertising Standards Code Section 2 Nr. 6.
480. Rule 23.2. In addition Rule 23.1 provides that so-called. "advertorials" have to comply with the general rules of the Code like the prohibition against misleading content and form.
481. Section 2.1.1 Television Advertising Standards Code; Sec. 2 Nr. 1 Radio Advertising Standards Code.
482. Section 5.4.5 Television Advertising Standards Code.
483. For the Radio s. the Radio Sponsoring Rules, <www.ofcom.org.uk/radio/ifi/cr/codes/adv_sponsorship_code.pdf>; for TV Part A of the ITC Code on Programme Sponsorship, <www.ofcom.org.uk/tv/ifi/codes/code_prog_sponsor/>.
484. Part B No. 15.1 ITC Code on Programme Sponsorship; Radio Sponsoring Rules at the end.
485. Section 15 ITC Code on Programme Sponsorship.
486. Section 16 ITC Code on Programme Sponsorship.
487. Common law may protect against certain cases like trespass to land or even trespass to goods, e.g. unsolicited cleaning of windows of cars. Many repeated telephone calls may be regarded as nuisance, Schricker/Ohly, Rdnr. 89 ff.
488. See below under Direct Marketing.
489. S. (before implementation of the Comparative Advertising Directive) *British Airways* v. *Ryan Air*, [2001] F.S.R. 541, where the air carrier BA was named "expensive ba . . . rds". The court found this "vulgar" but not "malicious".
490. Art. 3a(1)(e) Directive on Misleading and Comparative Advertising; Sec. 4A(1)(e) Control of Misleading Advertisings Regulations as amended 2000.
491. As well as in the ITC Code for TV advertising Sec. 5.4.6.
492. Rule 20.1 British Code of Advertising, Sales Promotion, and Direct Marketing.
493. S. BBC's videofilms of prohibited and allowed shocking advertising under <news.bbc.co.uk/1/hi/magazine/3306723.stm>.

have been sponsored. There are no special regulations for print media and advertising in movie theatres;[494] so the general rules apply.[495] Outdoor advertising is regulated through the Town and Country Planning (Control of Advertisements) Regulations of 1992.[496]

According to the Tobacco Advertising and Promotion Act 2002,[497] which is supplemented by additional regulations, all advertising of tobacco products is prohibited.[498] Also prohibited is the advertising on television for tobacco and brand-sharing products.[499]

Product-specific prohibitions are also in place for other goods and services on commercial television.[500] Television advertising for pharmaceutical products, medical treatments, health services, food, dietary products as well as dietary counseling, financial services, alcoholic beverages, education, dating services, telephone services, mail-order sales, lotteries, and bingo, among other things are not completely forbidden, but are regulated.[501]

Advertising for pharmaceutical products to consumers is largely prohibited throughout the media.[502] Other regulations exist for food stuff,[503] consumer credit,[504] package holidays,[505] lotteries and bingo.[506] Further product-specific regulations exist in the ASA/CAP Code.[507]

4. Direct marketing

Great Britain has implemented the EC Directives regarding door-to-door sales,[508] distance selling[509] and e-commerce.[510] In the field of direct marketing, self regulation

494. Schricker/Ohly, note 145 f.
495. For publishing houses the Newspaper Society has established a division that examines the legality of ads on demand, <www.newspapersoc.org.uk/nsservices/pera/legal-advice.html>.
496. On the basis of Sec. 220 ff. Town and Country Planning Act.
497. In force since 14.2.2003, before the Directive No. 2003/33/EG of 23.5.2003.
498. S. the web site of the Ministry of Health <www.dh.gov.uk/PolicyAndGuidance/ HealthAndSocialCareTopics/Tobacco/fs/en>. New regulations on brandsharing came into force on 31.7.2005 and on point of sale advertising on 31.12.2004.
499. According to Broadcasting Act 1990, also implementing Directive No. 97/36/EEC "Television without Frontiers" which in Art. 13 contains a prohibition of tobacco advertising and in Art. 17(a)(2) a prohibition of sponsoring by the tobacco industry.
500. ITC Code Sec. 3.1. (unacceptable products and services).
501. Section 8 to 11. A similar list exists for radio advertising, Appendix 3 (Prohibited Categories) of the Code.
502. Medicines (Advertising) Regulations 1994 und Guidance Notes der Medicines Control Agency dazu unter <www.mca.gov.uk/inforesources/publications/gn23/medic.htm>.
503. S. Sec. 14 and 15 des Food Safety Act 1990 and the regulations passed on this basis.
504. Consumer Credits (Advertisements) Regulations 1989.
505. Package Travels, Package Holidays and Package Tours Regulations 1992.
506. Betting, Gaming and Lotteries Act 1963 and Gaming Act 1968, which was in part made more liberal through Deregulation (Betting and Bingo Advertising etc.) Order 1997.
507. Rules 46-55.
508. Directive 85/577/EEC, implemented through Consumer Protection (Cancellation of Contracts Concluded Away from Business Premises) Regulations 1987.
509. Directive 97/7/EC, implemented through Consumer Protection (Distance Selling) Regulations 2000, in force since 31.10.2000.
510. Directive 00/31/EC, implemented through Electronic Commerce (EC) Regulations 2002, in force since 21.8.2002.

remains the most important aspect in practice. In addition to ASA/CAP Code, the Code of Practice of the Direct Marketing Authority (DMA[511]) applies, and is binding for association members.[512] Furthermore, the Direct Selling Association has a Code of Ethics[513] that binds its members and a Code of Practice for Consumers[514] that is aligned with the OFT.

Unsolicited telephone calls, faxes, emails (spam), and text messages as well as the creation of cookies on a customer's computer are regulated by the Privacy and Electronic Communications (EC Directive) Regulations (PECR).[515] The enforcement is incumbent on the Office of the Information Commissioner.[516] Again the self-regulation authorities (Direct Marketing Authority (DMA)[517] and ASA) are the places to turn first with complaints. For individual consumers, individual business owners and partnerships, the "opt-in System" applies to unrequested emails and text messages.[518] Emails must contain a recognizable sender, a valid address where the recipient can request to be spared from further emails.[519] Furthermore, the nature of the email as advertisement must be clearly distinguishable without opening up the message body.[520] Before cookies are stored on the consumer's computer, an option to decline must be displayed. The opt-in system also applies to automated phone calls and unsolicited faxes.[521] For unsolicited phone calls[522] and unsolicited mail,[523] the opt-out System applies. The "Robinson lists" are maintained by the so-called "Preference Services",[524] which are institutions of the DMA.

Extensive duties to inform exist for door-to-door sales.[525] According to ASA/CAP Code, visits by a sales representative must be announced[526] and the option to decline must be given.[527]

The recipient of unsolicited goods is not obliged to make any payments and can keep them as free gifts;[528] the sender becomes criminally liable if he sends an invoice. For some products, the unrequested advertisement or delivery is prohibited.[529]

511. An independent organisation established by the direct marketing industry, <www.dma.org.uk/content/Pro-Authority.asp>. The two codes overlap partly but the DMA Code contains further regulations e.g. for telemarketing. S. ASA/CAP Code Sec. 41.1.
512. For other businesses the ASA/CAP Code applies.
513. <www.dsa.org/ethics/ethics.htm>. A.1. forbids misleading, illegal and unethical practices towards consumers.
514. <www.dsa.org/ethics/consumers.htm>.
515. In force since 11.12.2003. The PECR transposes Directive 20238/EC. It replaces the Data Protection and Privacy Regulations of 1999.
516. Formerly the Data Protection Commissioner.
517. <www.dma.org.uk/content/Pro-Authority.asp>.
518. Section 22(2), (3) PECR.
519. Section 23 PECR.
520. Section 8 Electronic Commerce (EC Directive) Regulations 2002 und ASA/CAP Code Rule 22.1.
521. Section 20(1), (2) PECR.
522. Section 21(1) PECR.
523. Section 11 Data Protection Act 1988, in force since 1.3.2000.
524. For normal mail (MPS), Fax (FPS), Telefon (TPS) und Email (e-MPS).
525. Consumer Protection (Cancellation of Contracts Concluded Away from Business Premises) Regulations 1987, in implementation of Directive 85/577/EWG.
526. Even when a consumer answers an advertising.
527. Rule 42.7. S. also Sec. 48 ff. Consumer Credit Act 1974 and Sec. 56 Financial Services Act 1986.
528. Unsolicited Goods and Services Act 1971 und 1975, amended by Consumer Protection (Distance Selling) Regulations 2000, S.I. 2000 Nr. 2334, implementing the Distance Selling Directive of the EU.
529. For example creditcards and advertising for loans directed to minors. Schicker/Ohly, note 90 f.

Deceitful pyramid schemes are difficult to differentiate from legitimate multi-level marketing systems.[530] Legitimate distribution systems are permitted in accordance with the regulations of Part XI of the Fair Trading Act[531] and the Trading Schemes Regulations 1997. Pyramid schemes, however, violate the codex of ASA/CAP and DMA.[532]

5. Sales promotion

Premiums, rebates and special sales events are largely permitted and subject to only few legal restraints.[533] Within the scope of self-regulation, however, the ASA/CAP code regulates such marketing measures.[534] Just as for advertising, these must be legal, decent, honest and truthful[535] and respect the principals of fair competition.[536] In the area of rebates trading stamps were regulated by the Trading Stamps Act of 1964 which, however, was repealed on 6 April 2005.[537] The Code of Practice for Traders on Price Indications, which regulates the prohibition of misleading price indications in regards to special sales, must be followed.[538] Furthermore, the seller is obliged to supply the anticipated demand for goods.[539] The ASA/CAP code on advertising and sales promotion permits free offers, free trials or premiums, as long as the general provisions against misleading advertising etc. are respected.[540]

The ASA/CAP Code also regulates the advertising with promotions with prizes.[541] Information regarding conditions for participation and chances of winning must be provided. Deceitful practices, or "scams", do not only violate general criminal provisions, but also the Regulations on misleading advertising and the ASA/CAP Code.

6. Defamation, disparagement

The common law suits of defamation or injurious falsehood can be used against disparagement and defamation.[542] Rule 20.1 of the ASA/CAP Code prohibits unfairly attacking or discrediting companies or their products. When comparative advertising is used, defamation and disparagement of the products, characteristics and activities of competitors is prohibited.[543]

530. See the differences from the point of view of the World Federation of Direct Selling Associations under <www.wfdsa.org/legal_reg/ge_ppaper1.asp>. and <www.wfdsa.org/legal_reg/ge_ppaper3.asp>.
531. Amended by the Trading Schemes Act 1996.
532. S. information about scams under <www.consumerdirect.gov.uk/general/scams/index.shtml>.
533. Circus/Painter, Sales Promotion Law, London (1989); Ulmer/v.Westerholt, no. 513 ff...
534. Rules 27 bis 38.
535. Rule 2.1. these terms are explained in Rules 4 to 7.
536. Rule 27.4.
537. Trading stamps schemes are now covered by general consumer protection laws, <www.dti.gov.uk/ccp/topics1/pdf1/tradstampsguide.pdf>.
538. In addition to this, the Price Marking Order 1999 (Statutory Instrument No 3042) which implements EC Directive 98/6/EC entered into force on 18.3.2003.
539. Rule 30.
540. The term "free" is explicitly regulated by Rule 32.
541. Rule 33bis 35.
542. S. above.
543. Rule 20.1.

7. Danger of confusion

Danger of confusion may lead to the common law suit of passing off. The benchmark for confusion is (as in Trade Mark Law) the average consumer who is reasonably attentive and circumspect. The mere effect of enticing is not considered enough, if the wrong impression is corrected before the sale. Therefore look-a-likes (same get up but distinctively different marks) are largely considered legal.[544]

8. Misappropriation

There is no special prohibition under unfair trade practices law beyond the industrial property law and copyright law that prohibit imitation.[545] If imitation causes danger of confusion, a suit can be brought under the general conditions, especially passing off.[546] There is no cause of action in common law regarding the exploitation of reputation. However, the ASA/CAP Code prohibits taking unfair advantage of brand names, business names, indications of origin or other characteristics of a competitor's product.[547]

9. Impediment of competitors

The enticing away of customers or employees (and their employment in violation of an effective non-competition covenant) can be considered inducement or procurement of breach of contract and the wronged party can bring suit.[548] Know how is protected by contract and tort law. Therefore, secrecy clauses are recommended. Sometimes secrecy obligations can be derived from an employees general duty of allegiance. The common law cause of action is "breach of contractual obligation of fidelity" or "abuse of confidential information". The incitement to betray secrets is considered a tort if the inciter knows of the contract and has the mens rea of recklessness. A lawsuit based on conspiracy is also possible.

10. Breach of law

The common law has a cause of action known as "breach of statutory duties". In practice, however, it is difficult to determine the rights being protected by the violated norm and to prove that this claimant and his damages are covered by it. The Trade Description Act has thus so far not been considered a protective law.[549]

11. Enforcement

Where common law principles have been violated, an action for damages is possible. The claimant has the burden of proof; when encountering difficulties calculating

544. As to the requirements of pasing off see above.
545. Kamperman Sander, p.53 f.
546. S. also Rule 21 ASA/CAP Code.
547. Rule 20.2.
548. Cornish/Llewelyn, 2-15. S. as an example the case *Unique Pub Properties* v. *Beer and Minerals*, [2003] All E.R. (D) 314 (June), where beverages had been supplied to pubs despite knowledge that they had exclusive dealimg agreements with other supliers.
549. Ohly, Richterrecht, p. 37 ff.

the damages such as to goodwill, the court can help with estimations.[550] Instead of compensation, the claimant can request an account of profits, although it is within the discretion of the court. Punitive damages may apply in case of defamation. Aggravated damages can apply to situations that involve extremely malicious motives or behavior. A publication of the verdict can be ordered by the court.

In practice, injunctive relief is most important, and most proceedings are concluded after such a decision. The court summarily tests the merits of the case and weighs the interests of the parties. In especially urgent cases, an interim injunction without participation of the defendant can be achieved. The search order is a distinctive feature of the British system; it gives the claimant extensive rights to preserve evidence.[551]

The Trade Description Act and the Consumer Protection Act have penal sanctions. Criminal proceedings can be initiated by the regulatory authority. In English law,[552] private persons have this right as well. In simple cases, the criminal court can also order the compensation of the claimant.

In case of a violation of state regulations, the regulatory authority can request a cease and desist order from the court. The Stop Now Orders (E.C. Regulations) 2001[553] make it easier to request a cease and desist order for a cross-border violation of European consumer protection regulations.[554] A violation of judicial rulings is punishable by monetary penalty or imprisonment as contempt of court.

Rulings of the ASA are published. It also can demand changes to or withdrawal of ads. If such a demand is refused, the OFT can step in and request a court to give a cease and desist order. The media will not publish such ads. For association codes, the severest sanction is expulsion from the association. OFCOM can prohibit the broadcast of such advertising in television and radio. An even more effective measure is to take away the license in extreme cases.

In common law, the injured party has standing to sue in civil cases. In criminal or administrative actions, the authorities bring suit. In some circumstances, private claims are also possible in the criminal court. Consumers and competitors may submit complaints to authorities and self-regulation organs.[555] In criminal suits, a company can be sued as a legal person.

XI. GREECE

Selected Literature: Alexandridou, *Die Beurteilung der Zugabe nach griechischem Wettbewerbsrecht*, GRUR Int. 1977, 298; Alexandridou, *Die gesetzgeberische Entwicklung des Verbraucherschutz- und Wettbewerbsrechts in Griechenland*, GRUR Int. 1992, 120; Alexandridou, in: Ulmer (ed.), *Das Recht des unlauteren Wettbewerbs in den Mitgliedstaaten der EWG*, Vol. VII, *Griechenland*, 1994; Alexandridou, *The Greek Consumer Protection Act of 1994*, GRUR Int. 1996, 400; Alexandridou,

550. With the possibility to grant only nominal damages, Schricker/Ohly, note 166 ff.
551. Ch. 12, sec. 7 Civil Procedure Act 1997 (formerly called "Anton Piller Order").
552. Scottish law is different in this respect.
553. S.I. 2001/1422 implementing EC Directive 98/27/EC.
554. In principle, this is restricted to "Community infringements" (Definition in Sec. 212 Enterprise Act 2002), i.e. infringements of EC law or its implementation acts into national law.
555. Section 11 and Sec. 205 Enterprise Act 2002 provide for "super complaints" through recognised consumers associations to OFT or other agencies if certain markets in their entirety show properties that might lead to substantial damages for consumers.

To dikeo tou ilektronikou emporiou, 2004; Georgakopoulos, *Egchiridio emporikou dikeou. I empori, Geniko meros* Vol. I, 1984; Gouskos, *Die Beurteilung des Verkaufs mit Zugaben nach dem griechischen Gesetz gegen den unlauteren Wettbewerb*, GRUR Int. 2000, 38; Keßler/Alexandridou, *Greece*, in: Micklitz/Kessler (ed.), *Marketing Practices Regulation and Consumer Protection in the EC-Member States and the US*, 2002, p. 128; Kotsiris, *Dikeo Antagonismou*, 4th ed. 2001; Liakopoulos, *Viomichaniki Idioktisia (Industrial Property)*, 5th ed. 2000; Marinos, *Arthemitos Antagonismos*, 2002; Panagiotidou, *Sigkritiki diffimisi*, 2000; Papathoma-Baetge, in: Papagiannis (ed.), *Griechisches Wirtschafts- und Unternehmensrecht*, 1997, p. 55; Rokas (ed.), *Athemitos Antagonismos*, 1996; Selekos, *Die Preisunterbietung als Mittel des unlauteren Wettbewerbs nach griechischem Recht*, GRUR Int. 1994, 212.

1. Sources of law

Nomos peri Athemitas Antagonismou (Law No. 146/1914 against Unfair Competition) from 12 December 1913/17 January 1914 (UWG); Nomos peri prostasias ton Katanaloton (Consumer Protection Law No. 2251/1994) from 11 November 1994. (Consumer Protection Act)

2. Greek unfair competition law in a nutshell

Greek unfair competition law[556] is based on two pillars: The Law No. 146/1914 against unfair competition (UWG)[557] on the one hand and the Consumer Protection Act No. 2251/1994[558] in its version from 12 July 2000 on the other hand. The UWG deals with unfair competition in a broad sense while the Consumer Protection Act, which is supplemented by Law No. 2328/95,[559] mainly regulates advertising. Both laws overlap to a large extent and are generally applied parallel to each other.

The Greek UWG corresponds in large parts to the German UWG from 1909. It contains a general clause in § 1 which prohibits any competitive act in business that violates "bones mores". The general clause is followed by some specific causes of action; among others § 3 (misleading indications), § 7 (clearance sales), § 11 (defamation), § 13 (danger of confusion), and § 16 et seq. (protection of trade secrets).

The most important regulation is the general clause. The term "bones mores" is interpreted according to existing social values ("decency of those who do business and think fairly and justly").[560] Case law refers also to internal legal principles, namely the Constitution,[561] the fundamental principles of anti-trust law, the European directives, the jurisdiction of the ECJ and guidelines by the Greek self regulation such as the

556. Greek unfair competition law is discussed in detail in German by Alexandridou, in: Ulmer (ed.) Das Recht des unlauteren Wettbewerbs in den Mitgliedstaaten der EWG, Griechenland (1994); Papathoma-Baetge, p. 55 ff. The leading treatises in Greek are by Kotsiris, Marinos and Rokas. As to Greek law in general see Kerameus/Kotsiris (ed.), Introduction to Greek Law, 2nd ed. 1993.
557. A German translation can be found in Alexandridou (fn. 556), p. 241. The UWG is supplemented by several decrees; see Parakis, in Rokas (ed.), p. 15.
558. FEK (Official Publication A, 191); German translation in GRUR Int. 1995, 894. The reform through the Decree No. Z 1-496 of 7.12.2000 concerned comparative advertising.
559. The Law No. 2328/95 regulates advertising in broadcasting and the protection of personality, honor and privacy.
560. Papathoma-Baetge, p. 60; Alexandridou (fn. 556), No. 35.
561. Alexandridou (fn. 556), No. 40; Liakopoulos, Viomichaniki Idioktisia (Industrial Property), p. 418; First Instance (single Judge) Athens 17500/1993, Armenopoulos 1994, p. 819, 820.

"Code of advertising ethics".[562] The general clause is also the basis for general "case groups" developed by jurisprudence and legal literature.[563]

The application requires a competitive act in business and a competitive relationship between plaintiff and defendant. This is interpreted rather strictly; for example, a competitive relationship is deemed not to exist between different levels of trade.[564] Independent professions are not included.

The protective goal of the UWG originally only covered competitors. In recent years, it was suggested in legal literature and also by some courts to broaden the concept in order to include the interests of the general public and the consumers.[565] However, only competitors, their associations and the chamber of commerce have standing to sue.[566]

The Consumer Protection Act of 1994[567] regulates misleading, comparative and otherwise unfair advertising as well as other causes of action that are relevant to consumers (such as discrimination, advertising aimed at children, and direct marketing). The purpose of the Consumer Protection Law is to "ensure the health and safety of consumers and protect their economic interests". Enforcement is mainly through civil suits: Consumer associations and the chamber of commerce have standing to sue for injunctive relief per Art. 10 para. 8, 9, 10 and 15. In the area of direct marketing, individuals also have standing to sue,[568] as do competitors in the central regulation of Art. 9.[569] The latter can use both legal foundations in reference to the overlapping causes of action; claims for compensation, however, are only considered under the UWG. The proper defendant, too, is different; the independent professions are not included in the UWG (but included in the Consumer Protection Act).

The UWG partly supplements the regulations of the intellectual property laws.[570] When interpreting the individual causes of action, the valuations of anti-trust law may also need to be taken into account.[571]

562. Regarding self regulation, see Alexandridou (fn. 556), No. 303. Kostopoulos, Diafinisi ke Ellinikos Kodikas diafimisis, 1999, p. 225; The Code mostly regulates misleading, concealed and "indecent" advertising as well as advertising aimed at children.
563. Regarding the individual "causes of action" based on the general clause see Papathoma-Baetge, p. 61 et seq. The "case groups" correspond mostly to the "Fallgruppen" created under § 1 of the German UWG of 1909.
564. Athens 18743/1992, EEmpD 1993, p. 141; see also First Instance Athens (Chamber) 2339/1997, DEE 1997, 470 (no competitive relationship between a seller of CD-players etc. and a publishing company that offered such items as premiums); Cocalis, p. 124; Karakostas/Tzouganatos, Prostasia tou katanaloti (Consumer Protection), 2nd ed. 2002, p. 292.
565. See, for instance, Alexandridou (fn. 556), No. 24 ff.; Papathoma-Baetge, p. 57; different Cocalis, p. 126. Court decisions that have included the protection of the consumer are, for instance, Athens 97/1986, EEmpD 1986, 703, 706, 710; Kavala 410/1994, EEmpD 1995, 510, 512.
566. See Alexandridou (fn. 556), No. 107.
567. See fn. 557.
568. Cf. Karakostas/Tzouganatos, p. 303.
569. This is not undisputed; see, for instance, Marinos, Athemitos Antagonismos (Unfair Competition), 2002,No. 646 and Liakopoulos, p. 473 on the one hand and Alexandridou, GRUR Int. 1996, 400, 402 on the other hand; see also First Instance Athens (Chamber) 2339/1997, DEE 1997, 470, 471 (only for comparative advertising).
570. Regarding IP-protection in Greece, see the leading treatises by Rokas, Viomichaniki Idoktisia, 2004 and Liakopoulos,Viomichaniki Idoktisia, 5th ed. 2000; in German Alexandridou (fn. 556), No. 69; Karatidis, in: Papagiannis (ed.), Griechisches Wirtschafts- und Unternehmensrecht, 1997, p. 441; Möhring/Schulze/Ulmer/Zweigert (ed.), Quellen des Urheberrechts, Vol. 2; furthermore Manual Industrial Property, Vol. 3 (1997).
571. Anti-trust law from 26.9.1977 (No. 703/1977); see Alexandridou (fn. 556), No. 40, Papathoma-Baetge, p. 55, 69 et seq.

Decisions regarding unfair competition law are relatively rare in Greece. However, the interpretation of the UWG is very similar to the German UWG, and the EC-Directives give some guidelines for interpretation in some areas.

3. Regulation of advertising

a. Misleading advertising

Article 3 UWG contains a broad prohibition of misleading statements. It is supplemented by a criminal cause of action in Art. 4 and by a regulation of misleading bankruptcy sales in Art. 6 UWG. The Consumer Protection Act prohibits also misleading advertising. The text in Art. 9 No. 1-3 corresponds to Directive 84/450/EEC but adds to it additional causes of action in No. 4.

Irrespective of the legal foundation, misleading advertising is interpreted according to the same principles. It requires a "statement", which must be intended for an audience consisting of a greater number of people.[572] A danger of misleading exists if the statement can be interpreted in a way that does not correspond to reality; the benchmark is the average addressee of the advertisement who acts with average attentiveness.[573] Under which circumstances advertising exaggerations are taken seriously is difficult to determine; case law is not quite consistent on this point.[574] The relevance of the misleading statements as regards its impact on the commercial behavior of the addressee and the quota of persons that have to be influenced is hardly discussed in Greek decisions: It is understood, however, that misleading advertising must be capable of affecting the decision-making of consumers.[575]

In practice, cases of misleading advertising often occur in regard to the price.[576] In addition to Art. 3 UWG and Art. 9 Consumer Protection Act, Art. 7(12) UWG applies to special offers (see below 5). Of importance is also the protection of indications regarding geographic origin.[577] Art. 9 No. 4 b Consumer Protection Act prohibits advertising using statements about the geographic origin if "the method of convincing the consumers is based on the assumption that the technology or science of a certain country which is not the country of origin would have an influence on the quality of the advertised goods". In practice, this cause of action often deals with English expressions; here it is difficult to separate real indications of origin from

572. Messages to individual persons or a limited group of people are not included; see Alexandridou (fn. 556), No. 276, 278.
573. Alexandridou (fn. 556), No. 280.
574. It depends on how much the consumers are used to such exaggerations; see Alexandridou (fn. 556), No. 280; the court of first instance Athens (27080/1995, DEE 1996, 517 and 114/1996, DEE 1996, 519—"Slim") has, for instance, considered as misleading an advertisement for a "slimming panty hose", while the advertising slogan for a IBM-computer "No box can hit this system" was considered as harmless puffing (Athens 4543/1991, EEmpD 1992, 667—"IBM").
575. For the Consumer Protection Act this follows already from the definition of misleading advertising in Art. 9(2), which states that misleading advertising "... is capable of influencing the economic behavior of the targeted consumers"; see also Liakopoulos, p. 462; First Instance Athens (Single Judge) 27080/1995, EEmpD 1996, 495. Article 3 UWG requires an "exceptional good offer", see Alexandridou (fn. 556), No. 281 with reference to First Instance Athens (Single Judge), 288/1987, EEmpD 1987, 663.
576. See Alexandridou (fn. 556), No. 287.
577. See Alexandridou (fn. 556), No. 315.

Anglican terms that have been incorporated into the common Greek language ("style", "fashion", etc.).[578]

Also considered misleading advertising, per Art. 9 No. 4 a Consumer Protection Act, is the use of expert opinion by people that lack the claimed scientific qualification, specialization or authority (testimonials) or who did not approve use of their statement in advertising. The same applies to scientific terms, test results or quotations which are intended to give advertising a "scientific touch" (see under 3c).

The courts normally determine themselves if a case qualifies as misleading advertising. A reversal of the burden of proof does not occur.

b. Comparative advertising

According to Art. 9 No. 8 Consumer Protection Act, comparative advertising—mostly in conjunction with Directive 97/55/EC—is permitted if it "compares the basic, similar, verifiable and impartially selected characteristics of the advertised goods or services in an objective manner", does not mislead consumers, does not cause danger of confusion, is not "depreciatory, defamatory or disparaging" and does not "aim at exploiting the reputation of a brand name or a characteristic of a competitor". Furthermore, limitations regarding indications of origin and "imitations" must be observed. Product tests conducted by a third party can only be used, according to No. 9, with a written permission by the person in charge of the tests; the advertiser is liable for content of tests as if he had conducted it himself. Few cases are known today regarding this regulation; which was only introduced in 2000.[579]

c. Concealed advertising

Greek law prohibits concealed advertising through various provisions. According to Art. 9 No. 6 d Consumer Protection Act, subliminal advertising is prohibited. No. 4. lit c. states that an advertisement may not appear to be a scientific statement, journalistic research or commentary. Article 9 No. 5 forbids the concealment of the advertisement in another advertisement. The court of first instance Athens has, for example, prohibited statements of Phillip Morris regarding the dangers of smoking on the basis that they could be confused with scientific opinions.[580]

On television, program and commercials must be clearly separated and surreptitious advertising is prohibited. For the internet, extensive transparency duties exist for commercial communication according to Art. 5 of the Decree No 131/2003, which transposed the transparency requirements of the Commerce Directive 2000/31/EC into Greek law.

In addition to this, the concealment of the commercial character violates the general clause of Art. 1 UWG.

578. See Alexandridou (fn. 556), No. 326.
579. But see Panagiotidou, Sigyritiki diafimigi, 2000, and the decision of the court of first instance Kavala 410/1994, EEmpD 1995, 510 ff.—"Viesmann". The court prohibited a comparison of clearly misleading indications as to the superiority of the advertiser's product (and the inferiority of the competitor's product).
580. First Instance Athens (Single Judge) 26583/1996, DEE 1997, 84—"Phillip Morris".

d. Aggressive advertising

The general clause of Art. 1 UWG also applies to harassment.[581] Additionally the Consumer Protection Act provides (for) a strong protection against harassment by direct marketing (see under 4,5).

e. Product and media specific advertising regulations

Advertising, teleshopping, and sponsoring in broadcasting are regulated by Law No. 2328/95, which also transposed the requirements of the Television Directive.[582] Furthermore, the prohibition of surreptitious advertising of Art. 9 no. 4 Consumer Protection Act also applies (especially for the press, see under c).

Product specific advertising regulations exist especially for pharmaceuticals,[583] foodstuff,[584] and alcohol.[585] Advertising for tobacco products is forbidden on television.[586] According to Art. 9 No. 14 Consumer Protection Act, the Minister of Commerce can promulgate regulations for advertising of specific goods or services so that the consumer can better judge the quality and price of the good or service offered.

f. Other advertising regulations

Article 9 No. 5 Consumer Protection Act forbids advertising that violates "bones mores". According to No. 6, the following forms of advertising are considered unlawful: (a) advertising that leads to or misuses feelings of fear, superstition or prejudice or encourages criminal behavior; (b) advertising that discriminates on the basis of sex, race, nationality, heritage, belief, or physical or psychological characteristics; (c) advertising that gives the impression of an excessively enticing offer, especially if directed towards children, youth and other groups that require special protection; (d) advertising that indirectly points towards goods other than the ones that are the obvious content of the advertisement, without disclosing that this information is a inseparable part of the message.[587]

581. See Kotsiris, Diyeo Antagonismou, 2001, No. 140 who refers to the German jurisdiction and the balance of interest that is necessary.
582. See Keßler/Alexandridou, p. 135. The Decree No. 100/2000 also regulates advertising in television, sponsoring and teleshopping.
583. According to the Decree No. 96/1973 in the version of the Decree No. 1316/1983; cf. Chryssospathis, p. 83. See also Art. 21 of the Minister Decree No. Y 6a/776/1993, and Art. 5 No. 7 of the Decree No. 100/2000 about advertising for drugs.
584. According to Art. 10 of the Code for foodstuff and beverages of 1987 in the version of 1995.
585. TV-advertising for alcohol is restricted according to Art. 5(8) and (9) of the Decree No. 100/2000; in addition a new Minister Decree from 2003 deals with the labelling and advertising.
586. Warnings are mandatory according to Decree No. 1591 from May 1989.
587. There are few decisions on the basis of Art. 9 Consumer Protection Act. The Court of first instance of Athens has, for example, forbidden the advertisement for a computer play "Crash dummies" in which a doll was slaughtered, Athens 335/1995, DEE 1996, 515—"Crash dummies". As to the prohibition of indirect advertisements see Karakostas/Tzouganatos, Prostasia tou katanaloti (Consumer Protection), 1997, p. 164.

4. Direct marketing

As a general rule, Art. 9 No. 13 Consumer Protection Act requires that direct marketing occur so that "the private life of the consumer is not disturbed".

For mail-order sales, comprehensive protections exist for the end user.[588] According to Art. 4 No. 4 Consumer Protection Act (and Art. 1 UWG), the sending of unordered goods is forbidden when this would cause the recipient to believe that he must pay, keep or return the goods.[589] Door to door sales are not per se forbidden, but may not under any circumstances intrude on the private life of the consumer. The mailing or depositing of advertising material is allowed so long as the addressee does not request otherwise.[590]

Advertising aimed at the consumer per telephone, fax, email, automated calls, or other electronic means of communication is under Art. 9 No. 10 Consumer Protection Law only allowed when explicitly agreed to ("opt-in"). According to No. 11, consumers may only be directly contacted when a commercial relationship already exists (or the consumer explicitly agreed to allow this contact). Information must be given further for the purposes of direct marketing and the data must be erased upon request.

Pyramid schemes are forbidden under the Regulation from 9 September 1926 and under § 1 UWG; any contracts on this basis are invalid.[591]

5. Sales promotion

Advertising with free gifts etc. is not separately regulated in Greek law.[592] Promotional incentives and price reductions are generally allowed, as are sales at a loss.[593] They are mainly judged on the basis of the prohibition on misleading advertising and, in particular, on the basis of Art. 9 No. 6 c Consumer Protection Law. According to that provision, the "impression of an excessively enticing offer" may not be given, especially "towards children, youth and other groups that require special protection". This is found to be true for very valuable (or rare) gifts and significant price reductions or when the "allocation" is dependant on chance.[594] For example, premiums like contact lenses (in connection with the sale of glasses), computers (in connection with the sale of high priced software), or four volumes of a historical book (in connection with the subscription to a newspaper) were considered illegal.[595]

588. Keßler/Alexandridou, p. 133 f.
589. Keßler/Alexandridou, p. 137.
590. The Court of first instance Athens has awarded punitive damage of 5869 Euro to a consumer whose explicit wish not to be harassed by unsolicited advertising material was not respected. Athens 1988/20002, 2003, p. 79, No. B.
591. Keßler/Alexandridou, p. 137; Marinos, in: Rokas (ed.), Ahtemitos Antagonismos, 1996, Art. 1 No. 62.
592. See Bodewig/Henning-Bodewig, WRP 2000, 1341, 1352 f.
593. They can in individual situations violate Art. 1 UWG, see Keßler/Alexandridou, p. 140; further Selekos, Die Preisunterbietung als Mittel des unlauteren Wettbewerbs nach griechischem Recht, GRUR Int. 1994, 121, 124 f.; First Instance Kavala (single Judge) 478/1984, EEmpD 1985, 359, 360.
594. Cf., for instance, Thessaloniki 1344/1985, Armenopoulos 1985, 484 with note Alexandridou; as to the wide spread practice of premiums in the press see Athens 17500/1993; Armenopoulos 1994, 819 and Gouskos, GRUR Int. 2000, 38, 40.
595. Pireaus 335/1995, EEmpD 1995, p. 515; Athens 3946/1996, EEmpD 1997, p. 128, Athens 16530/1993, EEmpD p. 1994, 482; see also the older decision of Kilkis 104/1984, EEmpD 1985, 184 (free development of films linked to the purchase of new films).

Lotteries[596] are forbidden under Art. 8 of Law 2515/97. In addition, Art. 9 No. 6 c Consumer Protection Act applies (see above). According to that law, games of chance may not be coupled with the sale of goods which includes the use of psychological pressure. It is unclear whether this also applies for competitions based on skill; in any event, if the solution is very simple and the price very valuable, such promotional games could be unfair under Art. 9 No. 6 Consumer Protection Act. Regardless of this limitation, newer decisions are predominantly liberal; for instance, a "psychological pressure to buy" was denied in a game directed to traders of chocolate and in a promotional game by a TV-magazine which involved valuable prices.[597]

Article 7(12) UWG forbids special sales events "for single or limited amounts of goods which serve to lure the public and exploit them by selling other goods in the store at a regular price". This regulation is broader than the prohibition of misleading advertising with loss-leader. Article 9 No. 6 c Consumer Protection Act, which prohibits disproportionate luring of customers through the giving of advantages, can also apply here.

Article 6 UWG regulates going out of business sales; Art. 7 UWG contains the requirements for a permissible clearance sale. Article 7(10) UWG allows seasonal sales, which are more closely regulated in a Decree.

6. Denigration, disparagement

Outside the area of comparative advertising (see above, 3b), denigration and disparagement are forbidden under Art. 11 UWG;[598] in addition, the general clause of Art. 1 UWG can apply. Article 15 UWG contains a corresponding criminal cause of action.

7. Danger of confusion

Bringing about a danger of confusion is forbidden under Art. 13 UWG.

8. Misappropriation, imitation

The imitation of products, services, etc. can be a violation of "bones mores" in the sense of the general clause of Art. 1 UWG. Unfair competition is normally assumed if the imitation leads to a danger of confusion or an exploitation of a competitor's reputation, but case law also considers aspects such as the intent of the imitator, the means of the adoption, and the level of investment and amortization (although no clear criteria have been established).[599] In the area of design, unfair competition law protection against imitation is especially important since the requirements for protection under intellectual property law are not always met in practice.[600] Computer programs are also protected in this manner.[601]

596. See Keßler/Alexandridou, p. 141.
597. Alexandridou (fn. 556), No. 372; Marinos, p. 376 who refers to Court of Appeals Athens 59/1968, EEN 1968, p. 384 and Court of First Instance Athens (Single Judge)8734/1992, EEmpD 1993, p. 504.
598. This provision corresponds to § 14 of the German UWG of 1909.
599. Keßler/Alexandridou, p. 145 f.; Alexandridou (fn. 556), No. 197 ff.; see also Arfios Pagos (Supreme Court) 15/1972, EEmpD 1972, 400.
600. Cocalis, p. 137.
601. See First Instance Thessaloniki (Single Judge), 1971/89 EEmpD 1991, 157.

9. Impediment of competitors

Obstruction of competitors' products or services is one of the main causes of action of the general clause of Art. 1 UWG (see above, 2). The following causes of action are also included: interception of customers, discrimination, boycott, undercutting sales, and inducing breach of contract[602] or domain grabbing.[603] Protection of trade secrets is regulated in Art. 16-18 UWG. [604]

10. Breach of law

The breach of laws outside of the UWG violates the general clause of Art. 1 UWG if the law has the goal of regulating competition or is based on ethics; for example, if it is aimed at protecting the health of the consumer (foodstuffs, cosmetics). For other norms, the defendant must have gained an unlawful competitive advantage.[605] Greek law is relatively strict on this issue.[606]

11. Enforcement

The UWG and the Consumer Protection Act mainly provide for civil law sanctions (see above, 2). Enforcement of the Consumer Protection Act is also provided for by the consumer associations (which can also claim immaterial damages[607]) and the "General Secretariat for Consumer Protection" that was established in 1997 at the Ministry for Development. In 2004, a new administrative agency—the Greek Consumer Ombudsman—was created.[608] In addition, self regulation through the "Simvoulio Eleghou Epikinonias" (SEE) which began its work in 2004 seems to gain importance in practice.[609]

XII. HUNGARY*

Selected Literature: Dietz, *Die Einführung von Gesetzen gegen den unlauteren Wettbewerb in ehemals sozialistischen Staaten Mittel- und Osteuropas*, GRUR Int. 1994, 649; Bacher/Bárdos/Stadler, *Hungarian National Report*, LIDC, 2002; Boytha, *Versenyjogi ismeretek (Matters of Competition Law)*, 1998; Cseres, *The Hungarian*

602. First Instance Athens (Singel Judge) 22493/1994, EEmpD 1994, p. 656; see also Alexandridou (fn. 556), No. 389 (p. 215).
603. First Instance Athens (Single Judge) 3359/2003, EEmpD 2003, 695—rolex.gr.
604. Alexandridou (fn. 556), No. 204.
605. Cf., for instance, first instance (Chamber) Thessaloniki 14944/1997, EEmpD 1997, 802, 807 with note Rokas and Mikroulea.
606. See, for instance, Court of Appeals Athens 5489/1991, EllDni 1993, p. 610 (bakery without administrative permission), Athens 11081/1995, EEmpD 1995, 516 (advertisement for glasses sold in pharmacies).
607. See Karabostas, Dikco prostasias katanaloti, 2004, p. 405.
608. Law No. 3297/2004; FEK A 259 from 23.12.2004.
609. The SEE has replaced the former organs of self regulation. It was established through Law 2863/2000; for details see www.see.gr.

* This report is authored by Dr. Bakardjieva Engelbrekt, University of Stockholm. The author wishes to thank Dr. C. Cseres, University of Amsterdam, Dr. J. Firniksz and Dr. R. Grimm, Hungarian office for Economic Competitions, for valuable information and comment.

Cocktail of Competition Law and Consumer Protection: Should it be Dissolved?, JCP 2004, 43; Fazekas, *Some facts about pyramidal sales in Central and East European Countries*, CLJ 1998, p. 495; Kajdiné Suhajda/Kardos, Reklámjogi és reklámetikai kézikönyv (Handbook of advertising law and advertising ethics), 1998; Kaszainé Mezey/Miskolczi Bodnár, *Versenyjogi kézikönyv (Handbook of competition law)*, 1997; Maniet, *Consumer Protection in Hungary*, in: Alexiev et al., *Consumer Protection in Bulgaria, Czech Republic, Estonia, Hungary, Latvia, Lithuania and Romania*, CICPP No. 4, p. 107; Sárközy (ed.): *Versenyjog (Wettbewerbsrecht)*, 2001; Vörös, *Länderbericht Ungarn*, in: Beier/Bastian/Kur (eds.), *Wettbewerbsrecht und Verbraucherschutz in den Länder Mittel- und Osteuropas*, 1992; Vida, *Schutz gegen unlauteren Wettbewerb in Ungarn*, WiRO 1993, 257; Vida, *Wettbewerbs- und Warenzeichenrecht in der ungarischen Rechtsprechung*, GRUR Int. 1991, 791; Vida, *Das Recht des unlauteren Wettbewerbs in Ungarn*, WRP 1991, 465; Várady, *The Emergence of Competition Law in (Former) Socialist Countries*, Am. J. Comp. Law 1999, 229.

1. Sources of law

Versenytörvény (Act LVII on the Prohibition of Unfair and Restrictive Market Practices) of 1996 (VT); Reklámtörvény (Act LVIII on Business Advertising Activity)[610] of 1997 (RT)

2. Hungarian unfair competition law in a nutshell

The main legal source of Hungarian unfair competition law is the Act LVII of 1996 on the Prohibition of Unfair and Restrictive Market Practices (Competition Act, Versenytörvény, VT).[611] The VT is a comprehensive act on regulating market conduct and is very broad in scope. The most distinctive feature of the approach taken by the Hungarian lawmaker is that the objectives of free and fair competition are integrated in one and the same piece of legislation. According to the Preamble of VT, the Act protects the public interest in the maintenance of market competition, serving economic and social progress, the interests of the undertakings in observing the requirements of business integrity, as well as the interests of consumers.

Another characteristic of the Act is that it introduces a division between competitor-related and consumer-related unfair marketing practices. The main provisions on unfair competition affecting competitors' interests are to be found in Chapter II VT entitled "Prohibition of Unfair Competition". The consumer-centered rules are listed in Chapter III ("Prohibition of the Unfair Influencing of Consumer Decisions"). Of central importance in the first group of competitor-oriented rules is the general clause of Art. 2 VT. Under this clause it is prohibited to conduct economic activities in an unfair manner violating or jeopardizing the lawful interests of competitors and consumers, or in a way which is in conflict with the requirements of business

610. The text of the two acts in English translation as well as other legal materials can be found on the website of the Office for Economic Competition (GVH) <www.gvh.hu>

611. An earlier precursor of the present Competition Act was Act LXXXVI on the Prohibition of Unfair Market Conduct of 1990 (German translation in: Beier/Bastian/Kur, 1992, p. 307). It is also worth noting that Hungary was one of the few former socialist countries of Central and Eastern Europe to enact a statute against unfair competition already during the years of command economy, namely Act IV of 31.10.1984 on the Prohibition of Unfair Economic Activity.

integrity. The general clause is exemplified by relatively few specific factual situations constituting unfair market conduct (see Art. 3-7 VT).

The consumer-related rules are divided into two categories. The first one addresses different forms of consumer fraud (Art. 8) and the second one concerns business methods restricting the freedom of consumer choice (Art. 10). Although the general clause of Art. 2 defines as an act of unfair competition also acts infringing upon consumer interests, the clause can be invoked only in relations between competitors and cannot be applied to situations of consumer deception.[612]

The VT represents an idiosyncratic mix of civil and administrative law characteristics. The provisions on unfair competition in Chapter II are enforced chiefly by private law means upon the initiative of the interested parties in proceedings before the ordinary courts (Art. 86 VT). The consumer-oriented provisions as well as all rules concerning restrictions on competition are in turn enforced by way of administrative proceedings.

The integrated approach to antitrust and unfair competition law in the Competition Act explains the central position of the Hungarian Competition Authority (Gazdasági Versenyhivatal, GVH) in the process of implementation and enforcement of the VT (Art. 33 VT). Within the structure of GVH there is a separate body, the so called Competition Council, which performs the actual decision-making functions in individual cases and enjoys a considerable degree of independence (Art. 35 VT).

Despite the already existing provisions on consumer deception in the VT, the Hungarian lawmaker found it appropriate to adopt a separate Act LVIII of 1997 on Business Advertising Activity (Advertisement Act, Reklámtörvény, RT), setting out to implement the relevant EC Directives in the field of advertising. Also this Act is of mixed, partly administrative and partly private law, nature.

Further rules on consumer protection are integrated in the comprehensive Act CLV of 1997 on Consumer Protection[613] (Törvény a fogyasztóvédelemröl, FTT) as well as in a number of Governmental Decrees on specific consumer protection topics (for instance distance selling or doorstep selling). The FTT is enforced with the active involvement of the Bureau of Consumer Affairs (Fogyasztóvédelmi Föfelügyelöség, FVF).

Due to its close relationship with antitrust law and consumer protection, the connection of Hungarian unfair competition law with intellectual property law is less apparent. However, the provision on imitation of distinctive signs and product characteristics in Art. 6 VT can be used as a complement to trade mark protection and can be applied in parallel to the protection by exclusive intellectual property rights.[614]

3. Regulation of advertising

The rules on advertising are scattered in a number of laws, forming different—and often overlapping—layers of regulation.[615] The most comprehensive treatment of

612. The opposite was true for the general clause of the 1990 Competition Act, which could be applied to consumer-related situations. See Cseres, 2004, p. 58; Bacher/Bárdos/Stadler, p. 5.
613. The text of the Act in English translation can be retrieved from the website of the Consumer Protection Inspectorate <www.fvf.hu/gicp.php3?page=2>. For a German translation see GRUR Int. . . .
614. The rules and sanctions pertaining to industrial property rights take, however, precedence over rules on unfair competition law. See Bacher/Bárdos/Stadler, p. 4.
615. This is partly a consequence of the efforts to bring Hungarian law in conformity with the Community "*acquis*", in particular those in the area of consumer protection. Initially, the main provisions on

advertising is offered by the RT. Concurrently to RT, Art. 8 VT ensures a well-developed protection against consumer fraud. Furthermore, the FTT sets out to prevent consumer deception caused by insufficient, incorrect or misleading labeling and product designation.

a. Misleading advertising

Article 8(1) VT prohibits explicitly the deception of consumers in economic competition. The concept of deception is broadly defined and covers not only advertising claims, but also designation of goods as well as the dissemination of any other information (Art. 8(2)(a) RT). Not only false or misleading information, but also deception by omission is subsumed under the prohibition (Art. 8(2)(b) RT). The deceptive claims, information and presentation may relate to the price or to any other essential aspect of the product. It should be noted that the effects of a product on health or on the environment are particularly mentioned as essential features (Art. 8(2)(a) RT).[616]

Article 8 requires that the deceptive information shall be relevant for consumer choice in order to be prohibited. This is evident from the emphasis on "essential features" in Art. 8(2)(a), as well as from the explicit condition in lit. c that the factors related to the sale and distribution of the goods shall be influencing the decision of consumers.

The standard of deception in the practice of the Competition Council is high. Exaggerations are not tolerated if they concern verifiable information.[617] But even claims like "the best" and "finest" can constitute acts of unfair competition, unless they are supported by convincing evidence. In the opinion of the Competition Council a claim of superiority could reasonably be used in advertising only if such claims are proven by means of objective scientific tests of sufficient certainty.[618]

The Competition Council proceeds in its assessment of advertising from the average consumer reasonably circumspect and informed under the circumstances. If the advertising targets a group of consumers who are more vulnerable, for instance sick people or children, then the average consumer from the targeted group is used as a benchmark.[619] Stricter standards apply also where environmental arguments are used in advertising.[620]

advertising of a general nature were concentrated in the Competition Act. With the VT of 1996, however, the rules on misleading and comparative advertising were transferred in the RT. See Cseres, op.cit., p. 51.

616. The enumeration is by no way exhaustive, something confirmed by Art. 8(2)(c) RT, which defines as deception also information about factors related to the sale and distribution of the goods, and in particular the method of distribution, terms of payment, gifts associated with the goods, discounts, or the chance of winning.
617. For instance claims of having the largest selection of pop-rock, classical and other music was qualified as misleading since the advertiser was not in a position to furnish evidence in support of its claim. See Case No. Vj-245/1995/28—"Fotex Records" under the Competition Act of 1990.
618. An opinion poll, showing that a certain brand of yoghurt is most popular among the interviewed consumers was not accepted as sufficient evidence, since it reflected subjective judgment. See Case No. Vj-140/1994—"Danone" under the Competition Act of 1990. See also the dispute between Colgate and Procter & Gamble as to the superior qualities of tooth-paste containing calcium. Since the scientific evidence was non-conclusive the unconditional superiority claims made by Colgate were found unjustified and constituting act of unfair competition, Case No. Vj-81/1994—"Colgate".
619. See Annual Report of GVH, 2002, under 3.2.4.2.
620. See Case No. Vj-290/1996, reported by De Caluwe, Les regles de concurrence dans le monde, evolution recénte, 190 Revue International de la Concurrence 1999, issue 3, p. 4, at 30.

An additional set of rules on deceptive advertising is included in RT (Art. 7). In substance these rules do not differ much from the rules in the VT. The main explanation for this duplication is apparently the desire to furnish the FVF with enforcement powers in the field of misleading advertising.

The RT envisages a possibility, if justified, to compel the advertiser to substantiate the statements in his advertisement (Art. 17(3) RT). In this way the requirement of reversed burden of proof in Directive 84/450/EEC is fulfilled.

b. Comparative advertising

The VT does not explicitly regulate comparative advertising as such. According to Art. 3, however, it is prohibited to injure or jeopardize the reputation of competitors by making or spreading false allegations or by falsifying facts, or by other practices.

A more detailed regulation of comparative advertising can be found in Arts. 7a-7c RT. These provisions serve the transposition of Directive 97/55/EC in Hungarian law. Although the Hungarian law-maker has chosen to follow the text of the Directive, in some respects the implementation is not literal. For instance Art. 7a divides the conditions for permitted comparative advertising into two groups—positive (Art. 7a(3) RT) and negative (Art. 7a(2) RT). Among the positive requirements, one can note the requirement that the comparative advertising shall objectively exhibit the price, where applicable (Art. 7a(3)(c) RT). In respect to legitimate comparative advertising, the RT provides explicitly that the holder of the trademark shall not contest its use if such use is appropriate, essential and not excessive (Art. 7a(4) RT).[621]

Very often comparative advertising is based on misleading claims. In such cases, the general rules on consumer deception of the VT may be invoked. Thus, the Competition Council condemned as misleading the advertising employed by two hypermarkets "Auchan" and "Tesco" in the course of a fierce price war between the two competitors. Claims of being cheaper were treated as verifiable statements in need of substantiation.[622]

c. Disguised advertising

Covert and subliminal advertising is explicitly prohibited in Art. 6(1) of the RT. The use of such advertising could arguably be also qualified as a method restricting the freedom of choice of consumers under Art. 10 VT. Specific rules on separation between advertising and program content are established in Act No. 1 on Radio and Television Service of 1996 (Rádiózásról és televíziózásról szóló törvény, RTT).[623]

621. Comparisons with fictitious product or company, with a product that is not available in commercial circles, with a product or a company that cannon be clearly identified, with a product or a company not of a similar nature are forbidden (Art. 7c RT).
622. See Vj-209/2000—"Auchan"; Vj-217/2000—"Tesco". The cases are reported by Cseres, op. cit., p. 64.
623. As a matter of general principle advertising shall be identifiable as such. Advertisements shall be clearly separated from the program (Art. 10(3) RTT). Hidden and subliminal advertisement is impermissible (Art. 10(5) RTT).

d. Intrusive advertising

The use of business methods that manipulate consumers and interfere with their privacy are certainly to be considered falling foul of Art. 10 VT, since such methods significantly limit consumers' freedom of choice. The RT in addition explicitly prohibits advertising infringing on personal rights, on the respect for the deceased, or on rights related to the protection of personal data.[624]

e. Product- and media-specific advertising regulation (references)

Specific restrictions on advertising for certain product categories and in certain media are to be found in a number of legislative acts and governmental decrees. Of more general nature is the rule of Art. 6(2) RT prohibiting the advertising for goods whose production or marketing is illegal.

The RT introduced restrictions for display of alcohol and tobacco advertisements at certain public places (Art. 12(2)(e) RT). In 2002 an almost total ban of tobacco advertising was explicitly introduced in the RT.[625] Pornographic advertising and advertising for sexual services are forbidden by force of Art. 5a RT, with the exception of advertisments in sex shops or attached to sex goods.

Advertising in the electronic media is subject to detailed regulation under the RTT. The rules follow closely the Television Without Frontiers Directive (TWFD).[626] The RTT exempts broadcasters from liability for the advertisements, with the exception of intentional deception (Art. 10(1) RTT).[627]

Act CVIII of 2001 on electronic commercial services and on matters relating to information society services sets out to bring Hungarian law in compliance with the E-commerce Directive 2000/31/EC. It applies the "country-of-origin" principle and implements the information requirements set forth in the Directive.

f. Other regulations on advertising

The RT prohibits a number of unfair or otherwise improper methods of advertising upon threat of administrative penalties. For instance, advertising shall not encourage violence or generate sense of fear (Art. 4 RT). Advertising targeting children may not be published if it may harm their physical, intellectual or moral development. In particular it is forbidden to show children and juveniles in dangerous or violent situations or in situations with sexual emphasis (Art. 5 RT). Some of these restrictions

624. In the practice of the Competition Council there are numerous cases when doorstep selling or aggressive methods of direct marketing were qualified as unjustifiable intervention in the private sphere of the consumers and limiting their freedom of choice.
625. See Annual Report of the Consumer Protection Inspectorate, 2002, under 3.1.
626. Chapter IV of the RTT contains a long catalogue of advertising restrictions and prohibitions. Apart from a total ban on the advertisement of tobacco and of prescription drugs, the RTT prohibits unconditionally the advertisement of fire-arm explosives (Art. 13(1) RTT). The advertising of alcoholic drinks is subject to similar restrictions as those set up in the TWFD as is advertising directed to children (Art. 14 RTT). In addition, alcohol advertising shall not be broadcasted in prime broadcasting time with the exception of drinks of low alcohol content (Art. 13(2)(a)-(f) RTT).
627. The supervision of the Act is entrusted to the National Radio and Television Commission, which can impose fines in case of violation. The Commission can initiate proceedings involving consumer protection issues and against practices of unfair market competition (Art. 41(1)(k) RTT).

are obviously inspired by the rules on advertising in TWFD, but are then extended to the whole field of advertising irrespective of form or medium.

4. Information requirements

The issue of consumer information is taken particularly seriously by the FTT. This statute comprises a list of mandatory information requirements for the labeling and designation of products. In respect to consumer credit a duty for the seller to provide clear information as to the full cost of the credit is established in Art. 6(4) RT.

5. Direct marketing, specific marketing methods

As in other countries in transition to a true market economy, also in Hungary pyramid sales have been a wide-spread plague. Legally such schemes have been often qualified as constituting both consumer deception under Art. 8 VT, and a business method restricting unjustifiably the freedom of consumer choice under Art. 10 VT.[628] In 1997 moreover the Hungarian Criminal Code (IV Act of 1978) was amended to include a special provision on pyramid sales and games, causing significant damage. Pyramid games and similar arrangements are now punishable as a felony with imprisonment of up to three years (See Art. 299 c).[629]

Government Decree 44/1998 (III.1) regulates door to door selling, while Government Decree 17/1999 (II.5) is devoted to distance selling.[630] Act CXIX of 1995 contains a definition of direct marketing. Act CVIII of 2001 contains rules on direct mail and unsolicited commercial e-mails.

6. Sales promotion

Rebates and free gifts are in principle allowed, unless they employ deceptive information, for instance about the terms of payment or the gifts associated with the goods (Art. 8(2)(c) VT), or unless they make the objective appraisal of goods and offers more difficult and thus restrict consumer freedom of choice (Art. 10 VT).[631] The same applies to promotional games. The organizer must not use deceptive information, in particular as to the chances of winning. If the game is marketed in an excessively aggressive manner, it may be seen to fall foul of Art. 10 VT.

7. Disparagement

According to Art. 3 VT jeopardizing or infringing the reputation of a competitor is prohibited as an act of unfair competition. Such is always the case when false allegations are made about a competitor or when facts are falsified.

628. See Fazekas, 1998, p. 495 with reference to the decision of the Competition Council in the Case "BC Pyramid Game" No. Vj-105/1994 imposing a substantial fine.
629. Fazekas, Ibid.
630. For references see Cseres, op. cit., p. 54.
631. Concerning special offers made in the context of comparative advertising see Art. 7 b RT.

8. Passing off, imitations

Art. 6 prohibits the use in one's business of the distinctive signs (name, mark of designation) of a competitor, i.e. signs by which the competitor or its goods are recognized by consumers. This provision has been interpreted by the Supreme Court to extend even to situations of exploitation of goodwill without evidence of confusion.[632]

The same provision (Art. 6 VT) also addresses imitation of the appearance, the packaging or designation of a product. Two qualifying conditions apply, namely that the appearance or the packaging is characteristic and that it serves to recognize the products or a competitor.

9. Obstructive competition

Article 4 VT protects business secrets. It is prohibited to acquire such secrets in an unfair manner or to disclose them in an unauthorized way to third parties or to the public.[633] Unfair appeals to other persons to disrupt their economic relationship with third parties or to prevent the creation of such relationships is likewise prohibited as an act of unfair competition (Art. 5).

10. Breach of statutory duty

Hungarian unfair competition law does not comprise an explicit and general provision on breach of statutory duty as a *per se* act of unfair competition. Such act may, however, be considered as being within the scope of the general clause of Art. 2 VT.[634]

11. Remedies, procedure

According to Art. 86 VT the party injured by an act of unfair competition may claim injunction, restoration of the *status quo* prior to the infringement, receiving satisfaction (apology) and where appropriate obliging the infringer to give publicity to the satisfaction and compensation for damages. Proceedings are instituted before the ordinary courts under general rules of civil procedure.

In proceedings before the GVH on the basis of the consumer-related provisions of the VT the Competition Council, hearing cases in three-member panels, has the competence to issue a cease-and-desist order, to order the publication of a corrective statement and to impose a fine on the infringer. (Art. 77 VT)

632. See Vida, WiRO 1992, p. 258, reporting on a decision by the Supreme Court (Bírósági Határozatok 1993, p. 27 ff, AZ Pf IV 20 672/1992) based on the identical provision of the Competition Act of 1984. The case concerned the marketing by a Hungarian company of accessories for the well-known Barbie-doll. See also GRUR Int. 1989, p. 235—"FABULAND-Märchenfiguren I".
633. The manner of acquiring a business secret is deemed unfair also if access to it was obtained without the consent of the holder and with the assistance of a person who was at the time of the acquisition of the business secret, or in a period prior to it, in a confidential relationship or business relationship with him.
634. Bacher/Bárdos/Stadler, p. 4. On the basis of the Competition Act of 1990 the Competition Council on several occasions condemned as acts of unfair competition advertising campaigns carried out in violation of the legislative prohibition on alcohol and tobacco advertising. See the decisions reported by Vida, WiRO 1993, p. 260 f.

The enforcement of the RT may follow several different avenues. Competitor-related infringements of the provisions on misleading and comparative advertising (Art. 7 and 7a RT) are under the jurisdiction of the ordinary courts. Consumer-related offences of these provisions are within the competence of the Competition Council (Art. 15 RT). The overall monitoring of advertising is entrusted to the FVF and to the local consumer protection inspectorates (Art. 15 RT). These bodies can initiate advertising control proceedings for violation of all other provisions of the RT and impose penalties or issue cease-and-desist orders, including interim injunction, if this is urgently needed for protection of legal and economic interests of the parties concerned. The proceedings are initiated either ex officio, or upon the application of affected parties, including consumer organizations (Art. 16 RT) and follow the rules of administrative procedure. Finally, in case of infringement of personal rights, private parties can claim their rights directly before the courts in accordance with the general rules of civil law and procedure (Art. 15(3) RT).

XIII. IRELAND

Selected Literature: *Barrett/Voigt*, *Ireland*, in: Micklitz/Keßler (ed.), Marketing Practices Regulation and Consumer Protection in the EC Member States and the US, 2002, p. 149; *Forde*, Commercial Law, 2nd ed. 1997. *Maguire*, Consumer Law Handbook, 2000; *McNeece* (ed.), Commercial Law, 2001.

1. Sources of law

Common law: passing off, injurious falsehood, defamation; Statutes and Regulations: Consumer Information Act 1978; European Communities (Misleading Advertising) Regulations 1988; Self Regulation: ASAI Code of Advertising Standards und Code of Sales Promotion Practice

2. Irish competition law in a nutshell

Even though the Republic of Ireland has been independent since 1921, its shared legal tradition and economic ties with Great Britain have lead to the Irish law being rather similar to that of Great Britain.[635] This is seen especially in case law; although British decisions are not binding in Irish law, they are strongly probative. Further, the Irish Parliament often uses British references for its own legislation.

These similarities also extend to the approach to combat unfair competition.[636] As Great Britain, Ireland has no comprehensive specialized body of law called unfair competition law comparable to that of most continental European countries. Rather, the relevant law is mainly case law of general applicability, usually in the area of tort law, which largely protects businesses. The passing-off suit is directed against danger of confusion, the torts of injurious falsehood and defamation largely cover slander.

635. "Irish Law" refers here to Republic Irland. In North Ireland British Law applies. For an excellent guide to Irish law in general (with many links) s. Whelan, *Guide to Irish Law*, <www.ucc.ie/law/irishlaw/guide/>.

636. With due prudence it may therefore be referred to the chapter on British Law.

A broader tort, such as misappropriation of good will (without a danger of confusion) does not exist.

In addition, there are some specific criminal and administrative laws and regulations that cover certain elements of unfair competition from the point of view of consumer protection.[637] The most important of these is the Consumer Information Act of 1978, which prohibits misleading advertising of any kind, but does not provide for private actions.[638] Rather, enforcement is up to the "Office of Director of Consumer Affairs". (OCDA).[639]

Corresponding to the British example, the central role of self regulation by business is stressed and puts governmental enforcement into a rather secondary role. In practice, standards such as the "Code of Advertising Standards for Ireland" (CASI) and the "Code of Sales Promotion Practice",[640] which are promulgated by the Advertising Standards Authority for Ireland (ASAI) supplement the scarce statutory basis and are usually the first recourse for competitors and consumers. These and other standards[641] have the effect that many conflicts can be settled through self regulation. Their purpose is primarily to protect the consumer,[642] although indirectly business is protected as well.

3. Advertisement

A general civil law prohibition of misleading advertising does not exist. However, the passing-off suit has its widest applicability here. If a misrepresentation of origin is

637. For a comprehensive list of all legal provisions which regulate advertising and Sales Promotion in the different branches s. <www.asai.ie/codes_2002/appendix.html>.
638. According to common law, however, natural persons act as a prosecutor in criminal proceedings. In such proceedings Irish courts, furthermore, may order damages for victims in simple cases, s. Criminal Justice Act 1992. It is, however, to date unclear in how far this rule originally created with rape victims in mind can be applied generally.
639. The OCDA is in charge of the prosecution of the criminal provisions against deceptive advertising as well as the information of consumers as to unfair practices, the enforcement of safety rules for consumers and the information about the consumer's contractual rights, <www.odca.ie/>. The enforcement agency for Ireland's antitrust law, the Competition Act 2002, is the Competition Authority, <www.tca.ie/>.
640. S. under <www.asai.ie> (Code of 2001). Both codes are modelled after the British Codes and the Code of the ICT.
641. The complete list under <www.asai.ie/codes_2002/appendix.html>: Animal and Plant Health Association—Code of Practice for the Animal Health Industry with guidelines for TV and Radio advertising; Central Bank of Ireland—Advertising Requirements applicable to Credit Institutions; Drinks Industry Group—Code of Practice (Naming, packaging and merchandising of single-serve alcohol beverages in the Republic of Ireland); Irish Association of Investment Managers—Code of Advertising Practice; Irish Brokers Association—Code of Conduct for Insurance Intermediaries; Irish Direct Marketing Association—Code of Practice on Direct Marketing; Irish Direct Marketing Association—Code of Practice for Data Protection; Irish Direct Marketing Association—Code of Practice on Telemarketing; Irish Insurance Federation—Code of Practice on Advertising and Sales Material; Irish Mail Order Association—Code of Practice on Catalogue Mail Order Trading; Irish Pharmaceutical Healthcare Association—Code of Standards of Advertising Practice for the Consumer Healthcare Industry; Minister for Arts, Heritage, Gaeltacht and the Islands—Code of Standards, Practice and Prohibitions in Advertising, Sponsorship and Other forms of Commercial Promotion in Broadcasting Services (and Codes made thereunder by RTE and IRTC); Regulator of Premium Rate Telecommunications Services—REGTEL Code of Practice; The Dental Council—Guidelines on Public Relations and Communications; The Medical Council—Guide to Ethical Conduct (Advertising and the Media); The Opticians Board—Rules relating to Advertising.
642. S for the ASAI Code Chap. 1, Sec. 8.

involved, passing off can play a role, besides or instead of an action for trademark infringement.[643] Furthermore, suits under "injurious falsehood" and "defamation" are possible.

In statutory law, the Consumer Information Act of 1978 and the European Communities (Misleading Advertising) Regulations of 1988 provide for criminal and administrative law sanctions in order to protect consumers against misleading advertising. Section 8 of the Consumer Information Act of 1978 forbids every advertisement that is misleading and could lead to substantial loss, damages or injury to members of the public. The applied test used is an objective one; it depends on the impression of the advertisement on the targeted consumer groups. Common and easily recognized exaggerations are allowed. The enforcement of the law by the ODCA has in practice only subsidiary importance next to self regulation; the number of cases correspondingly is low.[644]

The European Communities (Misleading Advertising) Regulations 1988[645] transpose Directive 84/450/EC nearly word-for-word.[646] The ODCA enforces this regulation as well, and can give cease-and-desist orders and enforce them in court if necessary. Contrary to English law, the Irish legislature granted the right of action for injunctive relief to every interested person, i.e. competitors and consumers, without having to show proof of personal damages.[647] The practical importance is relatively low, however, because of the traditionally primary role and the efficiency of self regulation.

For self regulation, the Code of Advertising Standards for Ireland (CASI) in its 2001 version is of special importance; it is overseen by ASAI. The area of application is wide: It includes not only advertising in print media, on billboards, etc., but also radio, television, and movie theater advertising.[648] Advertisements must, according to the code, be "legal, decent, truthful and honest".[649] These terms are each defined and expanded upon.[650] Obvious lies or exaggerations are allowed as long as there is no real danger of misleading. Additionally, a kind of general clause requires that every advertisement must respect "the principles of fair competition generally accepted in business".[651] However, this clause does obviously not have independent legal significance as a catch-all basis for claims that would otherwise fall outside of the code. When judging advertising, the totality of all circumstances must be considered.[652] The ASAI's decisions are seen as relatively strict.

643. S. the decision of the High Court (cited at Grehan, No. 24) concerning an advertising for a detergent as "Mild Green Fair Liquid" which created confusion with "Mildly Green Friary Dishwashing Liquid".
644. According to the annual report for 2002, p. 6, the ODCA has received 289 complaints against allegedly misleading advertising, which all could be settled amicably with the parties. Of the 238 complaints concerning misleading indications of prices: only 4 could not be settled so that the Director had to resort to a sanction.
645. S.I. No. 134/1988
646. For price indications furthermore the European Communities (Requirements to Indicate Product Prices) Regulations 2002 apply.
647. Sec. 4 European Communities (Misleading Advertising) Regulations 1988.
648. This extents also to commercial e-mails towards customers, see Case Report in the matter of Ryanair, Batch No: 147, Ref: CB/0311/1175.
649. Sec. 2.1 Code of Advertising Standards for Ireland.
650. Sec. 2.12^{bis} 2.24.
651. Sec. 2.3.
652. Among them are the characteristics of the target group, the media, the context of the advertising and the special features of the advertised product; Sec. 1.5 c.

Special rules exist to protect against misleading use of "testimonials and endorsements" by celebrities, experts, and consumers.[653] Price indications must, among other things, refer to the actual product displayed and include sales tax.[654] It must also clearly be specified which costs may not be charged to the customers when the term "free" is used.[655] Section 7 Consumer Information Act of 1978 also contains specific provisions for different kinds of advertising with statements of price.[656]

For television advertising the "Codes of Standards, Practice and Prohibitions in Advertising, Sponsorship, and other forms of Commercial Promotion Broadcasting Services" of the ministry in charge apply.[657] Beyond the general prohibition of misleading advertising, advertising must be recognizable as such, Section 2.53, and be clearly segregated from editorial content, Section 2.54.

A specific implementation of Directive 97/55 regarding comparative advertisement has not occurred. Ireland, after consulting the Commission, is of the opinion that the Consumer Information Act of 1978 already contains the relevant principles of the directive, which are thereby a component of Irish law. Under Section 14 of the Trade Marks Act of 1963, comparative advertising using registered trade marks was strongly limited. Section 14(6) of the new 1996 Trade Marks Act specifically permits the use of trademarks to identify goods or services of the registered owner or its licensee. As in England, the use must be "in accordance with honest practices in industrial or commercial matters" and should not "without due cause, take unfair advantage of, or be detrimental to the distinctive character or reputation of the Trade Mark".[658] A more precise interpretation of this rather general prohibition by the Irish courts does not yet exist.[659]

The common law grounds for a civil suit (passing off, injurious falsehood, defamation, slander of goods) can also be used against comparative advertising if their specific elements are met. Defamation, for example, can occur if the comparison is based on competitor's circumstances that have nothing to do with its commercial activity.[660] In practice, however, such suits play only a small role.

More important is the Code of self regulation, which regulates in some detail the use of comparative advertising: the terms barely differ from that of the British standards.[661] Correct comparisons are generally allowed.[662] However, they must be fair and may not give the advertiser an undue advantage through its choice of compared features. Denigration and disparagement should be avoided. Factual assertions must be able to be substantiated. The "goodwill" of the competitor may not be taken advantage of in an unfair fashion.

653. Sec. 2.33^{bis} 2.37.
654. Sec. 3.38^{bis} 2.40.
655. Sec. 2.41 und 2.42.
656. Grehan, Rdnr. 31.
657. <www.bci.ie/promob.html>. The Broadcasting Commission of Ireland (BCI) has the authority to set up new Codes. Complaints as to the infringements of codes may be directed to the Broadcasting Complaints Commission (BCC). They are published as well as the decisions by BCC under <www.bcc.ie/decisions.html>.
658. See AIPPI, Country Report Ireland, question 168.
659. But see the decisions of the ECJ in the matters of Toshiba and Pippig; discussed in chapter 3 IV, 4.
660. As to this and other common law cases (but before implementation of the EC Directive) see AIPPI, Irland, Question 140, Yearbook 1998 IV, S. 108 ff.
661. Sec. 2.47^{bis} 2.50 Code of Advertising Standards for Ireland.
662. *Joseph O'Connor (Nenagh) Ltd & Ors.* v. *Power Supermarkets Ltd.*, see Grehan, p. 372, 375 f.

Nuisance advertising also has no general and complete regulation in case law or statute. However, certain kinds are covered. Directive 2001/31/EC regarding electronic commerce was transposed into Irish law on February 26, 2003.[663] According to that law, unrequested advertising emails (spams) must be clearly marked as such and the advertiser must check the "opt-out" register frequently. An opt-out system also applies for unrequested telephone calls in direct marketing. For unrequested faxes and automated telephone calls, the opt-out system only applies to businesses; natural persons must "opt-in".[664] The Opt-Out-Register is controlled by the Commission for Communications Regulation.[665]

Different kinds of nuisance advertising are dealt with by various Codes for special branches.[666] The advertising standard for the banking industry, for example, prohibits unrequested telephone calls and home visits by sales representatives, except to customers or non-customers that expressly requested such contact.[667]

According to the ASAI Code, advertising may not cause fear or distress[668] without good reason, or bring forth violence or anti-social behavior[669]. As to shocking and offensive advertising which is neither regulated by law, nor covered by common law, the ASAI Code contains some generally phrased prohibitions. According to Rule 2.13, an advertisement may not contain anything that would cause grave and widespread offense. Offensive or provocative material should not be used for the sole purpose of catching attention, Rule 2.17. Advertising must respect the inherent dignity of all persons and may not discriminate against, disparage or insult discrete groups; nor can such material be misused for purely advertising goals, Rules 2.14–2.16.

Disparaging, insulting, and malicious advertising is not fully regulated in statutes or in case law. Civil law remedies against cases of defamation or injurious falsehood, however, can apply. Although the EC Directive regarding comparative advertising was not explicitly transposed, the Consumer Information Act must be interpreted according to the Directives standards. Thus, comparisons may not denigrate or disparage trademarks, company names or other identifying symbols, nor the goods, services, operations or standing of a competitor.[670]

Media specific advertising regulations do not exist for print media; instead the entire ASAI code applies. For television, the "Code of Standards, Practice and Prohibitions in Advertising, Sponsorship, and other forms of Commercial Promotion Broadcasting Services" applies.[671] Generally, misleading advertising is forbidden here as well (Section 6). The separation principle between commercials and general programming is found in Section 7 ff.; for sponsoring, specific regulations are found

663. Through the European Communities (Directive 2001/31/EC) Regulations 2003, amended through the European Communities (Electronic Communications Networks and Services) (Data Protection and Privacy) Regulations 2003 (S.I. No. 523 of 2003) in implementation of EC Directive 2002/58/EC.
664. 8th Report on the Implementation of the Telecommunications Regulatory Package, Ireland, 92, http://europa.eu.int/information_society/topics/ecomm/all_about/implementation_enforcement/index_en.htm.
665. <www.comreg.ie>.
666. It should, however, be noted that chapter 8 of the ASAI Code concerning Direct Selling (especially mail order business) does not concern advertising but rather deals with the obligation of parties after the placement of an order.
667. Sec. D Advertising Requirements Applicable to Credit Institutions, published by the Irish Financial Services Regulatory Authority, <www.ifsra.ie/data/in_car_files/Advertising_reqs.pdf>.
668. Rule 2.26.
669. Rule 2.28.
670. See Art. 3a (1) (e) of the Directive discussed in Chapter 2, III.
671. <www.bci.ie/promob.html>.

in Part II of the "Codes of Standards, Practices and Prohibitions relating to Sponsorship in Broadcasting Services". Product placement (surreptitious advertising) is prohibited, as is subliminal advertising. Special regulations exist for advertising during children's programs, as well as for advertising of alcoholic beverages and various other goods and services. Advertising of tobacco products is forbidden. (Section 18 and Appendix 1).

Product specific advertising regulations exist for an entire array of goods and services. The regulation of tobacco advertising following the EC Directive 2001/37/EC had a complicated legislative history.[672] A new regulation, the Public Health (Tobacco) (Amendment) Act 2004,[673] which implements Directive 2003/33/EC, came into force 2004 and forbids, with narrow exceptions, tobacco advertising and sponsoring of events by tobacco companies.

Privisions issued regarding advertising for Concert and Theater events,[674] Gasoline[675] and Plane Tickets[676] supplement the Consumer Information Act of 1987. Special regulations also exist for the advertisement of alcoholic beverages, pharmaceutical products, cosmetics, health and beauty services, financial services,[677]employee placement services, etc. Advertising by solicitors[678] is strictly regulated both in style and substance. For example, slogans such as "no win no fee", "most cases settled out of court", or "first free consultation" are forbidden.[679]

4. Sales promotion

A general statutory regulation of sales promotion activities does not exist. However, an individual ASAI Code of Sales Promotion Practice applies.[680] Included in this are premium offers, reduced price and free offers, the distribution of vouchers, coupons and samples, personality promotions, charity-linked promotions, prize promotions. For such sales promotion measures, as for other advertising, the general regulations of the ASAI apply foremost, such as against misleading advertising (Section 12.3). A more detailed definition of this general prohibition is found in Section 2.41; it contains the conditions for when an offer may be marked as "free". Discounts and bonus gifts as well as special sales are otherwise allowed. Stamps, coupons, vouchers, tokens or similar devices which are delivered to any person upon the purchase of goods and is redeemable by that or some other person have a special regulation in the Trading Stamps Act 1980,[681] according to which a certain minimum amount of information is required. Section 2.43–2.46 of the ASAI code require that for advertised special discounts an appropriate amount of those goods can be delivered.

672. The Public Health (Tobacco) Act 2002, which contained a broad prohibition of tobacco advertising had to be withdrawn because the Act was not correctly notified with the European Commission.
673. <www.irlgov.ie/bills28/acts/2004/a604.pdf>.
674. Consumer Information (Advertisements for Concert or Theatre Performances) Order 1997 (S.I. No. 103 of 1997).
675. Consumer Information (Diesel and Petrol) (Reduction in Retail Price) Order 1997 (S.I. No. 179 of 1997).
676. Consumer Information (Advertisements for Airfares) Order 2000 (S.I. No. 468 of 2000).
677. S. dazu den Consumer Credit Act 1995 (No. 24 of 1995), der die Verbraucherkreditrichtlinie umsetzt.
678. Solicitor's (Advertising) Regulations 2002, in force since 1.2.2003.
679. <www.venables.co.uk/n0301irishsolicitorsadvertising.htm>.
680. Chapter 12 of the ASAI Code (2001).
681. The Act excludes a stamp, coupon, voucher, token or similar device which is redeemable only from the seller of the goods, or his supplier, or the person who provides the services.

Sweepstakes can be split into two categories. Lotteries in which success is largely dependant on luck and that do require consideration (e.g. the purchase of a product) to participate, are governed by the Gaming and Lotteries Act of 1956 and are, with some exceptions, prohibited.[682] According to precedent, a prohibited lottery exists even when only the first step is decided by chance and the second step requires participants to give some knowledgeable answer.[683] When sweepstakes depend in large part on the knowledge or skill of the participant, they are permitted. The ASAI code defines rules for a fair process (Section 12.44 to 12.55).

The problem of pyramid schemes is handled in Ireland by the Pyramid Selling Act of 1980.[684] According to the statutory definition,[685] it is a criminal act to invite other people to become a participant in a scheme, to accept payments for recruiting people or to accept payments in order to change the status of a promoter.

5. Direct marketing

Ireland has transposed the Door to Door Sales Directive,[686] the Long Distance Sales Directive,[687] and the E-Commerce Directive;[688] thus the respective information duties and advertising requirements are applicable. According to these laws, unsolicited e-mails must be clearly marked as advertising and the advertiser must consult and abide by the "opt-out" register on a regular basis. For direct marketing, the consumer has the right to be removed from address lists. The Irish Direct Marketing Association (IDMA) is responsible for the execution. The IDMA also issues a Code of Practice and an addendum codex for telemarketing and data protection which are binding on its members.[689] Section 8 of the ASAI Code contains special regulations regarding distance selling, which apply as a supplement to the general regulations.

6. Disparagement, denigration and misappropriation

The common law grounds of defamation and injurious falsehood can be used against disparagement and insults. For misappropriation, however, there are no specific grounds upon which to bring an action. The ASAI Code contains in Section 2.53 a prohibition of exploitation or unfair use of goodwill of another party which is associated with its trademark, name, slogan, or advertising campaign. Section 2.54 forbids imitation of advertising that could cause danger of misleading.

682. S. "Review of the Gaming and Lotteries Act 1956–1986" on the Website of the Ministry of Justice <www.justice.ie>.
683. *Flynn* v. *Denieff*, [1990] ILRM 391.
684. <www.irishstatutebook.ie/ZZA27Y1980.html>. S. also the "Explanatory Memorandum" under <www.entemp.ie/tcmr/memopysell.doc>.
685. Sec. 1, which distinguishes Pyramid Schemes from Multi Level Marketing.
686. European Communities (Cancellation of Contracts Negotiated away from Business Premises) Regulations, 1989, (S.I. No. 224 of 1989).
687. European Communities (Protection of Consumers in Respect of Contracts Made by Means of Distance Communications) Regulations, 2001, (S.I. No. 207 of 2001).
688. European Communities (Directive 2001/30/EC) Regulations 2003.
689. <www.idma.ie/legal/>. S. also Barrett/Voigt, pp. 164 ff.

7. Danger of confusion

In defining danger of confusion Irish courts traditionally use an objective standard based on the average consumer under both common law and the Consumer Information Act. The ASAI roughly applies the same standard for self regulation.

8. Misappropriation; imitation

Outside of specific regulations regarding intellectual property, imitation as such is not forbidden. However, inasmuch as the imitation creates a danger of confusion, it may violate the general principles, e.g. as passing off.[690]

9. Impediment of competitors

The enticing away of customers or employees and their employment in violation of a valid contractual prohibition of competition can—as in Great Britain—lead to a claim of inducement to or procurement of breach of contract. The protection of "know-how" is not specially regulated, but a matter of contract law. Confidentiality agreements with employees and business partners are, therefore, essential to such a claim, as breach can be actionable as breach of contractual obligation of fidelity or as abuse of confidential information.

10. Breach of the law

As in England, the tort of breach of statutory duties covers the compensation of damages caused by the violation of legal requirements which were supposed to deter exactly such damages.

11. Enforcement

In civil law cases, the primary sanction is compensatory damages. The provisions of the Consumer Information Act and the European Communities (Misleading Advertising) Regulations of 1988 protecting consumers are enforced primarily through cease-and-desist orders of the ODCA[691] and the courts. The ODCA has standing to sue and according to the Regulations also the individual consumer.[692] The court can order publication of its decision. Violation of laws and regulations are punishable.[693] Such Criminal proceedings can also be instituted by private persons.

The sanctions of the ASAI generally include the publication of cases with the names of the advertiser and the advertising agency. If an advertisement or sales promotion measure violates the ASAI Code, it must be withdrawn or changed. The media

690. S. f.i. ASAI Code 2,54, imitation of another's advertising.
691. Sec. 9 Consumer Information Act; Sec. 4(2) Regulations.
692. Sec. 4 (1) Regulations.
693. Sec. 17 Consumer Information Act (fine and imprisonment); Sec. 6(5) Regulations (fine). In practice, criminal proceedings will be instituted only in exceptionally grave violations.

will otherwise refuse to promulgate it.[694] Members who do not follow the decisions of the ASAI can be punished by fines and/or be expelled from the association.

According to common law rules, the injured party in civil claims has standing to sue.[695] In general, this will be the competitor which has been harmed. Under the criminal and administrative provisions of competition and consumer law, the enforcing authorities, generally the ODCA, also may bring an action. For violations of Regulations regarding misleading advertising, both the competitor and the consumer have standing to sue for cease-and-desist orders. Private suits can also be brought before the criminal court, which in simple cases can award compensation. Finally, advertisers and consumers can submit complaints to the ASAI.

XIV. ITALY

Selected Literature: Abriani/Cottino, *La concorrenza sleale*, in: Abriani/Cottino/Ricolfi, Diritto industriale, 2001, p.271; Auteri, *La concorrenza sleale*, in: Trattato di diritto privato, ed. Rescigno, vol. 18, p. 341(1993) Alpa, *Il diritto de consumatori*, 2002; Alpa/Radeideh, Italy, in: Micklitz/Keßler (ed.), *Marketing Practices and Consumer Protection in the EC Member States and the US*, 2002, p. 201; Auteri/Floridia/Mangini/Olivieri, *Ricolfi/Spada, Diritto Industriale, Proprietà intelletuale e Concorrenza*, 2nd ed. 2005; Bastian, Italien, in: Schricker (ed.), *Recht der Werbung in Europa*, 1997; Berruti, *La concorrenza sleale nel mercato: guirisdizione ordinaria e normativa antitrust*, 2002; Bodewig/Henning-Bodewig, *Rabatte und Zugaben in den Mitgliedstaaten der EU*, WRP 2000, 1341; Figurelli, *Le nuove leggi civili commentate*, 2001; Francetti, *Italy*, in: Campbell (ed.), Unfair Trade Practices—The Comparative Law Yearbook of International Business, 1996, p. 209; Fusi, in: Greffe/Greffe (ed.), *La publicité et la Loi*, 9th ed. 2000; p. 845; Ghidini, *La concorrenza sleale*, 2002: Hofer/Lösch/Torricelli/Genta, *Werberecht in Italien*, in: Schotthöfer (ed.), Handbuch des Werberechts in den EU-Staaten, 2nd ed. 1997, p. 389; Liuzzo, *Prozessuale Aspekte des italienischen Werberechts*, GRUR Int. 1992, 599; Magnani, *Appropriazione di Know-how, concorrenza parasitaria e sfruttamento di lavori altrui, Responsabilità civile e previdenza*, 1997; Ubertazzi, *Commentario breve al diritto della concorrenza*, 3rd ed. 2004; Padovini, *Konsumentenschutz und Zivilprozeßin Italien nach dem Gesetz* 281 Vol. 30. July 1998 (Gesetz zum Schutz der Rechte der Konsumenten), ZfRV 1999, 9; Preussler, *Das Wettbewerbsrecht in Italien*, in: Heidelberger Kommentar zum Wettbewerbsrecht, 2000, 727; Quiring, *Die sklavische Nachahmung im italienischen Wettbewerbsrecht*, 1989; Ruggero, *Le vendite a prezzi predatori e le strategie di marketing, Giur. comm.* 2003, p. 165; Schaltenberg, *Die Bekämpfung irreführender und unlauterer Werbung in Italien*, 1988; Schricker, Italien, in: Ulmer (ed.), *Das Recht des unlauteren Wettbewerbs in den Mitgliedstaaten der EWG*, Vol. V, 1965; Somarriello, *Vergleichende Werbung in Italien und Deutschland*, 2002; Somarriello, *Vergleichende und irreführende Werbung in Italien nach Umsetzung der Richtlinie 97/55/EG*, GRUR Int. 2003, 29; Vanzetti/Di Cataldo, Manuale di diriHo industriale, 4th ed. 2003.

694. ASAI Code Kap. 4 Sec. 16, Kap. 1 Sec. 5.
695. The first translation is per the Romain legal dictionary, the second is the common US term for a party who can bring suit.

1. Sources of law

Article 2598-Art. 2601 Codice Civile (CC); Legislative Decrees No. 74 of 25 January 1992 and No. 67 of 25 February 2000 (Decree 74/1992); Codice di Autodisciplina Pubbicitaria (CAP)

2. Italian unfair competition law in a nutshell

Although the notion of unfair competition ("concorrenza sleale")[696] is well established in Italian law, there is no uniform, coherent regulation In practice, several sets of regulations must be considered.

The civil law protection against unfair competition is found in Art. 2598 to 2601 Codice Civile (CC). According to the prevailing opinion, this law is limited to suits brought by competitors. Article 2598 CC bans the following business practices, "without prejudice to the provisions concerning the protection of distinctive signs and patent rights":

- Creating of confusion, including by slavish imitation
- Disparaging and appropriating the merits of a competitor's product
- Using any other means which do not conform with the "principle of professional correctness" and are likely to damage another's business (general clause).

A second set of regulation is found in the Legislative Decree No. 74 from 25 January 1992 regarding misleading advertising, which was expanded in 2000 to include comparative advertising.[697] In this decree Council Directives 84/450/EEC and 97/55/EC were adopted nearly word-for-word, but the Italian legislature took the opportunity to regulate other aspects as well. For example, the second sentence of Art. 1 states that every advertisement must be "clear, truthful and correct". Decree 74/1992 also regulates concealed and subliminal advertising, the use of certain terms such as "guarantee, advertising of dangerous items, and advertising for or with children. The Italian anti-trust authority ("Autorità Garante della Concorrenza e del Mercato") is in charge of enforcing these rules.[698]

In addition to these legal possibilities, self-regulation is of special interest in Italy.[699] Based on the frequently revised "Codice di Autodisciplina Pubblicitaria" (CAP),[700] the rules are also used to define the "general clause" of Art. 2598 No. 3 CC.[701]

696. A comprehensive overview of Italian unfair competition law can be found in the commentary of Ubertazzi and in the treaties of Abriani, Auteri and Ghidini; as to the literature in German see Bastian and Schricker.
697. A consolidated German translation can be found in GRUR Int. 2003, 51.
698. The division's authority was expended to include such powers in 1992. The Autorità Garante handles about 400 to 500 cases per year, and is considered especially efficient.
699. In the past, self regulation sometimes took over the function of the courts because of the difficulties and length of time of legal proceedings. Although the importance of self-regulation has receeded somewhat according to the successful establishment of the Autorità Garante, nearly 80% of all advertising disputes are still handled through the "Giurf"; see Somarriello, GRUR Int. 2003, 29.
700. The newest revision is available over the internet at www.iap.it. Although the CAP is only binding for its members, it is generally respected by all market participants. The "submissions clause" is used in nearly all standard contracts in the advertising area; see Somarriello, GRUR Int. 2003, 29.
701. See, e.g. Corte di Cassazione 15.2.1999, No. 1259; Court of Appeals Milan 30.7.1999 (RIC 196,2001, p. 31).

The "Instituto di Autodisciplina Pubblicitaria" enforces the standards set out in the CAP, with the "Guirí" as decision-making body. The decisions of the Guirí are in practice given the same respect as decisions from the courts and the Autorità Garante.

The various possibilities to fight unfair competition overlap partly.[702] The protective aims vary: Art. 2598 CC protects individual claims of competitors, and is in some aspects related to Intellectual Property laws, [703] now regulated in the new Codice della proprietà industriale.[704] On the other hand, the provisions regarding advertising in Decree No. 74/1992 serve the interests of consumers, businessmen and the public in general; since they are enforced by a branch of the Competition Authority, they have some connections with antitrust law.[705]

3. Regulation of advertising

a. Misleading advertising[706]

The traditional legal protection against misleading advertising for business consists of civil law actions on the basis of Art. 2598 No. 3 CC ("professional correctness"). However, successful actions directly based on Art. 2598 are rare, due to the fact that the civil courts traditionally consider consumers as smart enough not to trust any advertising. As long as the assertions in the advertisement stay relatively vague, even clear untruths are tolerated.[707]

Thus, the main basis for fighting misleading advertising is, since 1992, Decree 74/1992.[708] It is closely modeled on Directive 84/450/EEC and uses the same protective purpose clause (protection of persons carrying on a business, consumers, and the general public) and the same definition of advertising.[709] The Autorità Garante, which is responsible for implementing this regulation, has broad powers and enforces the laws rather strictly. Misleading advertising furbidden by Decree 74/1992 constitutes unfair competition in the sense of Art. 2598 CC.

In determining whether an advertisement is misleading, the Autorità Garante usually refers to the target group. Depending on the group, the Autorità Garante will—contrary to the civil courts—also take the benchmark of a less experienced consumer.[710] Exaggerations are rarely considered as harmless "puffing", not even

702. This can lead to differing decisions on one and the same matter. See Somarriello, GRUR Int. 2003, 29.
703. For a discussion of Italian intellectual property law in English, see Jacobacci & Partners, Manual of Industrial Property all over the World (2003), p. 2399; for a discussion in Italian, for instance Albriani/Cottino/Ricolfi; Auteri/Florinda/Mangini/Oliver/Ricolfi/Spada; Vanzetti Di Cataldo.
704. Approved by decree No. 30 of 10 February 2005.
705. For a discussion of Italian anti-trust law, see Beck, Das italienische Kartellgesetz—überblick und erste Erfahrungen, WuW 1991, 707; Pera, Das neue italienische Kartellgesetz, Jahrbuch für italienisches Recht, 5 (1992); Giammarco, Die Generalklausel des unlauteren Wettbewerbs als Grundlage kartellrechtlicher Entscheidungen in Italien, GRUR Int. 1989, 29.
706. On the topic of misleading advertising, see in German Schaltenberg; Bastian, No. 30; Schricker, GRUR Int. 1990, 112.
707. In recent years, however, the courts seem to apply stricter standards, most likely due to the influence of the decisions of the Autorità Garante.
708. See *supra* at 2.
709. The key element under Art. 2 (1) is the subjective intent of promoting goods or services. Where this exists, written/picture advertising, direct advertising, and image advertising are likewise included.
710. Especially if the advertising is aimed at "impressionable" consumers or deals with topics not easily understood by normal consumers. For example, an advertisement for an internet provider promising that "the Internet will be 200 times faster" was held to be misleading, since consumers could

in the field of diet pills[711] and cosmetics.[712] Advertisements aimed at children and youth have to fulfill strict requirements; Art. 6 expressly forbids the exploitation of gullibility and inexperience. Only if the target group consists of specialists, the Autorità Garante generally expects a higher level of awareness and ability to make a decision. Advertisements with guarantees have to comply with especially strict rules (Art. 4 Sec. 2).

Misleading of consumers can also occur by leaving out essential information for the target group ("half-truths"). For products which could endanger the health or safety of consumers, Art. 5 requires explicitly that the danger be pointed out.

The misleading must be capable of influencing the economic actions of the consumer. The possibility of enticement is considered decisive; disclaimers at the point of sale are not always sufficient. For example, the Autorità Garante held that an advertisement for a weight-loss drink was misleading due the lack of information in the advertisement about the necessity of healthy eating to achieve the desired results. It was not considered sufficient that this information be in or on the packaging.[713]

To determine whether an advertisement is misleading, Autorità Garante itself generally completes a formal analysis of the words in the advertisement. Empirical evidence such as surveys are allowed, but not often used. The Autorità Garante may order the advertiser to prove the factual accuracy of the statements in the advertisement (Art. 7, Sec. 4).

The third route to fight misleading advertising is self-regulation. The enforcing body, the "Giurí", has developed an abundant body of decisions.[714] Like the Autorità Garante, the "Giurí" is generally rather strict as far as misleading advertising is concerned.

b. Comparative advertising

The area of comparative advertising was included in 2000 into the Decree No. 74/1992.[715] The statement of purpose in Art. 1, No. 2, whereby every advertisement must be "clear, truthful, and correct", also applies to comparative advertising. As to the rest, Directive 97/55/EC was incorporated nearly word-for-word. The rules on comparative advertising are also enforced by the Autorità Garante.

When first implemented, it was disputed whether "indirect comparative advertising" also belonged in this area. Indirect comparative advertising is advertising that merely compares kinds of products or systems.[716] According to Autorià Garante's understanding, however, only "direct comparison" falls under Decree No. 74/1992.[717]

understand this as referring not only to the speed with which a consumer would be connected to the internet, but also the transmission speed once connected. Autorità Garante No. 909, Vol. 12/2000.

711. See the decision No. 10372, Boll. 4/2002, dealing with an advertisement for a "Body Slim" corset, which claimed to cause drastic weight loss without dieting or exercising. The court emphasized the fact that the product was advertised on TV and consumers thus could not inspect it before buying.
712. See the decision No. 747, Boll. 21/1992, dealing with an advertisement for an "anti-aging" crème, which claimed that "Pharmacists and scientists agree".
713. Autorità Garante, No. 848, Boll. 24/1992.
714. For an overview of the powers of the "Giurí" in the area of misleading advertising, see Somarriello, GRUR Int. 2003, 26.
715. For a complete description, see for instance Figurelli, Le nuove leggi civili commentate, 2001, p. 883.
716. Somarriello, GRUR Int. 2003, 30.
717. See Autoritá Garante's position and it's decision on this issue in Somarriello, GRUR Int. 2003, 29, fn. 14.

All other forms of comparison, such as system comparison and advertising with superlatives are dealt with by the Civil Court on the basis of Art. 2598, No. 2 and 3 CC.

For an advertisement to be considered a "direct" comparison, it needs to identify its competitor. This is defined relatively broadly. For example, Autorità Garante held that a telephone-company advertisement using a dog similar to the long-time mascot of a competitor was a comparative advertisement.[718]

According to the Autorità Garante, comparative advertisement must in particular not be denigrating to competitors or misleading to consumers. The above-noted "commercial with the dog" was considered misleading because the services advertised were not fully comparable to that of the competitor. (On the other hand, it was not found as an exploitation of the reputation of the competitor, because the advertiser, as a newcomer, only tried to gain a foothold on the market.[719]) Generalizing and vague statements as to a competitor or his product are rarely tolerated; often also on the grounds that they do not discuss relevant, typical, verifiable and objective characteristics.[720]

Self-regulation is, as far as the aspect of denigration or exploitation of goodwill is concerned, even stricter than Autorità Garante, since it is geared primarly towards the protection of businessmen.[721] For example, the advertisement discussed in paragraphs 15 and 16—using a similar mascot to compare telephone companies—was held by the "Guirí" (but not the Autorità Garante!) to be an exploitation of the competitor's reputation.[722]

c. Concealed advertising

Subliminal and concealed advertising ("pubblicità nascosta") is forbidden under Art. 4 of Decree No. 72/1992. Every advertisement must be "clearly recognizable as such". Although Art. 4 is aimed at the media—print advertisements must be distinguishable from other forms of non advertising communications through the use of graphical elements which are of immediate recognition,[723]—all forms of advertisement are generally included in this prohibition. For example, an offer for a subscription to a newspaper that is presented in the form of an "official letter" was forbidden. Special rules exist for television advertising (see under f).

Self-regulation also forbids concealed advertising (Art. 7 CAP). All media must clearly separate advertisement and other forms of content through proper means.

718. Autorità Garante 18.1.2001, No. 9127 Boll 3/01. The same case was also decided by the "Giurí" (30.4.2000, No. 148/00; see No. 17); for a discussion of both decisions see Somariello, p. 35.
719. Somarriello, GRUR Int. 2003, 29, 35.
720. For instance, the Autorità Garante forbid an advertisement with a famous actor who had formerly promoted the competitor and who simply stated that the advertised service provider was "better". *Autorità Garante* v. 23.1.2001, No. 9143, Boll. 4/01. Similar the "Giurí" as to general disparaging remarks (about dissimilar food products); *Barilla Alimentare spa, Bauli spa, Gruppo Biondí* v. *Danone*, 18.11.03, No. 201/2003:
721. The CAP, in earlier versions, forbid all (direct) comparative advertising as well as every unauthorized use of trademarks and the like.
722. Giurí 30.4.2000, No. 148/00; for a detailed discussion see Somarriello, GRUR Int. 2003, 29, 35.
723. The key issue is often defining the line between journalistic free speech and advertising. The tendency to promote sales of a named company must be "predominant". According to the Autorità Garante, the following factors can show such predominance: accepting money or similar consideration for a representation; the suggestion of surreptitious advertising in television (product placement); the excessive emphasis on the characteristics of a single product; and the closeness of the economic relations between the beneficiary and the media company as regards advertising.

d. Aggressive advertising

A general ban on annoying, aggressive or intrusive advertising does not exist in Italy. This aspect plays mainly a role for certain types of media and direct marketing.

e. Other advertising regulations

According to Art. 1 of Decree No. 74/1992, every advertisement must be "clear, truthful and fair". However, since this is seen as a mere goal, claims can not be based on a breach of this requirement.

Article 6 of Decree No. 74/1992 forbids the exploitation of lack of business knowledge and gullibility of children and youth as well as the exploitation of "the natural feelings that adults have for the young". It is sufficient that the advertisement has unwanted effects on children and youth; a corresponding intent is not necessary. For example, the Autorità Garante forbid the Benetton advertisement with a picture of a dying AIDS victim in part due to the psychological damage it could cause to children.[724] The protection of children and youth is also emphasized by self-regulation standards (Art. 11 CAP corresponds largely to Art. 6 of Decree No. 74/1992[725]). Of special note are Art. 8(1) of (law) No. 2223/1990 (Advertising in Radio and Television) as well as Art. 3 of Regulation No. 525/1991, with which the child protection provisions of the Television Directive were put in place. Advertising which violates the general sense of decency is forbidden under Art. 15 of (law) 74/1948 (media law).[726] Finally, certain Criminal Code regulations are applicable to indecent advertising.[727]

Fear in advertising and the exploitation of superstitions or gullibility are contained in the self-regulation standards (Art. 8 CAP).[728] According to Art. 9 CAP, the advertisement may not approve of or portray physical and psychological violence, nor may it show behaviors which according to the taste and the perception of the consumer are seen as inappropriate, vulgar, or disgusting.

f. Media- and product-specific advertising regulations

Italian law has an abundant number of regulations that specifically deal with certain media or products.[729] As in other areas, legal regulations and self-regulating standards overlap.

724. Autorità Garante, No. 1752, Boll 4/1994.
725. The "Giurí" has, for instance, forbidden "provocative" advertising (people forming letters of the alphabet in an obscene manner), Benetton Group spa, Giurí vom 14.11.2003, No. 199/2003.
726. Bastian, No. 128.
727. See, e.g., Art. 565 Criminal Code (forbidding representations which offend family values), Art. 402 Criminal Code (offending the religious beliefs of the Catholic church); see also Fusi, No. 1910.
728. Case law on the topic is rare, since other aspects are usually considered decisive. The Tribunale di Milano in 1964 forbid an advertisement using fear on the basis of Art. 2598 No. 3 CC ("normal" coffee was shown as an oversized injection of caffeine and then compared to the low-acid Kaffee Hag). However, the individual interests of the producers of "normal" coffee were at the center of the decision.
729. See Bastian, No. 179 and Fusi, No. 1919.

Radio and television advertising is regulated in the Broadcasting Code, as well as in several related decrees.[730] This regulation contains, among other things, the enactment of provisions of the Television Directive. For the press, Statute No. 74/1948 applies.

Product specific advertising and marketing regulations exist especially for food-stuff.[731] Television advertising for alcoholic beverages is very limited;[732] for all media types, the self-regulation standard of Art. 22 CAP applies. Advertising for presciption drugs must have a prior approval by the responsible authorities according to Art. 201 of Regulation No. 1265 from 27 July 1934;[733] this is complemented by self-regulation standards (Art. 25 CAP). Cosmetics are regulated by Statute No. 713/1986.[734] According to Law No. 52/1983, tobacco advertising is generally prohibited;[735] this also applies to "alibi products", i.e. products other than tobacco which carry the tobacco brand name.[736]

4. Direct marketing

The delivery of unrequested goods is per Art. 19 CAP (self-regulation) prohibited, if it is not clearly stated that there is no obligation to pay for or return the goods. Addressing consumers on the street is generally allowed. However, Decree No. 15 (15 January 1992), which transposed Directive 85/557/EEC, controls sales contracts made outside of places of business.[737]

Unsolicited advertising via telephone using automated calling systems and via fax is as a rule prohibited without prior consent per Art. 10(1) of Decree No. 185 of 22 May 1999 and Art. 130 of the "Codice in Matercia di protenzione dei dati personali", approved with Decree No. 196/2003. In all other cases, the "opt-out" solution applies (provided the conditions of Decree 196/2003 are respected) and the commercial goal of the call or fax is directly and clearly laid out. At this point, there are no laws regarding advertising via email.[738]

Pyramid schemes are prohibited.[739]

5. Sales promotion

Italian law has no specific regulations regarding sales promotions.[740] However, sales promotion techniques must not be misleading and they must be in accordance with

730. Frignani, GRUR Int. 1994, 33.
731. Regulation No. 109/1992 contains a general prohibition of misleading advertising for food products, which among other things regulates the information on and design of labels; see Bastian, No. 225. In addition Art. 13 of Law No. 283 of 30.4.1962 applies.
732. Law No. 425 from 30.11.1991; see Bastian, No. 197.
733. See Fusi, No. 1921; Bastian, No. 242.
734. Fusi, No. 1922; Bastian, No. 253.
735. Fusi, No. 1922; Bastian, No. 253.
736. See Corte di Cassazione 6.10.1995, Foro it. 1995, I, 3458. The decision of the United Senate ended the earlier disjointed case law by holding that the distribution of student pencil cases in the shape of cigarette packs violates the prohibition of tobacco advertising. Previously, the Corte di Cassazione (11.7.1990, Giust.civ. 1991, I, 650) had, for example, prohibited the advertising by a travel agency of "Camel-Trophy" Adventure Trips, but not the advertising for clothing with a Marlboro label (Corte di Cassazione 27.4.1990. Giust. it 1990, I, p. 1, 1574).
737. See Alpa/Radeideh, p. 210 f.
738. Alpha/Radeideh, p. 206.
739. According to Decree No. 175 of 12 August 2005.
740. Bodewig/Henning-Bodewig, WRP 2000, 1354; Alpa/Radeideh, p. 212; Francetti, p. 236.

Decree No. 118/1998,[741] which deals with indication of price and "special sales" (clearance sales, going out of business sales, seasonal sales, and special discounts).[742] Furthermore, discounts can lead to a sale at a loss which is forbidden in some cases.[743]

Premiums, free gifts, joint offers and package deals are generally allowed,[744] as long as they are not misleading and respect the "principles of professional correctness" (Art. 2598 No. 3 CC).[745] Pursuant to Art 21 CAP (self-regulation) certain informational obligations must be met (transparency requirements). The advertiser must pay the shipping costs of any free gifts offered over the television.

Lotteries are regulated according to the Presidential Decree No. 430/2001. Promotional games are not forbidden, but must follow transparency regulations under both the Presidential Decree and Art. 21 CAP (self-regulation). Persuant to Art. 12, any interested person can demand an examination by the Ministry of Commerce. Taking advantage of gambling instincts in order to promote sales is generally considered "dishonest".[746] It is unclear whether the law prohibits the tying of promotional games, especially games of chance, to the purchase of goods.[747]

6. Disparagement and denigration

The term denigration ("denigrazione") is used for both one-sided criticism as well as comparative advertising.[748] Traditionally, both were judged on the basis of Art. 2598 No. 2 CC. Since comparative advertising is now regulated in Decree 72/1992,[749] the main focus today of Art. 2598 No. 2 CC is one-sided criticism and indirect comparative advertising as to procedures or systems.[750]

Article 2598 No. 2 CC includes in this both factual claims as well as value judgments as to professional relations that are made accessible to an unknown number of people.[751] Even true statements are not allowed to be expressed in an unnecessarily aggressive, suggestive, or otherwise disparaging manner; here the general clause of No. 3 ("professional correctness") may also apply. Warnings against infringement of IP-rights are only allowed if the claimed protected right (or decision) actually exists

741. See Hofer/Lösch/Torricelli/Genta, p. 413 ff.
742. According to Regulation No. 80/1980, special events must be advertised to the community in which they are to occur. Under Art. 9, the organizer must prove that the truth of the statements. See also Art. 20 CAP (forbidding the false impression that the sale is out of the ordinary).
743. Per Art. 15(8) of Regulation No. 114/1998, sales at a loss are controlled by Regulation No. 218 (6.3.2001). As to whether such sales violate the principles of professional correctness of Art. 2598 CC, see Ruggero, Giur. comm. 2003, 165.
744. Such sales are considered as part of freedom of commerce, and thus protected by Art. 41 of the Constitution.
745. Alpa/Radeideh, p. 214; Francetti, p. 243
746. Francetti, p. 214; Alpa/Radeideh, p. 214; Fusi, No. 1927.
747. The decisions until now focused more on the aspect of deceit; see for instance, Tribunale di Milano 9.2.1976, Giur. Ann. Dir. Ind. 1976, p. 808; Autorità Garante 17.3.1993, No. 1020; and 14.9.1995 No. 3266. The first decision dealt with an advertisement in mail-order business that suggested that the consumer could win valuable prizes by ordering the items listed on the attached form. In the second decision, the court invalidated the supposed win of a vacation, whereby the winner would have to bear most of the costs.
748. Bastian, No. 88; Schricker, No. 146.
749. Although competitors and their associations can base claims regarding comparative advertising on Art. 2598 No. 2 CC, an advertisement which is found to be lawful under Regulation No. 74/1992 cannot be prohibited under Art. 2598 CC. Insofar, there is now one unitary standard.
750. See No. 12 ff.
751. Somarriello, GRUR Int. 2002, 29, 31.

and the means of communication do not go beyond what is absolutely necessary.[752] This also applies to the announcement of court rulings which are not required by the court.

7. Misappropriation, imitation, risk of confusion

Under Art. 2598 No. 1 CC unfair competition can be caused by: (1) one who creates danger of risk of confusion by using distinguishing marks of a third party (including domain names or magazine titles), (2) slavish imitation of a competitor's products, (3) or by any other means commits acts that result in confusion with the products and the activities of a competitor.[753]

In practice, the imitation of the get up, the product itself and its packaging, is mainly forbidden. If a danger of confusion would ensue.[754] This requires a certain amount of originality in the copied achievement and an imitation of more than merely technical aspects.[755]

The imitation of products (in a broader sense) which are not or no longer protected under special laws is in principle permitted. However, it can go against the principle of "professional correctness" in Art. 2598 No. 3 CC to exploit the hard-won and expensive achievements of a competitor in order to save on one's own expenses (parasitic competition).[756] In this case "special circumstances" must be proven, such as a systematic imitation,[757] or other obstructive practices.[758] Actions based on the Codice Civile are restricted to competitors (see above, 2), but Art. 13(1) CAP (self-regulation) forbids slavish imitation of a commercial[759] even between non-competing products.

8. Impediment of competitors

Practices such as boycotts or refusals to deliver are regulated under No. 287 Cartel Law of 10 October 1990.[760] The practice of head-hunting only violates the principle of "professional correctness" of Art. 2598 No. 3 CC when the means used are objectionable,[761] such as when specific highly qualified and indispensable employees are

752. See Bastian, No. 90.
753. Regarding slavish imitation, see Quiring, p. 90; Florinda, in: Auteri/Florinda/Mangini/Olivieri, p. 331; and Vanzetti Di Cataldo, p. 47.
754. As to the question of risk of confusion, the impression of the public is determinative. The risk of confusion can be excluded when other consumer groups are targeted and/or differing additions ensue. Tribunale Padova 11.1.1995 refered to in RIC 196, 3.2001, p. 31 f.
755. RIC 184, 3.1997, p. 27 f. The imitation of miniature automobiles was allowed because they only copied the "original"; Tribunale di Firenze 17.4.1995. The fact that there were already many copies on the market does not per se invalidate the right to protection; see Tribunale di Firenze 23.1.1996 and Tribunale de Napoli 8.11.1996, both discussed in RIC 190, 3.1999, p. 36.
756. Corte di Cassazione 17.4.1962, GRUR Ausl. 1964, 515; Corte di Cassazione 20.4.1996, No. 3787 and Tribunale di Napoli 23.10.1995, Foro Padano 1996, I, p. 80; see also Maggi, Riv.dir.ind. 2001, III, p. 364, 368 who refers to Tribunale di Milano 9.3.2001 (slavish imitation of design fashion).
757. The imitation of only one cloth(ing) design from 50 was, for example, not considered sufficient. Tribunale Verona 17.7.1998, RIC 196, 3.2001, p. 34.
758. See for instance Corte di Cassatione 20.4.1996, No. 3787 (Imitation of technical aspects, know-how, etc., under the direction of a former employee).
759. Regarding imitation of commercials, see Bastian.
760. See Francetti, p. 217.
761. Francetti, p. 229.

enticed away.[762] The same rules apply for the enticement of consumers; for example the "detour" of telephone calls meant for competitors onto one's own line was considered as being against "professional correctness".[763]

Judgment as to protection of trade secrets and know how were originally only based on the general clause of Art. 2598 No. 3 CC ("professional correctness").[764] After the enactment of Regulation No. 198/1996 according to Art. 6bis patent law and the enactment of the Codice della proprieté judustial (Art. 98, 99) these legal basis has to be considered too.

9. Breach of the law

The infringement of other regulations violates the general clause of Art. 2598 No. 3 CC if the infringed regulation also aims at regulating the "professional correctness".[765] This is found to be true, for example, for bribing employees into giving up secrets or for violating European or Italian cartel law.

10. Indications of geographic origin

According to Art. 31 of Regulation No. 198/1996 and Art. 29, 30 of the Codice della proprietà industriale, the use of misleading geographic indications is unfair competition as understood in Art. 2598 CC. Inasmuch as such assertions lead to "appropriating the merits of a competitor's product"—which is only possible for representations as to quality that are relevant to a buyer—Art. 2598 No. 2 CC is directly applicable.[766]

11. Enforcement

The protection granted by the Codice Civile (Art. 2598-2601 CC) is of a civil nature.[767] In principle, there must be a competitive relationship or the potential thereof between the plaintiff and the defendant.[768] Commercial associations also have standing to sue (Art. 2601 CC). The plaintiff can bring an action for a cease-and-desist order,

762. Corte die Cassatione 9.6.1998 No. 5671, RIC 196, 3.2001, p. 34; Corte di Cassazione 16.4.1983, No. 3365, Giur.Ann.Dir.Jur. 1983, p. 1596.
763. Francetti, id. See also RIC 190, 3.1999. See also Tribunale di Verona 30.4.1996, where a former employee targeted customers of his former employer without mentioning that he no longer worked for him. Regarding the misleading impression that one has sole power of distribution, see also Tribunale di Monalo 28.11.1996, discussed in RIC 190, 3.1999, p. 36.
764. See Auteri, *Commentary on the regulation No. 198/1996*, in: Le nūove leggi civili commentate, 1998, p. 71 and 124.
765. Corte di Cassazione 23.2.1976, No. 582; Giur. Ann. Dir. Ind. 1976, p. 783; 8.4.1978, No. 2220, Giur. Ann. Dir. Ind. 1978, p. 1001.
766. The advertisement of butter with the false statement of origin of "Vipiteno" is not a forbidden preemption of preferences, since consumers would not think of this area as having any special quality. Corte di Appello di Roma 24.2.1975, Giur.ann.dir.ind. 1975, Nr. 703. As regards the (indirect) assertion that the advertised wine has all of the qualities of Champagne, see Tribunale di Milano 16.10.1978. Giur.ann.dir.ind. 1978 N. 1086
767. See Bastian, No. 264; Francetti, p. 245; Preussler, p. 729.
768. A competitive relationship was found to exist between a foreign company that had a license to sell its goods in Italy and an imitator. The licensee would also have standing to sue; see RIC 196, 3. 2001, p. 32.

abatement, damages, and publication of judgments (Art. 2599 CC). Injunctions may be rendered in a preliminary proceeding according to the regulations of Art. 700 Codie di Procedura Civile. The regional courts have jurisdiction.

The violation of Decree No. 74/1992 (misleading, comparative or other unfair advertising) is dealt with by the "Autorità Garante della Concurrenza e de Mercato" (see above, 2). This authority has the power to make final cease-and-desist orders, as well as preliminary ones in emergency cases (Art. 7(6)). It may order its ruling to be published or make a public notice correcting the misleading information (Art. 7(6)(3)). Competitors, consumers and their organizations also have standing to sue. (Art. 7(2),(12)).[769] The decisions of the Autorità Garante can be appealed to the administrative courts (Art. 7(11)).

XV. LATVIA[770]

Selected Literature: Dietz, *Die Einführung von Gesetzen gegen den unlauteren Wettbewerb in ehemals sozialistischen Staaten Mittel- und Osteuropas*, GRUR Int. 1994, 649; Torgans, Consumer Protection in Latvia, in: Alexiev et al., *Consumer Protection in Bulgaria, Czech Republic, Estonia, Hungary, Latvia, Lithuania and Romania*, CICPP No. 4, 143; Cambier, *Comparative and Misleading Advertising Legislation in Central and Eastern Europe*, CICPP No. 12.

1. Sources of law

Konkurences likums (Competition Act) of 2001 (KL); Reklams likums (Advertising Act) of 2000 (RL).[771]

2. Latvian unfair competition law in a nutshell

The Latvian lawmaker has chosen to address the problems of fairness and freedom of competition in an integrated manner. The Competition Act of 2001 regulates different forms of restrictions on competition along with unfair commercial practices (Art. 2 KL). It opens avenues for administrative law enforcement before the Competition Council (Konkurences Padome, KP) as well as for private law enforcement.

The rules on unfair competition are concentrated in Ch. V KL. Article 18(1) and (2) KL form a broad general clause against unfair competition. According to Art. 18(2) acts of unfair competition are actions, as a result of which regulatory enactments or the fair practices of commercial activities are violated and which have created or could create a hindrance, restriction or distortion of competition. The general clause is complemented by a catalogue of prohibited unfair commercial practices (Art. 18(3) Nrs. 1-5 KL).

769. The right of commercial associations to bring suit is in practice limited to cases where the interests of the association are harmed; Corte d'Appello di Roma 30.1.1995. Locus standi of consumer associations based on the Law of July 1998 is disputed.
770. The report was authored by Dr. Antonina Bakardjieva-Engelbrekt, University of Stockholm. The author is grateful to Inese Grunde and Ineta Krodere-Imsa, attorneys-at-law, Riga, for providing valuable information and language assistance.
771. The texts of these legal acts in English are retrievable from the website of the Competition Council <www.competition.lv>. A database on Latvian legislation in English can be found at: <www.ttc.lv>.

Of relevance for unfair competition law is the Advertising Act of 1999. Rules on consumer information are included in the Consumer Rights Protection Law of 1999 (Patērētāju tiesibu aizardzibas likums, PTAL).

3. Regulation of advertising

The main legal source for the regulation of advertising is the RL. The concept of advertising is defined in Art. 1 RL. Article 3 RL provides a general clause on advertising activity, according to which all advertising shall be lawful, truthful and objective and in accordance with ethical advertising practices (see also Art. 3(2) RL). It shall not reduce public confidence in advertising and shall comply with principles of fair competition.

a. Misleading advertising

A general prohibition on misleading advertising is established in Art. 8 RL.[772] The definition of misleading advertising is taken literally from Directive 84/450/EEC[773] and includes a requirement of relevance of the advertising message for consumers.

In its practice the KP proceeds from the benchmark of the average consumer, referring expressly to the ECJ judgment in the case C-220/98 *Estee Lauder*. The average consumer is characterized by the KP as intelligent, well informed, careful, observant and cautious person.[774] However, the standard applied to superlative advertising is rather strict. Claims of superiority like "the best" or "the cheapest" are not allowed unless they can be substantiated.[775]

b. Comparative advertising

Comparative advertising is any advertising using a comparison which directly or indirectly indicates a competitor or goods or services offered by a competitor (Art. 9(1) RL).[776] Comparative advertising is permitted if it meets the requirements in Art. 9(3) RL, whereby the burden of proof is on the advertiser.[777] The rules are modeled after Directive 97/55/EC.

772. In the catalogue of acts of unfair competition the KL also contains a prohibition of the dissemination of false, incomplete or distorted information, however, only as far as such information concerns other market participants (Art. 18(3) Nr. 3 KL).
773. According to Art. 8(2) RL misleading advertising is advertising that in any manner, including its manner of presentation, is (or may be) directly or indirectly misleading and due to its misleading character, may affect the economic behavior of a person, or is harmful or may be harmful to a competitor (Art. 8(2) RL).
774. The threshold is thus arguably set higher than in ECJ jurisprudence. See decision of the KP No. 770/03/10 of 22.12.2003—"Pampers".
775. See decision of the KP No. 102/03/07/7 of 14.4.2003—"SIA BT 1".
776. In the "Pampers" case the KP held that the comparative test with an anonymous non-branded diaper did not allow consumers to identify a competitor or his products, neither directly nor indirectly. See decision of the KP No. 770/03/10 of 22.12.2003.
777. See decision of the KP No. 800/03/09/11 of 11.9.2003 —"Telekom Baltija".

c. Concealed advertising

The RL establishes a general duty of advertising disseminators in all media to separate advertising from other forms of information (Art. 12(3) RL).[778]

d. Product- and media-specific advertising regulation

The Alcoholic Beverages Act of 2004 (Alkoholisko dzērienu aprites likums, ADAL) prohibits among other the display of alcohol advertising in residential and education institutions, in cultural and sporting events (Art. 58 and 59 ADAL).[779] Advertising of medicinal products is strictly regulated, whereby advertising to the public of prescription drugs and narcotic substances, is not permitted.[780]

Specific conditions and requirements for radio and television advertising and teleshopping are included in the Radio and Television Act of 1995 (Radio un televizija likum, RTL), which for the most part follow Directive 89/552/EEC, as amended.

e. Other regulations on advertising

According to Art. 4 RL violence and war propaganda in advertising is not permitted. Prohibited are also all forms of discriminatory advertising, advertising that exploits people's trust, lack of experience or knowledge. Advertising directed to children must comply with conditions, seeking to safeguard the rights and interests of children in view of their vulnerability as a target audience (Art. 5 RL).

4. Information requirements

The PTAL proclaims freedom of choice and will, and the right to information as general consumer rights (Art. 4 PTAL). Corresponding to these rights is the duty of sellers to furnish consumers with complete information regarding the goods, services, contract performance and liability (Art. 4(2) PTAL).[781]

5. Direct marketing, specific marketing methods

The PTAL contains rules and information requirements on doorstep selling, distance selling, and time-share contracts, all in line with respective Community Directives (see Ch. 9-11 PTAL). For advertising via facsimiles, automatic answering machines and distance communication techniques, which involve individual contact with a consumer, a general "opt-in" principle applies (Art. 10 PTAL).[782]

778. For advertising in electronic media see Art. 22(1) and (3) Radio and Television Act.
779. See Art. 24(1) and (2) RTL on tobacco and alcohol advertising in television broadcasting.
780. See Art. 7 Regulation Nr. 41 of 2001 on Procedures for the Advertising of Medicinal Products.
781. This general duty is fleshed out by specific mandatory information requirements in Ch. IV PTAL.
782. See also Cabinet Regulation No. 207 of 28.5.2002 Regarding Distance Contracts, setting forth additional information requirements and implementing Directive 2000/31/EC.

6. Sales promotion

Article 6 RL sets forth detailed information requirements for the advertising of special offers. Such advertising shall in particular indicate the subject of the offer, the date it starts and ends and the conditions on which it depends (Art. 6(2) RL).

7. Disparagement

According to Art. 18(3) Nr. 3 KL it is an act of unfair competition to disseminate false, incomplete or distorted information regarding other market participants. In parallel, and pursuant to Art. 4(2) Nr. 5 RL, it is prohibited in advertising to defame, disparage or ridicule another person, or his activities, name, products, or marks.

8. Passing off, imitation

The KL comprises two provisions that interface with trademark protection. The first addresses the use or imitation of distinguishing signs that may create confusion as to the identity of an enterprise. The second provision addresses imitations that may cause confusion as to the origin of the goods (cf. Art. 18(3) Nr. 1 and 2 KL).

Independent of the KL, Art. 4(2), Nr. 6 RL sets forth a non-qualified prohibition to exploit in advertising identifying designations (including a trade mark) of another entrepreneur, which appears to apply irrespective of the risk of confusion.[783]

9. Obstructive competition

Business secrets are protected under Art. 18(2) KL.[784] Exerting coercion on employees of another enterprise through threat or bribery is another example of obstructive unfair competition under Art. 18(2) Nr. 5. Sale below cost is not prohibited unless the undertaking is in a dominant position.[785]

10. Breach of law

The general clause on unfair competition in KL explicitly refers to breach of statutory enactments as an act of unfair competition.[786]

11. Enforcement

The KP is entitled to establish violations of the rules against unfair competition, to impose legal obligations on the infringer and considerable administrative fines (Art. 19 KL). Concurrently, the civil courts can adjudicate civil claims, e.g. for damage compensation (Arts. 20, 21 KL).

783. In addition, Art. 4(2) Nr. 7 protects advertising (in text, slogan, visual representation, audio or other special effects) from imitation, which may create confusion.
784. See also Art. 19 Commercial Code (Komerclikums) of 2000 on the legal protection of commercial secrets.
785. See decision No. 45 of 10.31.2002 of KP, Annual Report of the KP for 2002, p. 12.
786. Also Art. 3 RL establishes a general requirement that all advertising shall be lawful.

The RL is under the supervision authority of, among others, the KP and the Consumer Rights Protection Centre (Art. 13 RL, cf. Art. 25 PTAL). These institutions are entitled to enjoin the advertiser from further dissemination of the advert, to order the publication of corrective advertisement, to recall the advertising or to impose administrative penalties (Art. 15 RL).[787] The decisions of the supervisory bodies are subject to appeal, but the appeal shall not suspend the execution of the decision (Art. 17 RL). The PTAL employs a rich variety of civil, administrative and criminal sanctions and remedies (see Art. 25(8), Art. 33 PTAL).

Persons whose interests have been adversely affected by an act of unfair competition or unlawful advertising can claim compensation for damages on the basis of the Civil Law Act (Civillikums).

XVI. LITHUANIA[788]

Selected Literature: Dietz, *Die Einführung von Gesetzen gegen den unlauteren Wettbewerb in ehemals sozialistischen Staaten Mittel- und Osteuropas*, GRUR Int. 1994, p. 649; Viitanen, Consumer Protection in Lithuania, in: Alexiev et al., *Consumer Protection in Bulgaria, Czech Republic, Estonia, Hungary, Latvia, Lithuania and Romania*, CICPP No. 4, p. 171; Cambier, *Comparative and Misleading Advertising Legislation in Central and Eastern Europe*, CICPP No. 12.

1. Sources of law

Konkurencijos Ástatymas (Competition Act VIII-1099) of 1999 (KA); Reklamos Ástatymas, RA (Advertising Act VIII-1871) of 2000; Civil Code VIII-1864 of 2000; Vartotojø teisiø gynimo ástatymas (Consumer Protection Act) of 1994 (VTGA).[789]

2. Lithuanian unfair competition law in a nutshell

Lithuania belongs to the countries that regulate free and fair competition in a coordinated manner. The Competition Act of 2001 has as its main objective to protect freedom of fair competition and provides the legal basis for control of competition restrictions as well as of unfair competition (Art. 1 KA).[790] The rules on unfair competition form Chapter III KA and apply only in business-to-business relations. Of central importance is the general clause against unfair competition, which prohibits as an act of unfair competition any act contrary to honest business practices if such act may be detrimental to competition interests of another undertaking. (Art. 16(1) KA). This abstract provision is fleshed out by a non-exhaustive catalogue of examples of acts of unfair competition (Art. 16(1) Nr. 1-7 KA). The KA can be enforced by way

787. See decision in Annual Report of the Competition Council for 2002, p. 12.
788. The report was authored by Dr. Antonina Bakardjieva-Engelbrekt, University of Stockholm. The author wishes to thank Dr. V. Mizaras, Associate Professor at the Univesrity of Vilnjus, for valuable information.
789. A database on Lithuanian legislation in English can be found at: <www3.lrs.lt>.
790. The present Competition Act has its precursor in the Act on Competition and Restriction of Monopolies of 3.12.1992. The text of the law as well as other legal materials are retrievable from the website of the Competition Board <www.konkuren.lt>.

of civil lawsuit before the ordinary courts and by way of administrative proceedings before the Competition Council (Konkurencijos Tarba, KT).

The Civil Code (Civilinis Kodeksas, CK) stipulates a general prohibition against exercising civil rights in bad faith, with the intent of unlawfully limiting competition or in abuse of dominant position in the market (Art. 1.137 CK). The Code regulates sales promotions, special offers and distance selling and lays down liability for damages caused by misleading advertising. Of relevance for the regulation of advertising is further the Advertising Act of 2000 as well as the Consumer Protection Act of 1994.

3. Regulation of advertising

The basic legal framework for regulation of advertising is provided by the RA, but is complemented by provisions in the KA, CK and VTGA. The definition of advertising is borrowed from Directive 84/450/EEC (Art. 2(7) RA).

a. Misleading advertising

Misleading advertising is prohibited pursuant to Art. 5(1) RA. In parallel, KA proclaims misleading of undertakings, as well as advertising claims which are considered misleading under other Lithuanian laws, as acts of unfair competition (Art. 16(1) Nr. 2, 7 KA).

The definition of misleading advertising in Art. 2 Nr. 7 RA follows strictly the wording of Art. 2(2) Directive 84/450/EEC. When judging whether an advert is misleading account shall be taken not only of its accurateness but also of its comprehensiveness. The law thus explicitly recognizes the possibility of misleading by omission (cf. Art. 2(2) Nr. 2 RA). The perceptions of the average consumer are expressly set out as a benchmark for the overall assessment of the advertisement (Art. 5(4) RA). Article 5(2) RA introduces a reverse burden of proof.

b. Comparative advertising

The RA provides the legal basis for regulating comparative advertising. The definition of comparative advertising (Art. 2(5) RA) and the conditions that have to be satisfied for it to be permitted (Art. 6(1)1-8 RA) are as a whole equivalent with those in Directive 97/55/EC.

c. Concealed advertising

Advertising in all media shall be clearly recognizable as such (Art. 3(2) RA). Surreptitious advertising is banned (Art. 8 RA, see also Art. 4(8) RA).

d. Product- and media-specific advertising

The RA includes some product-specific restrictions and prohibitions. It bans advertising of weapons and ammunition (Art. 16 RA). Restrictions are set forth for advertising of health care services (Art. 15 RA) and for foodstuffs advertising (Art. 14

RA). Tobacco advertising is prohibited with some minor exceptions under Arts. 17-18 Tobacco Control Act of 1995.[791] The restrictions on the promotion and advertising of alcoholic beverages are laid down in Arts. 28-29 of the Alcohol Control Act.[792]

Rules on radio and television advertising are established in Arts. 39 and 40 of the Act on Provision of Information to the Public of 1996. Advertising in movie theaters and outdoor advertising are regulated in Art. 11 and 12 RA.[793]

e. Other regulations on advertising

The RA establishes a number of general requirements relating to the ethical aspects of advertising. Advertising shall not: violate public and moral principles; degrade human honor and dignity; incite national, racial, religious or other hatred; promote behavior that presents threat to security; abuse superstitions, people's trust and their lack of experience or information (Art. 4(2) Nr. 1-6 RA). Advertising directed to children shall not cause them moral or physical damage and shall comply with other requirements (Art. 7 RA).

4. Information requirements

Chapter II VTGA is devoted to consumer information. Article 5 establishes a right of consumers to obtain full information on the purchased goods and services and a duty of sellers to provide such information. This general duty is complemented by specific requirements, e.g. on indication of prices (Art. 5(5) and (6) VTGA).[794]

5. Direct marketing; specific marketing methods

Pursuant to Art. 13 RA advertising by telephone, fax and electronic mail may only be supplied with the consent or upon the request of the consumer ("opt-in" principle). All other direct marketing to individual consumers is subject to an "opt-out" rule (Art. 13 RA). Doorstep selling and distance selling are regulated in the VTGA (see Ch. V, VI) as well as in the CK (see Art. 6.356 CK on doorstep selling, Arts. 6.366 and 6.367 CK on distance selling and Art. 6.368 CK on supply of unsolicited products). The provisions generally follow the respective Community directives.

6. Sales promotion

Free gifts, price reductions and other sales promotion methods exerting pressure on consumers to buy, are restricted according to Art. 6.350 CK.

791. Act No. I-1143 of 20.12.1995, last amended as of 20.11.2003.
792. Act No. I-857 of 18.4.1995, last amended as of 9.3.2004. Initially the Tobacco and Alcohol Acts advanced a total ban of direct and indirect tobacco and alcohol advertising, respectively. Such extensive prohibitions were, however, declared unconstitutional by the Lithuanian Constitutional Court. See Decision of 13.2.1997 in Case No. 6/96 -10/96.
793. Act No. I-1418 of 2.7.1996, last amended as of 27.4.2004.
794. A similar catalogue of mandatory pre-purchase information exists in Art. 6.353, Book Six, Part IV, Ch. 23, Section IV of the Civil Code concerning consumer sales contracts.

7. Disparagement

According to Art. 16(1) Nr. 6 KA providing incorrect or unsubstantiated information about another undertaking is prohibited as an act of unfair competition.

8. Passing off, imitation

Two of the provisions of the KA have close kinship with trademark law. Article 16(1) Nr. 1 prohibits as an act of unfair competition the unauthorized use of a mark identical or similar to the name, mark or other distinguishing reference of another undertaking. However, this is so, provided that the use may cause confusion, seeks to take undue advantage of, or may cause injury to the reputation of that undertaking.

Art. 16 prohibits close imitations of products and product packaging of another undertaking by copying the external shape or packaging color or other distinguishing feature of the product, where there is a risk of confusion, or where the act amounts to goodwill exploitation (Art. 16(1) Nr. 5 KA; but cf. Art. 16(5) KA).

9. Impediment of competitors

Business secrets are protected under Art. 16(1) Nr. 3 KA[795] as well as under Art. 1.116 CK. Inducing employees of a competing undertaking to breach of contract with a view of extracting benefits for oneself or afflicting damages to the competitor is also banned as act of unfair competition (Art. 16(1) Nr. 4 KA.

10. Breach of law

Violations of legal duties and prescriptions may arguably be found to be against honest commercial practices (Art. 16(1) KA). Pursuant to Art. 9 RA all advertising of illegal and prohibited goods, services and activities is prohibited.

11. Enforcement

Competitors whose legitimate interests are violated by acts of unfair competition are entitled to claim injunction, compensation for damages, obliging the infringer to issue a corrective statement and seizure or destruction of goods or their packaging under certain circumstances (Art. 17(1) KA). Similar rights of action, with the exception of the right to claim damage compensation, are granted to business and consumer associations. The KT has powers to investigate acts of unfair competition, but only where these acts violate the interests of a number of undertakings and consumers (Art. 17(4) KA). The KT is authorized to impose administrative fines of considerable size as well as other penalties and measures (Art. 19 (1) KA).

Compliance of undertakings with the requirements of the RA is controlled by different institutions, the leading role being assigned to the state Consumer Protection Council (Vartotojø Teisiø Gynimo Taryba, VTGT) and the KT. There is a division of labor between the two agencies, whereby the rules on misleading and comparative

795. See also Art. 16(3) KA establishing a one-year non-disclosure duty for former employees.

advertising are within the supervisory powers of the KT, while the implementation of the other bans and requirements established by RA is supervised by the VTGT (Art. 17 RA). The KT has the right to issue a cease and desist order, including an interim one, to order the issuance of corrective statement and apply other administrative penalties (Art. 19(2), Nr. 1-6 RA). Persons whose rights and interests are violated can seek injunction, compensation for damages and corrective advertising in the ordinary courts (Art. 26 RA, see also Art. CK). Consumer associations, organizations representing advertising operators and self-regulatory institutions have likewise the right to claim cessation of unlawful advertising and corrective statement. The status and powers of the VTGT in the field of consumer protection are regulated in Ch. IX VTGA.

XVII. LUXEMBOURG

Selected Literature: Birden, Das Wettbewerbsrecht in Luxemburg, in: *Heidelberger Kommentar zum Wettbewerbsrecht*, 2nd ed. 2005, 731; Emering, *Dokumentation der Besonderheiten des Wettbewerbsrechts in Europa*, WRP 1991, 72; Henning-Bodewig/Decker, *Luxemburg*, in: Schricker (ed.), *Recht der Werbung in Europa*, 2002; Henning-Bodewig, *Das Wettbewerbsrecht in Luxemburg*, GRUR Int. 1994, 808; Radeideh/Schmitz, in: Micklitz/Kessler (ed.), *Marketing Practices Regulation and Consumer Protection in the EC Member States and the US*, 2002, p. 220; Schricker/Francq/Wunderlich, *Belgique, Luxembourg*, in: Ulmer (ed.), *La répression de la concurrence déloyale dans les Etat Membres de la Communauté Economique Européene; Tome II/1*, 1974.

1. Sources of law

Loi du 30 juillet 2003 réglementant certaines pratiques commerciales et sanctionnant la concurrence déloyale (Act to regulate certain trade practices and to sanction unfair competition) of 30 July 2002 (LPC)

2. Luxembourg's unfair competition law in a nutshell

At the core of Luxembourg's unfair competition law is the "Loi réglementant certaines pratiques commerciales et sanctionnant la concurrence déloyale" (LPC) from 30 July 2002.[796] As in Belgium, the LPC is predominantly sanctioned by civil law and aims at a comprehensive regulation of the entire market activity. The LPC 2002 equally protects businesses (including independent professions) and consumers.[797] At least some causes of action still require an act of competition and a competitive

796. Announced in the Mémorial (Official Gazette of the Grand Duchy Luxembourg) from 21.8.2002, p. 1830. The (unchanged) legal draft from 17.9.2001 can be found (in French) in the No. 4844/delegate paper from 10.2.2001 which also includes the reasoning. The previous Act from 1986, which has been incorporated at least in part, is published (in German) in GRUR Int. 1994, 144 and discussed in detail by Henning-Bodewig/Decker.

797. The former LPC (1986) was mainly aimed to protect business—despite giving consumer associations standing to sue. The new regulation takes the interests of the consumers into more consideration, although the official reasoning (p. 8) only mentions the "public" in general.

relationship.[798] Thus, the editorial work of the media and product test by consumer associations do not fall into the area of application.

Although the goal of the reform of 2002 was mainly liberalization—for example, the prohibition of premiums was repealed—the LPC is still considered more of a restrictive regulation. The first chapter contains an extensive regulation of "certain business practices", including seasonal clearance sales, liquidation sales and others. The second chapter is intended to fight "certain abuses" of competition. It contains in Art. 14 LPC a broad general clause, which is similar to Art. 10bis Paris Convention ("usages honnêtes"). In the LPC of 1986, the general clause was exemplified by a catalog of 13 examples.[799] This catalog was completely removed in the reform of 2002. However, the official statement regarding the legal draft emphasizes that the former examples, if not expressly replaced by new provisions, are now to be subsumed directly under the general clause. Replaced by new provisions were, above all, the regulation of advertising[800] especially regarding comparative advertisement.

Luxembourg's unfair competition law traditionally has close ties with the laws of intellectual property,[801] especially the Unified Benelux trademark law,[802] but certain references also exist to the Trade Name Act from 10 August 1915,[803] to the anti-trust law from 16 June 1987,[804] as well as to the Consumer Protection Act from 1983 which mainly deals with consumer protection in contractual relationships.

Case law exists mainly in the area of commercial practices that are regionally restricted (sales, special offers, etc.). On the whole, there is relatively little (published) case law based on the LPC.[805] Belgian case law and legal literature are often used to interpret the provisions of the LPC, although the former similarities between the statues in Belgium and Luxemburg have diminished since the passing of the Belgian Unfair Trade Practices Act of 1991.

3. Regulation of advertising

a. Misleading advertising

The regulation of misleading advertising in Art. 17 LPC corresponds almost literally to Art. 2 Nos. 2 and 3 of the Misleading Advertising Directive. The term "advertisement" is defined in Art. 15.[806] The official explanation emphasizes that misleading statements regarding health-improving effects, environmental aspects and chances of winning

798. The condition for a competitive relation for the law of 1986 was mostly derived from the general clause which remained unchanged.
799. These were a wide choice of causes of action, such as danger of confusion, defamation, special offers, rebates, joined offers.
800. In the 1986 Act, multiple causes of action were applicable to particular aspects of advertising. This rather confusing approach has now been replaced by a comprehensive regulation on advertising.
801. Regarding Luxembourg's IP law see (in English) "Manual Industrial Property", Vol. 4 (1998); as to copyright law (in German) Möhring/Schulze/Ulmer/Zweigert (ed.), Quellen des Urheberrechts, Vol. 4.
802. See Braun, Précis du Droit de Marques, 4th ed. 2004.
803. See Hillebrand, Das Firmenrecht in Frankreich, Belgien und Luxemburg, 1974; Elvinger, La protection de la dénomination sociale en droit luxembourgois, in: Jura vigilantibus, Lacier, 1994.
804. Birden, p. 733.
805. Suits that involve cross border practices are often brought before the French or Belgian courts.
806. Any communication that occurs during the commercial, industrial, technical or free-lance activity which serves the purpose of promoting sales. The official explanation expressly refers to other definitions of advertising, for example in the area of television.

are covered. Furthermore, it is to be expected that all misleading aspects regulated in the 1986 LPC are still included under Art. 17, for instance bait and switch offers, special offers (if the demand cannot be met within a day) or claims falsely referring to wholesale property. Although advertising statements do not have to be complete, the omission of important information was considered by more recent case law to be unfair competition.[807]

As Art. 17(1) LPC of the former LPC 1986 (false indication about origin or source) was completely discarded, it is to be assumed that indications of geographic origin are now primarily judged under the aspect of misleading and on the basis of the general clause (here especially under the aspect of exploitation of reputation; see under 7).

As to the determination of misleading, in principle the same criteria apply as under trademark law.[808] The benchmark is the reasonably well-informed, observant and circumspect average consumer. Earlier Luxembourg case law[809] was relatively hesitant to find advertising being misleading. In more recent decisions, however, it has been emphasized that the consumer has no obligation to carefully "analyze" the content of advertisement, but can rely on the obvious statements and the overall impression. How many of the targeted consumers have to be misled is rarely specified in Luxembourg decisions.[810] Intent etc., is not necessary on part of the advertiser; advertisement made in good faith can also be misleading.[811]

The burden of proof lies with plaintiff. However, pursuant to Art. 288 Code Procedure Civil the court may order the dependant to participate in the gathering of evidence (which is relatively often done).

b. Comparative advertising

In Art. 18 LPC, Directive 97/55/EC was transposed word-for-word. Comparative advertising is thus permitted if the requirements in Art. 18 (2) LPC are met. Since comparative advertising was strictly forbidden until 2002, the former—not very substantial—case law is of only limited usefulness.[812] The term comparative advertising is broadly interpreted, for instance the question whether an individual competitor could be identified is also determined by the situation in the market.[813] Considering the

807. For example the advertising of a telephone service provider with extremely cheap rates which did not mention that they only applied to certain times of the day; Cour d'appel de Luxemburg 18.2.1998—Mobilux./. CMDSA (unpublished)
808. See the decisions cited by Henning-Bodewig/Decker, No. 43.
809. See Henning-Bodewig/Decker, No. 43
810. According to the ECJ, a "significant part of the targeted consumers" must be mislead; see the "Nissan"—decision; discussed in this book in Chapter III, 3.
811. Under the 1986 Act, it was unclear whether the good faith of the advertiser could be a defense to a claim of misleading advertising.
812. This may be different as to the decisions after the enactment of the Directive but before the transposition into the Luxembourg law. For instance, the simple comparison of telephone rates was considered permissible (President of the Commercial Court Luxemburg 25.4.2001, not published), but the advertising of a publishing company with the statement that a competitor was "30% more expensive and less comprehensive", was prohibited as disparaging; President of the Commercial Court Luxemburg 9.10.2001—"Editpresse Luxembourg SA./. Saint Paul Luxemburg SA" (unpublished).
813. The word "Premier" in an advertisement for a mineral water was considered comparative advertising, because there was only one large competitor in the Luxembourg market. Also the claim of a mobile phone provider "we are the cheapest" was considered a comparison because there were only

traditionally strict interpretation of defamation and disparagement, it is to be expected that Luxembourg case law (like Belgian case law) will regard comparative advertising critically mainly under the aspect of disparagement.[814]

c. Concealed advertising

Article 28 Media Law from 27 July 1991 in its version from 2001[815] requires a clear separation of television advertising from other parts of the program and expressly prohibits surreptitious advertising. Article 47 of the Electronic Trade Act from 14 August 2000[816] states the basic principle that all commercial communication must clearly be recognizable as such. For the press, this principle is derived from Art. 11 of the ICC-Codex of the International Chamber of Commerce.

d. Aggressive advertising

The harassment of consumers by advertisement or sales promotion is not regulated expressis verbis. It can, however, be subsumed under the general clause of Art. 94 LPC.[817]

e. Product- and media-specific advertising regulations [818]

Advertising for pharmaceutical products is regulated in the law from 11 April 1983 in its version from 6 January 1995 which is supplemented by several decrees. A preventive duty to control (Art. 19(2)) exists for advertising directed to the general public (with the exception of mere recall advertising). Advertising for food products falls under the regulation from 16 April 1992 as well as several special regulations; it also includes alcohol. The advertising for tobacco products is restricted by the Tobacco Act.

Advertising in broadcasting is regulated by the Media Law from 27 July 1991; it contains in transposition of the television directive advertising restrictions for potentially dangerous products (tobacco products, pharmaceutical products, alcohol) as well as requirements as to the content of television commercial. The Electronic Trade Act from 14 August 2000 (see above, 3c) applies to the "commerce électronique".

four other providers in Luxembourg. President Commercial Court Diekirch 23.11.1990, Pas.Lux. 1992, 92 No. 76; President Commercial Court Luxemburg 29.10.1997—Mobilux SA./. CMD SA (unpublished).

814. For example, a television commercial for Pepsi in which a dancer threw a red can behind him while the music "I don't like that feeling" was playing in the background was considered disparaging (the decision was based on the general clause). President of the Commercial Court Luxemburg 18.10.1991—"The Coca Cola Comp. et SA Sountérage Luxembourg./. SA RTL" (unpublished).

815. Loi du 27 juillet 1991 sur Res medias, Mémorial A-N. 42 from 30.7.1991, p. 9.

816. Loi du 14 août 2000 relative au commerce électronique, Mémorial A-No. 96 from 8.9.2000, p. 2177.

817. The official reasoning (fn. 796) explicitly states that under the general clause, in principle, also aggressive commercial actions towards the consumer can be subsumed; the corresponding prohibition in the Swiss law is referred to.

818. See Henning-Bodewig/Decker, No. 86. The statues can be found in the Annex. The regulation of advertisement for alcohol and tobacco is also discussed by Radeideh/Schmitz, p. 231.

4. Direct marketing

Article 8 of the law regarding door-to-door sales prohibits unrequested commercial telephone calls and faxes that are not deemed necessary for the targeted consumer's profession.[819]

According to Art. 48 of the Electronic Trade Act the "opt-out" solution applies to any unsolicited commercial communication via e-mail.[820] At this point, however, such registers have apparently not been set up.

Door-to-door visits are prohibited by Art. 8 of the "Colportage"-Act from 16 July 1987[821] if they concern contracts about goods and services that are not necessary for the commercial activity of the consumer. Contracts that have been concluded in spite of this are not valid. The demarcation to the permitted sales at the location of the consumer ("démarchage domicile") is not totally clear. Special regulations for the mailing of advertising material do not exist.[822]

Pursuant to Art. 22 LPC chain sales ("vente en chaine") or similar commercial practices are explicitly prohibited.[823]

5. Sales promotion

Free gifts, premiums, promotional gifts and all other types of sales promotions are generally permitted.[824] They are to be measured by the prohibition of misleading indications. If and under which conditions the general clause of Art. 14 LPC might apply is not yet known.[825]

Rebates are not permitted when they would lead to a sale at a loss (Art. 20 LPC). This prohibition also applies to wholesalers for rebates directed towards individual traders who are in a legal or economic dependency.[826]

Lotteries for promotional purposes, games of chance ("jeux-concours") and raffles are only allowed under the conditions listed in Art. 21 LPC. They must be reported to the authorities and may not lead to any confusion as to the amount and value of the price or the conditions of receipt. Participation may not be dependant on financial

819. Radeideh/Schmitz, p. 222. A draft law requires the prior agreement of the consumers when automated calling systems are used ("opt-in").
820. Radeideh/Schmitz, p. 222. In addition, transparency requirements must be met according to Directive 30/2000/EC (see Chapter 3, II.). Directive 2002/58/EC has not yet been transposed into Luxembourgian law; it would require the establishing of an "opt-in"-system, see Chapter 3, IV.9.
821. Loi du 16.7.1987 concernant de colportage, la vente ambulante, l'étalage de marchandises et la sollicitation de commandes.
822. In the literature, an analogue application of the law regarding door-to-door sales is considered possible. This would lead to an "opt-out" solution.
823. "Vente en chaine" consists in the creation of a network of sellers, in which each seller gets advantages by expanding the network rather than by selling goods or services to a third party. A direct reference to pyramid schemes is made in para. 3. Para. 4 prohibits the conscious participation in such systems. MLM systems are not included because the assumed advantage results from selling good or services to third parties. Since 1999, there is a direct marketing association (Association pour la Vente Directe) which created a self regulation code that fits "home parties".
824. The former very restrictive, regulation was repealed in 2002.
825. The official explanation mentions that the general clause also covers overly aggressive marketing practices towards consumers.
826. Permitted are sales at a loss in cases mentioned in para. 3; for example, goods that go bad quickly, products whose value decreases because of changes in technology, or where the price must be adjusted because of necessary competitive action.

participation which includes the requirement of purchase.[827] The certificate of participation must be clearly separated from any eventual order form. If the impression is given through the conception or presentation of the communication that a consumer won a prize, the organizer is required to actually give the prize to that consumer.

Sales promotion measures in the internet must state the requirements of participation in easy to find, precise and unmistakable language, according to Art. 47 Electronic Trade Act on e-commerce (see above, 3e).

The LPC 2002 contains extensive regulations regarding special events (seasonal sales), street sales, and the public auctioning of new items.

6. Denigration and disparagement

Disparagement of a competitor through false or not provable statements regarding the person, company, or wares is seen as a violation of the general clause of Art. 14 LPC. The same applies for true statements that are unnecessarily aggressive in their phrasing.[828] The prohibition of denigration is generally strictly enforced in the law of Luxembourg.[829]

7. Misappropriation, exploitation of reputation, imitation

Exploitation of reputation is judged on the basis of the general clause of Art. 14 LPC. The main area of application (outside of comparative advertising) is the comparisons of systems or statements as to the geographic origin. For instance, the description of a cheese as "type trappiste" was considered not only misleading but also an exploiting of reputation and thus a violating of the general clause.[830]

According to Art. 17(f) of the LPC 1986, it was forbidden to cause confusion with the person, product, service or business of a competitor. Although this provision was repealed, such situations are now directly covered by the general clause of Art. 14 LPC. An imitation of products or trade marks which leads to a danger of confusion is thus clearly against the "usage honnêtes". However, in cases where a protection under Benelux-Trademark Law or the Benelux-Design Law is possible, these laws have precedence as lex specialis if the claim is based on the imitation ("contrefaçon") as such.[831] Art. 14 LPC is often the basis for a protection of advertising material against imitation[832] and for confusingly similar trade names.[833]

827. Since contests not based on luck do not fall under the term "lotteries", "jeux-concours", or "tombolas publicitaires", a coupling with the sale of products seems to be permissible.
828. The LPC 1986 contained in Art. 17h an explicit prohibition of disparagement which according to case law included true but unnecessarily denigrating statements, see Henning-Bodewig/Decker, No. 63. According to the official explanation, the cases that used to be listed as examples of the former general clause are now subsumed directly under the general clause of Art. 14 LPC 2002.
829. Henning-Bodewig, No. 60 ff.
830. Cour d'appel de Luxembourg 14.4.1986, Pas. Lux. 1992, 83 Nr. 43. The court saw the description "trappiste" as a statement of origin. The goodwill and reputation of the Trappiste Monks was unfairly exploited.
831. Both laws contain a "blocking provision" that prohibits unfair competition protection for trade marks and designs that are capable of protection under the Benelux Trademark or Design Act.
832. The imitated advertisement must be sufficiently distinct (and elaborate), which is often implied when an imitating action exists.
833. See above (fn. 9).

In special situations, the parasitic exploitation of another party's commercial achievements (without exploitation of reputation and danger of confusion) may be considered as being against the "usages honnêtes" and thus be subsumed under the general clause.[834]

8. Impediment of competitors

According to Art. 309 Criminal Code, an employee is forbidden for two years after the termination of the contract to reveal trade secrets, when this would cause a distortion of competition and was done with the intent to gain a personal advantage or harming another. Furthermore, the use of models, examples, technical measurements, forms, or documents of any kind of a competitor which were entrusted for purposes of work, a test, or a bid violates the general clause.

The poaching of employees can be unfair competition if it is accompanied by a breach of contract (competition clause).

9. Enforcement

The LPC is (like the Belgian law) first and foremost a civil law. It is sanctioned through a special injunctive suit ("action en cassation"). The "action en cessation" must be brought in a preliminary procedure ("référé"), but leads to a final judgment. Proof of urgency is not required. The President of the Commercial Court has exclusive jurisdiction in the first instance; he can order collateral through coercive payment. Suits for damages must be brought on the basis of the general tort clause of Art. 1382 Code Civil.

An injunctive suit requires a danger of repetition to be proven by the plaintiff. This is assumed when violations already exist. Only in exceptional cases a removal of the danger of repetition was considered,[835] mainly for third parties such as a publishers.[836]

Every person, trade organization and consumer association represented in the Price Committee has standing to bring an "action en cessation". This includes in theory also the individual consumer. However, for a suit based on the general clause, the claimant must be a businessman, craftsman, industrialist, or belong to a free profession. In practice, most claims are brought by competitors.

The proper defendant is anyone who committed the objectionable violation of the LPC. For the advertising causes of action in Art. 16 et seq. LPC, however, a "cascade form liability" exists.[837] The "annonceur" or advertiser is liable first, i.e. the person that commissioned the advertising and who benefits from it. Other people have subsidiary liability, that is, they are liable when the advertiser has no place of business in Luxemburg nor any agents.[838]

834. The reasoning given for the draft regulation (p. 18) includes as examples that are now directly subsumed under Art. 14 also the former Art. 17 k, which prohibited the use of material, packaging, or container of the product of a competitor, even if this was done without the intent of misappropriation or causing confusion.
835. Thus it is not sufficient that the defendant ends the act in question and that repetition appears unlikely. The way that written statements are formulated, the distain the parties have for each other, the sharp competition or the general behavior of the defendant are all indications of the danger of repetition.
836. See Henning-Bodewig/Decker, No. 139 ff.
837. See Henning-Bodewig/Decker, No. 150.
838. For instance, a Luxemburg television station was convicted for airing a commercial of a foreign company; see fn. 814.

According to Art. 25 LPC, the most important regulations of the law are also criminally sanctionable. Under Art. 25(1) LPC, each subsequent violation of a cease-and-desist order can be punished by monetary fines.

A link between unfair competition law and civil law in general, esp. contract law, is the Law regarding the Legal Protection of the Consumer from 25 August 1983. According to Art. 11, every description of features and attributes of a product or a service in an advertisement is considered a material part of the contract for this product or service.

XVIII. MALTA

1. Sources of law

Consumer Affairs Act of 1994; Art. 32 Commercial Code.

2. Maltese unfair competition law in a nutshell

Maltese law has no comprehensive regulation against unfair competition, but rather various statutes[839] that cover certain aspects of unfair competition. Next to the "Competition Act" of 1994 (last changed in 2000, chapter 379), which deals with issues of cartel law, the key regulation is the "Consumer Affairs Act" of 1994,[840] which criminally sanctions certain unfair competition practices in order to protect consumers. The interests of competitors are mainly protected through Art. 32 et seq. of the Criminal Code, which contains regulations similar to British common law torts, especially "passing off". In spite of these similarities, Maltese law has a written law tradition and goes back to the Napoleonic Code.

The "Consumer Affairs Act" contains a catalog of consumer rights, especially those that relate to contract law, and arranged for the establishment of the "Consumer Affairs Council" as well as the "Consumer Claims Tribunal" and consumer associations. Most EC-Directives in the field of consumer protection against unfair business practices were transposed into the Consumer Affairs Act. In Part VI ("unfair practices"), Directive 84/450/EEC regarding misleading advertising was transposed nearly word for word (Art. 47-48), as was the Directive regarding comparative advertising (Art. 49-50). Sales promotions with gifts and prizes is not forbidden, but under Art. 51 there is an obligation to provide the gift as offered, to clearly disclose all the terms and conditions for obtaining it, and to give a clear and full description of the free item. Pyramid schemes are forbidden (Art. 52). A violation of these laws can lead to monetary sanctions being imposed (Art. 54). Further regulations in the Consumer Affairs Act concern misuse of standard term clauses in consumer contracts, commercial guarantees and liability for defective products.

Enforcement of the consumer protection and competition aspects of the Consumer Affairs Act rests with the "Consumer and Competition Division" of the "Ministry of Finance and Economic Affairs" with the central figure of the "Director

839. All laws and regulations of Malta can be found at the internet site www.justice.gov.mt/legalservices.asp in the "Laws of Malta" section (numbered by chapters).

840. Last amended in 2001. Of importance is in particular Chapter 378. The Consumer Affairs Act is available under <docs.justice.gov.mt/lom/legislation/english/leg/vol_10/chapt378.pdf>.

General of the Consumer and Competition Division". While the "Commission for Fair Trading" deals with cartel law complaints, the "Information and Client Affairs Directorate" allows for amicable settlements of disputes between individually harmed consumers and the merchant. If such a settlement cannot be reached, the consumer has the right to bring his claim to the "Consumer Claims Tribunal". Registered consumer associations can also submit complaints regarding violations of the Consumer Affairs Act to the competent authority (Art. 37 Consumer Affairs Act).

According to Art. 94 of the Consumer Affairs Act, the Director General may, in the public interest and of his own initiative or on an application, issue a compliance order to any person to stop misleading or illegal comparative advertising. A person against whom a compliance order has been made may institute an action in court.

On the basis of the statutory power in Art. 7 of the Consumer Affairs Act, the Distance Selling Regulation[841] was promulgated, which transposed the regulations of the Distance Selling Directive, as well as the Consumer Affairs Act (Price Indication) Regulations.[842]

Other special laws also pertain to competition law, such as the Trade Descriptions Act (1986, last modified in 2000, Chapter 313), the Doorstep Contracts Act (1987, last modified in 2000, Chapter 317), the Medicines Act (2003, Chapter 458) with regulations regarding pharmaceutical products, the Tobacco (Smoking Control) Act (1986, modified 2003, Chapter 315) with general and media-specific regulations for tobacco advertisements,[843] and the Broadcasting Code for the Protection of Minors (2000, Subsidiary Legislation 350.05) which protects minors from television advertisements.[844]

The Electronic Commerce Act (2002, Chapter 426)[845] gives the Minister the power to transpose the E-Commerce Directive and especially to legislate informational requirements for commercial communications.

The protection of businesses from individual acts of unfair competition, especially those that have to do with the individual impediment of competitors, is regulated in Chapter 13 of the Commercial Code[846] under the title "Of limits of competition" (Art. 32-37). The use of trade marks and other distinguishing marks that could cause confusion between the marks, as well as false statements of origin are forbidden under Art. 32. This article contains the important "passing-off" protection and is closely related to the IP Laws, especially trademark law.[847] Denigration is also forbidden; companies may not make public statements for commercial purposes that would harm the business of another (Art. 34), and they may not poach

841. Subsidiary Legislation 378.08.
842. Subsidiary Legislation 378.09. Both Acts are available under <docs.justice.gov.mt/lom/Legislation/English/SubLeg/378/08.PDF and -09.PDF>.
843. Chapter 313, 315 and 317 can be found under <docs.justice.gov.mt/lom/legislation/english/leg/vol_7/chapt313.pdf> respective-315.pdf and-317.pdf; the "Medicines Act" (Chapter 458) under <docs.justice.gov.mt/lom/legislation/english/leg/vol_14/chapt458.pdf>.
844. <docs.justice.gov.mt/lom/Legislation/English/SubLeg/350/05.pdf>.
845. <docs.justice.gov.mt/lom/legislation/english/leg/vol_13/chapt426.pdf>.
846. <docs.justice.gov.mt/lom/legislation/english/leg/vol_2/chapt13.pdf>.
847. "Trademarks Act" (2000, reformed 2003, Chapter 416), "Patents and Designs Act" (2000, reformed 2003, Chapter 417), available under <docs.justice.gov.mt/lom/legislation/english/leg/vol_13/chapt416.pdf> respectively -417.pdf, and "Industrial Property (Protection) Ordinance" (1899, last changed in 2000, Chapter 29), at the <clea.wipo.int/PDFFILES/English/MT/MT002EN.PDF>. An overview over industrial property law in Malta is given in "Manual Industrial Property", Vol. 4 (2000).

another company's employee with the goal of thus also gaining that company's customers (Art. 35). A violation of these regulations gives rise to the right of the competitor to bring a claim for damages; fines ("penalties") can also be imposed (Art. 37).

XIX. NETHERLANDS

Selected Literature: Baeumer/van Manen, *Nederland*, in: Ulmer (ed.), *Het recht inzake oneerlijke mededinging in de lidstaaten der Europese Economische Gemenschap; Deel II.2.*, 1974; de Vrey, *Verglijkende reclame: da vergelijking opgelost?, IER* 2001, 4, 164; Heerkens, *De juridische positie van gedupeerden van het piramidespel in Nederland en Europa, Jaarboek Consumentenrecht* 1998; Henning-Bodewig, *Das neue (alte) Recht des unlauteren Wettbewerbs der Niederlande*, GRUR Int. 1993, 126; Henning-Bodewig/Verkade/Quaedvlieg, *Niederlande*, in: Schricker (ed.), *Recht der Werbung in Europa*, 1995; Holzhauer, *Ontoelaatbare reclame*, 1994; Hondius, *Niederländisches Verbraucherrecht—vom Sonderrecht zum integrierten Zivilrecht*, VuR 1996, 295; Hondius/Rijken (ed.), *Consumentenrecht*, 1996; Kabel (ed.), *Praktijkboek Reclame- en Aanduidingenrecht (PRAR)*, loose leaf edition; Kabel, *Grensoverschrijdende reclame en oneerlijke mededinging, AA* 1993, 74; Kabel, *Reclamerecht online, IER* 2001, 257; Kamperman Sanders, *Unfair competition law: the protection of intellectual and industrial creativity*, Oxford 1997; Mok, *Kartelrecht I*, 1998; van Nispen, *Artikelgewijs commentaar, Onrechtmatige Daad, Ongeoorloofde mededinging (loose leaf edition)*; Nillessen/van der Zandt, *The Netherlands*, in: Campbell (ed.), Unfair Trade Practices—The Comparative Law Yearbook of International Business, 1996,; Quaedvlieg, *Leistungsschutz in den Niederlanden*, GRUR Int. 1997, 971; Radeideh/de Vrey, Netherlands, in: Micklitz/Kessler (ed.), *Marketing Practices Regulation and Consumer Protection in the EC Member States and the US*, 2002, p. 238; Ribbink, Werberecht in den Niederlanden in: Schotthöfer (ed.), Handbuch des Werberechts in den EU-Staaten, 2nd ed. 1997, p. 445; Verkade, *Ongeoorloofde mededinging*, 1986; Van Engelen, *The Misappropriation Doctrine in the Netherlands*, 22 IIC 11 (1991); Van Veen, *Das Wettbewerbsrecht in den Niederlanden*, in: Heidelberger Kommentar zum Wettbewerbsrecht, 2nd ed. 2005, p. 735.

Sources of Law: Art. 6:162; Art. 6:194-196 Burgerlijk Wetboek (Civil Code) (BW); Nederlandse Reclamecode (NRC)

1. Dutch unfair competition law in a nutshell

Although recognized as a separate legal subject ("ongeoorlofde mededinging"),[848] the Netherlands have no coherent legal regulation to fight unfair competition. Only misleading and comparative advertising is expressly regulated in Art. 6:194 et seq. Burgerlijk Wetboek (= BW). As to the rest, the law of unfair competition has its foundation in general case law on the basis of the general tort clause (Article 6:162 BW) as well as an exceptionally strong self-regulation.

848. An overview (in Dutch) can be found in the leading treatises by *Verkade*, v. *Nispen* and Holzhauer as well as in the loose leaf edition PRAR, edited by Kabel. An excellent overview of the most recent court decisions is given in the yearly articles "Van de Brug af gezien" in the law journal IER (where unfair competition law is discussed by Kabel). As to a discussion in German see Henning-Bodewig, and Henning-Bodewig/Verkade/Quaedvlieg.

In spite of this rudiment legal foundation, all acts of unfair competition that have an effect on Dutch business or consumers[849] can at least in theory be subsumed under the general tort clause of Art. 6:162 BW. Although at the beginning solely intended to serve the individual rights of honest businessmen, the Dutch Supreme Court (Hoge Raad) has broadened the scope of the general clause considerately. As early as 1919[850] the acting, or failing to act, contrary to what is, under unwritten law, proper behavior in society was also considered a tort. In 1992, this jurisdiction was incorporated into the wording of Article 6:162 BW. Although the term "ongeorloofde mededing" is not mentioned the general clause is thus flexible enough to cover most relevant groups of cases of unfair competition.[851] Under the modern view, the protective aim even includes the interest to consumers.[852] A competitive relationship is not required. The standard of protection is high, although in Dutch legal practice there is a tendency towards reluctant application of the general clause in cases that can be dealt with otherwise. This is partly due to a strong self regulation on the one hand, and the traditional extensive protection by IP-laws,[853] especially trademark law, on the other hand.

As mentioned above, self regulation plays an important role in the Netherlands. It bases its decisions on a tight network of various codes with the Dutch Advertisement Code (Nederlands Reclame Code = NRC)[854] as the most important one. Even though the decisions of the "Reclame Code Commission" are not legally binding, they are generally recognized and are in practice of almost equal importance as court decisions.

2. Regulation of advertising

a. Misleading advertising

As of 1980, Art. 6:194 et seq. BW contains a regulation concerning misleading advertising which partially goes beyond Directive 84/450/EC. It applies to all statements ("mededinging") that are made public in the exercise of a profession or a business. Article 6:194 BW is not only applicable to the person who makes the statement, but also to the one who profits from it.[855] Not included however, are messages of ideological or political nature as well as the statements by consumer organizations or the media.[856] It is disputed whether information provided after the conclusion of a contract falls under these special regulations.[857]

The term misleading advertising is not defined in Art. 6:194 BW. From the context, especially the regulation of the burden of proof, it can be concluded that the

849. For a discussion of Dutch private international law see Kabel, Grensoverschrijdende reclame en oneeerlijke mededediging, AA 1993, 714; *Baeumer/v. Manen*, No. 132.
850. Since the fundamental decision of the Hoge Raad, NJ 1919, 161—Lindebaum/Cohen; discussed, for instance by Kamperman Sanders, p. 39; Henning-Bodewig, GRUR Int. 1993, 126.
851. See, for instance, examples of "Ongeoorloofde mededinging" given by Verkade; Henning-Bodewig, GRUR Int. 1993, 126.
852. See Van Nispen, IV., No. 9.
853. As to the Benelux trade mark law see Braun, Précis du Droit de Marques, 2nd ed. 2004.
854. The NRC (and various specific Codes) is available in English under <www.reclamecode.nl/pdf/DAC.pdf>.
855. It is irrelevant if the statement was done on behalf of someone else; see Verkade, No. 82.
856. These statements are directly judged on the basis of the general clause in Art. 6:162 BW; see Henning-Bodewig/Verkade/Quaedvlieg, No. 247.
857. The wording of the law does not use the expression "advertising"; cf. Henning-Bodewig/Verkade/Quaedvlieg, No. 65 ff.

statement must contain verifiable information that is at least capable of creating a false impression.[858] This can also apply to accurate information, especially in the case of "half-truths", if an incomplete statement can be misunderstood by the "target group". Dutch legal practice refers to the view of the average consumer, of whom a great deal of attention is often demanded (although the requirements may vary depending on the target group). Exaggerations in advertising such as "huge", "super" or claims of product uniqueness ("x is as always the cheapest") are often tolerated as harmless puffing.[859]

As a general rule the overall impression received by the target group, is decisive. This overall impression is often determined by eye-catching statements, although certain disclaimers are also taken into account.[860] The statement is interpreted according to the normal language of the target group and (especially in cases of incomplete information) supplemented by "normal experience".[861] As can be drawn from the wording of the burden of proof (see below), the advertisement must at least be sufficiently complete so that no misleading general impression is created.

As to the specific reference points of misleading that are mentioned in Art. 6:194 BW as examples, a wide variety of court rulings (and decisions by the "Reclame Code Commissie") exist.[862] They often deal with special offers,[863] the price and its calculation,[864] sales,[865] guarantees,[866] or statements of geographic origin.[867] Advertising in the Netherlands is always judged strictly when it concerns aspects that are important to consumers. In addition to the price and the quality, such aspects are health, safety and environmental friendliness. In these areas also advertising with "self-evident facts" is prohibited.[868]

The misleading information must be capable of affecting the commercial behavior of the target group. The Hoge Raad[869] originally hinted that even a false statement that does not affect the purchase behavior could be misleading. This position, which

858. Henning-Bodewig/Verkade/Quaedvlieg, No. 92 ff.
859. In general, a statement is taken seriously if it is substantiated through verifiable claims, see Verkade, No. 15; Case law is not always consistent on this point. For instance, a mere exaggeration was seen in the slogan "CA is still cheaper", but not in the slogan. "Finally clarity for wearers of glasses: Fielman is always the cheapest". Hof Arnhem 19.11.2002, IER 2003-2, 134 (the first instance, Rechtbank Amelo 8.4.2002, IER 2002, 266 with note Kabel, had held this also to be mere puffing).
860. See Verkade, No. 119.
861. For example, an advertising for a ski-overall "in all sizes" was interpreted in accordance with life experience as "in all common sizes". The advertising of an automobile insurance company with "40% no claim" was interpreted in the sense that this only applies in certain conditions; see Henning-Bodewig/Verkade/Quaedvlieg, No. 124 ff.
862. They are almost completely documented in PRAR II (Praktijkboek Reclame en Aanduidingsrecht), edited by Kabel.
863. A possible limitation in stock must be clearly indicated (although no fixed dates are given).
864. See Henning-Bodewig/Verkade/Quaedvlieg, No. 184.
865. Which are no longer regulated through special provisions since the "Uitverkoopwet" was repealed.
866. Advertising referring to a "guarantee" must—as explicitly stated in Art. 11 NRC—contain the range, coverage and the length of time of the guarantee unmistakably. If the legal warrenty is in fact limited, the term warranty or guarantee may not be used.
867. Regarding indecent geographic origin see Henning-Bodewig/Verkade/Quaedvlieg, No. 213.
868. For example, the advertising slogan "without artificial coloring" (for potato chips) or "without hormones" (for meat products) was held to be unlawful because the competitor's products were also without artificial coloring. In the field of environmental protection, Art. 5 NRC prohibits all claims that wrongly suggest the competitors products contain elements harmful for the environment (as compared to the non-existence of such elements in the advertiser's product).
869. Hoge Raad GRUR Int. 1986, 348—"Substral".

was disputed in the Dutch legal literature anyway, [870] should now be obsolete since the Nissan-decision of the ECJ.[871]

Pursuant to Art. 6:195(1) BW, the burden of proof[872] for the truth and completeness of all factual claims lies on the advertiser, unless the courts consider such a reversal inappropriate (e.g. where the plaintiff seems to be mainly interested in the defendant's business secrets). If the plaintiff sufficiently substantiates that the advertising is misleading, the defendant must prove that this is not the case. Para. 2 contains a second reversal of the burden of proof for fault which is necessary for claims for compensation.[873] Both reversals of the burden of proof are only valid in the principal proceeding. In the preliminary proceeding ("kort geding", see under 9), the judge is anyway not bound to such rules but generally follows Art. 6:195 BW.

b. Comparative advertising

The Directive 97/55/EC regarding comparative advertising was not implemented until 2002.[874] In addition to Art. 6:194 BW (prohibition of misleading advertising), Art. 6:194 (a) BW was included, which contains in § 1 the definition of comparative advertising, in § 2 the basis for admissibility of a comparison and in § 3 "special offers". The wording is largely the same as in the EC-Directive but Art. 195 BW contains a mandatory reversal of burden of proof for misleading comparisons: The advertiser is obliged to "provide evidence within a short period of time proving the material correctness and completeness of the actual facts".[875]

As can be seen in the wording of the burden of proof, comparative advertising is strictly judged under the aspect of misleading.[876] This applies also to "omissions". For example, a price comparison between two providers of Online-Services was prohibited as misleading because a low-priced special service of the competitor was not mentioned.[877] The courts also considered misleading a comparison between grocery stores with a picture that showed only a shopping cart full of products (so that it was unclear what was being exactly compared)[878] as well as an advertisement of a maker of eyeglasses which compared "generic lenses" with "brand name lenses".[879] More generous was the ruling regarding a "taste test" for dog food which—even though

870. See, for instance Verkade, No. 110.
871. Discussed in this book in Chapter 3.IV.3.
872. Regarding the reversal of burden of proof see Henning-Bodewig/Verkade/Quaedvlieg, No. 133 ff.
873. The party that "created or determined the content or presentation of the information completely or in part or ordered it to be created" (with the exception of media) has the burden of proof that there is no intent or negligence.
874. Until the enactment, comparative advertising was permitted under the aspect of unfair competition law, but often prohibited as a trademark infringement (Art. 13 Benelux-trademark law); see de Vrey, IER 2001, 164; Henning-Bodewig/Verkade/Quaedvlieg, No. 256. The leading case was the "Substral"-case; see fn 869.
875. See Verkade, BIE 2001, 75. For ordinary advertising a time span is not given.
876. As the differences in the burden of proof already indicate, the judgment is apparently stricter than in cases of non-comparative advertising.
877. Rechtbank Amsterdam 16.4.2003, IER 2003-6, p. 388—"KPN".
878. The indication of a link to a website that was supposed to provide more information was considered not sufficient; Rechtbank Amsterdam 3.12.2003—"Albert Heijn/Laurus".
879. Hof Arhem, 19.11.2002, IER 2002-3, 134—"Specsavers / Fielmann" with note Kabel in IER 2002, 266 (regarding the first instance).

not all details seemed to have been stated correctly—was overall still considered "impartial" and thus not misleading.[880]

The response of a manufacturer of eyeglasses to the comparative (misleading) advertising of a competitor using the slogan "ben je belazerd?" (roughly: "am I stupid?")[881] was considered denigrating, as was the advertising slogan "Why pay too much at Albert Heijn?" (also because it was considered too vague and unspecific)[882]

c. *Concealed advertising*

Advertising and marketing measures in which the commercial character is not recognizable are sometimes subsumed under the prohibition of misleading advertising in Art. 6:194 BW ("purpose of the offer").[883] A misleading commercial offer for a brand research, for example, was prohibited on this basis because it created the impression of an invoice.[884] According to Art. 7 NRC, anonymous advertising is prohibited irrespective of the media involved. Additionally, Art. 13 of the Code for the printing business[885] applies to the press; Art. 52j of the Media Decree from 1987 to the area of broadcasting.

d. *Aggressive advertising*

Harassing advertising seems to be without relevance outside the area of direct marketing. (see under 3)

e. *Other advertising*

Advertising exploiting sentiments of fear,[886] appealing to the subconscious, abusing feelings of social responsibility or exploitating of the inexperience (especially of children and minors), as well as "shocking", violent, or discriminating advertising is predominantly judged on the basis of the NRC. Article 2 and 3 NRC prohibit any advertising against "good taste and honest practices".[887] In addition to this basis Code, special codes apply. For example, advertisement with "social sponsoring" must also meet the strict requirements of the "Milieu Reclame Code"[888] when it refers to the protection of the environment.

880. Hof Den Bosch 24.3.2003, IER 2003-4—"Royal Canin/Hill's Pet" (different the first instance which held it partially as a misleading advertising).
881. See fn. 879.
882. See fn. 878.
883. See Henning-Bodewig/Verkade/Quaedvlieg, No. 534.
884. Hof Amsterdam BIE 2001, 239. In addition to a cease-and-desist order, the court ordered corrective advertising which had to include the information that payments that had already been made would be reimbursed.
885. See Rechtbank van Koophandel Amsterdam 7.12.1995; Henning-Bodewig/Verkade/Quaedvlieg, No. 532.
886. According to Art. 13(2) Mediawet, advertising using fear is expressly prohibited.
887. This principle is rather strictly enforced; see the decisions discussed in PRAR II; furthermore Holzhauer, p. 135.
888. The Code can be found on the Internet address stated in fn 854; see also PRAR II 56 ff.; Holzhauer, p. 168.

f. Product- and media-specific advertising regulations

Dutch law contains a wide variety of product specific advertising regulations[889] that are supplemented by "special codes" of the self regulation. Food advertising is mostly regulated through the "Warenwet" and the decrees based on it.[890] Health claims are judged especially strictly;[891] a special "Code voor Zoetwaaren" from 1991[892] regulates advertising for sweets and has extensive duties to inform. Advertising for tobacco products is prohibited in broadcasting in accordance with the "Tabakwet" of 1988 and, since 1994, also has to comply with the strict "Code voor Tabakwaren".[893] The so-called "Alcohol Code" requires restraint in advertising for alcohol products, especially when it may reach young consumer.[894] The advertising for pharmaceutical products[895] that is directed to the general public, is partly subject to a preventive control.[896]

A press law does not exist in the Netherlands, while advertising in broadcasting is extensively regulated.[897] Most regulations affecting advertising can be found in the media law ("Mediawet") and the decrees etc. that were passed on its basis. In public broadcasting, an advertising monopoly of the "Stichting Ether Reclame" (STER) exists, which makes all advertising subject to a preventive control. Internet advertising falls under the Telecommunications Act which is supplemented through a "special code" from 15 August 2000.[898]

3. Direct marketing; special sales methods

Commercial phone calls using automated calling systems and advertising via fax are only permissible when there is a prior agreement.[899] In all other cases (including e-mail advertising) the "opt-out" solution applies;[900] in addition to this, the advertising may not lead to an impediment of competitors or a harassment of consumers. Also using the "opt-out" solution are Art. 7:46 BW (the transposition of the Distant Contracts Directive) and the "Code for Unsolicited Advertising". The law to protect personal data from 6 July 2000 regulates the use of personal data collected by means of mail-order business.

Door-to-door sales are regulated through the so-called "Colportagewet" from 1973. The sending of unrequested goods is prohibited by Art. 7 of the "Code regarding

889. Henning-Bodewig/Verkade/Quaedvlieg, No. 386; regarding the latest developments, see the annual overview in the law journal comments IER.
890. Henning-Bodewig/Verkade/Quaedvlieg, No. 414.
891. Self-regulation, for example prohibited slogans such as "tasty healthy". Case law has, however, become more generous now, see PRAR II A.
892. Henning-Bodewig/Verkade/Quaedvlieg, No. 441.
893. Henning-Bodewig/Verkade/Quaedvlieg, No. 443; Radeideh/de Vrey, p. 258.
894. Henning-Bodewig/Verkade/Quaedvlieg, No. 496; Radeideh/de Vrey, p. 257.
895. The problem is often the demarcation between advertising and information, for example, when advertising gives "impartial" suggestions to avoid obesity, etc. See the decisions cited by Hoogenraad, IER 2002, 79.
896. Advertising for pharmaceutical products is hard-fought in the Netherlands; the pharmaceutical industry mostly settles its arguments through the Code Commissie of the "Stichting Code Geneesmittel Reclame"; see Hoogenraad, IER 2002, 79.
897. Radeideh/de Vrey, p. 244 ff.; Henning-Bodewig/Verkade/Quaedvlieg, no. 536.
898. The Code was created by the DMSA (Dutch Association for Direct Marketing, Distance Sailing and Sales promotion). See Radeideh/de Vrey, p. 243, Kabel, Reclamerecht online, IER 2001, 257.
899. According to Art. 11 of the Telecommunications Act from 19.10.1998; see Radeideh/de Vrey, p. 241.
900. The Directive 2002/58/EC—discussed in this book in Chapter 3, IV.9—has not yet been transposed.

Direct Marketing", unless it is unmistakably clear that there is neither an obligation to pay nor an obligation to send them back.[901] The sending of unaddressed advertising material is permitted if the sender is clearly identifiable (see above, No. 13)[902] and the recipient did not refuse such material by posting a sticker on his or her mailbox.[903] Pyramid schemes are prohibited under the Gambling Act.[904]

4. Sales promotion

Sales promotion only have to comply with the general regulations, especially the prohibition of misleading advertising (see above, et seq.).[905] The advertiser that promotes lower prices must be able to prove that the higher price was actually claimed during an adequate time span. The start and end dates of special offers must be indicated (which is expressly regulated for comparative advertising). Sales at a loss are neither prohibited under the aspect of unfair competition nor by anti-trust regulations.

Games of chance require approval by the state in accordance with the Gambling Act.[906] Theoretically, this includes promotional games that depend on luck, such as sweepstakes.[907] However, a liberalization is expected and the prohibition appears to not have been strictly enforced. Independent of this, a special "Code for Sweepstakes" has extensive duties to inform and prohibits linking participation with a purchase.[908]

5. Disparagement

False statements or statements that can not be proven regarding other market participants violate Art. 6:162 BW. The same applies to truthful statements for the purpose of competition that unnecessarily damage the goodwill of another party or are capable of doing so, as well as objectively denigrating statements that are irrelevant, overly aggressive, etc.[909] A reference to personal circumstances (religion, race, moral conduct) in a deprecatory context is always prohibited. Warnings against infringement of industrial property rights are only permitted, if they are kept objective and not overly "revaling" and are limited to those who might be affected by the violation of the property right.

901. Radeideh/de Vrey, p. 241.
902. Radeideh/de Vrey, p. 251.
903. Radeideh/de Vrey, p. 249.
904. "Wet op de Kansspelen",version from 12.12.2001 (Stbl. 664); see also Radeideh/de Vrey, p. 253.
905. For certain products (health products, tobacco), special regulation exists, for example the Reclamesbeluit Geneesmiddelen contains a prohibition of "gunstbetooning", see Bodewig/Henning-Bodewig, WRP 2000, 1341; Hoogenraad, IER 2002, 79.
906. See Radeideh/de Vrey, p. 254; Kabel, IER 2002, 77; Gerechtshof den Bosch 18.6.1988, NJ 1999, 726; regarding games of chance in the internet see Koning/Wisman, NJB 2001, 1235.
907. See Hoge Raad 19.12.1989, IER 1990, 28 with note Verkade, PRAR VIII C 7; Hoge Raad 19.11.1991, IER 1992-8, 113; Holzhauer, p. 32; Valkenbuts, Rechtsverglijkende onderzoek van sweepstakes, Jaarboek Konsumentenrecht 1991, 283 ff.; PRAR XII D 1.
908. Cf. Radeideh/de Vrey, p. 254.
909. See the fundamental "Felix Kattenbrood"-decision of the Hoge Raad (1941). The aspects of disparagement and imitation also play an important role in the decision making process of the Reclame Code Commissie; see Henning-Bodewig/Verkade/Quaedvlieg, No. 239.

6. Misappropriation, exploitation of reputation, imitation

The unauthorized use of the reputation of a third party ("aanleunen") is to be judged on the basis of the general clause of Art. 6:162 BW. Outside of trademark law and comparative advertising, an exploitation of another's goodwill mainly occurs in cases of geographic origin[910] and imitation (see under No. 25). In any event, the "aanleunen" must go beyond the normal measure of imitation.[911]

The unauthorized use of the popularity of well-known personalities for the purpose of competition is considered as a form of misappropriation dealt with under the genral clause of Art. 6:162 BW. This type of suit however, features also traits of right of privacy and falls under Art. 19 et seq. of the Copyright Law (the so-called "portrait law").[912]

Protection against imitation based on the general clause of Art. 6:162 BW requires that the imitated product is sufficiently "distinctive" and that there are "other circumstances" in addition to the imitation.[913] Such circumstances include most of all causing a danger of confusion which could have been avoided without affecting efficiency or practicability. Without danger of confusion—under the aspect of parasite exploitation—protection against misappropriation is granted only in exceptional cases. The commercial achievements must be "of such a nature that it can be put on one line with objects for which an intellectual property right is justified".[914]

7. Impediment of competitors

The protection of know-how is not regulated coherently in Dutch law.[915] Article 273 Criminal Code covers the deliberate disclosure of commercial secrets by an employee or former employee. In all other cases, for example regarding the use of the know how, secret, the tort law general clause of Art. 6:162 BW may apply. [916]

The poaching of employees by competitors is only considered unfair competition in exceptional cases, such as when it occurs in conjunction with disclosure of company secrets or the participation in a breach of contract. Sending of mass emails for commercial purposes was prohibited under the aspect of obstruction.[917] An individual

910. For example, the presentation of cheese in the shape of champagne bottles was prohibited (but not that of a margarine product that looked similar to butter, because there is no "butter image"); Rechtbank Den Haag 6.12.2000, BIE 2001, 424; Kabel, IER 2002, 78.

911. See the "Substral" decision (fn. 869).

912. Cf. for instance, Hoge Raad, NJ 1979, 383; Henning-Bodewig/Verkade/Quaedvlieg, No. 309.

913. Dutch case law and literature emphasizes the so-called "negative reflex effect" of the special regulations of intellectual property law. Additionally, the Unitary Benelux Trademark Law as well as the Unitary Benelux Design Law contain a provision that blocks unfair competition law protection for marks, models etc. that are capable of registration. "Landmark decisions" are Hoge Raad 26.6.1953, NJ 1954, 90—"Hyster Krane"; Hoge Raad 8.1.1960, NJ 1960, 415—"Scrabble" and most of all Hoge Raad 27.6.1986, BIE 1986, 280—"Decca/Holland Nautik"-decision. The decisions are discussed by Kamperman Sanders, p. 39; Nillessen/van der Zandt, p. 265 and van Engelen in IIC.

914. So the Hoge Raad in the "Decca/Holland Nautic"-decision. The threshold is normally very high. For example, the broadcasting of a soccer match by the Dutch Broadcasting Corporation was not considered a parasitic exploitation of the commercial achievements of the Dutch soccer association; Hoge Raad 27.10.1987, NJ 1988, 310—"*KNVB* v. *NOS*".

915. *Baeumer/v. Manen*, No. 260 ff.; Verkade, No. ....

916. *Baeumer/v. Manen*, No. 181 f; Quaedvlieg, GRUR Int. 1997, 971; GRUR Int. 2003, Nillessen/van der Zandt, p. 259.

917. See Hof Arnhem 4.2.2003, NJ 2004/54—"Rath ./. Nederlande"; Rath, who was involved indirectly in the promotion of pharmaceutical products, sent 604 million emails to members of the Dutch

boycott is only unfair competition if the person that is boycotted does not have other alternatives.[918]

8. Breach of the law

In theory, the violation of any norm can also be considered as a tort in the sense of Art. 6:162 BW. According to the "protective norm theory", the violated regulation, however, must be intended to protect especially the claimant from the consequences of the infringement.

9. Enforcement

Dutch unfair competition law is sanctioned by civil law.[919] The most important remedy is the suit for injunctive relief which is independent of fault. In cases of misleading and comparative advertising, correcting advertising may be order by the courts (Art. 6:198 BW). A claim for enquiry is permitted under certain circumstances.[920]

In claims for injunctive relief because of misleading and comparative advertising, special procedural requirements exist (see above, 2a,b). In principle, every party that was affected by the unfair act has standing to sue; a competitive relationship between plaintiff and defendant is not required. Associations (if they meet the requirements of the Act Regarding Association Claims[921]) and theoretically even individual consumers[922] also have standing. The proper defendant is every party that committed the unfair act or contributed to it.

In the Netherlands, most unfair competition claims are brought to court in the so-called "kort geding"-procedure, a preliminary procedure for injunctive relief.[923] In practice, the parties are often satisfied with the outcome of the kort gedings. Lawyer's fees are covered by each party themselves.[924]

Procedure before the Reclame Code Commissie (in the second instance: "College van Beroep") can be brought forth by anyone and is very popular (also with competitors) because of its effectiveness (and low fees). The sanctions, although limited to public or confidential "recommendations" are generally respected by all market participants.

parliament to complain about the European regulation for vitamins. The court held this to be a commercial communication and prohibited the sending of additional emails because of obstruction. In another case, Hof Amsterdam 18.7.2003—"Adfah" the court considered that the limit of harassment by emails (which are generally subject to the "opt-out" solution, see above, 3) was not reached. (the Hoge Raad decision is expected soon).

918. For example, the refusal of the Dutch Collecting Society BUMA to accept certain artists, see Verkade, No. 198.
919. See Henning-Bodewig/Verkade/Quaedvlieg, No. 595 ff; Verkade, p. 7..; as to the procedure and costs Van Veen, p. 737.
920. To name supplies, buyers, etc.; see Van Veen, p. 737.
921. Law from v. 6.4.1994; see Rechtbank Rotterdam, IER 1991, 70; Hondius, p. 26.
922. Decisions regarding this are not known.
923. It is introduced in the first instance to the president of the Rechtbank van koophandel and is valid primarily for cease-and desist claims. In obvious cases of breach of law and fault, an advance payment for compensation can be granted. The "kort geding"—procedure can be moved into the main case at any point, see Henning-Bodewig/Verkade/Quaedvlieg, No. 629.
924. See Van Veen, p. 739.

XX. POLAND[925]

Selected Literature: Dietz, *Die Einführung von Gesetzen gegen den unlauteren Wettbewerb in ehemals sozialistischen Staaten Mittel- und Osteuropas*, GRUR Int. 1994, 649; Kępiński, *Geographical Indications Under Polish Industrial Property Law*, IIC 2003, 751; Kępiński (ed.) *The Evaluation of the New Polish Legislation in the Matter of Consumer Protection from the European Perspective*, 2001; Łętowska, *Ochrona niektórych praw konsumentów*, 2001; Nowińska, *Zwalczani nieuczciwej reklamy*, 1997; Nowińska/Skubisz, *Reklama porównancza, Panstwo i Prawo 1995*, p. 26; Skubisz, *The Polish Law on combatting unfair competition of April 1993*, IIC 1995, 498; Skubisz, *Das Recht des unlauteren Wettbewerbs in Polen*, GRUR Int. 1994, 681; Szwaja (ed.), *Ustawa o zwalczaniu nieuczciwej konkurencji. Kommentarz*, 2000; Szwaja, *Die Genese der Generalklausel des neuen polnischen UWG*, GRUR Int. 1996, 484; Walczak, *Prawne aspekty reklamy w ustawodawstwie polskim, europejskim i mjedzynarodowym*, 2001; Wiszniewska, Polen, in: Schricker (ed.), *Recht der Werbung in Europa*, 1999; Wiszniewska, *Novellierung des polnischen Gesetzes über die Bekämpfung des unlauteren Wettbewerbs*, GRUR Int. 2001, 213.

1. Sources of law

Ustawa o zwalczaniu nieuwczciwej konkurencij (Act on the Combating of Unfair Competition) of 16 April 1993 (ZNKU);[926] Ustawa o ochronie konkurencji i konsumentów (Act on Protection of Competition and Consumers) of 15 December 2000 (OKiKU)[927].

2. Polish unfair competition law in a nutshell

Modern Polish unfair competition law builds on the Act on the Combating of Unfair Competition of 1993. The main objective of this act is stated to be "to prevent and combat unfair competition . . . in the interest of the general public, of traders and their customers, particularly the consumers" (Art. 1 ZNKU). The Act thus acknowledges the classical triad of interests, recognized among others in Directive 84/450/EEC.[928]

The ZNKU is based on a general clause on unfair competition (Art. 3). It defines as an act of unfair competition any act that is contrary to law or to *bonos mores* if it impairs or infringes upon the interests of another enterprise or customer. This definition although proceeding from the concept "act of unfair competition" is broad and does not seem to require a competitive relationship. Apart from infringements on *bonos mores* the general clause explicitly covers acts of competition involving breach of statutory duty (see below Nr. 28). The concept *bonos mores* is interpreted taking into account the prevailing ethical standards in business, but also considering

925. The report is authored by Dr. Antonina Bakardjieva-Engelbrekt, University of Stockholm.

926. Dz. U. 1993 Nr. 47 poz. 211. The Act entered into force on 1.1.1995. It has undergone several amendments: in 1996, 1998, 2000, 2002 and 2003, 2004 and 2005.

927. Last amended in 2003, Dz.U. 2003, Nr 86, poz. 804.

928. Interestingly, the pre-war Unfair Competition Act of 1926 in its civil law part was never formally abolished during the times of command economy. See decision of the Constitutional Court of 1991, GRUR Int. 1991, p. 654; cf. Wiszniewska, 1999, Nr. 26. Since some of the basic principles of the 1926 Act were taken over in the 1993 ZNKU, decisions pronounced on the basis of the 1926 Act are still quoted as source for interpretation of the ZNKU.

the interests of the general public and of consumers, as well as general principles of law.[929]

The general clause is complemented by a catalogue of specific factual situations listed in Art. 3(2) ZNKU and elaborated in more detail in Chapter 2 ZNKU. The catalogue is not exhaustive, but rather regulates the most frequent and typical acts contrary to honest commercial practices. The relationship of these special provisions to the general clause is two-folded. On the one hand the catalogue rules represent exemplifications of the general clause and thus give substance to the abstract standard of "*boni mori*". On the other hand, the general clause acts as a safety net, catching even situations, which do not fall within the scope of the special provisions.[930]

Originally the ZNKU was conceived as a private law statute and was enforced exclusively upon the action of individual competitors and business or consumer associations. Despite the proclaimed objective of protecting the interests of consumers and of the general public there were only limited means for representation of these interests before the courts. This situation was considered unsatisfactory and after amendment of ZNKU in 1996, the President of the Polish Office for Protection of Competition and Consumers (Urzad Ohrony Konkurencij i Konsumentow, UOKiK) was granted standing to sue in certain matters of unfair competition where consumer interests are seriously impaired. In 2002, as a result of the implementation of the Injunctions Directive 98/27/EC, the direct right of action of consumer associations under the ZNKU was abolished (Art. 19 ZNKU). Instead, consumer associations, together with the so called local consumer ombudsmen, the Ombudsman for citizens' rights and the ombudsmen of the rights of the insured were furnished with rights to institute proceedings before the UOKiK for protection of collective consumer interests, including certain factual situations under the ZNKU.[931]

Systematically, Polish unfair competition law is treated as part of private law. It is closely related with intellectual property law and in particular with trademark law. The leading case law under the 1926 Unfair Competition Act established the principle that trade mark protection and protection under unfair competition law could be claimed cumulatively for one and the same infringement. Conversely, in a decision after the transition to free market economy (but still based on the 1926 Act) the Supreme Court held that the Trade Mark Act should be seen as *lex specialis* in relation to the Unfair Competition Act and should therefore exclude the application of the latter.[932]

As to the relationship with antitrust law, in a decision of 1991 the Antimonopoly Court held that the two legal fields should be regarded as separate. Antitrust law aims at protection of the independence and decision-making freedom of economic actors, and focuses on the structure of competition. It does not deal with the fairness of competitive relations or fairness of advertising, which are the sole subject of unfair competition law.[933] At the same time, the UOKiK, which is the main governmental

929. Wiszniewska, 1999, Nr. 48; Szvaja, 2000, p. 41.
930. This function of the general clause is, however, not fully recognized in Poland, see Wiszniewska 2001, p. 215.
931. See Part V, Proceedings before the President of UOKiK, Chapter 4 Proceedings concerning practices infringing on collective consumer interests, Art. 100a ff. OKiKU.
932. This restrictive position has been criticized in legal doctrine; see Wiszniewska, 1999, Nr. 185 ff. A new and comprehensive Industrial Property Act (IPA) was adopted in Poland in 2000, Act of 30.6.2000, Dz.U. 2001, No. 49, Poz. 508, effective since 22.8.2001. On the relation between the IPA and the ZNKU see Kępiński, 2003, p. 751
933. Judgment of the Antimonopoly Court of 19.9.1991, XVIi Amr 9/91—"Westa/PZU", OG 1992, Nr. 3 p. 24 ff. See Wiszniewska, 1999, Nr. 36.

agency entrusted with the enforcement of antitrust law, has broad competences in the area of collective consumer rights, including areas such as misleading advertising.

3. Regulation of advertising

Advertising is subject to various different rules and regulations scattered in several legal acts. The main provisions are to be found in Art. 16 ZNKU. Article 16(2), Nr. 1 has the character of a "small" general clause. It qualifies as an act of unfair competition any advertising, which is contrary to the law or to honest practices or offends human dignity.

a. Misleading advertising

Several provisions of the ZNKU are devoted to the suppression of misleading advertising. Of central importance is Art. 16(1) Nr. 2, which prohibits any advertising that is likely to mislead consumers and is material for their choice of goods or services. In assessing whether an advertisement is misleading all its components shall be taken into account and in particular the quantity, quality, components, way of manufacturing, usefulness, possible use, repair, maintenance of the products as well as the behavior of the customers (Art. 16(2) ZNKU).[934] In addition, Art. 10(1) ZNKU defines as an act of unfair competition the use of misleading product indications. This provision is to be regarded as a special application of the general rule on misleading advertising to product indications.

Another rule that addresses specific situations of deception is Art. 14(1) ZNKU defining as an act of unfair competition the dissemination of untrue or misleading information about one's own or someone else's undertaking.[935] The concept of dissemination of information is obviously perceived as broader than that of advertising, encompassing also the use of business correspondence, statements in the course of personal visits, telephone calls, etc. Another qualifying element is that the dissemination is undertaken in order to yield benefits or to bring detriment to a competitor.[936]

The ZNKU says nothing about the standard of deception. Judging from the opinions in legal doctrine it seems that the benchmark consumer in Polish law is close to the European standard of "the average consumer who is reasonably circumspect and reasonably well-informed". For instance advertising with superlatives is generally considered allowed since the average consumer will relate to it with certain skepticism.[937] Conversely, exaggerated advertising claims may be considered misleading if

934. In a judgment of the Appellate Court of Warsaw of 19.7.1996, I ACr 492/96—"Daewoo" the Court advanced a narrow interpretation of the concept "advertising" in Art. 16 ZNKU. The claim of the advertiser that he was the sole agent of Daewoo in Poland was not considered to constitute advertising, since it did not relate to the goods and services offered but to the status of the trader. See Wiszniewska, 1999, Nr. 75.
935. The information can concern the management staff, the goods and services offered, the prices charged or the legal or economic status of the enterprise. It may in particular consist in employing unlawful or inaccurate qualifications, university degrees, titles and other information on the professional skills of the employees; false certificates; unreliable research results; unreliable information on distinctions or indications of products or services.
936. In legal doctrine opinions divide on the interpretation of this requirement. Some authors draw the conclusion that Art. 14 requires malicious intent. Others do not see a difference from the conventional principle of non-fault liability in the law of unfair competition. See Wiszniewska, 1999, Nr. 71.
937. See Wiszniewska, 1999, Nr. 75.

they are verifiable and may be taken seriously by the addressees. If specific claims are made then the consumer is expected to trust the claim.[938] It is generally agreed that the standard of deception depends on the target audience, and is stricter when the advert addresses children, elderly or sick people who are more credulous or vulnerable. The relevance of the advertising for the consumer purchasing decision is one of the components that have to be established in order to substantiate infringement.[939]

In order to bring Polish unfair competition law in full conformity with European law, an amendment of the ZNKU introduced an explicit requirement of reversed burden of proof for situations of misleading advertising (Art.18a ZNKU).

b. Comparative advertising

Under the 1993 ZNKU in its original version, comparative advertising was as a rule prohibited unless it provided useful and correct information to the customers (ex Art. 16(1), Nr. 6).[940] In 2000 ZNKU was amended with the purpose to transpose Directive 97/55/EC into Polish law. Article 16(1), Nr. 6 ZNKU was repealed and replaced by a new Art. 16(3) ZNKU. The new provision follows closely the wording of the Directive with only some minor deviations. The Polish act thus requires that the comparison is material (Art. 16(3), Nr. 2 ZNKU) and extends the protection against imitations to all distinctive signs.[941] It may likewise be noted that, whereas Directive 97/55/EC states that comparative advertising is permitted if it fulfils the requirements in Art. 3a, the Polish ZNKU proceeds from a prohibition of all comparative advertising that is contrary to *bonos mores*. In a second sentence the Act provides that comparative advertising is not contrary to *bonos mores* if it meets the said requirements.[942]

c. Disguised advertising

Following Art. 16(1) Nr. 4 ZNKU disguised advertising is prohibited.[943] As disguised advertising counts any statement, which while stimulating towards the purchase of goods or services, creates the wrong impression of neutral information. In legal doctrine this provision is considered to apply, among others, to different forms of product

938. Thus the description of pasta as "8-egg macaroni" was considered misleading since the product consisted of only 1-2 eggs per kilogram of flour. See Wiszniewska, 1999, Nr. 71. Judgment of the Provincial Court (Wojewódzki) in Czêstochowa of 14.6.1996, V GC 4366/95, not published. The decision is also reported by De Caluwe, Les regles de concurrence dans le monde, Revue Internationale de la Concurrence 1999, p. 4 ff., 38.
939. The President of UOKiK has used his powers to claim injunction in several cases of deception. Some of these cases concerned health-related advertising claims, for instance exaggerated effects of weight-loss pills (e.g. "eat as much as you wish without gaining weight"), others addressed misleading product indications (e.g. the use of the designation "mineral water" for plain water and of the designation "wild cherry" for a wine produced of apple concentrate). See Wiszniewska, GRUR Int. 2001, p. 217.
940. Novińska/Skubisz, 1995, p. 26 ff. See also the decision of the Appellate Court of Warsaw in the case "Waagi" OSP 1993, Issue 2, poz. 24, p. 80 ff. with a comment by Novińska.
941. See Wiszniewska, GRUR Int. 2001, 214 ff.
942. The wording has most probably resulted from the attempt to fit the European provisions into the language and structure of the ZNKU, which builds on prohibitions.
943. See Skubisz, in: Szvaja, 2000, Nr. 120.

placement. For the particular fields of printed press and of radio and television broadcasting the principle that advertising should be recognizable as such is laid down in the Press Act[944] and in the Radio- and Television Act respectively.[945]

d. Intrusive advertising

Any advertising, which represents a considerable interference with the privacy of the customers, in particular by harassing customers at public places, by sending unsolicited goods at the expense of the customers and by misuse of technical means of information is prohibited (Art. 16(1), Nr. 1 ZNKU).[946] In legal doctrine this provision is interpreted broadly to comprise all forms of approaching customers at public places, convincing them to visit restaurants, shops or to buy goods or services. The unsolicited advertising per fax or telephone is clearly subsumed under the prohibition, thus implementing the requirements of the Distance Selling Directive 97/7/EC (see also below Nr. 20).

e. Advertising rules for certain products and media

Various administrative law provisions lay down restrictions on advertising about specific product categories and in certain media. Characteristic is the prohibition of tobacco advertising incorporated via Art. 28 ZNKU in the Tobacco Act. Article 8a of the Tobacco Act stipulates that advertising of tobacco products in television and radio as well as tobacco advertising in the press intended for children and youth is prohibited. Advertising for prescription drugs in mass media is prohibited.[947] Also alcohol advertising is subject to strict limitations.[948]

Certain media-specific restrictions as well as information and transparency requirements are set out in the Press Act and in the Radio and Television Broadcasting Act.

f. Other regulations on advertising

Art. 16(1) Nr. 3 ZNKU contains a special rule on emotional advertising. It prohibits as an act of unfair competition any advertising which by provoking fear, by abusing existing prejudice or the credulousness of children impacts upon the feelings of the customers. Under this rule are subsumed all situations where psychological pressure

944. Dz. U. 1984 Nr. 5 poz. 24 with many subsequent amendments. See Art. 12(2) Press Act prohibiting disguised advertising in the activity of journalists if they draw an economic or personal advantage thereof.
945. Dz. U. 1993 Nr. 7 poz. 34 with many subsequent amendments. The principle of separation between advertising and programme in radio and television broadcasts is laid down in Art. 16(1) of the Act; cf. Wiszniewska, 1999, Nrs. 121, 243, 261.
946. Skubisz, in: Szvaja, 2000, Nrs. 130.
947. See the Pharmaceuticals Act of September, 6, 2001; Skubisz, in: Szvaja, 2000, Nr. 130.
948. See Art. 13(3) Act on Moderation and Combating Alcoholism of 26.10.82, which bans all forms of advertising of beverages with alcoholic content of more than 1,5 per cent per volume (for a definition of the concept "alcoholic beverage" see Art. 46 of the same Act).

is exerted over consumers, limiting their decision-making freedom.[949] A provision of an even more general character is the prohibition of advertising which is contrary to human dignity (Art. 16(1) Nr. 1 ZNKU).[950]

4. Direct marketing, specific marketing techniques

In its original version, the ZNKU did not include provisions on direct marketing or on other specific promotional methods. With an amendment of 2002 several provisions were included in ZNKU concerning different categories of aggressive promotional techniques. The Act now prohibits expressly the organizing of pyramid (so called avalanche) sales as an act of unfair competition pursuant to Art. 17c ZNKU.

Article 17 b sets strict restrictions on promotional lotteries and games. It is an act of unfair competition to formulate the conditions of the offer in terms enhancing consumers' confidence of winning, provided that the consumer is required to order the good or the service that is object of the promotion, or to pay certain percentage of the price in advance.[951] Certainly, direct marketing and all methods of promotion are also subject to the general requirements of fairness and correctness as established by ZNKU.[952]

Distance selling and doorstep selling are regulated in Chapter 1 and 2 of the Act on Protection of Some Consumer Rights and on Product Liability.[953] According to Art. 6 of this Act a trader can use facsimile, automatic answering machines or electronic mail for directing an offer at a consumer only if the consumer has given his express consent to this. The Act on Provision of Services by Electronic Means of 28 July 2002 implements the E-Commerce Directive 2000/31/EC and sets forth in Art. 10 an opt-in regime for unsolicited advertising by e-mail.[954]

949. Advertising which promises the winning of prizes that are disproportionately high in comparison with the value of the main product, is in legal doctrine given as one example of such psychological pressure, see Wiszniewska, 1999, Nr. 128.
950. The Appellate Court of Gdansk has applied this provision in the case of a promotional game, which did not clearly state the conditions of participation and left the wrong impression that by solving a simple problem consumers would be entitled to receive a prize and not (as the case was) to only participate in the game. The Court concluded that the promotion would invoke in the average consumers feelings of disappointment, of self-despise and of being defrauded. See Judgment of the Appellate Court of Gdansk of 6.11.1996, I ACr 839/96—"Nagroda Roku" (Prize of the year); see Wiszniewska, 1999, Nr. 135.
951. To draw up the promotional offer in the form of an official letter issued in the name of the consumer is given as one example of formulating the offer in an unfair way (Art. 17 b(2) ZNKU).
952. One of the cases filed by the President of UOKiK concerned a mass promotional campaign by a company, appearing under different names, and sending personal letters to consumers' homes. The letters urged consumers to participate in games of chance promising considerable prizes in cash and containing many deceptive elements. The Regional Court of Warsaw banned the advertising as misleading and abusing consumers' emotions and light-mindedness under Art. 16(1) Nr. 2 and 3 ZNKU. See Wyrok Sada Okregowy w Warszawie Wydzial XV Gospodarczy, 5.10.2001—"ZXY".
953. Ustawa o ochronie niektórych praw konsumentów oraz o odpowiedzialnosci za szkode wyrzadzona przez product niebezpieczny, Dz. U. 2000 Nr. 22, poz. 271. See the commentary by Łętowska, 2001.
954. Ustaw o swiadczeniu uslug droga elektroniczna (Dz. U. 2002, Nr. 144, poz. 1204). See also decision of the UOKiK of 30.9.2003, Bulletin of the UOKiK (Dziennik Urzedowy) Nr. 1, 2004, poz. 277.

5. Sales promotion

Special offers in the context of comparative advertising are subject to detailed information disclosure requirements following the implementation of Directive 97/55/EC.[955]

The ZNKU amendment of 2002 introduced a ban on premiums in Art. 17a ZNKU. Premiums are defined as giving all or some consumers free goods or services other than those that are object of the sale. The ban does not apply to premiums of very low value or to product samples. Exempted are likewise promotional lotteries organized in accordance with the relevant laws, as well as promotional competitions where the outcome does not depend on chance (Art. 17a(2), Nr. 2 ZNKU).

6. Disparagement, exploitation of goodwill

As mentioned earlier, Art. 14 ZNKU prohibits the dissemination of untrue or misleading information about another's enterprise, with the purpose of drawing benefits for one's own business or afflicting damages to a competitor's business. This provision forms the basis for preventing and combating goodwill exploitation as well as disparaging advertising. For both situations the law provides remedies only where the information is false or misleading.

7. Passing off, imitation

Article 5 ZNKU is devoted to the protection of commercial signs in the broadest possible sense. According to this provision it is prohibited to use as designations the trade name, name, emblem, abbreviation in letters or other characteristic symbols that have previously been lawfully used to designate another enterprise in a manner which could mislead clients as to its identity.[956]

The ZNKU contains also a special rule on product imitations. According to Art. 13 the counterfeiting of the outer appearance of a ready-made product by technical means in a way that may mislead consumers as to the identity of the product or the producer is prohibited. This prohibition does not extend to the copying of the functional features of a product. However, if there is a risk that by copying the technical features one would create confusion among consumers, then the imitator is obliged to make appropriate indications on the product.

8. Impediment of competitors

Already in its original version the ZNKU addressed the problem of obstructive competition by impeding the access of individual competitors to the market, as a particular

955. According to Art. 16(4) such advertising shall clearly and unequivocally indicate the date on which the offer expires or shall contain information that the offer is valid until the stock of products is exhausted or till cessation of rendering services and, where the special offer is not binding yet, it should also indicate the date upon which the special price or other specific terms of the offer shall become binding.

956. There are additional provisions regulating disputes concerning trade names following the splitting or other restructuring of companies. The principle is that certain priority right is granted to the first user of the name. See Art. 7 ZNKU.

form of unfair competition (Art. 15 ZNKU). Article 15(1) Nr. 3 ZNKU prohibits sales below cost, when the purpose is to eliminate a competitor. The same applies to inducing breach of contract or inducing third parties to refrain from entering a contract with another enterprise (Art. 15(2) ZNKU). The differential treatment of customers without objective ground is also considered an act of unfair competition (Art. 15(3) ZNKU). Other factual situations explicitly regulated as acts of unfair compertition are the unauthorized disclosure of trade secrets (Art. 11 ZNKU) as well as inducing employees or customers of an entrepreneur to breach a contract (Art. 12 ZNKU).

With the amendment of 2002, Art. 15 ZNKU has been considerably extended to cover a number of new factual situations, serving the common objective of protecting small and medium-sized enterprises. The statute now prohibits as an act of unfair competition the obstruction of the access to the market of small enterprises through sales at a loss, irrespective the purpose, when such sales are conducted on business premises with a total surface of more than 400 m2 (Art. 15(4) ZNKU).[957] In the same category fall the new rules of Art. 15(2) and (5) ZNKU, which address trade with certificates, authorizing repeat purchases with the same retailer, or with an economically related entity. Such practices are estimated to hamper the freedom of choice of purchasers. In the course of the preparatory work these restrictive rules have been assessed as selling arrangements fully compatible with Community law, with reference to the *Keck and Mithouard* ruling of the ECJ.[958]

9. Breach of statutory duty

As mentioned above, the general clause of the ZNKU qualifies expressly breach of statutory duties as an act of unfair competition (Art. 3(1) ZNKU). Likewise advertising which infringes upon statutory duties is prohibited (Art. 16(1) Nr. 1 ZNKU). The provisions are broadly drafted and leave the impression that infringements of any law whatsoever would fall foul of the general clause of Art. 3 ZNKU, or of the rule on advertising, respectively. In legal doctrine the view prevails that despite the openness of the general clause there is an implied requirement of relevance of the infringement for the objectives pursued by the ZNKU, namely to safeguard fair competition.[959] More specific situations of breach of statutory duty concern the bribing of public officials for the purpose of extracting economic benefits Art. 15a ZNKU, and the marketing of legally prohibited equipment for circumvention of technological protection measures controlling the access to electronic services (15b ZNKU).

957. Some exceptions from this rule are allowed for season sales. The latter are however, strictly confined to one month, for summer and winter sales respectively. Exempted are also sales of goods with expiring fitness term or "best-before" date (Art. 15(5) Nr. 2 ZNKU), as well as clearance and bankruptcy sales under certain conditions (Art. 15(5) Nr. 3 ZNKU).
958. See Commission on European integration, Ministry of Foreign Affairs, Doc. DH/945/2002 of 10.4.2002.
959. See Wiszniewska, 1999, Nr. 45; Skubisz, 1994. One example of enforcing statutory obligations by way of ZNKU is the case filed by the President of UOKiK against a major beer-brewing company. The company had opened a limited-scale production of alcohol-free beer of the same brand as its alcohol containing products. It made massive advertising allegedly of the alcohol-free brand, attempting thus to circumvent the total ban on alcohol advertising under the Polish Act on Combating Alcoholism. See Wyrok Sad Apelacyjny w Krakowie, 26 pazdziernika 2000—"Okocimskie Zakady Piwowarskie".

10. Sanctions, procedural rules

The ZNKU is predominantly private law oriented and the emphasis is on the civil law instruments of enforcement. Competitors, whose interests have been infringed upon by an act of unfair competition have right to claim injunction, compensation for damages and the return of anything constituting unjust enrichment. In addition, they may seek that the court orders the restoration of the *status quo* prior to the infringement or obliges the infringer to issue a corrective statement (Art. 18 ZNKU). National and regional business associations can claim injunction, restoration of the *status quo* and corrective statement for some but not all infringements, constituting act of unfair competition.[960] The legislator has not considered it appropriate to grant *locus standi* to the individual consumer.[961]

With an amendment of the ZNKU of 2000 the Polish lawmaker added an original sanction to the arsenal of remedies under the Act. In a move to strengthen the effectiveness of the law especially with regard of the protection of consumer and general public interests, an opportunity was envisaged to impose a sort of civil law penalty; an adequate sum of money ear-marked for a social goal connected with the promotion of Polish culture or related to the protection of national heritage (Art. 18(1) Nr. 6 ZNKU). This sanction can be invoked only where the infringement has been deliberate or at least negligent (zawiniony).[962]

Many of the acts of unfair competition in ZNKU entail criminal sanctions (see Chapter 4 ZNKU Criminal provisions). Criminal liability is more specifically envisaged for disclosure of trade secrets in breach of contractual obligations or of illegally acquired trade secrets (Art. 23 ZNKU). The same applies for acts of counterfeiting, (Art. 24 ZNKU) as well as for organizing pyramid schemes in contravention with the legal prohibition (Art. 24a ZNKU). Fine and imprisonment are likewise envisaged for malicious use of misleading product indications or non-compliance with mandatory information disclosure requirement (Art. 25 ZNKU) as well as for the dissemination of false information (Art. 26 ZNKU), provided such conduct has resulted in considerable damage for the customers, in the first case, or for the trader, in the second case. All the criminal offences in the ZNKU are enforceable only upon the motion of the injured party and the misdemeanors—upon request of the injured (Art. 27 ZNKU).

Finally, infringements on the collective interests of consumers, including acts of unfair competition negatively affecting such interests, e.g. unfair or misleading advertising, can be prosecuted on the basis of the OKiKU (cf. Arts. 23a(2) OKiKU). The President of the UOKiK has a broad range of competences, among others to issue a cease-and-desist order upon penalty of a fine, to order the restoration of the *status quo* prior to the infringement, the provision of the necessary information or the publication of the decision at the expense of the infringer (Art. 23c and Art. 102(1)

960. Thus business associations cannot claim injunction under Art. 5-7 (confusing trade names, trade marks and other distinguishing signs), Art. 11 (trade secrets), Art. 14 (dissemination of misleading information) and Art. 15a (bribing of public officials in the course of business activity) (see Art. 19 Sec. 2 ZNKU). A right of action of consumer associations was initially foreseen, but was later on transformed into a right to lodge petition before the UOKiK (see Nr. 32 below). On the right of action of consumer associations see Judgment of the Supreme Court of 28.10.2000, Federacij Konsumentow w W., OSN, Nr. 4/01
961. However, in some cases of intentional deception that have caused serious damages which constitute an offence, a charge for criminal law penalties may be brought by any person who has suffered damages, including the individual consumer.
962. For criticism of this new sanction see Szwaja, 2000, p. 533.

OKiKU). Proceedings can be instituted *ex officio* by the President of UOKiK or upon a motion by the local consumer ombudsmen, the Ombudsman for citizens' rights, the ombudsmen for the rights of the insured or by consumer associations (Art 100a OKiKU). The decisions of the President of UOKiK are subject to appeal before the Court for Protection of Competition and Consumers, Warsaw (Art. 78 OKiKU), whereby the rules of the Civil Procedure Code apply.

XXI. PORTUGAL

Selected Literature: Ascensão, *Concurência desleal, Coimbra* 2002; Ascensão, (ed.), Concurrência desleal, Almedia 1997 Ascensão, *Legislação de dereito industrial e concorrencia desleal*, 3rd ed. 2003; Ascensão, *Portugal*, in: Ulmer (ed.), *Das Recht des unlauteren Wettbewerbs in den Mitgliedstaaten der EWG* 2005; Bodewig/Henning-Bodewig, *Das Recht der Rabatte und Zugaben in der EU, WRP* 2000, 1341; Da Costa/Mendes/Wollmann, Das Wettbewerbsrecht in Portugal, in: *Heidelberger Kommentar zum Wettbewerbsrecht*, 2nd ed. 2005, p. 752; Jalles/Dein, Werberecht in Portugal, in: Schotthöfer (ed.), *Handbuch des Werberechts in den EU-Staaten*, 2nd ed. 1997, p. 507; Kuhlmann, *Der unlautere Wettbewerb im portugiesischen Recht*, 1988; Loba d'Avila Lima, *Concorrência Desleal*, 1910; Schricker, *Einführung in das portugiesische Recht des unlauteren Wettbewerbs*, GRUR Int. 1994, 819; Voigt, Portugal, in: Micklitz/Keßler (ed.), *Marketing Practices Regulation and Consumer Protection in the EC Member States and the US*, 2002, p. 267.

1. Sources of law

Article 317, 318, 331 Código da Propriedade Industrial(Law regarding Industrial Property) of 5 March 2000 (CPI); Código da Publicidade (Advertising Act) of 23 October 1990 (Advertising Act).

2. Portuguese unfair competition law in a nutshell

Unfair competition law ("concorrência desleal")[963] in Portugal is closely tied to industrial property law[964] which was codified as early as 1894 in the "Código da Propriedade Industrial" (CPI).[965] Since that time, unfair competition law has been part of the Law regarding Industrial Property Rights. Until 2003, the edition of the Statute No. 15/95 from 24 January 1995[966] applied, which regulated unfair competition in one single provision—§ 260 CPI—, containing a general clause[967] and several examples of acts

963. An overview over "concurrência desleal" in Portugues can be found in the leading treaties by Ascensão and Loba d'Avila Lima; in German in Ascensão (ed.: Ulmer) and Schricker, GRUR Int. 1994, 819.
964. See Ascensão (fn. 1), No. 33; (in English) "Manual Industrial Property", Vol. 4 (1997); see also (in German) Schricker, GRUR Int. 1984, 819. The Portugues copyright law is discussed by Dietz, in: Möhring/Schulze/Ulmer//Zweigert, Quellen des Urheberrechts, Vol. 5 (1992).
965. Diário do Governo of 21.12.1894.
966. No. 15/95 from 24.1.1995, in German in GRUR Int. 1997, 698.
967. According to § 260 CPI, who ever commits a competitive act that violates the norms and honest practices of the respective trade with the goal of harming another or of procuring an unfair advantage over a third party will be punished by monetary sanctions or imprisonment.

against "honest trade practices" (confusion, imitation, disparagement, false statements and trade secrets). The offence was penally sanctioned.

In 2003 the CPI was newly promulgated by the Legislative Decree No. 36/03 from 5 March 2003. The regulations regarding unfair competition are now found in Art. 317, 318, and 331. Article 317 CPI contains the general clause, which has a partially new wording: It prohibits (as before) any violation of the norms and "usos honestos" in the respective business but adds the requirement of a "commercial activity" and takes out the former requirement of a subjective intent ("intent to harm another or of procuring and unfair advantage over a third party"). The special causes of action are still formulated as examples of the general clause but misleading advertising has been completely taken out and statements of geographic origin are now regulated separately under Art. 325 CPI. The former example of the protection of trade secrets also has become an individual provision, regulated in Art. 318 CPI. As regards the sanctions (Art. 331 CPI), the largest change can be found as the violation of unfair competition law has been "degraded" from an actual criminal act to a mere regulatory offense.

The regulations in the CPI are supplemented by the Cartel law, several specific consumer protection decrees, and especially the Advertisement Act ("Codigo de Publicidada")[968]—which aims at a comprehensive regulation of advertising.

The Portuguese Competition Law is thus based on multiple pillars:

- the regulations regarding unfair or dishonest competition in Art. 317, 318, 331 CPI;
- the Advertising Act from 1990;
- the Consumer Protection Act of 1996[969] and the statutory decree No. 143/2001 from 26 April 2001,[970] which regulates distance contracts, pyramid schemes, joined offers, door-to-door sales, etc; the EC-Directives regarding consumer guarantees, e-commerce, and distance contracts were recently transposed as well;
- the relatively young Cartel legislation;[971]
- Statute No. 253/86 from 1986,[972] which covers seasonal sales, clearance sales, sales below cost, and direct sales to the end user, among other things;
- the "Advertising Code" of the Portuguese association of advertising agencies.

The above regulations have differing goals. While Art. 317 et seq. CPI serves mainly the interest of the individual competitor, the Advertisement Act focuses on the protection of consumers, but also considers the interests of business and of the general public. The area of application is also different. Article 317 CPI requires a competitive action and a competitive relationship, namely an identity or kinship of business activity[973]. This latter requirement is narrowly defined; for example, it was not found to exist between the makers of cloth and the makers of clothes. The

968. Act No. 330/90 of 23.10.1990; in the version of the Act No. 74/93 of 10.3.1993; Act No. 6/95 of 17.1.1994; Act No. 275/98 of 9.9.1998; Act No. 332/01 of 24.12.2001; published in German in GRUR Int. 1994, 830.
969. Lei da Defeso do consumidor; see Voigt, p. 271 ff.
970. Decreto-Lei No. 143/2001 of 26.4.2001.
971. Decreto-Lei No. 371/93 of 29.10.1993; see also da Costa/Mendes/Wollmann, p. 752 f.
972. Decreto—Lei No. 253/86 de 25 de agosto—Annuncios de reducao de precos; see Ascensão, in Ulmer (ed.), No. 355.
973. Schricker, GRUR Int. 1994, 821 ff.; Ascensão No. 61 ff.

new regulations from 2003 has clarified that the law also applies to professionals. The area of application of the Advertisement Act is determined by the definition of advertisement which is rather broad, and also includes "advertising" for religious, ideological, charitable, social-political, or other community services reasons.[974]

The various regulations can generally apply parallel to each other, just like the numerous product specific rules. However, in the area of advertising, the regulations of the Advertisement Act have priority over the regulation in Art. 317 et seq. CPI (Art. 2 Advertising Act).[975]

3. Regulation of advertising

a. Misleading advertising

Misleading advertising was regulated under the former Art. 260(d) CPI in five individual causes of action. This regulation was repealed by the 2003 reform without substitution. Thus, the only law that currently applies to misleading advertising is the Advertising Act.[976] According to Art. 10, advertising must "respect the truth and may not distort the facts". Statements regarding the origin, nature, composition, characteristics of products and the conditions of sale must "be demonstrable at any time to the authority in charge". In addition to this, Art. 11 transposes the Directive 84/450/EEC, although the requirement of an impact on the commercial behavior was left out and the requirement that the consumer must be completely and honestly informed as to the main qualities of the item or service was added (Art. 9(1)).

How these far reaching provisions are applied in practice is difficult to determine. From the little published case law,[977] in this area it can be concluded that the Portuguese courts seem to favor the benchmark of an average consumer who is quite circumspect of advertisements. This has led (as in Spain) to a relatively tolerant attitude against exaggerations, superiority claims, etc.[978]

b. Comparative advertising

According to Art. 16 Advertising Act, comparisons are allowed if they are based on material, self-evident, and objectively provable characteristics of the item or service, and if they compare similar products. Article 317 supplements this requirement, forbidding reference to a third party's name without permission. As with misleading advertising, the exact contours of this regulation are not entirely clear given the lack of applicable case law. It can be assumed, however, that the interpretation follows Directive 97/55/EC and the relevant decisions of the ECJ.[979]

974. See Schricker, GRUR Int. 1994, 821; the term advertisement was newly defined through the law from January 17 1995; see Aktuelle Informationen, GRUR Int. 1995, 432.
975. The main point of overlap was in the area of misleading and false statements; this is no longer an issue as the 2003 reform took out those regulations from the CPI.
976. See Schricker, GRUR Int. 1994, 826 ff. (before the 2003 reform); after the reform see Ascensão No. 299.
977. Cf the decisions cited by Schricker, GRUR Int. 1994, 826 and Ascensão, in Ulmer.
978. Schricker, GRUR Int. 1994, 827.
979. Discussed in this book in Chapter 3, III. and IV. See also Ascensão, No. 286. (ed.), No. 299 ff.

c. Concealed advertising

Protection from "hidden advertising" which is even mentioned in the Constitution,[980] is regulated in the Advertising Act. According to Art. 8, the commercial character must be unmistakably recognizable. Radio and television advertisements must be clearly separated from the actual programs; Art. 9 forbids subliminal and surreptitious advertising.

d. Aggressive advertising

Harassing or intrusive advertising is as such not regulated. The aspect of harassment, however, plays an indirect role in several advertisement regulations, see under 3f, 4.

e. Product and media specific regulations[981]

Advertising for alcohol is forbidden between the hours of 7 a.m. and 9:30 p.m. in television and radio (Art. 17 Advertising Act). Further regulation largely aims at prohibiting the excessive consumption of alcohol. Advertising for tobacco, unless specifically allowed, is forbidden for all forms of media that are located in Portugal. The same applies under Art. 19 for prescription medications outside of expert circles.

Television advertising is regulated in the third chapter of the Advertising Act which is supplemented by Law 16/94.[982] Under these laws, advertising and programming must be clearly separated and commercials must be recognizable as such. Product specific limitations for medications also exist. For teleshopping, specific regulations exist in Art. 25(a). Radio advertisements must follow the Radio Act of 23 February 2001; commercial communications via internet have to comply with the Act No. 143/2001 which transposed the transparency requirements of the e-Commerce Directive.[983]

f. Other advertising regulations

Art. 7 of the Advertising Act forbids advertising that violates constitutionally protected rights. No advertisement may:

- contain an attack on human dignity;
- discriminate on the basis of race or sex;
- appeal to or stimulate violence or illegal or criminal activities
- contain disparaging references to national or religious institutions, symbols, or historical personalities;
- contain obscene language;
- encourage actions that would harm the environment.

980. Art. 60 of the Portuguese Constitution forbids "all forms of hidden, indirect or fraudulent advertising".
981. Cf. Salles/Dein, No. 40 ff.; Voigt, p. 280 ff.
982. See Voigt, p. 273. The regulations implement among others, the TV-Directive, discussed in this book in chapter 3, IV. 5.
983. Discussed in this book in Chapter 2, IV. 8.

Pictures of and statements by natural persons may only be used with permission; testimonials are only allowed under certain conditions (Art. 15). The use of foreign languages is only allowed when the advertisement is targeted solely or mainly at foreigners (Art. 7(3). According to Art. 13, advertising may not in any way encourage behavior that could harm the health or safety of the consumer; this is assumed when information regarding the potential danger of the product is not given. Strict requirements exist for advertising aimed at children and minors (Art. 14, Art. 13(3)).

4. Direct marketing

Door to door sales are allowed when the consumer is given certain information regarding the vendor (Art. 15(1) Law 134//2001).[984] The same applies for the sending of unordered goods, as long as the impression is not given that the recipient must conclude a contract, make a payment, or return the goods.[985]

Telephone advertising via automated calls and faxes require the prior consent of the consumer per Art. 11(1) Law No. 143/2001; the advertiser has the burden to prove that consent existed (Art. 12). For all other forms of direct marketing, Art. 11(2) of the Law 143/2001 establishes an "opt-out" system. The same applies for email advertising,[986] which in addition has to meet certain transparency requirements (see above, 3e).

5. Sales promotion

An explicit ban on reducing prices or giving incentives does not exist in Portuguese law.[987] However, Statute No. 253/86 from 25 August 1986 regarding price reductions, sales below cost, and direct sales regulates the advertising of price reductions. According to Art. 3, the advertiser must be able to prove the original price and have sufficient stock for the length of the sale (Art. 5). Sales below cost are forbidden under Art. 15. In addition, the general prohibition on misleading applies (see above, 3a).[988]

According to Art. 19 Advertising Act, games of chance are forbidden when they make up the "material part of the advertisement". Whether only games of chance as such, and not promotional games, are included, is unclear. A regulation of games based on skill does not seem to exist. The requirements under which seasonal sales and clearance sales are allowed to be held are found in Art. 8-13 Statute No. 253/86.[989] Pyramid schemes or similar systems are forbidden under Art. 27(2) Statute No. 143/2001.

6. Disparagement, danger of confusion

According to the general clause in Art. 137 CPI, it is considered as being against "honest practices" to give false statements in trade or industry with the goal of disparaging

984. Voigt, p. 275.
985. Voigt, p. 276.
986. Voigt, p. 273.
987. Ascensão, in Ulmer (ed.), No. 339 ff; 348 ff; 357 ff. Bodewig/Henning-Bodewig, WRP 2000, 1352; Schricker, GRUR Int. 1994, 829; Voigt, 275.
988. Schricker, GRUR Int. 1994, 828.
989. See Ascensão in Ulmer (ed.).

a company, goods or services or the reputation of a competitor. The objective discreditation thus does not suffice; it must have been intended.

Article 137 CPI further supplements trade mark law by forbidding actions that could cause confusion regarding the commercial achievements, products or services, or the reputation of a competitor. It requires that the commercial achievement, etc., at the time of the unfair action actually be sufficiently distinct.[990] Danger of confusion is determined according to trademark law principles, i.e. similarities are more important than differences etc.

7. Misappropriation, exploitation of reputation, imitation

According to Art. 317 CPI, the exploitation of another's reputation, even if it does not lead to a confusion, is not allowed, for instance, when the third party distinguishing mark is used with the addition of "type".[991] Slavish imitation as such is not regulated in Portuguese law. However, if it would lead to a danger of confusion, it is covered by one of the examples of the general clause in Art. 317 CPI; without danger of confusion it can, at least in theory, directly be based on the general clause in Art. 317 CPI under the aspect of a violation of "honest practices".

8. Impediment of competitors

As of 2003, the unauthorized appropriation, use or dissemination of trade secrets is regulated as a separate cause of action in Art. 318 CPI under the title "Protection of Unrevealed Information". This new regulation serves to transpose TRIPS but is also part of unfair competition law under Art. 317, 318 CPI.[992] The poaching of employees is only unfair if it aims at harming the competitor.[993]

9. Breach of law

Every violation of statutory consumer rights is simultaneously seen as a violation of the Advertising Act (Art. 12). It is unclear when and under what circumstances the violation of other regulations is considered a violation of "honest practices" under Art. 317 CPI.[994]

10. Enforcement

Violation of the CPI is, as of the 2003 reform, no longer criminally sanctioned but presents a regulatory offense. Monetary sanctions can be imposed ranging from 3,000 to 30,000 Euros for legal persons and 750 to 7,500 for natural persons (Art. 331 CPI). The specifics are based on the Legislative Decree 433/82 from 27 October 1982. Rights

990. The title of a television show "Telejournal" was held to be not sufficiently distinct, and thus not protected against the use of the exact name by another television broadcaster. See Oehen-Mendes, Portugal, in: Schricker/Stauder (ed.), Handbuch des Ausstattungsschutzes, 1986, p. 724; Schricker, GRUR Int. 1994, 824; RIC 184.
991. Cf. Schricker, GRUR Int. 1994, 825; Ascensão, No. 225.
992. lu extenso Ascensão in Ulmer (ed.), No. 269 ff., see also Schricker, id.
993. Ascensão, No. 95 ff.
994. See Voigt, p. 283.

to damages for the person harmed by the unfair competition act are possible on the basis of Art. 482 Codigo Civil. In an action for damages, suits for discontinuance may also be brought. Independent suits for discontinuance, in practice, do not seem to be very prevalent.[995]

The Advertising Act is sanctioned by administrative law. Various administrative authorities, such as the Consumer Protection Institute, have enforcement power. In addition to cease- and desist-orders, prohibition of the commercial activity, deprivation of public services, and the closing of business may be ordered (Art. 35(1)). The possibility of enforcement of claims for damages also exists (Art. 30).

XXII. SLOVAK REPUBLIC

Selected Literature: Dietz, *Die Einführung von Gesetzen gegen den unlauteren Wettbewerb in die ehemals sozialistischen Staaten Mittel- und Osteuropas*, GRUR Int. 1994, 649; Švidroň, in: Blanpain (ed.), *International Encyclopedia of Laws*, 2001, p. 189.

1. Sources of law

Zákon č. 513/1991 Zb. Obchodný zákonnik (Commercial Code) §§ 41-55 (C.C.); Zákon č. 147/2001 Z.z. o reklame (Advertising Law) from 5 April 2001.

2. Unfair competition law of Slovakia in a nutshell

The current unfair competition law of the Slovak Republic is based on two overlapping sets of regulations: §§ 41 et seq. C.C.,[996] on the one hand and the Advertising Law[997] of 2001 on the other hand.

§§ 41 et seq. C.C. regulate unfair competition as part of the Commercial Code. The relevant provisions are mainly based on the legislation of the former Federal Republic of Czechoslovakia from 1991,[998] which was transferred upon the establishment of the Republic of Slovakia. As this development is similar to that of the Czech Republic, the description there can be referred to for the development, materialization and basis of the C.C.-regulations. However, it should be noted that Slovakia has made some changes to §§ 41 C.C. since then.

In its current edition, §§ 41 C.C. contains, next to the general clause in § 44 with the cental notion of "dobré mravy" ("bones mores"), the following specific offenses: misleading advertising, deceptive description of goods or services, benefiting from the exploitation of a competitors reputation, bribery, disparagement, protection of trade secrets, and endangerment of health or the environment.

The regulations against unfair competition apply to all commercial practices. A competitive relationship between plaintiff and defendant is not required. For some

995. Kuhlmann, p. 188.
996. Zbierka zákonov c. 98/1991, strana 2474; see the first fn. of the Czech country report.
997. German translation GRUR Int. 2003, 714; see also Aktuelle Informationen, GRUR Int. 2001, 803.
998. Beier/Bastian/Kur (ed.), Wettbewerbsrecht und Verbraucherschutz in Mittel- und Osteuropa, p. 312; see also Knap, p. 105.

offenses, a close relationship to the laws regarding industrial property rights exists.[999] The values of the cartel law of 27 February 2001[1000] are also useful in interpreting the general clause, equally those of the consumer Protection Act No. 634/1992.

The Advertising Law of 5 April 2001 protects the interests of the consumer, the trader and the general public. It regulates a large number of offenses that have to do with advertising, such as misleading and comparative advertising. It also contains extensive product-specific advertising regulations. As in the C.C., there is a broad general clause in § 3(1), requiring advertising to be consistent with the regulations of business competition and "bones mores". Supervision over the law is incumbent upon various state entities, namely the Agriculture and Food Inspection authorities, the state institute for pharmaceutical product control, the state institute for control of veterinary medicine, and for the remainder of cases, the Slovakian Trade Inspection Authorities.

The regulations of the Advertising Law are subsidiary[1001] to §§ 41 et seq. C.C. which have priority if the two overlap. If they do not overlap, it is assumed that for both regulations the same criteria to determine unfairness apply. Also, a behavior that is forbidden under the Advertising Law is considered to be a violation of the general clause of § 44 C.C.

3. Regulation of advertising

Advertising is partly regulated in the Commercial Code and partly in the Advertising Law. When the term "advertising" is used, it is understood that under either regulation, the definition is determined according to the § 2(1) of the Advertising Law. According to this definition, advertising is the presentation of products in any form with the goal of establishing it in the market.[1002] The definition of "product" encompasses, according to para. 1(b) not only goods, but also services, real estate, trademarks, indications of origin, as well as other rights and obligations that are related to business activities. According to § 1(2), the following are not considered advertising: the address or location of a company or legal person, labels with business names or trademarks on letters or envelopes, legally regulated disclosures for products which have such requirements, and legally regulated annual reports regarding economic activity, audits, etc.

a. Misleading advertising

According to § 3(1) of the Advertising Law, advertising may not be misleading. As no further regulations on this subject exist in the Advertising Law, the main basis regarding misleading advertising must be seen in § 45 C.C. Under § 45 C.C., misleading

999. As to the industrial property rights laws of the Slovak Republic, see (in English) World Trade Executive, Inc (ed.), Intellectual Property law in the European Community, 2004, p. 319.
1000. See Aktuelle Informationen in GRUR Int. 2001, 802.
1001. GRUR Int. 2003, 714.
1002. Cf. Svidron, p. 191. On first glance, this definition seems to be narrower than that in Council Directive 84/450/EEC, which requires the intent to promote sales (and not to establish a place in the market). However, it is to be assumed that the courts will interpret the definition of advertising according to the Directive. Furthermore, the general clause of the C.C. applies, which could make the definition broader.

advertising is defined as advertising for goods, services, real estate, etc. that misleads or could mislead the person at whom the advertising is directed or who receives the advertising. The law further requires that either the economic activity of the addressee may be is influenced or that the advertisement has the ability to harm competitors or consumers. Para. 2 names three groups of reference points of misleading statements which approximate those in the Directive 84/450/EEC.

How these regulations are applied in practice, is difficult to assess due to the lack of published case law on this subject. However, it is well established that the question of the ability to mislead is determined according to the perception of the addressee of the advertising. Furthermore, the specific circumstances of the statement and the environment that determines its perception are to be considered. Although the benchmark of a reasonably attentive and circumspect "average consumer" is applied there is also an emphasize on the protection of children and minor in the Advertising Law and a specific prohibition of the exploitation of inexperience and lack of knowledge (§ 3(4)). Thus, it can be expected that the courts will consider the lack of experience of particular consumer groups as regards advertising practices and exaggerations in advertising.

b. Comparative advertising

Comparative advertising is regulated in § 4 Advertising Law. Its content and terminology largely corresponds to that of Directive 97/55/EC, although it has a slightly different structure. The question of special offers is not included in the regulations of comparative advertising, but rather as a subsection of the "general requirements of advertisements" in § 3(8) Advertising Law. Furthermore, para. 3 explicitly states that the only permissible forms of comparative advertising are those listed in para. 2. A certain textual difference to the Directive could be that the Directive refers to "competitors", while the Slovakian regulation refers to "advertisers", which, based on the interpretation of §§ 41 C.C., can be understood as including non-competing market participants.

As of now, there is little case law on comparative advertising. In view of the legal position of the former ČSFR up till now, however, it is expected that comparative advertising, especially the aspects of misleading and disparagement, will be relatively strictly judged.

c. Concealed advertising

According to § 3(3) of the Advertising Law surreptitious advertising is forbidden irrespective of the media involved. Furthermore, § 3 para. 4(j) of the Advertising Law forbids subliminal advertising.

d. Aggressive advertising

In addition to a specific regulation regarding telephone advertising (see under 4), § 3(7) of the Advertising Law contains a general prohibition of harassment through advertising. Under that regulation, "advertising may not be directed at persons who have previously declined such advertisement". How this "opt-out"-rule is applied in practice is unclear. The word "directed" seems to exclude advertising that reaches the addressee by chance, e.g. because the address unintentionally is not taken out of the computer. However, if the advertiser does not make an effective commitment to stop further advertising after he has been informed on the addressee's wish this can be seen as a violation of the general clause of § 3(1) Advertising Law.

e. Product and media specific advertising regulations

The Advertising Law contains detailed product specific advertising regulations. In addition to this, the general clause of § 3(1) applies.

According to § 5 of the Advertising Law, advertising of alcohol may not be portrayed as beneficial for physical or psychological benefits, nor may it encourage excessive consumption. It shall not portray abstinence as a flaw or stress the alcohol content. Advertising of alcohol may not be aimed at minors and no minors shall appear in the advertisement.

Advertising for tobacco products is forbidden in all media. The same applies for the distribution of samples in public and for publicly distributed advertising items. Para. 2 contains some exceptions (labeling on delivery trucks, advertising in stores where the items are sold, etc.)

Advertising for pharmaceutical products is, according to § 8 of the Advertising Law, completely forbidden for unregistered medications, those requiring a prescription, and specific types of medication. For drugs allowed to be advertised, there are extensive textual requirements. In para. 4, the requirement disclosures are listed. Exceptions exist under para. 7, such as giving certain information to experts and giving information at the same time as a person's health is discussed, as long as the person is not receiving information regarding a specific pharmaceutical product.

Regarding the marketing of foodstuffs, § 3(4) forbids presenting foodstuffs and nutritional supplements as if they had medicinal qualities. It is also forbidden to present products as good for one's health without being able to prove this through expert opinions (§ 3 para. 4(i), (h)). § 9 has extensive regulations regarding baby and child food. It is mainly aimed at not stopping mothers from breastfeeding.[1003]

It is forbidden to (publicly) advertise for weapons and munitions. (§ 7).

For the radio, Law No. 308/2000 applies. According to § 32(2), it supplements the regulations in the Advertising Law. For the internet, the law No. 610/2003 regarding electronic communications of 3 December 2003 has transposed the transparency requirements etc. of the Directive 2000/31/EC.

f. Other advertising regulations

According to § 3(4)(e) of the Advertising Law, commercial advertising may not exploit the trust, lack of experience or knowledge of consumers. Advertisement may not incite actions by minors that could lead to bodily or psychological harm (sub. l). Telephone, fax, or email advertisements for products that cannot be sold to minors are forbidden,

1003. The advertisement may only be appear in certain publications and may only contain statements that are accurate and scientifically proven. The use of certain words (e.g., humanized, materialized) is completely forbidden. The same applies for the distribution of samples, for rebates and premiums, and special sales.

as is the suggestion to encourage parents or others to purchase the product for the minor. Advertisements shall not violate human dignity, harm national or religious sentiments, or discriminate (c). It shall not encourage or sanction the use of force, vandalism, or vulgarity (d). Finally, it may not present the naked human body in an obscene fashion (e).

Advertising may not present any product whose means of manufacturing, sale or use is forbidden (b). The potential dangers for the environment and the health of people, animals and plants must be clearly disclosed (f). If products are put forth as promoting health, this must be able to be proven by expert opinion (h). The physical or psychological health of citizens may never be put in danger (g).

Personal data and statements of third parties may not be used in advertisements without the explicit approval of the party (k, l). More generally, an advertisement may not impair the rights of third parties. Pursuant to § 3(5) Advertising law, advertising must respect the Slovakian language, grammar etc. and must follow acknowledged terms of terminology.

4. Direct marketing

Advertising may not be distributed specifically to a person who has forbidden it (see under 3d). It can be assumed that this "opt-out"-rule applies in a generalized fashion for all methods of marketing. Marketing and advertisement against the declared will of the recipient constitute a violation of the general clause of § 44 C.C. ("bones mores"). Door to door sales, sending of unrequested advertising materials, etc., are also judged on this basis; the conctractual relationship is dealt with on the basis of the law 108/2000.

For advertising using automatic call systems, faxes and internet, the "opt-in" solution applies under § 3(6) of the Advertising Law. In other words, such advertising is only allowed with the prior approval of the recipient.

Pyramid schemes are forbidden based on the prohibition of exploiting gullibility and inexperience (§ 3(4)(a) Advertising Law) and on the general clause in § 44 C.C.

5. Sales promotion

Rebates, premiums, and free gifts are—except for certain products, see under 3e et seq.—not statutorily regulated. § 3(8) of the Advertising Law stipulates informational requirements for special sales,.

Advertising for sales promotion and promotional games are judged mainly on the basis of misleading and the prohibition of exploiting gullibility and inexperience (§ 3(4)(a) Advertising Law, § 44 C.C.).

6. Danger of confusion, disparagement, misappropriation of reputation, imitation, impediment of competitors; breach of the law

The judgment on the basis of §§ 44 et seq. C.C. largely corresponds to Czech law.

7. Enforcement

The regulations in the C.C. are sanctioned under civil law (see the Czech law for particulars).

The Advertising Law is sanctioned under administrative law. When a violation exists, the regulatory authorities (see above, 2) can forbid further or imminent distribution of the advertisement under § 11. The authorities can also publish the prohibition order or require an amended demonstration in the mass media. Monetary sanctions can also be imposed; for certain causes of action they can even be imposed against the advertising medium. For misleading and comparative advertising, the advertiser is required to submit proof of the accuracy of the factual assertions within fifteen days under § 11(2) Advertising Law.

XXIII. SLOVENIA

Selected Literature: Dietz, *Die Einführung von Gesetzen gegen den unlauteren Wettbewerb in ehemals sozialistische Staaten Mittel- und Osteuropas*, GRUR Int. 1994, 649; Grilc/Podobnik, *Das Wettbewerbsrecht in Slowenien*, in: Heidelberger Kommental 2nd ed. 2005, p. 1006; Puharic, Jugoslawien, in: Beier/Bastian/Kur (ed.), *Wettbewerbsrecht und Verbraucherschutz in Mittel- und Osteuropa*, 1992, p. 111; Krneta, *Die Neuregelung des Wettbewerbsrechts in Slowenien*, GRUR Int. 1994, 289; Straus, *Das Recht des unlauteren Wettbewerbs in Slowenien mit Hinweisen auf die Rechtslage in Kroatien*, GRUR Int. 1994, 700; Straus, *Die Entwicklung des jugoslawischen Wettbewerbsrechts und die Neuregelung von 1974*, GRUR Int. 1976, 426; Straus, *Das Wettbewerbsrecht in Jugoslawien*, 1970; Zabel, *Tržno pravo, Gospodarski veslunik*, Ljubljana 2000; Zabel, *Uvod* v. *gospodarsko pogoldbeno prava. Gospodarski vestnik*, 1986.

1. Sources of law

Zakon o varstvu konkurence (Competition Act) of 25 March 1993 (ZVK); Zakon o varstvu potrošnikov (Consumer Protection Act) of 1998 (ZVPot)

2. Slovenian unfair competition law in a nutshell

The Republic of Slovenia developed into an independent state through several phases, beginning in 1990, from the former Yugoslavia.[1004] In the first stage, the laws of Yugoslavia were incorporated in the Slovenian law, inasmuch as they conformed to the constitution and laws of Slovenia. In addition to the right to private property and free economic activity, the Slovenian constitution also contains the right of protection against unfair competition (Art. 47(2) Constitution).

At first, the Yugoslavian law from 8 August 1990 regarding trade which contained regulations to fight unfair competition[1005] was incorporated into Slovenian law. This regulation, however, was considered by scholars to be a regression compared to the

1004. Regarding the development and status of Slovenian law see (in German) Grilc/Podobnik; Straus, GRUR Int. 1994, 700; Krneta, GRUR Int. 1994, 289.

1005. See Puharic, p. 111.

former competition laws from 1974 and 1962. On 25 March 1993, the republic of Slovenia passed its own law to protect competition—the so-called ZVK[1006] —which became the main legal foundation to fight unfair competition in Slovenia. In addition to the ZVK, a consumer protection law (ZVPot)[1007] was enacted in 1998 which in its reform version from 2002 (also) regulates misleading and comparative advertising.

Originally, the ZVK from 1993 aimed to broadly protect the institution of competition under all relevant aspects.[1008] It not only contained anti-trust regulations and unfair competition regulations, but also provisions prohibiting speculations, competition-limiting practices of state-run institutions, dumping and misuse of subsidies. However, in 1999 the antitrust-regulations were drawn out and regulated in a new, specific statute.[1009]

The regulations to fight unfair competition are largely found in Art. 13 ZVK. They are primarily sanctioned by civil law. Article 13(2) ZVK contains a general clause as its most important regulation. It defines unfair competition as whether a company's act to access to the market violates "bones mores" and thereby harms or might harm other entities engaged in market operations.

The general clause in Art. 13 ZVK is supplemented by 14 specific causes of action, among these unfair advertising (false advertising, misleading comparisons, imitating, and discriminating advertising), bribery, false labeling of goods and services, concealment of faults in products and other deceptions of consumers, interference in business relations, unjustified failure to fulfill of contracts, termination of contracts, sham clearance sales, unauthorized use of trade marks, unauthorized use of services of sales representatives of other companies, bonus sales and violation of company secrets.

The relationship between the specific cases and the general clause is not completely clear—legal scholars argue that specific causes of action must also meet the requirements of the general clause.[1010]

The law is applicable to all natural or legal people that do business. The business has to at least happen mainly on the market, which is doubtful for the activities of the independent profession.[1011] The application also requires an act of business activity regarding the access to the market of a company but does not require a competitive relationship.[1012] The law is applicable to all activities that affect Slovenian territory. The purpose of protection is to protect all market participants, competitor and consumer[1013] and—as can be drawn from the context of the former regulation—competition as an institution. These goals of protection are also to be kept in mind when interpreting the term "bones mores" in Art. 13 ZVK.

As to the interpretation of the general clause and the examples of unfair competition, the connection to some of the newer laws is also of importance. In 2001, Slovenia passed the Law regarding industrial property,[1014] although it does not curtail

1006. The Act is available (in English) at <sigov.si/urk/ang/2legal/1basis-2.html (mg.rs.si/english/bodies/index.php)>.
1007. St. 20/1998; reform act 110/2002 of 18.12.2002; in force since 17.1.2003.
1008. See Grilc/Podobnik Straus, GRUR Int. 1994, 700; Krneta, GRUR Int. 1994, 289.
1009. Act No. 56/1999; last amended through Act No. 37/2004; the "Prevention of the Restriction of Competition Act" can be found in English over the website of the Ministry of the Economy (s. fn. 1006).
1010. See Grilc/Podobnik, p. 1099; Straus, GRUR Int. 1994, 700, 708.
1011. Straus, ibd.
1012. See Krneta, GRUR Int. 1994, 294.
1013. Krneta, ibd.
1014. See Aktuelle Informationen, GRUR Int. 2001, 803.

suits based on Art. 13 ZVK.[1015] The new Consumer Protection Act (ZVPot) from 1998 contains regulations on misleading and comparative advertising.

Since Slovenia's unfair competition law is relatively young, there is little established case law.[1016] However, the regulation of Art. 13 ZVK ties in with the former Yugoslavian law, especially the laws of 1962 and 1964 and German and Austrian court decisions are often used for interpretation. Insofar as European Directives have been transposed into Slovakian law, the interpretation by the ECJ also plays an important role in the interpretation of the relevant provisions.

3. Regulation of advertising

a. Misleading advertising

False and misleading advertising is regulated in multiple causes of action: Art. 13(3) sub 1 ZVK prohibits the advertisement, promotion or offering of goods or services using false or deceptive (confusing) data, information or statements. Sub 4 deals with sales using descriptions or data that can lead to a deception regarding origin, method of production, amount, quality or other product properties. Sub 6 prohibits the concealment of product defects or any other means of deception of the consumer. In addition to this, misleading advertising is regulated in Art. 12 b ZVPot which mainly transposes Directive 84/450/EEC. Case law which would lead to a detailed interpretation of these regulations is apparently not available.[1017] It can, however, be assumed that the interpretation follows the established principles developed by the ECJ in respect to Directive 84/450/EEC.

b. Comparative advertising

Art 13(2) sub 2 ZVK prohibits "promotion, advertising or offering of goods or services by stating untrue data or making use of the terms allowing the prestige of another company, its products or services, to be used or allowing the quality of products of another company to be evaluated or undervalued". As of 2000, comparative advertisement is (also) expressly regulated in Art. 12c ZVPot, which closely follows the words of Directive 97/55/EC.[1018] It can be assumed that the interpretation of both provisions is in line with the Directive and the jurisdiction of the ECJ.

c. Other advertising regulations

The regulations in Art. 13(8) and (9) ZVK also include a prohibition of imitation (exploitation of reputation) and of disparaging (defaming) advertising. Under Art. 13(2) sub 3 ZVK it is furthermore prohibited to disparage another company by referring to nationality, race, religion or political orientation. The last sentence in

1015. When IP-law remedies and unfair competitor law overlap, the defendant has the choice, s. Straus, GRUR Int. 1994, 707.
1016. See the (few) decisions cited by Grilc/Podobnik, p. 1011.
1017. See in this book Chapter 3, III.3. Some cases are cited by Grilc/Podobnik, p. 1099.
1018. Grilc/Podobnik, p. 1012; Krneta, GRUR Int. 1994, 294; see also Straus, GRUR Int. 1994, 709.

Art. 13 sub 1 ZVK expressly declares as unfair competition the "promotion, advertising or offering of goods or services ... by the abuse of ill-informed or gullible consumers. This could be interpreted to consider certain factual situations as unfair competition if interests of consumers are violated, even when there is no misleading. According to Art. 15 ZVPot any advertising exploiting the inexperience etc. of children and minors is prohibited. Advertising in the media is regulated in the so-called Zmed; advertisment for tobacco products in the ZOUTI; for cosmetica in the Zkos and for drugs in the ZZMP.[1019]

4. Sales promotion

According to Art. 13 sub 9 ZVK, a company may not advertise clearance sales or price reductions if it could lead to misleading of consumers. Furthermore, sub 13 ZVK prohibits attracting the buyers of goods or users of services by promising or giving gifts, bonuses, etc. if these advantages substantially exceed the value of the goods purchased.

5. Danger of confusion

According to Art. 13(3) sub 10 ZVK, the unjustified use of name, company, trade mark or otherwise business symbol is considered unfair competition if it creates a danger of confusion. In the former Yugoslavian law, this protection was granted relatively broadly. For example, the Supreme Court of Slovenia prohibited naming construction parts by a Slovenian builder LEGO based on a suit by the Danish toy maker.[1020]

6. Disparagement, exploitation of reputation

Defamation of another company (whether true or not) is unfair competition in the sense of Art. 13(3)(4) ZVO if there is a risk of a damage to the reputation (see above, 3f).

7. Slavish imitation

Imitation is not explicitly regulated. However, even if there is no danger of confusion or exploitation of reputation, it can in certain cases be prohibited based on the general clause.[1021]

8. Impediment of competitors

According to Art. 13(3) sub 7 ZVK acts are considered unfair competition if they are intended to terminate business relations of other companies or try to impede or obstruct such relations. The same applies, according to sub 8, for non-fulfillment or termination of contracts with the intention to sign the same or a similar contract with a different company. Sub 12 prohibits the unauthorized use of services of sales

1019. Discussed by Grilc/Podobnik, p. 1012.
1020. GRUR Int. 1977, 204—"Lego" with note Straus.
1021. Straus, GRUR Int. 1994, 700, 709.

representatives of another company. Sub 14 protects trade secrets in cases of illegally obtained knowledge and unauthorized use of confidential information.[1022]

9. Enforcement

Violations against Art. 13 ZVK result in claims for compensation, injunctions, removal and publication of the ruling. Article 26 states that each affected market participant has standing to sue. Violations of the Consumer Protection Act (ZVPot) are predominantly sanctioned through administrative law.

XXIV. SPAIN

Selected Literature: Alonso Espinosa/López Pellicer/Massaguer Fuentes/Reverie Navarro (ed.), *Régimen jurídico general de comercio minorista. Comentarios a la Ley 7/1996, de 15 de enero, de Ordenación de Comercio Minorista, y a la Ley Orgánica 2/1966, de 15 de enero, complementaria de la de Ordenación de Comercio Minorista*, Madrid 1999; Berg, *Das neue spanische Gesetz gegen den unlauteren Wettbewerb von 1991*, 1997; Bueso Guillén/Voigt, *Spain*, in: Micklitz/Keßler (ed.), *Marketing Practices Regulation and Consumer Protection in the EC Member Status and the US*, 2002, p. 301; De Los Santos, *Espagne*, in: *Greffe/Greffe, La publicité et la loi*, 9th ed. 2000, p. 751; Domínguez Pérez, *Nachahmung und ungerechtfertigte Ausnutzung fremder Leistungen im spanischen Recht gegen unlauteren Wettbewerb*, GRUR Int. 2001, 1017; Fischer/Fischer, *Spanisches Handels- und Wirtschaftsrecht*, 2nd ed. 1995; Freyer, *Das neue spanische Gesetz gegen unlauteren Wettbewerb, ZVglRWiss 91 (1992)*, p. 96; Fröhlingsdorf, Das spanische Wettbewerbsrecht, in: Löber/Peuster (ed.), *Aktuelles spanisches Handels- und Wirtschaftsrecht*, 1991, p. 497; Galán Corona, *The Spanish Unfair Competition Act of 10 January 1991*, RIC 173, I. 1994, p. 16; García-Durán/Goizuëta y Besaga/Iranzo Martín/Rodriguez Morullo y Otero/Sáez Septién/Sánchez Suarez/Schwarzt Girón, *La Regulación de comercio Minorista en las Comunidades Autónomas de España*, Madrid 2001; Knothe/Bellido Penadés, *Der einstweilige Rechtsschutz im spanischen Wettbewerbsrecht*, GRUR Int. 1998, 667; Leible, *Bedeutung und Bestimmung der Verkehrsauffassung im spanischen Recht des unlauteren Wettbewerbs*, WRP 1992, p. 1; Lema Devesa, *Der Schutz des Verbrauchers im allgemeinen Werbegesetz Spaniens*, GRUR Int. 1990, 208.; Massaguer Fuentes, *Comentario a la Ley de Competencia Desleal*, Madrid 1999; Otero Lastres, *Das neue spanische Gesetz gegen unlauteren Wettbewerb*, GRUR Int. 1992, 183; Pelau Ramírez, *Descuentos promocionales (Un análisis desde el derecho contra la competencia desleal y la normativa de comercio*, Madrid 1998; Piñar Mañas/Beltrán Sánchez (ed.), *Comentarios a la Ley de Ordenación del Comercio Minorista y a la Ley Orgánica complementaria*, Madrid 1997; Bercovitz Rodríguez-Cano/Leguina Villa (ed.), *Comentarios a las Leyes de Ordenación del Comercio Minorista*, Madrid, 1997; Röhrenbach/Meister, *Dokumentation der "Besonderheiten" des Wettbewerbsrechts in Europa—Spanien*, WRP 1999, 307; *Schiller* v. *Werberecht* in Spanien, in: Schotthöfer (ed.), *Handbuch des Werberechts in den EU-Staaten*, 2nd ed. 1997, p. 113; *Schricker*/v. *Bredow, Recht der Werbung in Europa*, Vol. 2, Spanien, 1990; Schulze, *Das spanische Kartellrecht*, WuW 1991, 993; Tato Plaza, *Das neue System*

1022. Krneta, GRUR Int. 1994, 295.

zur Selbstkontrolle der Werbung in Spanien, GRUR Int. 1999, 853; Vicent Chuliá, *Das spanische Gesetz gegen unlauteren Wettbewerb im Meinungsstreit*, GRUR Int. 1994, 14; Wirth, *Das neue Recht des unlauteren Wettbewerbs in Spanien. Eine Darstellung des Gesetzes 3/1991 Über unlauteren Wettbewerb mit rechtsvergleichenden Bezügen*, 1996; Wirth, *Die Werbeselbstkontrolle in Spanien*, WRP 1993, 94.

1. Sources of law

Ley de competencia desleal (Act Against Unfair Competition) of 10 January 1991 (LCD); Ley General de Publicidad of 11 November 1998 (Advertising Law)

2. Spanish competition law in a nutshell

Spanish unfair competition law ("competencia desleal") is based on several overlapping regulations. The most important regulations on the federal level are found in the

- Law No. 3/1991 against unfair competition (LCD)
- Law No. 34/1988 regarding advertising (Advertising Act)
- Law No. 7/1996 regarding the retail industry (LOCM)

Next to the regulations of the Spanish federal legislature, those of the 17 "Autonomous Regions" must also be considered.

The predominantly civil law sanctioned LCD[1023] was influenced by the German and Swiss Acts against Unfair Competition. It protects all market participants from unfair competition. The action must have a competitive purpose; this is assumed if it is objectively capable for competitive advancement (Art. 2(2) LCD). A competitive relationship is not required (Art. 3(2) LCD). The LCD is dominated by a general clause in Art. 5 forbidding all unfair competitive actions: A behavior is considered "unfair" that (objectively) does not comply with the demands of "good faith".[1024] In connection with the general clause several individual causes of action are regulated: creating of confusions (Art. 6) deception (Art. 7); free gifts, premiums, etc. (Art. 8); denigration (Art. 9); comparison (Art. 10); imitation (Art. 11); exploitation of reputation (Art. 12); violation of trade secrets (Art. 13); procuring breach of contract (Art. 14); violation of other norms (Art. 15); discrimination (Art. 16); and sales at a loss (Art. 17).

The equally civil law sanctioned Advertising Act of 1988[1025] protects business interests, the (collective) interests of consumers, and the interest of the public in the

1023. Act No. 3/1991 from 10.1.1991; amended through Act 1/2001 from 7.1.2001 de Enjuicianiento Civil and through Ley 39/2002 from 28.10.2002 and Ley 14/2003 of November 20, 2004. An overview in Spanish can be found in the leading treatises of Massaguer and Bercovitz; in German in the books by Berg and Wirth and the articles by Wirth, Freyer, Fröhlingsdorf, Leible, Otero Lastres and Schricker.

1024. According to the preamble, "good faith" is different from "honest practices" in that it does not refer to actual practices of certain trade circles. Case law has compared "good faith" to "honorable proper behavior"; it emphasizes the ethical element and the similarity between general and business behavioral requirements, see the decisions referred to by Otero Lastres, GRUR Int. 1995, 186.

1025. Act Nr. 34/1988 from 11.11.1988; in German GRUR Int. 1989, 904. As to the content see the overviews by Lema Devesa, Fuchs, Rauscher.

functioning of the market. Its scope is determined through the term "advertising". Misleading and comparative advertising is regulated, as is other unfair advertising (such as discriminatory, subliminal and denigrating advertising). Article 6(b) Advertising Act contains a kind of limited general clause: An advertisement is unfair when it violates "the norms of propriety and good business practices". Article 8 deals with product-specific regulations respectively the authority to pass such regulations. Advertising contracts are also regulated.

The Act to Regulate the Retail Industry from 1996 (LOCM)[1026] supplements the LCD and the Advertising Act. It legislates the legal framework for all sales of goods at retail stores and regulates seasonal sales, clearance sales, free gifts with sales, and all other sales which through lower prices or better conditions promote sales. A violation of the LOCM is a regulatory offense which is enforced by the "Autonomous Regions".

The "Autonomous Regions" ("Comunidades Autonomas = CA) are entitled to exclusive authority over the area of intrastate trade and consumer protection.[1027] Many of the seventeen autonomous regions have used this legislative authority, with the result that regional limitated regulations exist for nearly every advertising or marketing practice which affects consumer interests.[1028]

The relationship between the various sets of regulation is complicated. As concerns the LCD and the Advertising Act—which protect approximately the same commercial interests[1029] —the Advertising Law is more specialized. Both laws are, however, also applied cumulatively. The regulations in the LOCM, on the other hand, are partly subsidiary to those of the CA.[1030] Which regulation takes precedence in a concrete case is difficult to determine, as there is relatively little case law. In case of doubt, a specific competitive act should be measured under all of the applicable laws (including those of the CA).

Some of the regulations in the LCD (partly in the Advertising Act as well) exhibit some relationship to the laws of intellectual property, especially trademark law.[1031] Other prohibitions, such as sales at a loss, overlap with the Cartel Act of 1989[1032] and the Consumer Protection Act of 1984.[1033] Finally, there is the voluntary self-regulation of business by the "Autocontrol de la Publicidad" with the adjudicative organ "Jurado de la publicite" (CAP).[1034]

1026. See Bueso Guillén/Voigt, p. 312 f.
1027. The Spanish federal government, on the other hand, has the competence for general planning of economic activity.
1028. The regulations of the CA cannot be repeated here in detail; they are discussed in Spanish by Garcias-Duran/Goizuëta y Besaga Iranzo Martin/Rodriguez Morullo y Otero/Sáez Septién/Sánchez Suarez /Schwartz Girón (2001); and (partly) in English by Bueso Guillén/Voigt, p. 315 ff.
1029. Cf. Massaguer, p. 113 ff.
1030. As regards the relationship Advertising Act/LOCM see Tribunale supremo 17.6.2003—"RSDI, Red Digital de servicios integrados", Revista Jurídica de Cataluña 2003, IV.
1031. As to Spanish IP-rights see, for instance Bercovitz, in: Tirant lo Blanck (ed.), 2001; in English "Manual Industrial Property", Vol. 5 (2001); copyright law (in German) Möhring/Schulze/Ulmer/Zweigert, Quellen des Urheberrechts, Vol. 5.
1032. See Folguera Crespo, "Relación entre la Ley de Defensa de la competencia y la Ley de Competencia desleal. Falseamiento de la libre competencia por actos desleales", en "Protección penal, competencial desleal y tribunales de marcas comunitarias", ANDEMA, CGPJ, Madrid.
1033. Ley general para la Defensa de los consumidores, last amended through Act No. 23/2002.
1034. The JAP bases its decisions on the "Codigo de Conducta Publicitaria" from 14.4.1994. See Wirth, WRP 1993, 94, Tato Plaza, GRUR 1998, 85; Tato Plaza, Autoregulacion publicitaria y Código de conducta sobre publicidad en Internet, in: Gómez Segade (ed.).

3. Regulation of advertising

Article 2 Advertising Act defines the term "advertising" similar to Art. 2 of the Directive 84/450/EEC. A certain difference exists insofar as not the final element to promote sales, but the intent to conclude contracts is emphasized.

a. Misleading advertising

Misleading advertising is regulated in various provisions. Article 4 Advertising Act largely corresponds to Directive 84/455/EEC.[1035] A similar but shorter prohibition of misleading advertising can be found in Art. 7 LCD. The regulations of the CA address misleading statements (under the aspect of consumer protection) and often establish informational requirements. Overall, it is a rather confusing system.

It can be assumed that the various regulations are interpreted under approximately the same criteria. Thus, the suitability to mislead is based on the view of the target group.[1036] This view is generally not proven through demographic research but determined according to "judicial life experience" by the courts themselves. Traditionally, Spanish case law uses the benchmark of an average consumer who views advertising skeptically and is not easily deceived.[1037] In more recent decisions, however, courts have referred to more concrete knowledge and abilities.[1038]

Article 7 LCD as well as Art. 4 sent. 2 Advertising Act explicitly regulate misleading through omission. Under Art. 4 Advertising Act, the omission must be "substantial"; it must deal with a fact that is relevant for the purchase in question. The decisive factor is whether the omission causes a danger of misleading.[1039]

Article 4 Advertising Law requires that the misleading statement is relevant, i.e. has an impact on the economic behavior of the addressee. Article 7 LCD speaks of "advantages" to which the misleading statement must refer. The enticing effect is not presumed: The regional court in Barcelona, for example, held that the use of the sign "®" when the mark was not actually legally protected, was not misleading since no competitive advantage could be gained by its use.[1040]

The court can require the advertiser to prove the correctness of factual assertions. If such proof is not offered, the statements can be held to be untrue (Art. 29(b) Advertising Act, Art. 26 LCD).

b. Comparative advertising

Article 6bis Advertising Act contains regulations regarding comparative advertising as of 2002. It is by and large the same as Directive 97/55/EC,[1041] althoughit also defers

1035. Discussed in this book in Chapter 3, III.3.
1036. Cf., for instance Leible, WRP 1992.
1037. See Lema Devesa, 5 ADI (1978, p. 263, 275).
1038. Thus, an advertisement for a computer program as "gratis" was found not objectionable because the specialized addressees should know what was meant, Audiencia Provicial de Navarra 9.7.2002, ADI 2002—"Editorial Aranzadi, SA". On the other hand, an advertisement that seemed to promise a prize but in reality only entered the consumer in a raffle was forbidden as misleading; see also Audiencia Provincial de Asturias 17.6.2002, ADI 2002 (misleading advertising on a poster with a disclaimer in small print).
1039. See Audiencia Provincial Palma de Mallorca 26.3.2003, ADI 2002—"Sanitas" (omission of a nomination in a list of medicins).
1040. Audiencia Provicial de Barcelona, 18.6.1995, RIC 184, 3 1997.
1041. Discussed in this book in Chapter 3, III.4.

to specific legislations for certain product and media. In addition to this, Art. 10 LCD forbids comparisons that are misleading or disparaging or "based on factors that are not similar, relevant or able to be proven".

As regards the interpretation of the requirements for a permitted comparative advertising, earlier case law is still applicable, as the now defunct Art. 6(c) Advertising Act did not contain criteria that significantly differed from the current law.[1042] As before, courts[1043] and self-regulation[1044] determine the ability to identify a certain competitor with consideration of the situation in the relevant market. The standard as to misleading is rather strict: For example, a comparison of orange drinks which showed several other—untested—drinks of the advertiser at the end of the advertisement was held to be misleading.[1045] Comparison of singled out characteristics is not allowed when this could lead to an incorrect interpretation of the end result. In some decisions, the advertiser has had the burden of proof regarding the truth of the factual assertions.[1046] An advertisement for liquid laundry detergent that stated "Problem No. 16 of Powder detergent" was considered disparaging since it gave the impression of a large amount of problems.[1047] Advertising for cars with the slogan "the traditional cuisine is not comparable with the microwave cuisine either" was also considered disparaging, since the products of other manufacturer may not be used as a free ride for one's own advertisement.[1048] The same applies for the untrue suggestion that a competitor is closing shops.[1049]

c. Concealed advertising

Article 3(d) and Art. 7 Advertising Act expressly forbid subliminal advertising. All other forms of camouflage of the commercial character can be regarded as misleading advertising.[1050] According to Art. 11 Advertising Act, all media are required to clearly separate advertising from regular programming, and the advertiser must unmistakably disclose the commercial nature of the advertisement ("principo de autenticidad").

d. Aggressive advertising

Harassing advertising in Spanish law is judged on the basis of the general clauses in Art. 5 LCD and Art. 5 Advertising Act; in extreme cases also Art. 3(a) Advertising Act (injury to human dignity) can apply.[1051] As regards harassing in direct marketing, see under 4 and 5.

1042. See Berg, p. 236.
1043. Cf. for instance, Audiencia Provicial de Alava 22.2.2000—"Guiaraba"; commented by Domínguez Pérez, De nuevo sobre la publicidad comparativa comentario a la sentencia de la AP de Alava de 22.2.2000, ADI 2001, p. 547.
1044. Cf. for instante, JAP 25.6.20002—"Cruz del Sur", ADI 2002; JAP 2.12.1999—"Henkel Iberica".
1045. JAP 6.8.1999—"Don Simón".
1046. See for instance, JAP 23.6.19990—"Henkel".
1047. JAP 8.7.1999—"Wash and go"; as regards the aspect of denigration see also Tribunale Supremo 4.6.2002, ADI 2002—"Elg nou".
1048. JAP 2.12.1999—"BMW Ibérica" (although the identifiably of individual competitors seems questionable).
1049. ATS 4.6.2000.
1050. Cf. for instance, Lema Devesa, p. 210.
1051. See Audiencia Provincial de Santa Cruz de Tenerife 30.4.2001, ADI 2001; JAP 23.2.2000, ADI 2000—"Canon España, S.A"...

e. Product and media specific advertising Prohibitions[1052]

Advertising for foodstuffs is regulated by the Royal Decree 212/1992[1053] which, among other things, forbids advertising with truism and certain superiority claims. Advertising for pharmaceutical products is regulated by the Royal Decree 2730/1981 (from 19 October 1981, current edition from 17 September 1982); the advertising for certain drugs is subject to a preventative control. Advertising of alcoholic beverages with more than 20% alcohol content is generally forbidden in television, and limited in other media; it shall not induce excessive consumption or encourage drinking by minors (Art. 8 (3) No. 5 Advertising Act).[1054] A similar regulation can be found in Art. 8 No. 5 (1) Advertising Act for the advertising of tobacco products, which in addition is completely forbidden in television.[1055] Further advertising regulations exist for cosmetics, automobiles, toys, insurance and financial services, real estate, weapons, etc.[1056]

Of the media specific regulations, the regulations in Act 25/1994 (Broadcasting Act) are of special importance.[1057] This regulation is partially a transposition of the Television Directive and includes detailed requirements as to the content of TV-advertising;.[1058] The use of foreign languages is limited in certain circumstances according to Art. 2, as is advertising for certain products. For the press, the Royal Decree 2198/1976 applies; it regulates among other things that advertisements must be clearly recognizable as such.[1059]

f. Other advertising regulations

Article 3(d) and Art. 7 Advertising Act forbid advertising that violates human dignity or violates constitutional values and rights, especially those that serve to protect children, youth and women.

4. Direct marketing, special sales

Door-to-door sales, sending of unsolicited goods and addressing consumers in public areas are not expressly forbidden at the federal level,[1060] but can fall under the respective general clauses of the LCD and the Advertising Act (see above, No. 2 et seq.),[1061]

1052. *Schricker/v. Bredow*, No. 93 ff.; Bueso Guillén/Voigt, p. 350 ff. (as to alcolhol and tobacco); De Los Santos, p. 754. A special legal basis for potentially dangerous products: Art. 7 Nr. 1 Advertising Act.
1053. For labeling, an additional Decree from 1999 applies.
1054. Cf. Audiencia Provincial de Madrid 4.3.2002, ADI 2002—"Ron Barcardi"; Audiencia Provicial de Cádiz 9.7.2002, ADI 2002—"Así somos".
1055. See Bueso Guillén/Voigt, p. 352.
1056. Cf. for instance, De Los Santos, p. 754.
1057. The current edition of this law is available at <www.aap.es>.
1058. No inducement to violence or anti-social behavior; no exploitation of fear and superstition; no encouragement of abuse, carelessness, aggressive action, or destroying items of cultural significance or nature; no suggesting that one could lose social status due to non-use of a product; etc.
1059. An advertisement that is not otherwise clearly identifiable is to be marked with the word "Publicidad" and a graphic border.
1060. This follows indirectly from Art. 2 of the law from 21.11.1991.
1061. See Bueso Guillén/Voigt, p. 323.

for instance, if the impression is given that the recipient must keep the goods (Art. 42 LOCM) or if a certain degree of harassment is exceeded. In this area, the multiple provisions of the CA should be observed, as they often have stricter regulations.[1062] The same is true for advertising via telephone, fax, and email,[1063] which are not (yet) regulated on the federal level. Pyramid schemes, etc. are largely forbidden under Art. 22(f) LOCM, although to some extent, the broader regulations of the CA may also apply.[1064]

5. Sales promotion[1065]

The announcement and granting of rebates is generally[1066] only unfair if it leads to a deception, especially if it promises an advantage not actually given (Art. 7 LCD) or is an illegal sale below cost (Art. 17 LCD). For the sale of goods by retailers, Art. 27 LOCM contains special requirements,[1067] although they only apply in those CAs which have not enacted their own regulations.

According to Art. 8(1) LCD, the offering of presents for promotional purposes is forbidden when the means in which it is done urges the consumer to purchase the main item. Para. 2 forbids offering advantages or free gifts with a sale when the consumer could thus be misled as to the price of other goods or services of that company. Such an offer is also prohibited if it makes it more difficult to assess the actual value of the offer or to compare it with competing offers; this is assumed when the actual cost of the advantages is more than 15% of the price of the main item. Finally, under para. 3, package deals are considered unfair if they have amenities that have no connection with the reason for contracting and one of the factors of para. 2 exists. Article 32-34 LOCM (give-aways or promotional gifts by retailers) contain further regulations but only apply if the AC do not have any respective laws.[1068]

Promotional games of chance[1069] can be submitted to a special regulation according to the legislative power granted by Art. 8(1) LCD. However, this has not yet occurred. According to Art. 32 LOCM, promotional games of chance have to meet certain transparency requirements. Again, it should be kept in mind that the regulations of the autonomous regions may have stricter requirements.[1070]

The LOCM has detailed requirements for special sales by retailers such as seasonal sales (Art. 24 et seq.), the sale of surplus (Art. 28 et seq.), clearance sales (Art. 30 et seq.), and sales of items at lower prices or under better conditions to encourage sales (Art. 27).

1062. See Bueso Guillén/Voigt, p. 327.
1063. The legislative proposal to transpose Direct 2000/31/EC would institute the "opt-in" solution for electronic communication. This is currently suggested by the self regulation "Código de confianza on line", 2002. For data protection, Ley oriánica de protección de datos de caraácter personel (Act No. 15/1999) applies.
1064. Bueso Guillén/Voigt, p. 330.
1065. As regards sales promotions in general see Palau Ramírez, Descuentos promocionales, Madrid 1998; Alfonso Espinosa; Régimen jurídico general del comerco minorista.
1066. Special provisions exist, e.g. for books.
1067. Cf., in particular, Palau Ramírez, Descuentos promocionales.
1068. Some regulations of the CA can be found at Bueso Guillén/Voigt, p. 333.
1069. As regards the assessment of games of chance under the aspect of misleading see AD Barcelona (fn. 1040).
1070. See Bueso Guillén/Voigt, p. 345.

6. Danger of confusion

According to Art. 6 LCD and Art. 6(b) Advertising Act, any action that is capable of causing confusion as to the activity, the merits or the business establishment of a competitor is considered unfair competition.[1071] The risk of association as to the origin of the good or service is sufficient (Art. 6(2) LCD). The demarcation from the Spanish Trademark Law of 7 December 2001 is seldom discussed in detail; jurisdiction applies Art. 6 LCD parallel to or instead of trademark protection.[1072] The protection of trade names or advertising material is relatively often the issue in such cases.[1073]

7. Disparagement, denigration

Article 6(a) Advertising Act forbids every advertising that "by content or depiction directly or indirectly evokes discrimination, denigration or disparagement of a person, business, product, service or operation". The prohibition of denigration in Art. 9 LCD is narrower; it is limited to false statements (but also encompasses "statements regarding the nationality, the beliefs, the private life or strictly personal circumstances of the affected person").

8. Misappropriation, imitation

Article 12 LCD forbids the unjust exploitation of the reputation. As this section does not require a competitive relationship, it supplements the Spanish Trademark Act, which does not provide protection for such exploitation for dissimilar products or services.[1074] According to Art. 12(2) LCD, the use of third parties trademarks or statements of origins with additions such as "model", "system", or "type" is unfair competition. Protection against exploitation of reputation is also provided for by Art. 6(b) Advertising Act.

Article 11(1) LCD establishes the principle of freedom of imitation in all cases where no property right exists. Pursuant to para. 2 this principle does, however, not apply to imitations that cause a misleading association as to the origin of the product or may result in an unjust exploitation of the reputation or the commercial efforts of another", inasmuch as those risks are not "inevitable".[1075] Persuant to para. 3 the systematic imitation is unfair if it is aimed at obstructing sales and "goes beyond what, in those circumstances, can be seen as natural reaction of the market".[1076]

Spanish case law has until now rather generously granted protection against imitation, also under the aspect of unjust exploitation of another's efforts.[1077] In more

1071. See the decision referred to (in French) in RIC 184, 3.1997, p. 22.
1072. As regards the demarcation between unfair competition protection and trade mark law protection see the legal literature cited in fn. 1031, esp. Domínguez Pérez, *Comentario à la sencentica de TS* v. 18.10.2000—"Capdevila", CCJC 2001, p. 343. See, in particular, Court of Appeals of Barcelona of 7 June 2002 Pentathlon/Decathlon in which the court, after having denied a trademark infringement, applied Art. 6 LCD.
1073. See *Schricker/v. Bredow*; Tribunale Supremo 23.9.2003—"Tejano Pepe".
1074. See Domínguez Pérez, GRUR Int. 2001,1017.
1075. See Domínguez Pérez, GRUR Int. 2201, p. 107 ff.; *Audiencia Provincial de Toledo* v. 8.1.2002, ADI 2002.
1076. Tribunal Supremo v. 17.10.2002—"Modital", CCJC 2003, p. 197.
1077. Cf. Domínguez Pérez, GRUR Int. 2001, 1017.

recent decisions, however, the protection has been limited to cases of clear reproduction. For example, the Spanish Supreme Court has not forbidden the imitation of a label directly after the patent protection for the product expired,[1078] or the imitation of the get-up for a shampoo that did not cause a danger of confusion ("look alike").[1079]

9. Impediment of competitors

The violation of trade secrets is regulated in Art. 13 LCD; inducement of breach of contract in Art. 14 LCD. Inducement to a normal end of contractual relationship or the exploitation of the breach of contract by a third party is only unfair in exceptional situations, such as when the goal is to gain access to trade secrets, to mislead, or to cause market displacement.[1080]

10. Breach of law

Under Art. 15 LCD, the use of a significant competitive advantage in the market is considered unfair competition if it is achieved through violation of a regulation outside the LCD.[1081] Without such a competitive advantage, the unfairness depends on whether the legal norm in question "had the purpose of regulating competition". Further, an advertisement which violates product and service specific regulations (also those of the AC) is considered "unfair" under Art. 3(e) Advertising Act. Art 15(3) LCD expressly forbids the hiring of foreigners without working permission.

11. Enforcement

The LCD provides for cease-and-desist-orders, abolition, adjustment, damages, publication of judgments and restitution of unjust enrichment (Art. 18 LCD). [1082] Persons who take part in the market and whose commercial interests are harmed or are in danger of being harmed have standing to sue, including individual consumers and consumer groups (Art. 20 LCD). Generally anyone is responsible who took part in the act of unfair competition;[1083] although for employees who were acting in the scope of their employment, the suit should be brought against the employer.

The Advertising Act also provides for civil law sanctions, namely for injunctive relief, and/or correction of the advertising in questions. All persons who have a legal interest, as well as certain administrative organs and consumer groups, have standing to sue. A warning notice must be given before a suit is brought (Art. 26). In appropriate cases, the civil courts can order a reversal of the burden of proof.

1078. Tribunal Supremo 17.7.1997—"Esselte Busines System", abstract in RIC 190, 3.1999; p. 24; see also the note of Domínguez Pérez in RIC 1998, p. 7707.

1079. Tribunal Supremo 5.6.1997; RIC 190, 3.1999, p. 24 f.

1080. For instance, the distribution through a former employee of an American company (of similar products, through the same methods of sales and with similar advertisements) was held to be unfair; Audiencia Provincal de Barcelona 14.4.1995, see RIC.

1081. See Berg, p. 292. Violation of regulations for construction work is not sufficient; see Audiencia Provincal 1.9.1995, RIC 184, 3.1997, p. 23.

1082. See Masarary Marti/Schmid, p. 770; as to the preliminary proceedings cf. Knothe/Penadés, GRUR Int. 1998, 667.

1083. See Audiencia Provincial de Guadalajara 18.1.2002, ADI 2002:

XXV. SWEDEN

Selected Literature: Bakardjieva Engelbrekt, *Fair Trading Law in Flux? National Legacies, Institutional Choice and the Process of Europeanisation*, 2003; Bernitz, *Das neue schwedische Marktgesetz—insbesondere der Schutz von Gewerbetreibenden gegen Nachahmung*, GRUR Int. 1996, 433; Bernitz, *Marknadsföringslagen*, 1997; Bernitz, *The EC directive on comparative advertising and its implementation in the Nordic Countries. especially in relation to intellectual property, 42 Scandinavian Studies in Law*, 2002, p. 11; Fischler/Vogel, *Schwedisches Handels- und Wirtschaftsrecht mit Verfahrensrecht*, 3rd ed. 1978, Keßler/Edling, Sweden, in: Micklitz/Keßler (ed.); *Marketing Practices Regulation and Consumer Protection in the EC Member States and the US*, 2002, p. 285; Keyßner, *Täuschung durch Unterlassen—Informationspflichten in der Werbung*, 1986; Kur, *Das Recht des unlauteren Wettbewerbs in Finnland, Norwegen und Schweden*, GRUR Int. 1996, 38; *Kur*, Schweden, in: Schricker (ed.), *Recht der Werbung in Europa*, 1995; Levin, *Werbung und Informationsfreiheit—die Praxis des schwedischen Marktgerichts*, GRUR Int. 1987, 207; Nordell, *Marknadsrätten. En Introduktion*, 2nd ed. 2003; Nordell, *Marknadsrättens goodwillskydde*, 2003; Plogell, Schweden, in: Schotthöfer (ed.), *Handbuch des Werberechts in den EU-Staaten*, 2nd ed. 1997, p. 527; Svensson/Stendlund/Brink/Sträm, *Praktisk marknadsrätt*, 7th ed. 2002; Treis, *Recht des unlauteren Wettbewerbs und Marktvertriebsrecht in Schweden*, 1991.

1. Sources of law

Marknadsforingslag (Marketing Practices Act) of 27 April 1995 (MFG).

2. Swedish unfair competition law in a nutshell

The basic foundation of Swedish unfair competition law can be found in the Marketing Practices Act ("marknadsforingslag = MFG") of 27 April 1995.[1084] As the name indicates, the MFG deals not only with acts of competition but quite generally with all commercial activities (§ 2 MFG). According to § 3 MFG, marketing means "advertising and other measures within the scope of a commercial activity intended to promote sales and availability of products". The term "products" also includes services. Actions without a commercial purpose are not considered marketing practices. The MFG is thus not applicable to, for instance, articles in the press, which is also due to the strong constitutional protection of free speech and press in the Swedish law.[1085] Apart from this, the scope of application is very broad; the MFG requires neither a competitive relationship nor a competitive act, but affects all kinds of commercial activity, including that of professionals.

1084. SFS 1995:450. The MFG was reformed in 1996, 1999, 200, 2002. The current version is available (in Swedish) at the website of the consumer department <www.konsumentverket.se/Mallar/sv/artikel.asp?IngCategoryld=490>; in German in GRUR Int. 1997, 37. For an extensive overview regarding the MFG in Swedish see the treatises of Bernitz and Svensson/Stedlund/Brink/Ström; in German Kur in: Recht der Werbung in Europa (1995) and Treis (1991) (both refer to the former MFG 1975, but are still relevant); in English Bakardijieva Engelbrek and Kessler/Edling.

1085. The Market Court has, for example, refused the application of the MFG in regards to gender discrimination and shocking advertising, see under 3f. Regarding influence of constitutional rights to legal protection, Levin, GRUR Int. 1987, 207.

Of great importance in the MFG is the general clause. § 4 MFG demands two basic requirements for all marketing practices:

- The marketing must conform to good marketing practices and also in other respects be fair to consumers and businesses.
- The business owner must provide all information that is of particular importance from the consumer perspective.

To interpret these two requirements, the principles of the ICC-Code,[1086] the preparation work for the MFG[1087] and -most of all—the decisions of the Market Court[1088] and the guidelines of the Consumer Ombudsman[1089] are taken into account. The general clause (as well as all other provisions of the MFG) is interpreted in "ethical terms"; especially the social responsibility of business in regards to the consumer is emphasized.

The general clause is supplemented by a number of individual causes of action: Misleading advertising (§ 6), misleading packaging sizes (§ 7), misleading imitation of products (§ 8), comparative advertising (§ 8a) special sales (§§ 9-11), sending of unrequested goods (§ 12), special offers (§ 13), advertising with guarantees (§ 13a), and unsolicited advertising via faxes and emails (§ 13b).

Although the MFG from 1995 unmistakably emphasizes the protection of consumers, it is—unlike its predecessor from 1975—not solely a consumer protection law. As the protective purpose clause in § 1 MFG indicates, the MFG serves the interests of the consumer and business equally.[1090]

The MFG is predominantly sanctioned by civil law. However, also the Consumer Ombudsman—next to individual companies—is of special importance when it comes to enforcement of the MFG. He has substantial and wide-reaching authority (see under 10) and often deals with complaints in an informal, outside of court hearing.

The MFG is supplemented by a number of other laws, e.g. the Price Information Act from 1991, the Foodstuff Act of 1971, the Pharmaceutical Products Act of 1992, the Tobacco Act of 1993, the Consumer Credit Act of 1992, the Consumer Insurance Act of 1980 and the Product Safety Act of 1988.[1091] For some regulations in the MFG, the principles of intellectual property law are of special interest.[1092] For others, anti-trust considerations can indirectly play a role. [1093]

1086. Available at www.icc.wbo.org.
1087. For example, the commissary report SOU 1993:59 and the motives to the governmental draft (prop 1994/95:123), constitute an important foundation for interpretation.
1088. The jurisdiction of the Market Court is available on the website of the court since 2000: <www.marknadsdomstolen.se>.
1089. The Consumer Ombudsman heads the Consumer Department. The guidelines etc. of the Consumer Department are available at <www.konsumentverket.se/mallar/ehandel/bestallrsultat.asp? IngCategoryID=416&GroupID=12&/ordrby=a&odrsort=desc&noAction=?IngCategoryld=777>.
1090. The MFG of 1975 was criticized for being too focused on consumer protection; see Kur, No. 43 and Treis.
1091. These laws are available at the website of the Consumer Departement (see fn. 1089).
1092. An overview regarding Swedish law of industrial property can be found (in English) in the looseleaf-collection "Manual Industrial Property", volume 5 (1995); in Swedish in Koktevedgaard/Levin, Lärebok i Immaterialrätt, 7th ed. 2002 and Bernitz/Karnell/Pehrson/Sandgren, Immaterialrätt, 7th ed. 2001; Wessman, Varumärkeskonflikter, 2002.
1093. As to the Swedish anti-trust law, see for instance, Benitz, Den svenska konkurrenslagen, 1996. The official explanation SOU 1993:59, p. 198 stresses that the interpretation of the MFG shall not lead to a restriction of competition.

Overall, the Swedish unfair competition law is distinguished by its high standard of protection for all market participants.

3. Regulation of advertising

a. Misleading advertising

Misleading advertisement is mainly regulated in § 6 MFG. In addition to this, there are a number of causes of action that deal with specific misleading acts, e.g. misleading packaging sizes, § 7 MFG, misleading imitation, § 8 MFG, bankruptcy sales, § 9 MFG, clearance sales and other sales, §§ 10, 11 MFG. Furthermore, the prohibition of misleading indications has to be seen in connection with the suppliers' duties to inform in § 4(2) MFG. The non-binding guidelines of the Consumer Ombudsman (KOVFS 192:91) regarding price advertising are to also of importance.[1094]

According to § 6 MFG, misleading "assertion and depiction" in regards to one's own company or another company are prohibited. When determining the ability to mislead, Swedish jurisdiction pays special attention to the perception of the target group, the kind of product and the particular sales situation. The more sensitive the target group (e.g. adolescents, sick people), the more important the product is for that group (for instance, products relevant to the health, safety, environment), and the less the means of acquiring invites an intense involvement with the advertising (everyday products, distribution in grocery stores, etc.), the higher the requirements in terms of truth, clarity and unambiguousness of the advertisement are.

The jurisdiction in general acts on the assumption of a not too observant market participant who relies especially on headlines and other eye-catching elements.[1095] Even experts are not expected to study thoroughly a longer text in order to get a correct overall impression.[1096] Disclaimer in small print, for example on the packaging, are generally not seen as sufficient to counterbalance an otherwise misleading overall impression[1097] and "exaggerations", for instance superiority claims, are rarely treated as harmless puffing.[1098] Even though recent decisions seem to apply a less strict standard,[1099] Swedish law is especially strict in regards to misleading advertising.[1100]

The prohibition of misleading also encompasses misleading by omission. However, since this aspect can also be subsumed under the broader duties to inform in

1094. See fn. 1089.
1095. See, for instance, Market Court 31.10.2000, MD 2000; 25—"Hästens Sängar". In this case, the danger of misleading was denied because the potential purchaser of the product (mattress) were more likely to observe the details of the advertisement. As to other jurisdiction see MD 1975:20—"Philips".
1096. Market Court MD 1977:8, p. 432—"Expressen".
1097. A small print notice of the Swedish origin on a beer can that otherwise gave the impression of an English product was not considered sufficient; Market Court GRUR Int. 1983, 211—"Louis Light".
1098. This applies even for advertising slogans like "sensational" (MD 1975:24—"T J Vaba"), "hypereffektiv" (MD 1975:7—"Import-Export AB"); "guaranteed satisfaction" because the consumer considers it a promise of a special warranty (MD 2090:32 "Axel Optik"); different MD 19989:28—"Statens Infandraverk".
1099. C.f. MD 2003:3—"Ryanair". Expressions like "selected flights" and "the offer has certain limitations" in conjunction with advertising for cheap flights was considered sufficient for the "average intelligent consumer" to avoid misleading regarding the low price of the special offer.
1100. This is not seen as a contradiction to the benchmark used by the ECJ; so the Market Court in the Expressen-decision (fn. 13).

§ 4(2) MFG (see under 4), an exact demarcation between positive actions and omissions appears superfluous.

Misleading information must be capable of affecting the commercial behavior of a substantial part of the target group.[1101] In practice, however, this aspect is seldom expounded upon; the Consumer Ombudsman and Market Court determine the danger of misleading by their own judgment. Representative surveys are rare.

The advertiser has a special duty to the ombudsman to substantiate all information, § 34 MFG, and generally bears the burden of proof for all factual claims.[1102]

b. Comparative advertising

Although "correct" comparative advertising has been traditionally permitted under Swedish law,[1103] the Swedish legislature has included a special regulation on comparison in § 8 a MFG. It largely corresponds to Directive 97/55/EC but emphasizes that the main principles of the MFG (esp. "good marketing practice", "duty to inform") remain untouched. For application of § 8a MFG, the identifiably of one or more competitors suffices[1104] which is assumed, if the comparison concerns competing products. Comparisons as to systems or procedures are not included, but are judged according to similar criteria.[1105]

Swedish law judges comparative advertising largely on the basis of its truthfulness and correctness. Even though comparisons do not have to be representative, it must be clearly disclosed that certain aspects were singled out; furthermore the general impression may not be "skewed". The advertiser making the comparison has the burden of proof for all factual assertions. Exaggerating conclusions as to the superiority of the own product are not allowed. Disparaging,[1106] mocking statements or statements exploiting the competitor's reputation are already against the principle of "good marketing practice".[1107]

Price comparisons are only permitted if the prices are current and the advertised price is not a bargain or special price (and is being compared to the regular price of the competitor).[1108] Additionally, in order to prevent misleading overall impressions, sufficient information must be provided.[1109]

1101. See Kur, No. 71.

1102. For example, the Market Court (MD 1994:15—"Novaglass") held that claims like "absolutely leak-proof" and "the best grades for leak-proof material in the market" (regarding roofing) were misleading, because the advertiser could not prove the truth of the statements.

1103. See Bernitz, in: 42 Scandinavian Studies in Law, 2002, p. 11.

1104. Cf. MD 1996:98—"Pagema". A felt tip pen of the brand "Stanford Magnum 44" was compared to "a well-known pen on the market". The Market Court held this to be a comparison in the sense of § 8a MFG; it was prohibited because the claims of superiority could not be proven.

1105. MD 2002:20—"Champagne". The slogan "Yogurt with champagne flavor" was not considered comparative advertising according to § 8a MFL, but was nonetheless prohibited on the basis of the general clause because of unauthorized exploitation of reputation.

1106. MD 2003:29—"Motor AB". A criticizing comparison between taking a commuter train and driving a car was considered unnecessarily disparaging according to the general clause of § 4(1) MFL and § 8a MFL.

1107. MD 2003:33—"Ryanair"; MD 2003: 32—"Axet Optik".

1108. MD 2003:33 "Ryanair". The airline "Ryanair" was prohibited from comparing prices without stating clearly that the price comparisons do not refer to the lowest fares of the competing airlines.

1109. See the decisions in the footnote above.

c. Concealed advertising

According to § 5 MFG any kind of business behavior (which is serving a commercial purpose[1110]) must clearly be recognizable as such so that it leaves no doubt about its commercial character. For specific kinds of media more detailed reputation exists, see under 3f. For all cases of advertising and marketing, the general clause of § 4 MFG applies[1111] since the concealment of the commercial character is always against "good marketing practices".

d. Harassing, intrusive advertising

The harassment of consumers for marketing purposes is considered a violation of the general clause of § 4 MFG.[1112] In practice, this cause of action generally appears in conjunction with direct marketing. (see under 5)

e. Advertising regulations for specific products and media

For food[1113] and pharmaceutical products[1114] as well as health products, detailed advertising regulations exist. According to the Alcohol Act,[1115] advertising for alcohol in radio and television is prohibited; in print media, it is prohibited for beverages with an alcohol content over 15%.[1116] Advertising for tobacco products is prohibited outside the place of purchase according to the Tobacco Act.[1117] These prohibitions of alcohol and tobacco products also apply to the advertisement of other products in case of a suspected circumvention.[1118]

1110. The MFG is not applicable to presentations and statements that serve mainly non-commercial purposes. Since there is a strong emphasis on the freedom of speech in the media, only presentations with a clear commercial character are judged according to the MFG; cf., e.g. Market Court; MD 1987:27—"Radoninstitutet"; Kur, No. 192.
1111. Kessler/Edling, p. 288; as to product placement cf. e.g. MD 1992:19—"Hempel Färg" and Nordell, Marknadsföringens Öppenskrav—reklamidentifiering och sändarangivelse, SvJT 1999, p. 846 ff.
1112. See Kur, No. 175.
1113. See Kur, No. 336; the regulations can be found in the annex.
1114. See Kur, No. 358; the regulations can be found in the annex.
1115. Alcohol was regulated in the Alcohol Distribution Act (1978:763) until 1.1.2000. This law was annulled and the regulations were integrated into the "Alcohol Act" (SFS 19894:1738) as chapter 4 §§ 8-13; see Kessler/Edling, p. 297.
1116. According to the old version of the Alcohol Act, advertising in the print media was prohibited for beverages with alcohol content over 3.5% (and therefore only permitted at the "point of sale"). As a consequence of the ECJ decision in the "Gourmet" case (see in this book in Chapter 2.II. and the Swedish decision MD 2003:5—Gourmet II) the prohibition of advertising in print media was limited to beverages with an alcohol content over 15%. (see § 13 Alcohol Act, changed SFS 2003:166) Any type of advertising for alcoholic beverages, even those with lower alcohol content, is subject to strict requirements, and should comply with the principle of abstinence. Guidelines of the consumer department also apply; they describe the legal obligations in more detail. For example, outdoor advertising is prohibited. See Keßler/Edling, p. 297.
1117. Tobacco Act 1993:581; see Keßler/Edling, p. 286, 297; Kur, No. 413 ff.
1118. MD 180:18—"Grant's Scotch Whisky" (labeling of whisky glasses with whisky brand);on the other hand, the movie theatre advertisement for "Camel Adventure Tours", MG 1989:10 = GRUR Int. 1990, S. 479—"Camel Adventure Tour" was allowed (because of constitutional reasons), see Kur, GRUR Int. 1990, 442.

Advertising in the press is not regulated through special laws.[1119] Special regulation, however, exists for advertising in broadcasting.[1120] It emphasizes (in addition to aspects transposed from the directive for television[1121]) the protection of children and minors: a general prohibition of advertising targeting children under 12 years of age in conjunction with children's programming exists. As shown by the ECJ in the "de Agostini-case",[1122] this rule does not apply to advertising broadcasted from another EC-country into Sweden (even in the Swedish language) which meets the lower requirements of the country of origin.

The E-commerce Directive was transposed in the Act regarding Electronic Business and other Services of the Information Society (SFS 2002:562).[1123] The guidelines of the "Nordic Ombudsmen on E-Commerce" that contain extensive advertising regulations, should also be heeded.[1124]

f. Other advertising regulations

As mentioned earlier (see above, 2), Swedish law emphasizes the "social responsibility" for any kind of marketing. Exploitation of feelings of fear or superstition, depictions of violence, depictions that are questionable regarding safety and health issues, and generally aggressive acts of marketing are regarded as being against good marketing practices. The following, for example, were prohibited:

- Advertising for a "survival kit" in conjunction with the turn of the millennium[1125] and the television advertising of an insurance using people that were upset about their public pension funds.[1126]
- Advertising for shoes that created the impression that somebody was stepping on a human face.[1127]
- Television advertising (Teleshopping) in which the time limit for the offer was constantly (and in an unclear manner) lowered.[1128]

Special restraint is required for advertising addressing children and minors[1129] (under 16 years of age). For example, an advertisement involving a cartoon of a

1119. But see under No. 18. In cases involving the press, the question of whether the publisher or journalist is a proper defendant can be of importance; see Kur, No. 251.
1120. See Kur, annex and No. 274.
1121. Discussed in this book in Chapter 3, IV.5.
1122. Discussed in this book in Chapter 3, IV.9., see also MD 2000:4—"De Agostini".
1123. The Act transposes in §§ 8 and 9 the transparency requirements from the EC Directive which are considered a more detailed explanation of "good marketing practices" in the meaning of the general clause in § 4(2) MFL. Violations are therefore to be judged by means of the MFL (see § 155 SFSS 2002:562). Concerning the regulations of rebates and premiums in the E-commerce Directive, § 13 MFL (see under 6) is considered to sufficiently meet these requirements.
1124. The "Position Statement of the Nordic consumer Ombudsmen on e-commerce and Marketing on the internet" from 2000 is available in English from the Website of the Danish Consumer Ombudsman: <www.forbrugerstyrelsen.dk>.
1125. Market Court MD 200:8—"Bodion".
1126. Market Court MD 2001:17—"Wasa Livs Försäkringar".
1127. Market Court MD 1996:7 -."Unit".
1128. Market Court MD 2000:4—"TV-Shop".
1129. Market Court MD 1983:16—"Skanidinavisk Press Svenska försäljnings AB"; see also 1997:4, "Egmont Serieförlaget Ab"; MD 1999:26—"Svensk-norsk Idéköp" (prohibition of marketing directed towards children).

skateboarder not wearing a helmet was prohibited.[1130] However, due to constitutional issues, advertising that discriminates on the basis of gender and shocking advertising are not subsumed under the general clause,[1131] but are dealt with by the Council for Market Ethics (MER).

4. Information duties

Independent of misleading, § 4(2) MFG states the obligation to provide the consumer with all information that are "of particular interest"[1132] to him. In case of a violation, sanctions can be applied according to §§ 15, 16 MFG to require the information be provided in the advertising, on the goods themselves, at the "point of sale", or when requested.

What information is of "particular interest" mainly depends on the kind of product or service. Statutory information requirements are to be observed in any case[1133] as well as the guidelines of the Consumer Department[1134] (although the latter are in theory not binding).

5. Direct marketing, special methods of advertising

The general clause of § 4 MFG and its interpretation as "social responsibility" also apply to all kinds of direct marketing[1135] (see above, No. 3) Consequently, the Market Court has prohibited any direct marketing targeting youth (below 16 years of age)[1136] and any direct marketing for potentially harmful products (such as tobacco products, alcohol, and pharmaceutical products). Sending unrequested goods is prohibited according to § 12 MFG if the recipient is tricked into believing that there is an obligation to pay. The same applies to sending invoices and the like (§ 12(2)).[1137]

According to § 12a MFG (but also according to the general clause of § 4 MFG) unsolicited advertising via fax and telephone advertising using automated call systems are prohibited ("opt-in"). In all other cases the "opt-out" solution applies. Provided that telephone calls are permitted at all, the advertiser must reveal the commercial purpose immediately and may not harass the consumer under any circumstances. According to § 3(3) MFG, the "opt-out"-rule also applies to unsolicited e-mail advertising.[1138]

1130. Market Court MD 1979:24—"Don George".
1131. See Kur, No. 208; and Kur, WRP 1995, 789, Arn, La publicité choquante, 2001.
1132. As regards the information duties see Keyßner; and also Kur, No. 114.
1133. See the laws named above, 2; and Kur, No. 130.
1134. See fn. 1124.
1135. For example, the sending of advertising material to pregnant women and parents of children under 6 months of age was forbidden because it would have reached people whose children had died; Market Court MD 1988:3—"Bljölagret Nilsson".
1136. Market Court MD 1083:16—"Skandinavisk Press Svenska Försälinnings AB"; MD 1997:4—"Egmont Serieförlaget AB"; MD 1999:26—"Svens-norsk Idéköp".
1137. § 12 is only applicable if there is no legal payment obligation but the marketing intends to create such an incorrect impression. The regulation is not intended to transpose the directive regarding distance contracts.
1138. See Keßler/Edling, p. 291. The information duties of the service provider are regulated in the law regarding electronic marketing (see above, 3e). At least indirectly, the guidelines of the Nordic Consumer Ombudsmen apply.

The sending of advertising material via mail or by dropping it off directly is permitted, as long as the recipient does not object ("opt-out"). The commercial purpose must be recognizable already from the outside.[1139] Door-to-door sales are permitted in general, but must meet the requirements of the law regarding door-to-door sales.[1140] Pyramid schemes are normally considered as contradictory to "good marketing practices" in the sense of the general clause.[1141]

6. Sales promotion

Swedish law does not contain a general prohibition of premiums, promotional gifts or rebates;[1142] restrictions[1143] exist only for certain products (e.g. pharmaceutical products, alcohol, tobacco). However, all "special offers" must meet the information duties of § 13 MFG. The conditions, the quality, the value, and the time frame always have to be provided; for instance, the consumer must be capable of estimating the value of a premium.[1144]

Rebates are permitted, and are unlimited in terms of amount; sales at a loss are not prohibited. However, price reductions must be in accordance with the regulations for misleading advertising, which are especially strict in this respect, see above 3a.

Promotional games based on chance require state approval if they are regarded as "lottery", and are generally not approved.[1145] Promotional games that do not depend on luck, however, seem to be permitted even when they are linked to a purchase.[1146]

Special sales are not prohibited, but their presentation to the public must meet certain requirements. According to § 9 MFG, "bankruptcy sales" must be of products from actual bankruptcy assets. The term "clearance sale" (or "going out of business sale") is only permitted if it is of the entire stock or a very specific part of it, the time frame is limited and the prices are substantially lower than the normal prices. According to § 11 MFG, the term "seasonal sale" may only be used if the sale refers to the usual assortment of products of the business (and the prices are substantially lower than normal prices).

7. Disparagement, exploitation of reputation

False disparaging statements are prohibited already under § 6 MFG. The advertiser has the burden of proof, which results in a prohibition of all statements that can not be proven true. Even true statements can be against "good marketing practices"

1139. Kur, No. 185.
1140. See Keßler/Edling, p. 292.
1141. MD 1973:3—"Holiday Magic". As the Market Court pointed out inexperienced private people do not see through the purpose of such schemes. Permitted are, however, so-called "home-parties" if the purpose is clearly disclosed; Keßler/Edling, p. 293.
1142. The strict limitations of the MFL from 1975 were replaced by duties to inform; see Bodewig/Henning-Bodewig, WRP 2000, 1361.
1143. Bodewig/Henning-Bodewig, ibd.
1144. Market Court MD 2000:7—"Super Personal Computer Trading" (A special offer for internet users was prohibited because the description of the costs involved were not detailed enough); MD 1998:7—"Fritjdresor AB" (insufficient information regarding time frame and other limitations of a rebate offer; imposition of a penalty for market disturbance the market); MD 1997:18—"Spiesresor".
1145. Kur, GRUR Int. 1996, 48; Keßler/Edling, 295.
1146. Kessler/Edling, p. 295 (with reference to MD 1997:18—"Spiesresor"); different Kur, GRUR Int. 1996, 48.

(§ 4 MFG) i.e. if they appear unnecessarily aggressive or mocking. In case of comparative advertising, § 8a MFG applies.[1147]

The legal protection against exploitation of reputation used to be granted only reluctantly.[1148] In recent decisions, however, it is recognized that any exploitation of reputation (even without risk of confusion) is against "good market practices".[1149]

The protection against exploitation of reputation and disparagement in accordance with the MFG overlaps sometimes with trademark protection, which is also granted outside of the area of similarity.[1150] Both claims can be made in parallel suits because they are based on different premises (although not in the same procedure, see under 10).

8. Misappropriation, imitation

§ 8 MFG contains a prohibition of "misleading imitations of products"[1151] (which applies also to services, § 2 MFG). The imitated product has to have certain distinctive features, must be well established in the market and the imitation must involve a danger of confusion.

A product is considered "distinctive" if it has a certain amount of originality and—as is explicitly required by § 8 sent. 2 MFG—does not deal with a shape that primarily serves at making the product "functional".[1152] In general, Swedish courts are reluctant to grant protection merely based on the similarity in shape, while in all other cases (as long as it is not an everyday product) protection is granted rather generously. The degree of a required product recognition is hardly ever discussed; however, it is lower than the trade mark requirement of secondary meaning. It is considered sufficient that the imitated product has a certain distinctiveness, so that it can be related to a specific company. Danger of confusion is determined on the assumption of a rather not too observant consumer who is mainly influenced by a general impression.

The parasitic exploitation of the commercial achievement of another party (without danger of confusion) or systematic imitation can, at least in theory, be subsumed

1147. Concerning the aspect of disparagement, Swedish jurisdiction is rather strict, irrespective of the provision the claim is based on; see the decisions cited by Kur, GRUR Int. 1996, 46, especially Market Court MD 1987:11—"Armani" as well as "Boss" (fn. 1149).

1148. Kur, GRUR Int. 1996, 46.

1149. MD 1993:9—"Boss". A life insurance company advertised for an insurance called "Boss" with a graphically similar slogan as that of the clothing company "Boss" and a picture of a dog dressed in an elegant suit. The Market Court ruled that this exploitation of reputation violated "good marketing practice". (an unnecessary disparagement, however, was denied.). The Market Court has decided an increasing number of cases based on the regulations regarding exploitation of reputation; see, for instance, Market Court MD 2003:3—"Hästens IV"; MD 2002: 33—"Hästens III"; MD 2002:28—"Santa Maria AB"; MD 1999:21—"Robinson"; MD 1996:3—"Galiano"; MD 2001:14—"Svenska Spei". As to geographic origin see the "Champagner"-decision in fn. 1105.

1150. Supreme Court NJA 1995, p. 635—"Galliano I", see also Market Court 1996:3—"Galliano II" (GRUR Int. 1997, 1013 with note Wessman).

1151. See esp. Bernitz, GRUR Int. 1996, 433; Kur, GRUR Int. 1996, 46; furthermore Kur, in: Schricker/Stauder (ed.), Handbuch des Ausstattungsrechts, 1986, p. 590 ff.

1152. Case law is not always on this point. For instance, a similar combination of colors (as the "Knorr"—packaging) was prohibited; not, however, the copying of multiple elements of a marketing concept from another competitor (MD 1993:26—"Hemglass")

under the general clause of § 4 MFG. In practice, such claims are rarely successful.[1153] However, if the imitation is caused by disclosure of company secrets or an unauthorized use of confidential information, it could be prohibited in accordance with the Law regarding Protection of Company Secrets of 1990.[1154]

9. Breach of the law

The violation of regulations outside of the MFG that aim to protect consumers or business, is considered a violation of the general clause of § 4 MFG.

10. Enforcement

The MFG contains a wide choice of sanctions.[1155] Its most important sanction is the prohibition of the objectionable business practice (§ 14 MFG). This is supplemented by the option to impose duties to inform (§§ 15, 16 MFG), the prohibition of unfit products (§§ 17, 18 MFG) and the order to remove misleading descriptions (§ 31 et seq. MFG).[1156] In case of reckless violations against §§ 5-13 MFG—but *not* the general clause of § 4 MFG—compensation can be claimed or the business owner can be forced to pay a "market disturbance penalty fee" (§§ 22-28 MFG).[1157] Individual consumers are also entitled to compensation claims which could now be more important in practice because of the new Act on Class Actions. (SF 2000:599)

Business owners and their associations, consumers or employees as well as the Consumer Ombudsman have standing to sue for injunctions. The Consumer Ombudsman can (in less serious cases) also render a cease and desist order which becomes official through recognition by the affected party. There are extensive duties to inform to the Consumer Ombudsman. (§§ 34-37 MFG)

The city court of Stockholm has jurisdiction for claims for compensation and market disturbance penalty fees based on the MFG; the appeals court is the Market Court. For cease-and desist orders, the Market Court has jurisdiction at the first and last instance (§§ 38 et seq., 43 MFG). Consolidation or joinder with suits based on other laws, such as protection of intellectual property, is not possible, § 53 MFG.

1153. See MD 2003:22—"Fazer" and MD 2003:7—"Digestivekex". (Judgment due to misleading imitation of packaging of melba toast with the mark "Finncrisp" that was similar to the packaging of a well-known kind of shortbread).
1154. Bernitz, GRUR Int. 1990, 441.
1155. See MD 2002:15—"STOP I" and MD 2002:16—"STOP II".
1156. See Kur No. 446; Dahlbeck/Koch, p. 758.
1157. S. the decisions cited in fn. 1144. The fee is paid to the State and ranges from 5.000 to 5 Mio. Schwedish Kronen.

INTERNATIONAL COMPETITION LAW SERIES

1. Ignacio De León, *Latin American Competition Law and Policy: A Policy in Search of Identity* (2001)
(ISBN 90-411-1542-0)

2. Wim Dejonghe and Wouter Van de Voorde (Eds.), *M & A in Belgium* (2001)
(ISBN 90-411-1594-3)

3. Yang-Ching Chao, Gee San, Changfa Lo, Jiming Ho (Eds.), *International and Comparative Competition Law and Policies* (2001)
(ISBN 90-411-1643-5)

4. Martin Mendelsohn and Stephen Rose, *Guide to the EC Block Exemption for Vertical Agreements* (2002)
(ISBN 90-411-9813-X)

5. Clifford A. Jones and Mitsuo Matsushita (Eds.), *Competition Policy in the Global Trading System* (2002)
(ISBN 90-411-1758-X)

6. Christian Koenig, Andreas Bartosch, Jens-Daniel Braun (Eds.), *EC Competition and Telecommunications Law* (2002)
(ISBN 90-411-1814-4)

7. Jürgen Basedow (Ed.), *Limits and Control of Competition with a View to International Harmonization* (2002)
(ISBN 90-411-1967-1)

8. Maureen Brunt, *Economic Essays on Australian and New Zealand Competition Law* (2003)
(ISBN 90-411-1991-4)

9. Ky P. Ewing, Jr., *Competition Rules for the 21st Century: Principles from America's Experience* (2003)
(ISBN 90-411-2006-8)

10. Joseph Wilson, *Globalization and the Limits of National Merger Control Laws* (2003)
(ISBN 90-411-1996-5)

11. Peter Verloop and Valérie Landes (Eds.), *Merger Control in Europe, 4th edition, EU, Member States and Accession States* (2003)
(ISBN 90-411-2056-4)

12. Themistoklis, K. Giannakopoulos, *Safeguarding Companies' Rights in Competition and Anti-dumping/Anti-subsidies Proceedings* (2004)
(ISBN 90-411-2254-0)

13. Marjorie Holmes and Lesley Davey (Eds.), *A Practical Guide to National Competition Rules across Europe* (2004)
(ISBN 90-411-2295-8)

14. Sigrid Stroux, *US and EU Oligopoly Control* (2004)
(ISBN 90-411-2296-6)

15. Tzong-Leh Hwang and Chiyuan Chen (Eds.), *The Future Development of Competition Framework* (2004)
(ISBN 90-411-2305-9)

16. Phedon Nicolaides, Mihalis Kekelekis and Philip Buyskes, *State Aid Policy in the European Community, A Guide for Practitioners.* Second Edition (2005)
(ISBN 90-411-2394-6)

17. Doris Hildebrand, *Economic Analyses of Vertical Agreements – A Self-Assessment* (2005)
(ISBN 90-411-2328-8)

18. Frauke Henning-Bodewig, *Unfair Competition Law, European Union and Member States* (2006)
(ISBN 90-411-2329-6)